Shanghai
on Strike

p¹³

ELIZABETH J. PERRY

Shanghai on Strike:

THE POLITICS OF

CHINESE LABOR

STANFORD UNIVERSITY PRESS

STANFORD, CALIFORNIA

Stanford University Press
Stanford, California
© 1993 by the Board of Trustees of the
Leland Stanford Junior University
Printed in the United States of America

Original printing 1993
Last figure below indicates year of this printing:
03   02   01   00   99   98   97   96   95   94

Stanford University Press publications are
distributed exclusively by Stanford University
Press within the United States, Canada, and
Mexico; they are distributed exclusively by
Cambridge University Press throughout the
rest of the world.

CIP data appear at the end of the book

For Ellen

Preface

THIS BOOK REPRESENTS a kind of homecoming for me. Having been born in Shanghai shortly before the Communist takeover, I grew up (in Japan and the United States) with a fascination for the city where my parents had previously resided for twenty tumultuous years. Unable to return for 30 more years, I awaited the time when Shanghai might come to mean something more than just an entry in my passport. The first trip back, in the spring of 1979, was not only an opportunity for nostalgic indulgence; it also suggested promising research possibilities. But only after several more years and the assistance of many supportive individuals and institutions was I finally able to undertake a serious study in the city of my birth.

Topping the list of facilitators to this research effort are two agencies: on the Chinese side, the Shanghai Academy of Social Sciences (SASS), headed by President Zhang Zhongli (who, coincidentally, had studied with my father at St. John's University in Shanghai); and on the American side, the Committee for Scholarly Communication with the People's Republic of China (especially Mary Brown Bullock and Robert Geyer). Funding from the latter group enabled me to spend a full academic year (1986–87) as a visiting scholar at SASS.

The rich archival materials at SASS's Institutes of History and Economics are what really made possible this study of the Shanghai labor movement. Included among these materials are hundreds of transcripts of lengthy interviews with elderly workers conducted by Chinese researchers in the late 1950's and early 1960's. To be sure, the line of questioning in these interviews reflected a particular agenda; the aim was to uncover the proletarian base of the Communist revolution. And of course the memories of aging workers about events that occurred some years earlier were not always reliable. Nevertheless, despite such biases, these sources provided a unique opportunity to learn—through the words of the workers themselves—about the lives, working conditions, and protest activities of ordinary Shanghai laborers. Furthermore, certain discrepancies between the workers' statements and official Communist Party accounts of the same events seemed to confirm the candor of these interviews. It was just such inconsistencies that led me to the central arguments of this study—findings that are often at variance with published histories of the Shanghai labor movement. Although they are likely to disagree with many of my conclusions, I am deeply grateful to the scholars who helped to familiarize me with these invaluable sources: Chen Weimin and Zheng Qingsheng at the Institute of History and Chen Zengnian and Xu Xinwu at the Institute of Economics.

Important as they were, the workers' memoirs made up a small portion of the wealth of materials available to me in Shanghai. Indeed, my confidence in the basic authenticity of the interview transcripts was established only after corroboration with other archival and library sources. Factory archives—notably those of the British American Tobacco Company and the Shanghai Number Four Silk-Weaving Factory—proved to be treasure troves complete with detailed firsthand accounts by both management and workers. Government documents (which included strike statistics, police reports, and arbitration records) were made available by the Shanghai Municipal Archives. Dozens of valuable unpublished factory histories were consulted at the Shanghai Federation of Labor Unions. The Port of Shanghai provided additional materials. Key periodicals and survey data were furnished by both the SASS Library and the Shanghai Municipal Library. I am most grateful to the directors and staffs of these units for their cooperation and to the Foreign Affairs Office of SASS (especially Wang Dehua and Tian Guopei) for making the initial introductions.

Outside of Shanghai, several other archives and libraries were particularly helpful. The Number Two History Archives in Nanjing allowed me to consult many important government documents from the Guomindang era, as did the Party History Archives in Taipei. The Bureau of Investigation in Taipei provided valuable Communist reports. The Central Library in Taipei, the Toyo Bunko Library in Tokyo, the National Archives in Washington, D.C., the Hoover Institution at Stanford, and the University of Washington East Asia Library in Seattle were all unfailingly helpful. Again I express appreciation to the directors and staffs of these institutions and to the American Council of Learned Societies, whose financial support made possible this segment of the research.

Assistance with data collection at various stages of the project was provided by George Brown, Cai Shaoqing, Dai Yingcong, Neil Diamant, Jiang Kelin, Li Xun, Liu Chang, Liu Shih-chi, Kevin Marchioro, Shih

Chia-yin, Matthew Sommer, Tia Thornton, Xiao Gongqin, and Yang Jeou-yi. Helpful comments on papers related to this volume were offered by participants in seminars at Academia Sinica, the University of California, Berkeley, the University of Chicago, the University of Michigan, the Shanghai Academy of Social Sciences, National Taiwan University, the University of Washington, and Yale University. The bulk of the writing was completed during a sabbatical from the University of Washington in 1988–89. Insightful readings of an earlier draft were furnished by Marie-Claire Bergère, Charles Bergquist, Joseph Esherick, Mark Frazier, Ellen Fuller, Emily Honig, Andrew Walder, Jeffrey Wasserstrom, and Yeh Wen-hsin. Expert assistance in the formatting and publication process came from University of Washington China Program Secretary Laurie Pollack and Stanford University Press Senior Editor Muriel Bell. Credit for the index goes to Tia Thornton. Appreciative as I am for all this help, none of these individuals is responsible for the problems that remain.

This book, which focuses on the origins and political proclivities of the Shanghai work force, is the first in a projected two-volume study of Chinese labor politics. In the second volume I intend to pursue the relationship between the labor movement and the formation and transformation of the modern Chinese state.

E.J.P.

Contents

Tables, Figures, and Maps

Eight pages of photographs follow page 64.

Shanghai
on Strike

Introduction

A RECENT GENERATION of labor scholars, disappointed by the failure of twentieth-century workers to live up to the exalted expectations of Karl Marx and Friedrich Engels, has focused on the *limitations* of proletarian politics, with particular attention to the fragmented character of labor. Divided by gender, age, ethnicity, and skill, workers are portrayed as rarely acting in the cohesive, class-conscious fashion predicted by communist visionaries. Much of this analysis has a pessimistic tone, as students of labor reluctantly accept the shortcomings of their object of study. There is also a note of irony when scholars discover that the meager indigenous support for a radical labor movement tended to be concentrated in the most privileged sectors of the working class, far removed from the heroic proletariat envisioned in the *Manifesto*.[1]

In responding to the unfulfilled promises of Marxism, studies of labor have been obsessed with "why not" questions: Why did workers not develop a class identity? Why did workers, especially the most downtrodden, not flock to radical political parties? Why did working-class parties, especially in advanced capitalist societies, not engineer Marxist revolutions? Such questions prompt one to search for sources of weakness in the working class. The result has been sophisticated analyses of divisions within the European and American labor forces. A host of studies has convincingly demonstrated that contradictions between men and women, old and young, northern and southern European, black and white American, or skilled and unskilled have prevented workers from exhibiting the class-conscious party allegiances or revolutionary behaviors that might otherwise be expected of them.[2]

This line of analysis has resulted in a realistic appreciation of the powerful centrifugal forces at play within the modern working class. But must such intraclass divisions be seen only in a negative light, as obstacles to the fulfillment of the "true" mission of the proletariat? I would suggest instead that the fragmentation of labor can provide a basis for politically influential working-class action, not only in support of one or another political party but even in the emergence of new political regimes. Different segments of society and even different segments of one class within society may forge linkages with state officials that alter the fate of both parties. This is not to suggest that social groupings will always have their way; usually neither partner gets what it wanted or anticipated in these often uneasy relationships. Nonetheless, beginning our analysis from the ground up, taking seriously the political potential of fragmented subclasses, provides a concrete means of exploring patterns of state-society interaction.

Chinese workers, no less than their European or American counterparts, have been deeply divided, yet fragmentation does not mean passivity. Despite (and, in large part, because of) important distinctions along lines of native-place origin, gender, and skill level, the Chinese working class has shown itself capable of influential political action.

The Political Influence of Chinese Labor

Labor unrest has played a central role in the political transformations that have swept twentieth-century China. The 1911 Revolution toppling the imperial system, the May Fourth Movement ushering in a new political culture, the rise and demise of the Nationalist regime, the victory of the Communists, and even the shape of post-1949 politics have all been deeply affected by the Chinese labor movement.[3] Regardless of their relatively small numbers in a still overwhelmingly rural country, Chinese workers have, often in unforeseen or contradictory ways, exerted a powerful influence on the modern Chinese polity.

In no city of China has the influence of organized labor been more evident than in Shanghai, the nation's industrial capital. Over the past century, periodic upsurges, fueled by an alliance between Shanghai's workers and students,[4] have heralded major shifts in national politics. These events follow a regular temporal pattern, with a momentous outbreak occurring about every twenty years. Perhaps, as Thomas Jefferson prescribed for the United States, each new generation has found it necessary to undertake its own revolutionary struggles.

Shanghai's most famous upsurge, marking the beginning of these generational cycles, was the May Thirtieth Movement of 1925, followed closely by the Three Workers' Armed Uprisings of 1926–27. In these incidents, workers, stimulated by radical students, protested vigorously against Japanese and British imperialism and demanded an end to warlord rule. The takeover of Shanghai by Chiang Kai-shek's Northern Expeditionary forces in March 1927 was undoubtedly facilitated by this impressive labor support, but the Generalissimo was soon to perceive Communist-inspired workers as a threat to his new regime. The "white terror" that Chiang and his gangster allies unleashed against the labor movement in April 1927 irrevocably colored the character of the emerging Nationalist state.[5]

Two decades later, during the Civil War years of 1946–48, massive numbers of Shanghai workers and students took to the streets to protest the Nationalists. Inflation, corruption, and (to a lesser extent) American imperialism were issues that united the anti-Guomindang (GMD) coalition and helped prepare the way for the Communist accession to power.[6]

Although the new Communist regime was quick to pronounce itself a dictatorship of the proletariat, labor unrest did not disappear under its rule. The socialist state rewarded older workers who had contributed actively to the revolutionary movement with union positions and other perquisites, making newcomers to the work force feel neglected by comparison. When the Cultural Revolution opened the possibility of acting on their grievances, they did so vehemently. The years 1966–68 saw violent confrontations between "conservative" and "radical" factions in Shanghai. Mao Zedong's decision to back the challengers through student Red Guards and worker Revolutionary Rebels had fateful consequences for the subsequent direction of his polity.[7]

Even in the post-Mao era, labor unrest in Shanghai has had important political repercussions. Student demonstrations in 1986–87 elicited a strong reaction from the regime, in part because of fear that the intellectuals would be joined by disgruntled workers. When protesters gathered by the thousands at People's Plaza in the center of the city, a tight police cordon was formed around them to prevent the participation of anyone without proper student identification. Large numbers of workers stood just outside the police circle, throwing bread and cigarettes to the students and shouting, "Younger brothers, your elder brothers support you!"[8] Fear of labor unrest undoubtedly prompted the regime's decision to delay long-announced price hikes for foodstuffs and played a hand in the demotion of the Party's general secretary, Hu Yaobang. Two years later, the fall of Hu's successor, Zhao Ziyang, also followed on the heels of dramatic protests in major cities across the country. Zhao's replacement by Shanghai Party Secretary Jiang Zemin was obviously linked to Jiang's success in forestalling a general labor stoppage in China's most important industrial metropolis.[9]

Thus whether in the 1920's, 1940's, 1960's, or 1980's, protest in Shanghai has had momentous political ramifications. The rise and fall of parties, regimes, and personalities have been closely intertwined with collective action in the city. This is not to say, however, that workers (or their student allies) have always prevailed. On the contrary, fear inspired by the specter of a politicized working class has often led regimes—whether republican or socialist in appellation—to adopt policies that ran counter to the aspirations of many Shanghai workers. The point, then, is not that modern Chinese politics has directly reflected labor's demands but that labor has been an exceptionally important force in the definition and development of the modern Chinese state.

Political leaders in twentieth-century China have accorded the working class a prominent place in their vision of a new society. Modernization was seen as virtually synonymous with industrialization, and workers were esteemed as the agents of development. A party claiming to represent the forces of progress thus needed a working-class constituency. The labor movement's ideological significance gave it a far greater political voice than the relatively small size of the Chinese work force might otherwise warrant. But ideology was not the only explanation for the key role that workers came to play in political events. The capacity of organized labor to wreak serious economic damage has lent it a strength (in China as elsewhere in the world) out of proportion to its actual numbers. Whereas the late imperial and warlord regimes tried simply to contain the destructive potential of a restive work force, both the Nationalists and Communists made active efforts to channel this growing resource in directions favorable to their own political agendas.

Politics from the Ground Up

Important as the designs of Communist and Nationalist agents were to the development of the modern Chinese labor movement, neither of these parties—nor the states they spawned—was able to exert full control over Shanghai's workers. The problem was not merely competition from the rival party; historical circumstances gave both parties a chance at hegemony. Rather, the Shanghai labor movement had a life of its own, closely linked to the countryside from which its workers sprang. Having launched many a successful protest well before either political party appeared on the scene, Shanghai workers were heirs to a tradition of collective action that did not always fit easily with the plans of outside organizers.

To understand the politics of Shanghai labor, we must take into account this heritage of protest. The course of the labor movement cannot be explained simply by reference to the partisan strategies of outside cadres, however successful they may at times have been. Labor politics begins with the laborers themselves: their geographical origins, gender, popular culture, educational attainments, work experiences, and the like. These are the features of a worker's milieu that structure lasting traditions of collective action.

Most previous studies of the Chinese labor movement have been written as Party history (*dangshi*), the point of which is to illuminate the policies of the Communists (or sometimes the Nationalists) rather than to analyze the actions and motivations of the workers themselves.[10] This usually leads to the conclusion that the Chinese labor movement did not begin until 1921 with the founding of the Chinese Communist Party (CCP), or at best in 1919 with the May Fourth Movement. According to this common view, it was only when intellectuals, influenced by the Russian Revolution, began to take an active interest in organizing workers that a labor movement was born in China. Fang Fuan presented the conventional wisdom when he argued, in his classic study of Chinese labor, that students—enamored of European models—taught the workers how to strike.[11] As Nym Wales put it, "Except for the old guild tradition, chiefly in handicrafts, [Chinese labor] was virgin territory for a strong class movement. . . . The organizers had only to build, not to destroy first. . . . The students merely told the workers what unions were and the workers acted."[12] Similarly, Jean Chesneaux concludes that the Chinese labor movement "developed in close collaboration with the Communist Party and followed the party's lead. . . . The political aims of the Communist Party and of the working class were much the same."[13]

The Chinese labor movement certainly did undergo a major transformation when politically motivated intellectuals became involved in its direction. Furthermore, under the guidance of these student-cadres, labor played an important role in the development of both the GMD and the CCP. Thus the tendency to frame studies of Chinese labor within the perspective of Party history is not without justification. Indeed, Part II of this volume, "The Politics of Partisanship," remains well within this interpretive tradition. Nevertheless, Chinese workers were not a tabula rasa on which Party cadres could write whatever political messages suited their designs. Workers were heir to their own traditions of protest, rooted in native-place cultures and workplace experiences, which engendered a certain tension between them and student organizers and limited the directions in which labor could be led.

Along with the recognition that labor was not putty in the hands of Party cadres to be molded at will goes the further conclusion that workers themselves were not all of a piece. Just as workers differed from students by virtue of background, life-style, and values, so laborers themselves were divided along similar lines. The literate, well-paid mechanic from Ningbo who enjoyed a secure job at the Jiangnan Arsenal was a world apart from the uneducated young woman, fresh from the Subei countryside, who worked for a pittance under miserable conditions in a silk filature or cotton mill. The protests of such workers were as dissimilar in style and substance as the differences in their origins and work situations.

When student organizers developed a burning interest in the Shanghai labor movement, they soon discovered that only some segments of the work force reciprocated their enthusiasm. Initial reactions to the overtures of Guomindang and Communist cadres, and subsequent responses to the policies of Nationalist and Communist regimes, varied along lines that long predated these political phenomena. To make sense of the politics of the labor movement, we must begin at the beginning—with the origins of the Shanghai working class.

Part I of this book, "The Politics of Place," traces the geographical roots of the Shanghai work force to suggest that early labor protest in the city varied along native-place lines. Part II, "The Politics of Partisanship," follows the story of the Shanghai labor movement into the 1920's–1940's, to show how outside organizers were forced—sometimes against their ideological predilections—to come to terms with the traditions that antedated their arrival. In Part III, "The Politics of Production," the investigation moves into the workplace to discover how workers at different points in the production process responded to the political agendas of the day. With workers from particular geographical origins occupying specific productive niches in the Shanghai economy, identifiable political divisions developed among skilled, semiskilled, and unskilled laborers.

In this study I focus on a common form of collective action—the strike—as a vehicle for exploring political variation. Strikes can occur for a range of economic and social reasons: to demand a wage raise, to protest the dismissal of a fellow worker, or to secure improved labor conditions. But strikes can also reflect explicitly political concerns. Workers may withhold their labor as a means of expressing opposition to the ruling authorities or, alternatively, as a way of punishing enterprises that disobey government regulations. The strike leadership holds the key to much of the explanation for overtly political protest. Yet leaders are dependent on followers for their success. A good deal of comparative research makes clear that people differ systematically in their willingness to support one or another political cause. Understanding the sources of political constituencies thus demands attention to the habits and aspirations that link people together as communities—their cultures, as it were.

In choosing to focus on the strike as an exemplar of labor politics, I owe the reader a word of explanation. After all, the thrust of much of the "new" labor history is away from concern with unions and strikes toward a far broader definition of workers' politics. Similarly, the trend in studies of popular resistance in general is to eschew a focus on overt, organized protest in favor of less dramatic "everyday forms of resistance."[14] Though very much in sympathy with this effort to direct attention toward more mundane varieties of popular action, I also remain attached to the study of open protest. Precisely because of their dramatic character, confrontations such as strikes have a more immediate political effect than do such "nibbling" actions as absenteeism, pilfering, slowdowns, or sabotage. Moreover, as James Cronin has noted, "The amount of personal risk and commitment characteristically involved in even the most casual strike makes the pattern of industrial strife a better indicator of working-class attitudes and behavior than any other as yet available."[15] As Michelle Perrot shows in her perceptive study of French labor unrest, strikes are both a means of cultural expression and a calculated effort to change economic and political relationships. The language and symbolism give rich insights into labor mentality, while the formal demands reveal ways in which workers battle "rationally" for their own interests.[16] Fortunately, the generous availability of source materials on Shanghai strikes and the high quality of scholarship on strikes in other countries render this form of protest a particularly promising subject for comparative study.

The strike is only one weapon in the arsenal of workers, but it is an especially efficacious and important one.* Its value goes beyond the substantial economic costs a walkout can inflict on the targeted enterprise because strikes tend to invite state intervention. Even strikes based only on economic demands that proceed in an orderly, nonviolent fashion are frequently settled by the mediation of a government agency. The close relationship between industry and the modern state lends the strike its peculiarly political character. For someone interested in exploring the interaction between social protest and state formation, strikes are thus an especially fruitful avenue of investigation.

Recent studies have argued that a united working class is not an automatic by-product of capitalist development but a contingency whose

---

*Of the 2,291 strikes that occurred in Shanghai between 1918 and 1940, more than 65 percent resulted in either full or partial victories for the workers. The figures are from *Shanghai Strike Statistics, 1918–1940*, a computerized data set, entered into SPSS format by a research assistant under my supervision, which includes 2,291 cases and 35 variables drawn from the statistical compilations of the Shanghai Bureau of Social Affairs.

realization is dependent on workers' participation in successful collective action.[17] In this view, strikes and other public demonstrations are less the outcome than the precondition of working-class formation. As Gordon Marshall argues,

> An overemphasis on class imagery at the expense of class action can perhaps be attributed to the widely held belief among academic observers that it is somehow necessary for men and women to encompass society intellectually before they can attempt to change it. This premise is not confirmed by the history of class action on either a revolutionary or on a more modest scale. . . . Consciousness is generated in and changed by social action.[18]

In the three parts of this volume, working-class action is studied from three different, yet closely related, vantage points. In the process, I strive to integrate concerns that have typically been the purview of separate social science disciplines. Part I focuses on popular culture (defined by native-place origin), a topic central to the field of social history. Part II examines the strategies of party organizers and the pattern of inter- and intraparty competition, a familiar subject for political science. In Part III, attention shifts to the workplace—the realm of industrial sociology. I argue that these three arenas are inextricably linked. Cultural origins shape conditions of labor, which, in turn, generate support for various political agendas. The study of politics thus cannot be divorced from history, economics, and sociology. Political outcomes ranging from mundane protests to the formation of modern states are constructed from the cultural origins and working experiences of ordinary citizens.

This volume locates the sources of working-class differentiation (in the politics of place and production) and explores the implications of these divisions for political mobilization (or partisanship). In so doing, it attempts to lay the groundwork for an analysis of the role of labor in the formation of the modern Chinese state—the task of a companion volume to follow. Chinese states—imperial, republican, and Communist alike—have been commonly characterized as "despotic," "bureaucratic," "autonomous," or "totalitarian." Such designations imply a minimal place for social forces. By contrast, this study emphasizes the dynamic influence of local society, divided though it was, on state transformation.

The waves of repression that have rolled over the Chinese polity from the 1920's to the present have followed on the heels of popular protests in which labor strife was of major concern. Admittedly, the repressive response of the state demonstrates the severe restrictions on popular participation. But it also suggests the extent to which state policies are themselves shaped in reaction to this very participation. Although the outcome is certainly a far cry from the workers' paradise envisioned by Marx and Engels, it nevertheless bears witness to a more influential political role for workers than a recent generation of scholars in labor history have led us to expect.

PART ONE

The Politics of Place,
1839–1919

Do CAPITALIST CITIES PRODUCE cohesive proletariats, capable of militant action on behalf of their own collective interests? This question has absorbed the attention of more than a few social theorists, many of whom view the industrial strike as an indicator of the possibilities of working-class politics. Those of Marxist persuasion see capitalist exploitation as a proletarianizing force, which leads workers to forge a powerful new solidarity. As class consciousness grows, so too does workers' militance in the form of industrial strife. Modernization theorists, by contrast, suggest that capitalist cities bring not immiserated proletarians but contented members of a new middle class. Quiescence rather than militance is the result.[1]

Opposed as these viewpoints are, they share some common points of departure. Both emphasize the transformative effect of capitalism; whereas the precapitalist countryside is characterized as "traditional" or "feudal," capitalist cities—whether proletarian or middle class in composition—are seen as decidedly "modern." Moreover, in both analyses the process of industrialization is viewed as exercising a homogenizing influence over the working class; feudal distinctions disappear in a machine-made uniformity.

Recently, however, the scholarly world has grown skeptical of the dichotomous imagery underlying both Marxist and modernization theories. Increasingly we find evidence that "traditions" persist, not merely as archaic remnants but as central organizing principles of industrial life. The working class and its capacities for concerted action are thus the product not simply of capitalist transformation but of precapitalist practices as well. Mao Zedong implied this inverted relationship when he described the Chinese revolution as "villages surrounding cities" (nong-cun baowei chengshi). The metaphor is an apt one not only for his socialist revolution but (equally ironically) for capitalist revolutions as well. Rather than engender a uniform working class bereft of its rural heritage, capitalism is encircled by the imperatives of the countryside.

The carryover of rural practices into the industrializing cities ensures fragmentation as workers from different regions operate according to divergent norms. But fragmentation need not imply passivity. Just as rural dwellers—in China and elsewhere—were capable of staging massive protests to further their interests, so too were workers. Their strikes provide an indication of working-class politics, but in a manner that defies certain basic assumptions of the dominant paradigms of capitalist development.

Shanghai! The very name connotes capitalist cosmopolitanism. At the turn of the twentieth century, Shanghai was known as the Paris of the East, where sojourners from all corners of the globe converged to create one of the most dynamic and sophisticated capitalist entrepôts the world had ever seen. The diverse mélange of foreigners was matched by an equally multifarious assortment of Chinese residents. Many of these domestic immigrants, drawn from villages across the empire, found the move to the big city considerably more alien and unsettling than did their foreign counterparts.

Unlike most foreigners, the hundreds of thousands of Chinese who flocked to Shanghai in the late nineteenth and early twentieth centuries entered the lowly ranks of the working class.* Early generations of industrial workers in Shanghai, like their peers elsewhere in the world, were products of the countryside. Reared in an agrarian environment that bore only marginal resemblance to the urban setting in which they relocated, immigrants turned to native-place identities to soften their adjustment to the strangeness of city life. Seeking out fellow provincials for employment as well as camaraderie was an obvious and effective survival strategy in an unfamiliar setting. The result was a constellation of ethnic enclaves: entrepreneurs and employees from a particular region of the country lived and worked near one another. Laborers joined transplanted communities of fellow immigrants from the same native place. As William Rowe has observed, "Geographically determined subethnic distinctions . . . constituted the most important distinguishing feature between individual Chinese in the late imperial period."[2] In Shanghai, as in other urban centers, workers slipped easily into a "politics of place." Where one came from helped to decide a worker's reaction to the cosmopolitan challenges of the city.

---

*Some foreigners, especially the many destitute White Russians who fled to Shanghai after the Bolshevik Revolution in 1917, were ordinary workers.

Ethnic cultures in Shanghai did not, of course, simply perpetuate or replicate the age-old practices of people's rural heritage; urban life required new solutions to new problems. The construction of working-class cultures was thus not only derivative but dynamic. Nevertheless, the raw materials from which such innovations were fashioned issued in large part from people's culture of origin. As Peter Burke has noted for early modern Europe, so too for China: "Popular culture was perceived as local culture. . . . It was the region, or town, or even village which commanded loyalty."[3]

In emphasizing the interaction between rural loyalties and urban demands, I am indebted to an impressive body of scholarship on the popular culture of workers in Europe and the United States.[4] Shanghai, like New York or Chicago, was an immigrant society, although in Shanghai the working-class immigrants were primarily of domestic rather than international origin. In either case, workers carried to their new environment patterns of life and thought from their native locales. As Herbert Gutman has written in his classic study of U.S. labor:

> The American working class was continually altered in its composition by infusions, from within and without the nation, of peasants, farmers, skilled artisans and casual day laborers. . . . Men and women who sell their labor bring more to a new and changing work situation than their physical presence. What they bring to the factory depends, in good part, on their culture of origin, and how they behave is shaped by the interaction between that culture and the particular society into which they enter.[5]

To understand how and why workers engage in certain forms of politics, we must first know where they came from. Chapter 1, "A City of Immigrants," links the geographical origins of the Shanghai work force to its early styles of protest. The tendency for workers from different native places to become segregated into occupational slots intensified the influence of local cultures on working-class behavior. Chapter 2, "South China Artisans," examines the organizations and strike actions of skilled craftsmen, the majority of whom hailed from the Canton or Jiangnan regions. Chapter 3, "North China Proletarians," focuses on patterns of protest among unskilled laborers, most of whom were peasants from the northern countryside.

CHAPTER ONE

A City of Immigrants

THE RAPID DEVELOPMENT of modern Shanghai was inseparable from its status as a treaty port. The opening to foreign trade and residence in the aftermath of the Opium War (1839–42) allowed Shanghai to grow in the space of several decades from a prosperous domestic port into one of the truly great cities of the world. Located at the confluence of the Yangzi and Huangpu rivers near the major silk- and tea-producing regions of China, Shanghai was perfectly positioned to serve as a global commercial center. Within just a few years of its opening to foreign trade, the city accounted for most of the value of China's imports and exports.[1]

This international commerce attracted a growing number of foreigners to the new British Settlement (which in 1863 was amalgamated with the American district into the International Settlement) and French Concession. (See Map 1.) Situated to the north of the old walled city, these enclaves soon harbored thousands of foreign residents and boasted a European architectural style that bespoke a world of difference from the original Chinese settlement. The old city (walled in the mid-sixteenth century in defense against Japanese pirates) had been constructed to meet the needs of domestic trade. There small wooden shops fronted winding streets whose names revealed the products that could be found along them: salted meat and fruits on Salty Melon Street, legumes and grain on Bean Market Street, bamboo and wood on Bamboo Alley.[2] In the foreigners' quarters, by contrast, imposing Western-style office buildings, houses, churches, race courses, gardens, and clubs sprang up to provide places of work, residence, religion, and recreation for the growing expatriate community. Foreign-staffed governments—complete with councils, courts, and police—were soon installed to protect the interests of foreign business.

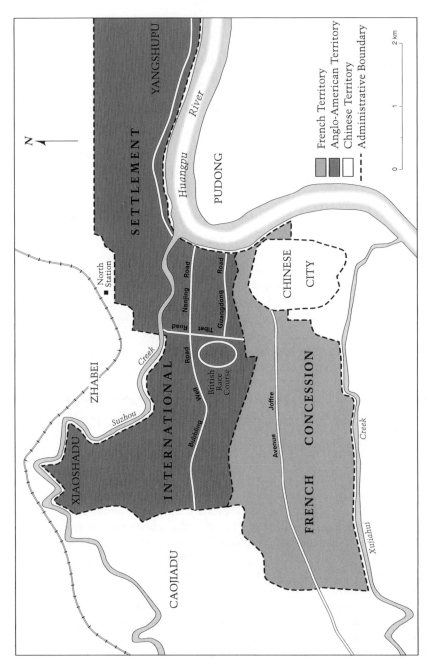

Map 1. Treaty port Shanghai, 1919. Adapted from Emily Honig, *Sisters and Strangers: Women in the Shanghai Cotton Mills, 1911–1949* (Stanford, Calif., 1986).

A local gazetteer described the city scene in the late nineteenth century:

> Exploring a corner of Shanghai is really like finding the whole world in a grain of millet. Disney Road, Peng Road, and Wusong Road in Hongkou are full of Japanese residents, just like in Japan. North Sichuan Road, Wuchang Road, Chongming Road and Tiantong Road are full of Cantonese, just like in Guangdong. The western section of Avenue Joffre is full of shops run by Frenchmen, just like in France. The foreign-goods stores outside Little East Gate are mostly operated by Fujianese, just like in Fujian. Salty Melon Street in Nanshi is full of shops run by Ningbo people, just like in Ningbo. Foreign residents and Chinese from every province and city all congregate here. So it is no exaggeration to describe Shanghai as a miniature world.[3]

If commerce played the leading role in the early development of Shanghai, industrial investment was not far behind. Established foreign companies vied with new domestic enterprises to produce the cotton and silk textiles, tobacco, machinery, and other goods for which Shanghai became renowned. The opening of the first (British-owned) steam filature in 1861 was followed four years later by the founding of the famous (Chinese-owned) Jiangnan Arsenal. By 1911, just over one-quarter of all China's factories—both foreign and Chinese in ownership—were located in Shanghai. By 1933, the proportion had risen to nearly half. On the eve of the Communist takeover in 1949, fully 60 percent of the nation's factories were concentrated in the city of Shanghai.[4] Industrial development brought a huge increase in the size of the city's population, especially its working class. A city that in 1852 had numbered just over 500,000 inhabitants grew to more than 5 million by 1949.[5]

Laborers to fill the ranks of the Shanghai work force were drawn from all over China. (See Map 2.) For its modern existence, then, Shanghai has been a city of immigrants. In 1885, non-natives made up 85 percent of Shanghai's Chinese population; in 1950, the number stood at 84.9 percent. Although immigration persisted, the proportions of various immigrant groups changed markedly over the years: Cantonese were surpassed by people from Ningbo, who were in turn eventually overtaken by arrivals from Jiangsu and other more northerly provinces.*

---

*In 1885, some 20 percent of the Chinese population was of Cantonese origin, 40 percent from Zhejiang, and 37 percent from Jiangsu. In 1935, only 4 percent of the city's inhabitants were from Guangdong, with 35 percent from Zhejiang and 53 percent from Jiangsu. The number of people from Anhui, Hubei, Shandong, and Hebei had also grown substantially. Although the percentage of non-natives fluctuated over these 65 years, never did the figure fall below 73 percent of the city's Chinese population (Zou Yiren, *Jiu Shanghai renkou bianqian de yanjiu* [Studies in the population change of old Shanghai] [Shanghai, 1980], pp. 112–15).

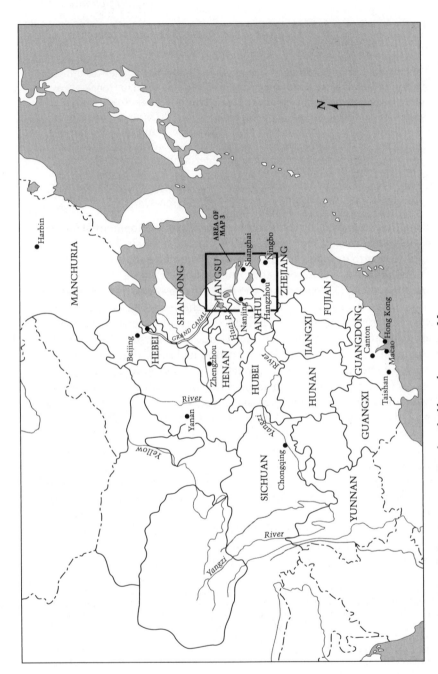

Map 2. Republic of China, ca. 1928. For detail of boxed area, see Map 3.

Cantonese Immigrants

In the period immediately following the Opium War, Shanghai's migrants hailed predominantly from the Canton (Guangzhou) region. Having served for many years as China's only entrepôt of international trade,
Canton had engendered a large work force geared toward the needs of
foreign business. When Canton was overshadowed by the opening of
Shanghai, tens of thousands of Cantonese—largely seamen and shipbuilders—headed north to ply their services in the new commercial and
industrial center. This migratory stream was further stimulated by the
appointment in 1843 of the pidgin-speaking Cantonese compradore Wu
Jianzhang as circuit intendant of Shanghai. Known as Samqua to the
foreigners, Wu settled down in the Hongkou district of the city, close to
the protection of his American and British friends.[6] By the early 1850's,
tens of thousands of his fellow provincials could be found in Shanghai,
living for the most part in Hongkou near Intendant Wu or along Guangdong Road next to the major shipyards. The large number of Cantonese
restaurants that sprang up in this area reflected the culinary preferences
of the district's new inhabitants.[7]

These Cantonese immigrants, like others who would follow in their
wake, continued the practice of founding native-place guilds to cushion
the move to an unfamiliar urban environment.[8] Such institutions served
both as employment agencies for recent arrivals and as welfare societies
in time of need. The more prosperous of these *gongsuo* or *huiguan*
(translated variously as "guilds" or "landsmannschaften") operated temples for the worship of familiar local deities, stages for the performance of
local operas, schools for the education of children or apprentices, savings
and loan associations, and burial grounds.[9]

Students of China are sometimes inclined to point to the proliferation
of native-place associations as an expression of the "uniquely" clannish
nature of the Chinese in general and the Cantonese in particular. Such
institutions, however, appeared in other parts of the world where migration encouraged comparable behavior. In the United States, for example,
associations of immigrant workers were also divided along ethnic and
regional lines. In 1914, more than 500 benevolent societies for fellow
townsmen could be found in New York City alone, "each providing job
opportunities (through employers from their village), insurance benefits,
aid to the sick, interest-free loans and cemetery rights."[10]

Native-place associations, whether in New York or in Shanghai, afforded displaced workers a sense of belonging. The migrant community
was not only a source of jobs and welfare but also a means of establishing
one's identity in an otherwise alien milieu. To this end, religious rituals

and communal feasts were important components of most *gongsuo* and *huiguan* activities. The group spirit engendered by such occasions contributed to distinctive patterns of collective action among the immigrant membership.

As early as 1853–55, Shanghai witnessed the explosive power of native-place identities in the Small Sword Rebellion.[11] Significant as this incident would prove to be in the course of Chinese history (disruption caused by the Small Swords' seventeen-month occupation of Shanghai resulted in a foreign takeover of the Customs Service, for example), it sprang from homely roots. Led by a pidgin-speaking, opium-smoking Cantonese member of the Triad secret society from the same village as Intendant Wu Jianzhang, the rebellion was based primarily on guilds from Guangdong (allied with those of Fujian).

By the mid-nineteenth century, the 3,500 seafaring junks operating out of Shanghai had attracted a burgeoning population of some 80,000 Guangdong natives and some 50,000 Fujianese to the entrepôt. Competition from foreign steamships after the Opium War put many of the old Chinese boats out of operation, rendering the now unemployed seamen ready recruits for protest. Contraction in the native shipping trade also undermined the fortunes of some of the guild directors, setting the stage for their participation in rebellion as well.

The main fighting force of the Small Swords was a motley crew of idled seamen, principally from Guangdong and Fujian, organized by *gongsuo* and *huiguan* leaders from their respective native places. Although these guild directors were prominent members of Shanghai's nascent treaty-port society, they were also local bosses who acted as patrons to their displaced fellow provincials. Li Shaoqing, director of Guangdong's Jiaying guild and an important early leader of the Small Sword Rebellion, served as protector to Cantonese opium smugglers in the Yangzi delta. The illicit opium trade was the crucial link that brought together urban and rural secret societies in the Shanghai area in common rebellion against the Qing state. Intendant Wu, himself from Jiaying County, had earlier lent his official approval to the formation of a guild-sponsored militia that, ironically, provided an organizational base for the subsequent rebellion. The involvement of guild-based militias in collective violence was a long-standing Cantonese practice, seen most recently in the Sanyuanli resistance to the British.[12]

On September 7, 1853, the militia rebels seized Shanghai's walled city of 200,000 in the space of a few hours. The magistrate was changing out of ceremonial dress following celebrations for Confucius's birthday when he was suddenly set upon by rebels and knifed to death in his yamen. The assassin turned out to be an erstwhile leader of Intendant

Wu's militia whom the magistrate had imprisoned some months before for instigating a fight. Wu was kidnapped by the rebels but soon turned over to the American authorities at their request. The sole opposition the Small Swords encountered in taking the city came from a group of 40 soldiers in the pay of the circuit intendant as his body guard, but of these all but 17 refused to fight because they were members of the Triad secret society fraternity.

Native-place identities enabled the initial organization of the rebellion, but they worked against its long-term endurance. Internal dissension among the rebels became apparent immediately after the occupation of Shanghai, when members of the Fujian and Guangdong factions feuded over disposition of the yamen treasury. Elements from Fujian loaded a share of the booty on board their junks and threatened to set sail. This faction advocated killing Circuit Intendant Wu and then escaping with the plundered cash to their native homes in the south. The Cantonese faction was more ambitious. As the grand marshal of the Small Swords informed the U.S. authorities, the Cantonese were willing to reinstate Wu Jianzhang as governor of the city if he would swear loyalty to their new Small Sword dynasty. The rebels would then proceed at once to Suzhou, to occupy the provincial capital. Unfortunately for these designs, the Americans released Wu, who subsequently played a role in the Qing government's suppression of the rebellion.

Although the Small Sword Rebellion eventually was undermined by state pressure as well as by escalating conflicts between its Cantonese and Fujianese membership, it opens a revealing window onto the complexity of Shanghai's treaty-port society. Scarcely a decade after the city's introduction to international trade and residence, evidence was present of processes that would shape the form of collective action for many years to come. The complicated interplay among foreigners, state officials, local strong men, and their working-class clients gave rise to enduring patterns of both crime and protest. Gangsters and rebels alike flourished in this hybrid environment. Periodically such figures joined hands to lead disgruntled or displaced workers in movements that assumed major political proportions, sometimes with strong nationalist overtones. Yet however large and ambitious these protests might become, they never entirely shed the influence of their native-place constituencies.

Ningbo Immigrants

The Small Swords were not the only rebels to challenge the Qing state in this period. To the west, the Taiping Rebellion established its Heavenly Capital in Nanjing and dispatched its armies to occupy much of the Jiangnan region.[13] In the spring of 1861, the Taipings took the treaty port of Ningbo.[14] Frightened landlords and merchants, loath to see their property confiscated by peasant rebels, flocked to the safety of Shanghai. This influx of Zhejiang notables, predominantly from the Ningbo area, buttressed the famous *Yongbang* (Ningbo clique) that had dominated Shanghai financial circles for decades.[15] The wealth of the recent arrivals was invested partly in new industrial enterprises and partly in traditional artisan crafts such as jewelry or carpentry, which supplied the luxury goods needed to maintain their upper-class life-style. Advantaged by more than eight centuries of experience in foreign trade and by the propinquity of their native place to Shanghai, Ningbo businessmen were soon able to surpass their Cantonese competitors in the Shanghai market.

Economic rivalry was intensified by cultural clashes. In the 1870's, writers of Ningbo origin published a series of articles in the local Shanghai press extolling the "refined" habits of their native region. By contrast, the figure of a Cantonese prostitute served in these essays to personify the alleged coarseness of her distant place of origin. The series resulted in a flurry of irate letters from offended Cantonese.[16]

Cultural distinctions were reflected in residential patterns. Whereas the Cantonese were concentrated in the Americanized Hongkou District, Ningbo immigrants tended to settle in the old Chinese city of Nanshi, close to the Ningshao dock, which was the lifeline of commerce between Shanghai and their native Zhejiang Province. Here genteel tea houses catered to their tastes. At these popular places of recreation, which numbered 64 in 1912 and 164 by 1919, Shaoxing opera* or Suzhou storytelling could be enjoyed over a cup of Hangzhou's famous Dragon Well tea. Some establishments also sold artwork, offered fortune-telling services, and provided a space for songbird enthusiasts to compare their pet birds. Teahouses were, moreover, centers for dispute mediation. Parties to a conflict would agree to "talk tea" (*jiangcha*) in the company of a designated mediator. When both disputants were satisfied with the settlement, they drank a cup of tea made of mixed black and green leaves to symbolize the newfound harmony.[17]

Interspersed with teahouses were the myriad guild halls where merchants and laborers from the same native place gathered to share both economic and social concerns.[18] These guilds institutionalized what Shiba Yoshinobu has characterized as the "fierce regional loyalty" of the Ningbo sojourners. Typically referring to themselves as "we fellows of

---

*On Shaoxing opera, see the footnote on p. 187.

common origin" (*ala tongxiangzhe*), Ningbo employers demonstrated a preference first for kinsmen, then for others from the same town or village, then for those from the same county, and finally for natives from other parts of the Ningbo region.[19]

The main guild for Ningbo sojourners in Shanghai, the *Siming gong-suo*, had been constructed in 1797 on land located just outside the north gate of the old city. Over the ensuing years, as the size of the Ningbo community increased, the guild greatly expanded its property. Recognition of its privileged status was conferred in 1844 when the Shanghai magistrate, a Ningbo native, declared the *Siming gongsuo* tax-exempt. Although the guild hall was destroyed ten years later in the fighting between the Small Swords and the Qing army, it was quickly rebuilt in even more impressive fashion. The new complex included a coffin depository, cemetery, meeting rooms, credit bureau, guest house, and temples for the worship of the earth god and Guandi. Annual ceremonies to honor the two principal deities brought together Ningbo sojourners in Shanghai from all walks of life.[20]

Even the powerful *Siming gongsuo* faced a formidable adversary after the French Concession was established on adjoining lands. Claiming that the guild's coffin depository and cemetery were a public health hazard, the French decided in 1874 to extend their territorial control by building a road right through the guild burial grounds. In reply, more than 1,500 Ningbo natives congregated at the *Siming gongsuo* to resist the foreign intrusion. Seven guild members were killed in the confrontation, sparking a vengeful riot in which numerous French homes and businesses were torched. Although the permanent usufruct rights of the Ningbo Guild were affirmed in the settlement of 1878, twenty years later the French consul again announced his government's intention to occupy the land in question. When French troops sallied forth to demolish the cemetery wall, the Ningbo community responded in unison. Ningbo workers in French employ indignantly walked off the job, and Ningbo residents refused to purchase Western goods or services. Thus ensued a six-month struggle—often hailed as the first patriotic strike in Chinese history—the success of which affirmed the political power of native-place loyalties.[21]

The militant response of the Ningbo community to the foreign assault on its burial ground reflected the centrality of death ritual in Chinese culture.[22] As a knowledgeable foreign resident commented on the incident, "To the Westerner, with his desire for that which is useful, it seemed absurd that the construction of a road should be held up by the unwillingness of the Chinese to remove some graves. To the Chinese, it seemed that the Westerner was wanting in respect for the dead, the strongest cult in China."[23] Funeral procedures were deemed sacred by elites and ordinary folk alike, and regional variation in such practices was a key marker of ethnic differentiation. By targeting property endowed with such deeply symbolic value, the French authorities stirred strong emotions within the Ningbo populace. Few if any issues could have operated more effectively to activate an emergent politics of place.

Jiangsu–North China Immigrants

Modern Shanghai's third wave of in-migration, which began in the 1860's and continued well into the twentieth century, was drawn from Jiangsu and other more northerly provinces. As refugees from the Taipings and subsequent military and natural calamities, these displaced persons included some wealthy Jiangnan landlords (especially from Wuxi and Suzhou) but were predominantly destitute peasants from Subei (northern Jiangsu), Shandong, Anhui, Hubei, Hebei, and elsewhere.[24] When their small riverboats reached Shanghai, most of the impoverished immigrants swarmed into shantytowns (penghu qu) along the canals. At first many of the refugees made their homes on their boats, stretching a thatched awning across the cockpit as some protection against wind and rain. Such an arrangement, though cramped and cold, ensured a ready means of transport back to the countryside if the need arose. Immigrants who found regular work along the docks or in the textile mills that bordered the canals usually moved out of the water, setting up tiny one-room shacks of bamboo and mud on nearby rented land.[25] For those whose wages and working conditions permitted, a move to a rented room or factory dormitory was the next step up, but often these quarters were no less crowded or unsanitary than the self-constructed shacks.[26]

As paupers' counterpart to the Jiangnan teahouses, shops known popularly as "tiger stoves" (laohu zao) appeared in the poor working-class neighborhoods to sell hot water for drinking and bathing. A section of these shops was furnished with stools so a worker might sit down to begin the day with a hot towel and friendly gossip over a cup of boiled water.[27] Food stalls offering inexpensive Yangzhou and Shandong fare could also be found in such areas to service rickshaw pullers and others who lacked access to a kitchen or cafeteria.[28]

The poverty of these northerners made it difficult for them to establish the fancy guild halls that afforded both community and connections to the immigrants from Canton and Ningbo. But if formal guilds were a luxury beyond the means of the poor docker or filature worker, local solidarities still found expression in the many native-place gangs (bang-kou) that formed easily among workers who shared a common geographical origin. Often these parochial ties gained greater institutional force through connections with the secret-society gangs (banghui) rampant along the city's waterways.

The Green and Red gangs, so prominent in the politics and economy of Republican-period Shanghai, had originated as protective networks for boatmen engaged in grain transport under the Qing. In the early nineteenth century, when the route of grain tribute shifted from the Grand Canal to the sea, Shanghai became a major hub in the network linking North China to the grain-rich Yangzi delta.[29] For the thousands of sailors who manned the grain boats—most of whom were northerners—quasi-religious gangs offered a measure of security and solace in their unsettled lives.

Although the Red and Green gangs grew out of Buddhist brotherhoods of transient boatmen, over time they came to assume a more powerful posture.[*] One reason for the transformation lay in the burgeoning opium trade. As we saw in the Small Sword Rebellion, opium smuggling and secret societies went hand in hand. It was a natural transition for groups that protected grain shipments to provide cover for opium cargo along the same waterways. Contraband opium grown in Yunnan or Sichuan was loaded on boats in Chongqing for the trip down the Yangzi River to Shanghai. Red Gang members protected the lading as far as Shanghai, where the Green Gang assumed responsibility for unloading the freight and delivering it to Cantonese opium den operators in the city. When the French Concession was established following the Opium War, the French became involved in this lucrative trade. In return for a cut of the proceeds, the French police permitted the gangsters to unload their valuable shipments at a conveniently located dock in the French Concession.[30]

The depredations of gangsters, often operating under police protection, lent the Shanghai waterfront its well-deserved reputation for unsavory activity. Native-place allegiances, mediated through gangs, structured

---

[*]David E. Kelley, "Temples and Tribute Fleets: The Luo Sect and Boatmen's Associations," Modern China 8 (1982): 361–91, provides an illuminating view of the early boatmen's associations, which were part of a lay-based Buddhist sect inspired by the teachings of Luo Qing, a sixteenth-century thinker. In the mid-seventeenth century, the sect was active among grain tribute boatmen from North China working along the Grand Canal far from home in Jiangsu and Zhejiang. By the nineteenth century the groups had changed from open welfare associations with religious affiliation to secret societies engaged in smuggling and extortion. For further discussion see Morita Akira, "Shindai suishu kessha no seikaku ni tsuite" [The nature of boatmen's associations in the Qing], Tōyōshi kenkyū 13 (1955): 364–76; Li Shiyu, "Qingbang, Tiandi hui, Bailian jiao" [Green Gang, Triads, and White Lotus Sect], Wenshizhe, no. 3 (1963): 67–78; and Chuang Chifa, "Qingdai Hongbang yuanliu kao" [Study of the origins of the Qing dynasty Red Gang], Hanxue yanjiu 1 (1983): 91–108.

much of the collective violence that was a constant feature of life on the Shanghai docks. As an observer described a common scene:

> At five o'clock yesterday afternoon, laborers of the Shandong group and the Hubei group, working at the wharf of the Butterfield and Swire Blue Funnel Line in Pudong, had a dispute about wages. . . . After work was finished, some thirty odd laborers of the Shandong group went out of the west gate of the wharf and a like number of the Hubei group went out of the east gate of the wharf, and meeting in the vacant field west of the Yizhong Machine Factory as if by appointment the two sides had another fight with iron bars, bamboo poles, and knives. The fight lasted a long time and members of both sides received severe wounds.[31]

Feuds among dockworkers were reminiscent of the armed vendettas (*xiedou*) so common in the rural villages from which these laborers had recently come and to which they frequently returned in times of urban unemployment or demand for agricultural labor.[32] Native-place rivalries among such workers were more than a matter of rural custom, however. Gangster labor contractors, who invariably hired workers from their own home villages, encouraged interregional conflict so as to expand their control at the expense of competing contractors.[33] An effective display of provincial loyalty on the part of the Hubei gang, for example, could block a rival Shandong contractor from access to a lucrative loading job. The expression of working-class culture, then, was closely related to the structure of the Shanghai labor market.

Native Place, Occupation, and Worker Solidarity

The intimate relationship between native-place identity and job opportunities meant that immigrant workers fell into occupational niches depending on their geographical origin. The Cantonese carpenter, Ningbo coppersmith, and Yancheng rickshaw puller became familiar figures in the working world of modern Shanghai. These occupational groupings were defined to some extent by conditions in the migrants' native places. Canton, which was opened to international trade long before other Chinese ports, produced a large number of skilled carpenters to repair the foreign ships that docked there. When the growth of Shanghai outstripped that of Canton in the mid-nineteenth century, Cantonese woodworkers gravitated naturally to the new metropolis and found employment on the basis of their artisan skills. Yancheng rickshaw pullers, originating as poor peasants forced by warfare or natural catastrophe to abandon farming, arrived in Shanghai with nothing to sell but their brawn. It was hardly surprising that so many of them ended up in the most physically taxing job to be found in the city.

If there was logic in the tendency for migrants from certain native places to fill particular job slots, the pattern was solidified by the personal intervention of labor contractors and local bosses. From Cantonese Intendant Wu Jianzhang to Ningbo guild leaders to Yancheng rickshaw magnates, native-place barons acted to funnel new arrivals from their home villages into lines of work over which they exercised some influence. Geographical origin was thus mediated through patron-client relations to generate the occupational niches with which various groups of immigrants became readily identified. The contacts and resources of their benefactors determined the opportunities available to workers in Shanghai.[34] The relatively affluent backgrounds and good connections of patrons from South China—the Cantonese and then, in much greater numbers, those from Ningbo and other Jiangnan locations—enabled workers from these areas to lay claim to the best jobs Shanghai had to offer. As a consequence, they tended to settle permanently in their new place of employment. Laborers from North China (especially Subei) were by contrast generally relegated to less skilled, less well paid, and less stable types of work. (See Map 3 for the location of Jiangnan and Subei regions.)

Over time, the outlines of a bifurcated working world became evident in Shanghai: skilled artisans from South China commanded the secure and high-paying jobs, while peasants from the North labored for starvation wages as rickshaw pullers, dockers, silk reelers, cotton spinners, and the like. Of course, occupational differentiation was in reality a good deal more complicated and fluid than a dichotomous regional model can capture. Within both regions, different counties and villages within counties provided labor power for different jobs. Moreover, native-place identity was not the only factor that consigned workers to particular occupations. Gender was certainly another critical determinant. For example, men from the Subei county of Yangzhou filled the ranks of Shanghai's barbers, bathhouse attendants, and butchers, whereas Yangzhou women often turned to prostitution.

The practice of hiring laborers (segregated by gender) from the same native place to perform the same type of work fostered strong solidarities among various groups of immigrants. These solidarities, I will argue, go a long way toward explaining why Shanghai laborers proved so prone to collective action. Previous scholars have also pointed to the importance of worker solidarity in giving rise to Shanghai's impressive record of labor unrest. In their view of solidarity, however, class consciousness usually figures at the center of the equation. They see native-place allegiance, gender identity, guilds, secret societies, and the like as "feudal" impediments to true working-class unity. Only because Shanghai

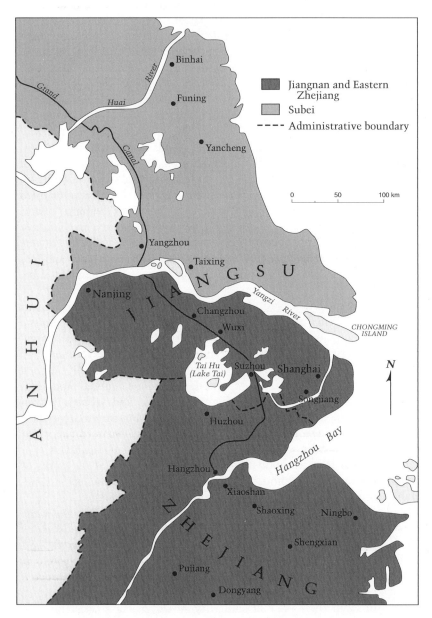

Map 3. Jiangnan and Subei. Adapted from Emily Honig, *Sisters and Strangers:
Women in the Shanghai Cotton Mills, 1911–1949* (Stanford, Calif., 1986).

workers, under outside leadership, were able to overcome such divisions was a "modern" labor movement made possible.

Two generations of Chinese scholarship and the one major Western study of the Chinese labor movement concur in attributing the rise of labor activism (which was most pronounced in Shanghai) to the growth of class consciousness among the workers. Although there is considerable debate over precisely *when* the workers became fully class conscious, Chinese analysts generally agree that the process was well under way by the mid-1920's. The French historian Jean Chesneaux reaches a similar conclusion: "In the course of its economic and political struggles between 1919 and 1927 the Chinese working class underwent profound internal changes. Conversely, it was its increasing class-consciousness and the rapid development and strengthening of its organizations that enabled it to undertake the struggles." Although Chesneaux recognizes regional and occupational divisions among Chinese workers, his emphasis is on the "advance in class solidarity" that accompanied the militant strikes of the 1920's.[35]

In contrast to this picture of growing class solidarity, recent studies by American historians have stressed the fragmented character of Chinese workers. Emily Honig identifies deep divisions, based primarily on native-place origin, among women in the Shanghai cotton mills, arguing that "women strikers of the 1920's showed little evidence of class consciousness or revolutionary commitment." Gail Hershatter's study of workers in Tianjin also finds "fragmentation, divisiveness, a changing sexual division of labor, and growth that proceeded in a distressingly nonlinear fashion."[36] Honig and Hershatter suggest that only during the Civil War years of the mid-1940's did Communist cadres manage to adapt and bridge intraworker differences so as to construct a successful revolutionary labor movement.

My approach builds on this recent line of analysis, highlighting divisions among Chinese workers and rejecting the argument that a monolithic working-class consciousness accounted for the rise of the labor movement.[37] More than previous authors, however, I stress a positive link between workers' fragmentation and their activism. Divisions among Shanghai laborers generated systematic and long-standing solidarities: immigrants of the same native place and gender engaged in common lines of work, thereby creating a potent basis for collective action. Rather than seeing such groupings as obstacles to be overcome by "modern" revolutionaries, it is perhaps more accurate to understand them as the very stuff of which labor activism was made.

Current theories of labor militance emphasize the importance of working-class culture in generating collective action. Cultural identity tends to be strongest among ethnically divided groups of workers. As John Cumbler has observed for the United States, "When an ethnic group dominated an industry . . . ethnic language, shared foods, traditions, histories, folklore and patterns of protest were welded into a powerful working-class culture."[38]

In urban China, as in many other immigrant settlements, native-place origin was closely associated with ethnic identity. As D. K. Lieu notes,

> From the points of view of dialect, customs, ceremonials, one locality in China is quite different from others. . . . So in all big cities there is a special feeling of brotherhood among people coming from the same native place; and to promote co-operation and mutual assistance, native clubs and guilds are organized. In Shanghai there are several hundred of these organizations. Aside from this, people from the same native place have the tendency to settle down in one place. . . . Concentration of residence of the people from the same native place leads to the establishment of particular types of tea-houses, restaurants, amusement places, catering mostly to patrons of one particular place. These places, on the one hand, are informal places for gatherings and discussions, disseminating news and promoting friendliness among people from the same native place, but, on the other hand, they are often trouble-breeding centers and rallying grounds for feuds and conflicts between people of different native-places.[39]

The solidarities forged by this politics of place facilitated militance, though not necessarily in a class-conscious fashion.[40] Sometimes, as in the Ningbo cemetery struggle, native-place identities could unite rich and poor in defense of their common cultural property. Sometimes, as in the Small Sword Rebellion or in dockworkers' feuds, such allegiances could turn one group of workers against another. In instances such as these, identification with place overrode identification with class. As we shall discover, however, this was not invariably the case. For skilled workers in particular, pride in one's own pedigree could at times be compatible with an ecumenical concern for the well-being of other, less fortunate laborers.[41] Moreover, even when class consciousness was not the driving motivation, at certain critical junctures (e.g., the May Fourth and May Thirtieth movements discussed in Chapter 4) workers of disparate origin—often led by native-place patrons—found it possible to coordinate their efforts in massive protests that changed the course of modern Chinese history.

The politics of place was thus a two-edged sword that both opened possibilities and set boundaries to the development of collective action. The emergence of working-class struggles in which issues of production became as, or more, salient than allegiance to place, seldom involved the abandonment of native-place identity. Instead, the fact that geographical origin acted to funnel laborers from the same regions into the same occupational niches meant that concerns of place and of production were usually mutually reinforcing. As I have suggested in this chapter, organizations that were at once communities of *immigrants* and collectivities of *workers* tightened the link between these two identities. For skilled laborers from the South, guilds performed this important function. For unskilled laborers from the North, gangs served as critical mediators. To be sure, the distinction was in practice not nearly so stark as the social science urge toward order might tempt one to assert. More than a few South China artisans joined gangs, just as native-place guilds rose to the defense of fellow workers from the North on more than one occasion. Even so, the difference was significant, and, as I shall detail in the two chapters to follow, it gave rise to distinctive repertoires of labor protest.

CHAPTER TWO

South China Artisans

CONTRARY TO THE COMMON view that the introduction of modern industry suddenly generated a new class of proletarians, devoid of skill or control over their jobs, most workers in China's first mechanized factories were artisans. Artisanal work is characterized by several features: skill developed through a period of apprenticeship, organization based on guilds, and control over admission of workers to the trade and over the labor process itself. The shipyards, arsenals, and machine works established after the Opium War hired experienced carpenters and metalworkers who commanded high wages from the foreigners and Chinese officials in whose employ they worked. Well-connected contractor-foremen recruited trained workmen from areas, almost invariably in South China, where skilled people could be found in ample supply.

Guilds and Artisan Community

In his study of nineteenth-century Hankou, William Rowe appropriately highlights the guild as "the most important element directing both social and economic life."[1] Most analyses of Chinese guilds have emphasized their role as *merchant* associations that had major implications for China's economic modernization.[2] Chinese guilds, however, were also *artisan* associations responsible for recruiting, training, and retaining skilled craftsmen of a particular trade. Thus, as in Europe, these organizations had important implications for the development of a labor movement.[3] More than their European counterparts, however, Chinese guilds typically limited their artisan membership to workers from a particular geographical region.[4]

A close relationship existed between the establishment of native-place guilds and the recruitment of skilled labor in the treaty port of Shanghai.

The first labor contractor for carpenters in Shanghai shipyards, for example, was a Cantonese who had worked as a carpenter himself in a foreign-owned shipbuilding company in Canton. After moving to Shanghai around 1850, contractor Li Rong made frequent trips home to his native county of Taishan. Within a few years, he had hired several hundred fellow Taishan carpenters (some as skilled master craftsmen, others as young apprentices) to work in the growing Shanghai shipbuilding industry. Subsequently another Cantonese contractor, Lu Wen, hired workers from counties other than Taishan. Whereas Li's recruits handled work on ships' hulls, Lu's labored in the holds. In 1858, Lu Wen collected three coppers from each of his employees for the purpose of founding a carpentry guild known as the *Lu Ban dian* after its patron deity, Lu Ban. Located in the Hongkou district, in the heart of the Cantonese residential area, the *Lu Ban dian* soon became a guild for all Cantonese carpenters, regardless of their native county or particular specialization. Any new arrival from Guangdong was required to join the guild before he could obtain work as a carpenter in Shanghai. For an entry fee and annual dues of 15 to 30 percent of their wage, members were guaranteed employment opportunities and welfare provisions in the event of illness or death.[5]

The success of the Cantonese carpentry guild prompted subsequent immigrants to follow suit. In 1866, woodworkers from Ningbo established their own *Lu Ban dian* in Shanghai. The new guild soon included some 600 members, of whom two-thirds worked in shipyards while the remainder moved about from job to job. Each spring, on the birthday of the patron deity Lu Ban, Ningbo labor contractors were invited to recruit apprentices—one per contractor—from among new guild members.[6]

Despite the advantages to be gained by guild membership, the system was not without its challengers. In January 1879, three Cantonese brothers who lived in Hongkou and worked as carpenters at the British-owned Pudong Shipyard and Engineering Works refused to remit the steep annual fee demanded by guild regulations. Claiming immunity because they were employed at a foreign firm, the brothers argued that the guild had no hold over them. This display of insolence was considered serious enough to draw the Guangdong native-place association into the conflict on behalf of the carpentry guild. Under pressure from the leaders of the local Guangdong community, the Shanghai magistrate issued an order requiring the carpenters to pay the guild fee. Because the carpenters resided in Hongkou where American authority prevailed, however, the signature of the U.S. consul was required before the magistrate's order could be delivered. Although Consul Bailey was willing enough to sign the document, he appended a proviso summoning the carpenters to appear before the city's Mixed Court, the joint Sino-foreign judicial body originally established in Shanghai in 1865 to try cases involving foreign interests. At the court hearing, the British managers of the Pudong Engineering Works testified that Chinese guild regulations impeded the rights of foreign businesses to hire workers. Honoring this opinion, the court ruled that the carpenters were exempt from guild demands and promised the brothers British police protection in the event of any further interference from the Cantonese *Lu Ban dian*.[7]

As this example indicates, guilds were not always able to exert unchallenged control in the heterogeneous environment of treaty-port Shanghai. Multiple sovereignties could work to undermine monopolistic claims on workers. Nonetheless, the power of guilds was considerable in large part because they protected the privileged position of skilled workers in the Shanghai labor market. The ability of guilds to limit participation in the trade guaranteed high wages for their artisan members. Well aware of this fact, workers sometimes banded together to enforce guild rules. In 1880, for example, the British-owned Shanghai Dock and Engineering Company pressed charges against six carpenters who had injured its foreman in retaliation for his having hired some workers from outside of the Ningbo carpentry guild. When the court hearing was convened, other craftsmen from the Ningbo *Lu Ban dian* surrounded the offices of the Mixed Court to add their voices to the clamor for guild control.[8]

Guild strength was reflected in architectural splendor. As a foreign observer described the woodworking guilds of Shanghai:

> A quarter of a mile along the Chinese Bund brings one to what appears to be a temple. It isn't. It is the guild-house of . . . Chekiang [Zhejiang]. There are two open courts, a theatre, a temple. The temple houses three gods, the principal one being Lu Pan [Lu Ban], to whom the wood merchants refer for the settlement of any disputes that may arise among them. . . . Proceeding, one finds among squalid tenements one of the most magnificent guild-houses in Shanghai . . . also a timber guild. Excellent examples of work in Chinese style are to be found in this guild with its red and gold temple and theatre, pewter storks and incense burners, and chequered patterned walls.[9]

The inclusion of temple and theater within its compound marked the guild as a community center. Religious ceremonies and dramatic performances enhanced the corporate spirit of guild activities. For most members, the highlight of the year was an annual banquet bringing together artisans from different enterprises. At the printers' guild, for example, skilled mechanics and typesetters from the Commercial Press, Zhonghua Book Company, and *Shen bao* and *Xinwen bao* newspapers assembled each fall around the time of the mid-autumn festival for a lavish vegetarian feast presided over by Buddhist monks chanting sutras. After the meal a theatrical performance and a game of mahjong completed the celebrations.[10]

Metalworking was another trade whose guild enjoyed strong membership support. Founded in 1800 as the Cassia Society by thirteen tinsmiths, the guild held its annual meeting in the fall at the time when cassia flowers were in full bloom. On this festive occasion tinsmiths would gather to honor their patron deity, Old Patriarch Li (*Li laojun*). Some years later, when Shanghai's copper and tinsmith shops began to amalgamate, the Cassia Society accepted workers from both trades. Following the Opium War, metalworking grew rapidly to accommodate the new shipbuilding industry. In an effort to ameliorate conflict and retain control, the guild promulgated a uniform price regulation and limited each workshop to hiring a single apprentice every three years.[11] By 1920, the metalworkers' guild owned considerable property and guaranteed a nine-hour workday to its 40,000 members, most of whom were well-educated craftsmen from Wuxi, Ningbo, and other Jiangnan locations.[12]

Powerful guilds fostered a "guild mentality" within the trades they served. At the beginning of their three-year training program, apprentices in metalworking shops were required to perform three kowtows with incense in hand both to their master and to Old Patriarch Li.[13] Similar customs prevailed even among metalworkers in Shanghai's most "modernized" factories. In 1920, a journalist reported with evident amazement on the persistence of "feudal guild relations" in one of Shanghai's largest and most profitable machine works. The imposing Western architectural style of the factory building belied a much more "traditional" pattern of interpersonal relations among the artisans who worked within its walls. New apprentices were made to "honor the master" (*bai shifu*) in a ceremony complete with candles, incense, and an improvised altar. After lighting a stick of incense, the apprentice kowtowed three times to the whitewashed wall to pay respect to the factory and then thrice more to the master craftsmen. Although the substitution of the factory wall for Old Patriarch Li suggests an important difference between the work cultures of shop and factory, the ritual continuities are unmistakable.[14]

For the skilled artisans who made up the majority of Shanghai's first generation of industrial workers, the move from craft shop to factory thus entailed less of a break with customary practice than might at first be imagined. The situation at the Jiangnan Arsenal, Shanghai's first mechanized factory, is illustrative. Founded in 1865 (some 25 years before the city's first cotton mill), the arsenal recruited most of its master craftsmen from foreign-owned shipyards and machine works in Canton and Hong Kong. Apprentices were also hired from afar, in part because of local rumors about the dangers of being swallowed by factory chimneys or beaten to death by factory machines. (The only local children who could be persuaded to work at the new establishment were those from a nearby orphanage for victims of the Taiping Rebellion.) Initially all workers were required to live at the factory dormitory, but the number of employees quickly outgrew the 1,500-person capacity of the dormitory, and many laborers moved into housing along Guangdong Road just outside the factory gates.[15] Workers from the same distant geographical region living and working in such close proximity fostered a tightly knit immigrant community among Cantonese craftsmen at the arsenal. Their native-place guild organizations (e.g., the *Lu Ban dian* for Cantonese carpenters) further solidified such networks. Over time, as immigration from other locations made possible the hiring of more non-Cantonese artisans, these newer employees formed their own neighborhoods and guilds to enhance security and competitiveness in the volatile Shanghai marketplace.

By the turn of the century, a clear hierarchy of occupational niches, closely associated with native-place origins, obtained at the Jiangnan Arsenal. Carpenters were from Canton, machinists from Ningbo and Shaoxing, and blacksmiths from Wuxi. In every case, entry to the trade was restricted by monopolistic guilds. To become an apprentice in the boilermaking shop at the arsenal one not only had to come from Wuxi but to be the son of a Wuxi boilermaker. Virtually all skilled jobs at the factory drew their artisans from a specific South China (especially Jiangnan) locale; master craftsmen refused to give workers from the North China area of Subei a chance to apprentice. Only in the poorly paid job of riveting could workers from Subei and Pudong ("the wrong side of the river" in Shanghai) be found.*

The importance of pedigree and connections in securing skilled positions suggests the arbitrary and subjective definition of "skill." Whereas most "skilled" jobs could be mastered during a relatively brief period of training, virtually every guild required a three-year apprenticeship to qualify for admission to the coveted ranks of its trade.† Skill was thus as

---

*Economics Institute of the Shanghai Academy of Social Sciences, ed., *Jiangnan zaochuanchang changshi* [Factory history of the Jiangnan Arsenal] (Nanjing, 1983), pp. 154–55; Li Cishan, "Shanghai laodong zhuangkuang" [Shanghai labor conditions], *Xinqingnian* 7, no. 6 (1920): 37. Li Cishan (p. 12) recounts the sorry tale of a hardworking and skilled apprentice in a cotton mill machine room who was maltreated because of his Subei origins. After suffering repeated curses in Wu dialect, the apprentice left the factory.

†As Peter Golas observes in his analysis of Chinese guilds, "The existence of an apprenticeship period and its length had usually only a very remote connection with the time required for a novice to learn a given trade" ("Early Ch'ing Guilds," in *The City in Late Imperial China*, ed. G. William Skinner [Stanford, Calif., 1977], p. 566).

much a socially and culturally constructed attribute as it was an embodiment of objective production abilities.

Occupational segmentation by native place, mediated through discriminatory guilds, fostered a sense of separateness and community among the artisans of a particular trade. Craftsmen tended to frequent the same teahouses located close to their respective guild halls, further cementing these solidarities. It may well be, as has been observed with respect to Chinese merchants, that native-place identity represented a hard-headed strategy for adapting to urban environments more than a sentimental clinging to traditional rural values: "The show of parochialism was in part an affectation, an air supplied to assure one's customers of impartiality and credibility. In this sense, clannishness was to business success in China what religious affiliation was to business success in frontier America."[16] Like the businessmen in whose employ they labored, workers in Chinese cities were forced to operate as part of native-place communities to ensure their economic survival. That such associations may have been generated as much by the imperatives of the urban marketplace as by some emotional attachment to one's home village did not, however, render them any less important as building blocks of collective action.

The link between community solidarity and a capacity for protest has been well established in the social science literature. Charles Tilly helped pioneer this approach, relating changes in protest repertoires to changing social organizations.[17] More recently, rational choice theorist Michael Taylor has argued, "Peasant collective action in revolutions and rebellions was based on community (as many historians have argued) and this is mainly *why* the large numbers of people involved were able to overcome the free-rider problem familiar to students of collective action (which has *not* been recognized by the historians)."* Strong communities, in other words, could override the otherwise "rational" tendency to withhold active participation in group endeavors. Although it is often suggested, à la Emile Durkheim, that urbanization spelled the end of the solidary peasant community and the onset of anomie among a rootless city population, this presumed distinction between "traditional" community and "modern" disunity is not always evident. Urbanites, too,

---

*Michael Taylor, "Rationality and Revolutionary Collective Action," in *Rationality and Revolution*, ed. Taylor (Cambridge, England, 1988), p. 64. Taylor suggests that when "traditional" peasant communities gave way to "modern" associations and organizations, the social basis for collective action was undermined, making "non-thin-rational behaviour more common and the success of collective action less predictable" (p. 93). My study disputes this alleged dichotomy between "tradition" and "modernity."

could form powerful communities just as capable of enforcing compliance as the rural villages from which they had come.

Early Artisan Protest

In large part because of the clannish nature of work, residence, and recreation among Shanghai's factory artisans, they quickly developed a reputation for staging group protests. In 1868, workers at the Shanghai Dock and Engineering Company struck to prevent a wage cut.[18] In 1879, ironsmiths at the Pudong Engineering Works walked off the job to complain against maltreatment by a foreign overseer.[19] In 1883, workers at the Jiangnan Arsenal rioted outside the offices of the general manager when a foreman at the factory tried to increase the length of the workday.[20] Two years later, they engaged in a slowdown to demand higher wages.[21] In 1890 a new general manager at the arsenal elicited a full-scale strike when he announced that the workday would be lengthened from eight to nine hours. On the morning the new schedule was to take effect, not a single worker entered the factory.[22]

These early protests were largely defensive in nature. Wage cuts, mistreatment, and extended work hours precipitated the confrontations. With the expansion of industry after the Sino-Japanese War of 1894–95, however, the pattern of artisan strikes changed noticeably. Increased demand for skilled workers encouraged a more aggressive style of protest on the part of this favored sector of the work force. Artisan strikes in the two decades leading up to the May Fourth Movement of 1919 were overwhelmingly offensive in character (see Appendix A). Demands for wage raises fueled the great majority of these incidents, but conflicts over guild rights, unionization, and factory discipline also occurred.

Of the 65 incidents for which we have data, more than 90 percent (59) were offensive strikes in which workers made new demands of their employers. The strengthened position of factory artisans in the Shanghai labor market had clearly led to more assertive protest.* The reports of these protests are too cursory to permit extensive analysis, but several themes do emerge. First, strikes repeatedly challenged the authority of

---

*The growing market for skilled workers is suggested by the rapid proliferation of factories whose work forces consisted largely of such employees: printing shops, machine plants, and tool factories. Whereas from 1875 to 1894 only 1 printing shop, 1 machine plant, and 2 tool factories were established in Shanghai, in the period from 1895 to 1919 some 72 printing shops, 224 machine plants, and 28 tool factories were opened. See Luo Zhiru, *Tongjibiaozhong zhi Shanghai* [Shanghai through statistical tables] (Nanjing, 1932), p. 63.

overseers and foremen. As certified professionals, skilled workers were quick to defend their control over the labor process in the face of unjust treatment or new impositions by authorities in the workplace. Second, in the few cases for which detailed accounts are available, the importance of native-place allegiance (typically mediated through guilds) is clear.

For example, in 1902 a British manager at the Shanghai Dock and Engineering Company testified before the Mixed Court that he had been summoned by the Guangdong woodworkers' guild to attend a meeting at their hall. When he arrived, he was greeted by a large number of Cantonese carpenters clamoring for a wage hike. To legitimate their demands, the woodworkers had forcibly prevailed upon their guild directors to affix the official seal of the Guangdong carpentry guild to the grievance petition. A guild director who also testified at the hearing noted that carpenters from Ningbo had continued to work throughout the dispute.[23]

A split between carpenters of different native-place origins occurred again a few years later when the thousand Cantonese woodworkers employed in both Chinese and foreign-owned shipyards went on strike to demand a 20 percent wage increase. Ningbo carpenters, whose normal wage was one-third less than that paid to Cantonese, served as scabs at several factories. Claiming that their superior skills were irreplaceable, the strikers threatened to leave Shanghai for Canton or other treaty ports where wages were higher and the cost of living lower. The threat may have been made more persuasive by Cantonese workers' history of returning home as an economic protest.[24] In any event, it was remarkably effective: within a week the shipyards signed an agreement raising the wage for Cantonese carpenters by 15 percent and pledging that every effort would be made to hire Cantonese, rather than Ningbo, woodworkers for any future openings.[25]

As these cases suggest, native-place identity certainly could encourage interworker competition. Even so, it would be a mistake to downplay the organizational potency of such parochial affiliations. Rather than dampen worker militancy, regional loyalty—divisive though it was—served as a rallying point for artisans' activism.

Politicization

Although the politics of place fostered fragmentation of the labor force, the result was not necessarily incompatible with support for wider political causes. Provincial allegiances were consonant with fervent nationalism, as was demonstrated in the Shanghai construction trade when carpenters and masons amalgamated into a single guild for the explicit purpose of preserving their market in the face of competition from the new, Western-style construction industry.[26] A stele inscription at the construction workers' guild, founded in 1906 exclusively for carpenters and stone masons from Shaoxing and Shanghai, demonstrates that native-place identity was no barrier to nationalist sentiment:

> The foreigners take advantage of our shortcomings to export their own products. . . . Our government offices have foreign personnel, our factories have foreign artisans, our schools have foreign teachers. The European influence is everywhere. . . . Our 400 million Chinese lack vigor. Only our construction trade is able to stand independently! Only when we stand independently can we be free. Only when we are free can we be strong. Only when everybody is strong will the nation and race be strong. A single person cannot be strong. Only after combining with millions of others can a person become strong. These millions must behave as a single person to become strong. Associations [tuanti] are the magical means to self-strengthening. . . . Wherein lies our spirit? In resisting foreign insults and cherishing our same kind. Wherein lies our lifeline? In uniting our resolve and sharpening our skills. . . . With these we can win out against the foreigners; with these we can survive in the international struggle.[27]

The notion that association (tuanti) provided a spiritual foundation for economic and political power reflected the artisans' organizational experience. Schooled in the corporate traditions of guild life, the construction workers of Shaoxing and Shanghai stressed associational bonds as the solution to the pressing problems of the day. Though parochial in tone, such sentiments did not necessarily stand in the way of political activism, even on behalf of revolutionary projects.[28]

Like nationalism, revolutionary participation could fit comfortably with native-place identification. On November 4, 1911, when troops of Sun Yat-sen's revolutionary army (made up overwhelmingly of Cantonese) surrounded the Jiangnan Arsenal, Cantonese carpenters helped them tear down the wooden fence and proceed to the arsenal warehouse. Weapons seized in this raid made an important contribution to the downfall of imperial rule in the city.* As soon as the victorious revolu-

---

*Economics Institute of the Shanghai Academy of Social Sciences, ed., *Jiangnan zaochuanchang changshi*, p. 165; *Xinhai geming zai Shanghai shiliao xuanji* [Compilation of historical materials on the 1911 Revolution in Shanghai] (Shanghai, 1981), pp. 675–76. The link between skilled Cantonese workers and support for the 1911 Revolution went deeper than this incident might suggest. Most of the early revolutionary leaders, including Sun Yat-sen, were Cantonese. They attracted a substantial following from fellow provincials employed as craftsmen at foreign-owned shipyards in Hong Kong and Canton. These literate, skilled workers, who were in direct contact

tionaries established their government, more than a hundred Cantonese workers rushed to military headquarters to enlist as soldiers under the new regime.[29]

The Revolution of 1911 marks a turning point in the history of Shanghai labor. With the overthrow of the Qing dynasty, a criminal code that had stipulated stern punishment for strikers was no longer in effect.[30] More important, the general politicization of urban discourse that accompanied the establishment of the new republic encouraged workers, especially skilled artisans, to frame their demands in more ambitious terms.

Political parties became actively involved in labor organizing as a result of the more permissive atmosphere following the downfall of dynastic rule. Chen Qimei, active in Sun Yat-sen's Revolutionary party and military governor-general of Shanghai for a brief period following the revolution, sponsored one of the more than 80 new parties that sprang up in Shanghai after 1911. That group, known as the Mutual Advancement Society (*Gongjin hui*), included workers and foremen with gang connections.[31]

More instrumental in promoting an assertive labor movement was the Republic of China Labor Party (*Zhonghua minguo gongdang*), which drew the great majority of its members from craftsmen in trades as diverse as jewelry making, hat making, carpentry, and machine building. A requirement for membership was secure employment and "the ability to stand on one's own feet."[32] Xu Qiwen, the worker who served as the guiding spirit behind the new party, persuaded several progressive industrialists (some of whom were also members of the Socialist Party) to lend their support. Naming Sun Yat-sen as their honorary chairman, members of the Labor Party promulgated a five-point platform calling for promotion of industrial development (through industrial exhibitions, model factories, product competitions, and technical schools), improve-

---

with foreign managers, were responsive to the message of nationalism and economic reform espoused by Sun and his comrades. Ma Chaojun, an early Xingzhong Hui member, had apprenticed as a mechanic at a Hong Kong shipyard. Later, while working in a San Francisco shipyard, Ma got to know Sun Yat-sen and was persuaded to follow him to Japan to study political economy at Meiji University and assist in the revolutionary enterprise. Returning to China in 1906, Ma helped to found the Guangdong Mechanics' Association—often hailed as China's first modern labor union. He also made extended trips to Wuhan and Shanghai to contact the many skilled Cantonese craftsmen employed in arsenals and shipyards in these cities. After the success of the 1911 Revolution, Sun Yat-sen placed Ma Chaojun in charge of the national labor movement. See Ma Chaojun et al., *Zhongguo laogong yundongshi* [A history of the Chinese labor movement] (Taipei, 1959), 5 volumes, 1:52; Su Qiming, *Beifa qijian gongyun zhi yanjiu* [A study of the labor movement during the period of the Northern Expedition] (Taipei, 1984), pp. 63–65.

ment of workers' knowledge (through schools, journals, and lectures), relief of workers' hardships (through credit unions, cooperatives, and charities), enhancement of workers' martial spirit (through establishment of a workers' militia), and encouragement of workers' political participation (through involvement in local assemblies and unions).[33]

More dramatically, the Labor Party offered assistance to several large-scale strikes—all of them involving skilled artisans—which erupted in Shanghai shortly after the 1911 Revolution. The first occurred in the foundry industry, a trade that had established a branch committee of the Labor Party known as the United Loyalty Association (*Tongyi hui*). Spurred to action by their new proto-union, foundry workers in the summer of 1912 submitted a demand for higher wages and fewer working hours. When the industry refused to accede to this ultimatum, workers walked off the job. Labor Party Chairman Xu Qiwen immediately organized a strike committee to provide financial assistance, convincing management to hand the strikers a complete victory in less than a day. Xu's negotiating skills were demonstrated again a few weeks later on behalf of Shanghai's bean curd makers, for whom he won a long demanded wage hike.[34]

A greater challenge to Labor Party leadership occurred in November in the form of another carpenters' strike.[35] That month some 7,000 woodworkers (excepting only those from Wenzhou, who remained at their jobs until forced to join in) struck to demand a 20 percent wage increase. When mediation by the county government failed to bring a settlement, the artisans turned to the Labor Party for assistance. Xu Qiwen's efforts on behalf of the strikers earned him the ire of the employers, who filed a lawsuit accusing him of "giving talks at several places and distributing leaflets to incite the ignorant workers so that he could personally profit from the situation." Although the district court dismissed the charge for lack of evidence, the Shanghai Garrison warned Xu against stirring up further trouble. The chastened Labor Party leader advised the carpenters to call off their strike, but it persisted until, in late January 1913, a 10 percent wage hike was finally granted.

The Labor Party enjoyed less success in the case of a strike launched by its branch association in the jewelry trade in December 1912.[36] To publicize the artisans' demand for a 10 percent wage increase, the party branch established a strike office which printed up handbills and distributed strike pay. Under the pressure of police interference and heavy fines, however, the office was forced to disband, and the protest ended in failure.

The declining efficacy of the Labor Party's support for striking artisans was a direct result of stepped-up state repression. Disturbed by Xu Qiwen's inroads among workers, particularly his unionization efforts, the Shanghai Garrison issued an order in late 1912 prohibiting the formation of labor unions. About the same time, Yuan Shikai's government in Beijing announced a national ban on strikes.[37]

Convinced that government opposition constituted the biggest obstacle to gains for labor, Xu Qiwen decided to take drastic action. On May 28, 1913, he participated in a daring assault on the Jiangnan Arsenal. Masterminded by none other than the erstwhile revolutionary Chen Qimei (who had also grown disillusioned with the repressive regime in Beijing), the uprising was envisioned as the first step in a coup attempt against Yuan Shikai. Carrying a white banner announcing his group as the National People's Army of the Republic of China (*Zhonghua minguo guominjun*), Xu and his artisan followers marched on the arsenal warehouse at one o'clock in the morning. Unfortunately for their ambitious plans, however, the general manager had received advance warning of the attack and was able to squelch the uprising in less than half an hour. Xu Qiwen was arrested on the spot and immediately sent to Beijing for execution. His Labor Party was outlawed.[38]

Artisans' assaults on the Jiangnan Arsenal marked both the beginning and the end of the brief flowering of political freedom enjoyed by Shanghai labor as a result of the 1911 Revolution. The demise of Xu Qiwen and his Labor Party signaled a much more restrictive attitude toward labor on the part of both local and national authorities.* Nevertheless, the organizational lessons which Xu had taught were not forgotten. In the many artisan strikes that swept Shanghai during succeeding years, demands for unionization, printing of handbills to gain public support, and collection of a strike fund were common features.

"Traditional" Radicalism

World War I, which ushered in China's "golden age of national industry," saw a noticeable rise in the level of strike activity. The proliferation

---

*After Yuan Shikai's death in 1916, the Labor Party was briefly revived under the leadership of Han Hui, a former 1911 revolutionary and anti-Yuan activist who also served as patriarch for Shanghai gang members following the assassination of Chen Qimei in 1916. (This linkage among revolutionaries, gangsters, and labor would resurface repeatedly throughout the course of the Republican period.) The constituency of the revived Labor Party was again largely skilled workers, organized by trade: printing, carpentry, painting, boilermaking, machinery, and so on. The reconstituted party focused on setting up savings banks and experimental factories and was active in only a few strikes. It ceased to operate after the execution of Han Hui by French police in 1917. See Fan Songfu, "Shanghai banghui neimu" [Inside the Shanghai gangs], *Wenshi ziliao xuanji*, no. 3 (1980), p. 155; *Minguo ribao*, Dec. 16, 1916, Jan. 4, 12, 17, Feb. 2, 15, 19, 25, Mar. 4, 9, 12, 13, 15, Apr. 15, 20, 22, 24, June 13, 17, 26, July 10, 29, Aug. 22, Sept. 18, 29, Nov. 2, 10, 1917; *Shi bao*, Nov. 27, Dec. 13, 14, 21, 24, 30, 31, 1916, Feb. 20, Mar. 14, 15, 20, Apr. 16, 26, May 10, 16, June 28, 1917.

of Chinese-owned factories—stimulated by the preoccupation of foreign capitalists with the war in Europe—generated a substantial increase in both the number of workers and the frequency of their protests. On the eve of the war, the industrial labor force of Shanghai stood at about 100,000; by the end of the war, the figure had doubled.* Their protests accelerated at an even faster pace: in the five years before the war (1909–13), Shanghai experienced 30 strikes; in the five years during the war (1914–18), some 86 strikes occurred—nearly a threefold increase over the preceding period.[39] The greater frequency of strikes was accompanied by a rise in their duration and size as well.[40]

Protest activity by artisans in particular in this period was marked by a noticeable increase in cooperation across trades. In November 1914, for example, carpenters and cement masons joined the city's painters in a united strike for higher wages. The unrest had begun the previous month when the painters—armed with garbage to heave at their employers if need be—convened a meeting at their local guild. The militance of the workers elicited a quick and favorable response from the employers. Pleased by the settlement, the painters hired a troupe of ballad singers to "repay the gods" (choushen) in a three-day celebration at the guild, after which they cheerfully returned to work. The following week, however, it became clear that the employers had no intention of living up to the terms of the agreement. Thus betrayed, the painters—more than a hundred strong—marched to the magistrate's yamen with incense in hand to plead their case on bended knee. Unmoved by this customary display of respect, the magistrate ordered the workers to behave in a more "modern" fashion by electing representatives and submitting a formal petition. Meanwhile, at the request of the employers, the Shanghai Garrison stationed troops at the guild hall to prevent the painters from meeting there.[41]

The spectacle of fellow artisans being forcibly turned away from their guild by soldiers aroused the sympathy of other craftsmen. On November 18, more than 100 representatives of Shanghai's cement mason and carpentry trades met at a teahouse in the International Settlement to

*Zhongguo jindai gongyeshi ziliao [Materials on the history of China's modern industry] (Beijing, 1957–61), 4 volumes, 2:1184–85, 1190; Li Cishan, "Shanghai laodong zhuangkuang." According to estimates by the Japanese scholar Furuya, in 1919 Shanghai had 261,785 workers employed in "modern" (i.e., mechanized) industries, 132,250 nonindustrial unskilled workers (including rickshaw pullers, dockworkers, and the like), 200,000 clerks and shop assistants, and 212,833 craftsmen. The total of 806,868 employed workers comprised fully 40 percent of the city's population of two million (T. Furuya, "Dai ichiji daisenki Shanhai no toshi keisei to rōdōsha jinkō" [Shanghai's city growth and labor population during World War I], Jimbun kagaku kenkyū [Niigata daigaku], no. 68 [1985]: 85).

𝓎.

draw up handbills pledging their support for the painters' strike. The next day, following the arrest of six carpenters charged with distributing pro-strike leaflets, more than a thousand masons and carpenters gathered at *Lu Ban dian*. Although initially locked out by the guild guard, the angry workers managed to force their way into the guild and seize the tablet honoring patron deity Lu Ban. Buttressed with this symbol of legitimacy, the protesters marched first to the home of the guild manager and then to the police station to demand the release of their arrested leaders. When the police fired blanks to disperse the crowd, the panic-struck artisans dropped the sacred tablet and scrambled to escape. Many were severely injured in the pandemonium. The sorry incident at the police station provoked a quick reaction from the city's carpenters and masons; the next day a general strike was declared.[42]

Despite the cross-trade character of the protest, its organizational foundation remained firmly rooted in native-place allegiances. Carpenters and cement masons from three areas—Shanghai, Ningbo, and Shaoxing—participated, and each chose representatives to negotiate demands. The city's painters also came overwhelmingly from Shanghai, Ningbo, and Shaoxing, which undoubtedly helped to facilitate the impressive display of artisan solidarity seen in this strike.[43]

That workers from Shanghai and the Ning-Shao region should find it easy to cooperate, even across trade lines, was not surprising in view of their common heritage and life-style. These craftsmen spoke more or less the same Wu dialect and frequented the same teahouses to listen together to Shaoxing opera over a cup of Zhejiang tea and conversation. Furthermore, Shanghai labor recruitment practices had resulted in a huge influx of Jiangnan artisans in recent years. Whereas during the nineteenth century, foreign-owned shipyards had relied heavily on Cantonese craftsmen, the subsequent blossoming of Chinese capitalism, which in Shanghai was engineered by industrialists from Jiangnan, saw a commensurate increase in the recruitment of skilled workers from that area.[*]

For the duration of the three-trade strike, participating workers gathered each day at neighborhood teahouses in the old Chinese city to listen to reports from their designated representatives. Finally, after a series of grueling negotiating sessions at *Lu Ban dian* with directors of the

---

[*]Population figures for Shanghai's International Settlement give a rough indication of the decline in the predominance of Cantonese workers. Cantonese residents made up 20 percent of the population in 1885, but the number had fallen to 8 percent by 1915 (Zou Yiren, *Jiu Shanghai renkou bianqian de yanjiu* [Studies in the population change of old Shanghai] [Shanghai, 1980], p. 114).

Ningbo, Shaoxing, and Shanghai cliques, the workers' representatives won an across-the-board wage increase.[44]

As the above case suggests, organizing along native-place lines did not inhibit strikers from forcefully pressing their demands, even against employers with whom they shared a common geographical origin. Native-place identity promoted camaraderie among workers in different trades, but it did not necessarily imply loyalty to native place above or in contradiction to craft or class interests. Seeing that their employers were profiting handsomely from the economic opportunities afforded by the war, artisans insisted upon a fair share of the largess. Native-place networks (inasmuch as they fostered cross-trade communication) worked to enlarge, rather than to forestall, artisan protest.

"Traditional" trappings in the form of native-place guilds, sacred tablets, incense, and religious celebrations should not blind us to the underlying radicalism of these early artisan strikes. Well before the May Fourth Movement or the birth of the Chinese Communist Party, Shanghai artisans were agitating for higher wages and organizational freedoms. Although guilds remained central to these struggles, striking craftsmen also began to join proto-unions. Moreover, within the guilds themselves a rift between the directors and the rank-and-file membership became evident. Workers felt increasingly free to challenge overtly the leadership of their native-place directors.

Craft and Class Consciousness

In some cases, craftsmen even established their own branch guilds in which membership was limited to workers. Painters in 1916 founded an "artisan guild" in the northern part of Shanghai to counter the leadership of the original "trade guild," which remained in the old Chinese city. That same year Cantonese carpenters opened a "public discussion hall," which operated a dormitory for bachelors and provided various social services to its membership. A few years later, the new organization agitated against its parent guild for a wage raise. Evidence suggests that even in the case of the Shanghai-Ningbo-Shaoxing carpenters, who remained an important part of their native-place guild, a spatial separation occurred: during a strike in 1918, artisans held all their meetings in the *Lu Ban dian* worship hall whereas guild directors met in the *gongsuo* offices next door.*

Shi bao, May 11, 1918; Economics Institute of the Shanghai Academy of Social Sciences, ed., *Jiangnan zaochuanchang changshi*, p. 168. A helpful discussion of the growing division between merchant and artisan guilds can be found in Zhuang Zexuan and Chen Xuexun, "Zhongguo zhiye tuanti de yanjiu" [A study of Chinese occupa-

A similar development in nineteenth-century France has been linked with the origins of working-class consciousness.[45] If class consciousness refers to an awareness of exploitation by owners and a propensity to redress grievances through independent collective action, then Shanghai artisans had shown tendencies in this direction years before Marxist intellectuals appeared on the scene. Although "modern" cadres would be quick to condemn native-place identities and guild associations as "feudal" impediments to true class consciousness, such institutions had played a key role in the development of artisan militance. Anxious as communist organizers were to deny this heritage, their subsequent success in organizing the Shanghai labor movement is incomprehensible without it.

The class-conscious leanings of Shanghai artisans were evident well before the May Fourth Movement. In 1912, a Workers' League of 200 skilled workers at the Jiangnan Arsenal issued a proclamation stating that "craftsmen [*gongjiang*] are like laborers [*laodongjia*] and the arsenal is like a capitalist [*zibenjia*]. The laborers must escape from the stranglehold of the capitalist."[46] Similarly, in 1916 a Sincere Comrades Society of skilled printers at the Commercial Press issued a founding manifesto which opened with the words, "Witnessing the oppression of capitalists and the bitterness of workers' life, several dozen comrades [*tongzhi*] have gathered to devise a strategy for liberation [*jiefang*]."[47]

The remarkably precocious language of these artisans is less surprising when placed in comparative context. As Ronald Aminzade notes of French craftsmen (who provided the major support for the early communist and socialist movements in that country), their "tremendous capacity for collective action was based upon the rich organizational and associational life that characterized artisan culture."[48] Similarly, William Sewell links the rise of French artisan radicalism to an inherited corporate tradition that emphasized mutual aid, veneration of a patron saint of the trade, group rituals, and the like. As Sewell has summarized the conclusion of a generation of research on the origins of the European working class: "The nineteenth-century labor movement was born in the craft workshop, not in the dark, satanic mill."[49]

---

tional associations], *Lingnan xuebao* 7, no. 1 (1947): 1–14. William T. Rowe, *Hankow: Conflict and Commerce in a Chinese City, 1796–1895* (Stanford, Calif., 1989), pp. 54–56, discusses the fragmentation of some late nineteenth-century Hankou guilds into separate organizations for employers and artisans. For an even earlier dating of this process in "more advanced sectors of the economy" (e.g., Suzhou cloth production), see Golas, "Early Ch'ing Guilds," p. 558.

CHAPTER THREE

North China Proletarians

THE PRIVILEGES AND securities of Shanghai artisans were not shared by the rank-and-file proletariat, who lived in constant fear of dismissal and replacement. Arbitrary as the definition of skill might be, its institutionalization in the form of apprenticeships and guilds guaranteed its claimants a range of benefits unavailable to the majority of laborers. Wages reflected this disparity. Around the time of the May Fourth Movement, the breakdown in Shanghai was as shown in Table 1.*

A substantial gap existed between the wages of skilled and unskilled laborers. As casual employees unprotected by guild institutions, unskilled workers wielded relatively little bargaining power regarding wages. Moreover, among unskilled workers gender and age were important determinants of wage rates: men were paid considerably more than women, and children received the lowest compensation.

Rural Roots and Gang Connections

The majority of unskilled workers were drawn from the ranks of destitute peasants, especially from the North China countryside. Forced by natural disaster or warfare to flee their native villages, these refugees

---

* *Wusi yundong zai Shanghai shiliao xuanji* [Collection of historical materials on the May Fourth Movement in Shanghai] (Beijing, 1980), p. 15. At this time the daily expenses of an unmarried unskilled laborer averaged 40 cents, while those of an unmarried skilled laborer averaged 64 cents. Expenses for a five-person family of unskilled laborers averaged 71 cents a day, whereas for a five-person family of skilled laborers they averaged $1.20 (ibid., p. 16). Although wages in Shanghai had increased very little in the years between the 1911 Revolution and the May Fourth Movement, consumer prices in the city had risen much more rapidly, including a 46 percent jump in the cost of cotton cloth and a 38 percent increase in the price of rice. See Liu Mingkui, ed., *Zhongguo gongren jieji lishi zhuangkuang* [Historical conditions of the Chinese working class] (Beijing, 1985), vol. 1, p. 483.

TABLE I

Workers' Wages in Shanghai, ca. 1919

Occupation	Daily wage (in yuan)
Skilled	
Mechanic	1.00–2.00
Cement mason	0.60–0.80
Carpenter	0.50–0.80
Painter	0.50–0.70
Bricklayer	0.50
Unskilled	
Male cotton mill worker	0.30–0.40
Male coolie	0.25–0.35
Female cotton mill worker	0.20–0.25
Child cotton mill worker	0.10–0.20

SOURCE: Liu Mingkui, ed., *Zhongguo gongren jieji lishi zhuangkuang* [Historical conditions of the Chinese working class] (Beijing, 1985), vol. I, p. 390.

arrived in Shanghai with few resources or contacts. Untrained for urban labor and unwelcome at the southern-dominated guilds that controlled entry to the skilled occupations, the peasant-workers were relegated to the worst paying and least secure jobs available.

Not surprisingly, many of the unskilled workers returned to the countryside whenever the opportunity arose. Their failure to adapt to urban life was often remarked upon by observers of the Shanghai labor scene. A. M. Kotenev, writing from the viewpoint of the foreign employers, noted in 1927 that "the formation of a . . . separate class of the proletariat as in Europe is not yet completed. Most of the labourers in Shanghai come direct from the countryside. . . . They are farmers, fishermen, or seasonal workers and it takes considerable time to train them in the essential discipline of labour." The situation was described somewhat more positively by Nym Wales, an advocate of labor protest: workers fresh from the countryside, she remarked, "had not yet been beaten down into passive wage slaves with no hope for better living conditions."[1]

Regardless of differences in perspective, observers agreed that close ties to the countryside rendered the unskilled workers of Shanghai an unruly lot. And in this assessment they were surely correct. From the earliest days of the Shanghai labor movement, unskilled workers compiled an impressive record of strikes. Of the more than 50 recorded industrial strikes in Shanghai between 1895 and 1913, at least 75 percent were launched by unskilled workers—most notably women in the silk filatures (which accounted for nearly 50 percent of all strikes) and cotton mills (which contributed another 20 percent).[2]

In explaining protest among artisans, I emphasized the importance of community bonds. How, then, do we account for strike propensity among unskilled laborers, whose mobility and exclusion from guild membership would seem to have undercut their potential for group cohesion? Is this simply a case of anomie, in which rude peasants unaccustomed to urban norms engage in spontaneous violence against the restrictions of city and factory life?

An examination of the structure of unskilled labor in Shanghai reveals forms of solidarity that, though very different from those that characterized artisan existence, were nonetheless capable of sustaining workers' strikes. Even the most transient elements of the unskilled labor force—beggars, night-soil carriers, and dockers, for example—were integrated into urban networks. Admittedly, their lack of skills and the divisiveness of native place, gender, and age did work against the development of a cross-occupational identity among unskilled workers, but an absence of class consciousness was no barrier to labor militance. The segmentation of a heterogeneous mass of workers into relatively homogeneous subdivisions provided a firm foundation for activism.

Unskilled workers often channeled collective action through gang affiliations. Especially after the 1911 Revolution, in which both Green and Red gangs were key players on the side of the revolutionary armies, these underworld organizations assumed a more aggressive role in the Shanghai economy.* Enriched by their control of the lucrative opium trade, gangsters began to meddle in the expanding labor market as well. Virtually every line of unskilled labor came to be ruled by native-place barons with gang connections—beggar chiefs, brothel madams, night-soil hegemons, wharf contractors, and factory foremen. Immigrants from the villages in search of work quickly discovered that employment opportunities in the city were dependent upon criminal ties.

The overlap between workplace relations and gang membership lent a highly authoritarian flavor to the lives of unskilled workers. The gangs themselves organized along strictly hierarchical lines according to

---

*The cooperation between the Red and Green gangs during the 1911 Revolution had resulted in a blurring of distinctions between these two major secret society networks and an enhanced position for both societies in the new republican order. Under the active patronage of Chen Qimei, gangs gained increased importance in the Shanghai marketplace, as was forcefully demonstrated in 1914 when the general manager of the Commercial Press fell victim to gangster assassins because of his resistance to Chen's monetary demands. On the role of the gangs in this period, see Jiang Hao, "Hongmen lishi chutan" [Preliminary discussion of the history of the Red Gang], in *Jiu Shanghai de banghui* [The gangsters of old Shanghai] (Shanghai, 1986), pp. 68–86; Xu Gengshen, "Jindai Shanghai de liumang" [The gangsters of modern Shanghai], *Wenshi ziliao xuanji*, 1980, no. 3, pp. 170–72; Fan Songfu, "Shanghai banghui neimu" [Inside the Shanghai gangs], ibid., pp. 155–56.

master-disciple relationships. Fellow disciples were expected to behave fraternally to one another and with filial piety toward their master. Initiation ceremonies symbolized these expectations. As a soldier from Subei described his induction into the entourage of Zhang Jinhu, a military official of Shandong origin who became a major Green Gang chieftain in the Shanghai area following the 1911 Revolution:

> Before I [and my commanding officer, Du] arrived at the Zhang residence, one of Zhang's longtime disciples, Luo Xinquan, was waiting for us in the living room. When we arrived, Luo went upstairs to notify Master Zhang, who only then joined us in the living room. Commander Du and I immediately performed three kowtows to Master Zhang as a greeting. (This was the ritual that Commander Du had previously explained to me.) Master Zhang then asked about my general history, my military experience, and my family situation. Luo Xinquan had already lit the candle and incense in front of the altar [on which were displayed wooden tablets representing the three patriarchs of the Green Gang]. When Luo intoned, "Young brother Cui, perform a ritual before the patriarchs," I bowed thrice and kowtowed nine times in front of the altar. Then he intoned, "Younger brother Cui, perform the ceremony of honoring the teacher." Again I bowed thrice and kowtowed nine times. Finally he intoned, "Perform the ceremony before elder brother Du," upon which I bowed once and kowtowed thrice. Then Commander Du instructed me to perform for elder brother Luo, and again I bowed once and kowtowed thrice. The initiation ceremony was thereupon completed.[3]

Simple as this rite of induction was, its careful distinction between ritual greetings to fellow—albeit senior—disciples (one bow and three kowtows), on one hand, and to the revered master (three bows and nine kowtows), on the other, reveals the centrality of hierarchical authority in Green Gang practices. Members were forever bound by the obligations established at the time of their initiation. One's gang master was often also one's labor supervisor, so these patriarchal relations permeated the workplace.

Interestingly, the Green Gang initiation ceremony was not unlike the rite to "honor the master," which marked the beginning of apprenticeship for new guild members in skilled occupations (see Chapter 2). There was, however, a critical difference in the authority structure of gangs and guilds. At the end of their three-year training period, guild apprentices would stand on a more or less even footing with their erstwhile masters. Consequently, guilds were marked by a somewhat more democratic culture than were the authoritarian gangs.* For unskilled workers, by

*By the early twentieth century, disputes within guilds were often settled after resort to majority vote. See *Shi bao,* May 13, 1918, June 17, 1920.

contrast, servitude to one's gang master was a lifetime sentence from which the only escape might be a return to the countryside. As long as one remained a member of the urban proletariat, obedience to the will of the chieftain remained an indispensable strategy for survival.

Nonfactory Laborers

Surely no Shanghai residents were more downtrodden than beggars, prostitutes, or night-soil carriers. Yet even among these "lumpenproletarian" elements a remarkable degree of organization existed. The networks that bound such workers to their occupations were authoritarian in nature, allowing little room for freedom of action on the part of the rank and file. But the very strength of these organizational bonds ensured a ready response to leadership initiatives.

By the twentieth century beggars in Shanghai were divided territorially (into north, south, east, and west districts of the city) as well as by native-place origin (into Fengyang, Huaiyang, Shandong, Subei, and Shanghai gangs). Each of the five native-place gangs was ruled by an "elder" (*laoda*) with full powers to negotiate with the eight "beggar heads" (*gaitou*) who presided over the four districts of the city. Elders supplied the labor force (numbering some 20,000 men, women, and children engaged in 25 identifiable styles of begging activity), while beggar heads were responsible for levying fees on shopkeepers and collecting a daily remittance from all mendicants operating within their territory. The regular income permitted beggar chiefs to oversee an impressive welfare system for those working under their jurisdiction. A survey of 700 Shanghai beggars revealed that nearly all the respondents were from peasant families in North China and had been pressed into mendicancy by natural calamities at home. Thanks to the sureties afforded by beggar chiefs, most of the informants said that they considered begging preferable to factory work. Such protection carried a price, however. Beggars were completely subservient to the dictates of their leaders, whose close ties with the Green Gang often involved them in criminal activity.[4] Shopkeepers or others who ran afoul of the gang were apt to experience firsthand the organized power of the city's beggar armies.

Prostitutes were another tightly organized component of the Shanghai underclass.[5] According to a 1920 survey by the Shanghai Municipal Council, the city was home to more than 60,000 prostitutes, divided into several grades according to price and quality of service.[6] Prostitutes lived and worked under the tight control of pimps and brothel madams, who in turn were closely integrated into the gangster network. Regular remittances to Green Gang leaders were an unavoidable operating expense for practitioners of this occupation.[7] Although the tyrannical system under which they labored rendered prostitutes virtually powerless to undertake collective opposition against their overlords, mass protest at the behest of their masters was within the realm of possibility. In 1948, for example, tens of thousands of dancing girls stormed the Shanghai Bureau of Social Affairs in a dramatic expression of dissatisfaction with a government ban on cabarets in the city.[8]

Night-soil carriers also fell under strict gangster domination. The several thousand workers who undertook the mundane task of emptying the city's public and private commodes constituted a true peasant-proletariat. Many of these laborers cultivated fruit and vegetable plots in the western outskirts of the city, selling their produce in Shanghai markets just before or after completing the daily collection rounds. Then they returned home with fresh fertilizer for their fields (or for sale to other peasants). The night-soil carriers were traditionally ruled by "manure heads" (*fentou*), who collected service fees and distributed wages. With the establishment of the republic in 1911, however, this lucrative business was contracted out to "manure hegemons" (*fenba*), who remitted a set fee to the government each month. To protest the unwelcome change, manure heads instigated a major strike by their night-soil carrier followers in the spring of 1912. For nearly a week, carriers refused either to empty toilets or to sell vegetables. Government authorities were unwilling to abandon their new plan, however, and the trade was captured by manure hegemons with gangster connections. For many years, the manure hegemon of the French Concession was none other than the paramour of Green Gang chieftain Du Yuesheng. Upon her death, the remunerative position was inherited by a son.[9]

Draconian controls limited opportunities for independent action on the part of the Shanghai underclass, but militance instigated by their overseers was feasible. Admittedly, it was a rare beggar chief or brothel madam who felt inclined to launch a protest movement. Manure heads, however, incited repeated (albeit usually fruitless) strikes by night-soil carriers to challenge increasing government intervention in the sanitation arena.[10]

Dockers, who numbered some 50,000 to 60,000 by the 1920's, were yet another group of peasant-workers whose feisty behavior was often encouraged by their supervisors. Although relations between wharf company owners and workers were usually distant, the gap was bridged by powerful labor contractors who did the actual hiring of employees. Most of the hirees were temporary workers (known as "wild chickens" or *yeji*), whose stints at the docks were interspersed with returns to the countryside. The rural origins of Shanghai dockers grew more pronounced

TABLE 2

Place of Origin of Shanghai Dockworkers

Year starting work	Village	Shanghai	Other city	Total
1918 or earlier	49 (58%)	33 (39%)	3 (3%)	85
1919–37	233 (86%)	10 (4%)	28 (10%)	271
1938 or later	4 (80%)	0 (0%)	1 (20%)	5
TOTAL	286 (80%)	43 (12%)	32 (8%)	361

SOURCE: Port of Shanghai survey, 1963.

over the course of the Republican period. A survey of 361 retired dock-workers conducted by the Port of Shanghai shows the trend (see Table 2). Villages in Subei, Hubei, Hunan, and Shandong were the principal source of these laborers. Many docks also had smaller crews of permanent workers, known as "loaders" (*duizhuang gongren*), who received higher wages and most of whom came from the port of Ningbo.[11]

By far the most common type of collective violence among dock-workers was struggles for turf.* Led by labor contractors, such scuffles took the form of armed confrontations between native-place gangs for hegemony over contested wharves or warehouses.[12] The importance of regional identities in these conflicts was underscored by the periodic intervention of native-place associations to demand or provide compensation for the families of victims.† But intraworker feuds were not the only collective action in which dockers engaged at the behest of their supervisors. Workers paid a set percentage of their wages to labor contractors as an employment commission so wage increases served the interests of both parties. Although contractors could ill afford to alienate wharf company owners by overtly advocating labor unrest, behind the scenes they often encouraged their underlings to strike for higher wages.

A major work stoppage among loaders at seventeen Shanghai docks in 1914–15 was promoted by labor contractors who advised the strikers on

*A parallel can be drawn with conditions on the New York waterfront. Daniel Bell writes, "Control of 'loading' and its lucrative revenues was the major prize over which the bloody pier wars were fought on the New York docks for thirty years" (*The End of Ideology* [New York, 1988], p. 183). Bell notes that loading wars were not a problem at the other major U.S. maritime ports and attributes the difference to spatial arrangements. New York lacked direct railroad connections to the piers and had congested, narrow streets so that loading became a serious problem. Similar conditions obtained in Shanghai.

†In July 1926, for example, the Jianghuai Native-Place Association agreed to pay 1,000 yuan in damages to the families of two Hubei workers killed in a melee with Subei dockers over unloading rights at a Pudong godown. A complaint by the Hubei Native-Place Association to the manager of the warehouse was referred to the Jianghuai Association, which assumed financial responsibility for the incident (*Minguo ribao*, July 8, 13, 1926).

the formulation of demands that stood a reasonable chance of acceptance. Finally, after 44 days without the help of their loaders, all but two
of the affected wharf companies consented to the contractors' modest
requests. The two holdouts, claiming that their contractors had seriously undermined the prerogatives of management, refused to honor the
agreement and summarily dismissed all loading contractors on charges
of having instigated the strike.[13]

The decisive role of contractors, foremen, and overseers in facilitating
or forestalling protest by their subordinates most clearly distinguishes
the militance of unskilled workers from that of the skilled. As David
Montgomery found in his study of American workers, peasant immigrants tend to work furiously when an authority figure is present and to
loaf in his absence, whereas the craftsman's ethic is to refuse to work
while the boss is watching.[14] Different cultures of workplace authority
are matched by different styles of protest. Artisan strikes are often directed against structures of authority in workshop or factory, whereas
the walkouts of unskilled workers are just as often directed by workplace
supervisors.

Subservience to overseers did not mean, of course, that strikes by
unskilled laborers posed no challenge to higher-level authorities. Such
protests often made demands of employers or state officials. But the
leadership role of intermediate authority figures, in the persons of labor
contractors or foremen, ensured that their interests were at least as
important as those of their followers in defining strike objectives.

The Industrial Proletariat

Because of their status as bona fide members of China's emerging
proletariat, unskilled factory workers have received a good deal of attention from Marxist-inspired historians of the Chinese labor movement.
Numerous studies give the impression of active, radicalized proletarians
of the 1920's, receptive to communist initiatives.[15] Industrial workers
were not a homogeneous group, however. Much of the support for the
communists would come from workers who lived and labored under
conditions vastly different from those experienced by the lower ranks of
the factory proletariat. The world of the unskilled industrial laborer (who
was typically female) was often much closer to that of the "lumpen"
beggar, night-soil carrier, prostitute, or docker than to the carpenter or
mechanic working within the same factory compound.

A 1922 survey of cotton workers in the western part of Shanghai
showed that the great majority were peasant refugees from Subei, pressed
by recent floods to leave the land. Because only a week of on-the-job

training was required for new workers, unskilled women and girls were hired at very low wages as spinners and weavers.[16] The hiring was usually done by labor contractors. As one cotton worker recalled:

> I'm from Subei. I lived in a village as a child. . . . We were very poor. When I was thirteen, a labor contractor from Shanghai came to our village to recruit children as contract workers. He said, "Shanghai is a wonderful place. You can eat good rice as well as fish and meat. You can live in a Western-style house and make money." So many parents in the countryside agreed to let their children go off as contract workers.[17]

As Emily Honig has shown, the conditions that cotton workers faced after their arrival in Shanghai were a far cry from the idyllic life promised by the contractor.[18] Nevertheless, the impossible situation in the countryside left them little alternative.

Workers seeking employment in the Shanghai mills were at the mercy of contractors and their gangster allies. Another former cotton worker recollected:

> If a young person wanted to work in a factory she had to pass through three "gates." First, to get from the countryside to the city, you had to have a friend take you. Second, once in Shanghai, if you wanted to get into a factory you had to go through a labor recruiter. Third, once in the factory, you were a stranger to the other workers in the workshop. Moreover, the manager purposely encouraged all sorts of "gangs" among the workers so they would be divided. New workers were beaten up and prevented from working. There was no choice but to ask for help from the friend who had brought you to Shanghai. All the friend could do was introduce you to a gang leader. The gangster would say, "Don't worry. They're all our people. Just treat everyone to a dinner and it will be all right." The new worker had to pay more than ten dollars to her new master and five or six dollars for the dinner. Adding this to the five dollars which she paid the recruiter, she was already out more than twenty dollars. Having taken a gang master, you were stuck in the relationship for a lifetime.[19]

In the early twentieth century, thousands of Shanghai cotton workers—especially those of Subei origin—joined the Green Gang. An offshoot of the gang known as the Mutual Advancement Party (*Gongjin dang*) was a particularly powerful presence in the cotton industry, enrolling a large number of Subei guards and foremen as well as ordinary workers. Male laborers (a minority within the cotton mills) were evidently more inclined toward active gang participation than were women, but subservience to workplace authorities was common to both.[20]

Unskilled factory employees, like their lumpen counterparts, labored under the stern control of overseers. In many factories these shop-floor bosses, known popularly as *namowen* or "Number Ones," were former women workers who had won promotion by force of personality. The character of the Number Ones is captured in an anecdote recounted by a foreign resident of Shanghai:

> The hiring of women and girls is generally committed to Chinese fore-women, who are responsible for keeping their full quota at work. These women are usually shrewd and business-like, with a full appreciation of the dignity of their position. One recently entered the first class compartment of a tramcar. She wore the loose blue gown, apron, and head cloth of the working people and when the Chinese conductor came by he addressed her gruffly. "Old woman, you belong in the third class. Get out of here." "Why should I get out?" she responded with spirit, "I have money to pay for a seat in the first class." The conductor changed his tone and manner at once, recognizing a dominant personality behind the coarse clothes. "Pardon me, Madame," he said meekly and took the proferred coins.[21]

Each workshop or work group within a workshop was ruled by a Number One who supervised the labor process and was empowered to impose fines and other punishments for rule infractions.[22] The control such shop-floor bosses exercised over their workers made them pivotal figures in the suppression or stimulation of labor unrest. According to former cotton workers, Japanese factories were particularly prone to suffer from protests because they paid Number Ones only slightly better than ordinary workers. The dissatisfied supervisors were consequently ready to lead their workers off the job on the slimmest pretext.*

Popular Culture

Subservience to the dictates of labor bosses was not all that unskilled factory workers and lumpen elements shared in common. Living conditions were also similar, or even identical in the many families in which husbands worked as coolies and wives as cotton mill or silk filature hands.† The tendency for all family members to contribute substantially

*Jiang Yuanqing and Song Sanmei, Sept. 12, 1957, transcript of interview, Labor Movement Archives of the SASS Institute of History. *Minguo ribao*, July 6, 1919, reported that a Number One from Hubei was sentenced to three years in prison for having incited a strike at the Japanese-owned Naigai Wata cotton mill. The Hubei Native-Place Association had hired a lawyer to defend the forewoman against the charges. See also *Minguo ribao*, Feb. 10–16, 1919, for a strike at the Japanese-owned Rihua cotton mill in which forewomen refused to obey orders from management to convince strikers to return to work.

†As a study of Subei people in Shanghai pointed out, Subei men tended to work as rickshaw pullers, road repairmen, and coolies, and women were employed as textile workers (Jin Yuan, "Jiangbeiren zai Shanghai" [Subei people in Shanghai], *Nüsheng*, 2, no. 14 [1934]: 10).

to household income was an important characteristic that distinguished the household economy of unskilled workers from that of skilled workers. Surveys conducted in 1930 showed this difference clearly. Among 100 factory workers' families in Yangshupu (the district of Shanghai where many of the cotton mills were located), husbands provided only 26 percent of family income, with wives providing 6 percent, sons 43 percent, daughters 9 percent, daughters-in-law 6 percent, and other sources 10 percent. By contrast, a study of 100 printers at the Commercial Press established that in the families of these skilled workers husbands contributed fully 97 percent of household income. Similarly, among postal workers—another skilled and well-compensated occupation—husbands were found to provide nearly 90 percent of family income.[23]

The comparatively large number of working family members did not guarantee the unskilled a comfortable life-style. A study of housing conditions among the working poor of Shanghai showed that the highest grade of housing to which they might aspire was two-story rental units shared by two to four families. Usually one water tap was provided for a row of apartments and there were no toilet facilities. Each family might have to make do with only a hundred square feet or so of space. More commonly, workers lived in the even more cramped and less sanitary conditions of factory housing or shantytowns.[24]

Working-class families in Shanghai averaged four or five members.[*] In the poorest households, sex ratios tended to be skewed, with males outnumbering females by a substantial margin. Young or middle-aged men were especially numerous, a reflection of the demand for unskilled male laborers in their years of prime physical strength. Older males, having exhausted their marketability in Shanghai, tended to return to the countryside when the opportunity arose.[†] Few working-class households claimed Shanghai as their native place. And despite diverse geo-

---

[*]A survey of 230 households in the western cotton mill district of Caojiadu found an average of nearly 5 members; a survey of 100 families in the eastern cotton mill district of Yangshupu found an average of 4.11 members (Yang Ximeng, *Shanghai gongren shenghuo chengdu de yige yanjiu* [A study of the standard of living of Shanghai workers] [Beiping, 1931], p. 18; Fang Fuan, "Shanghai Labor," *Chinese Economic Journal* 7, nos. 2 and 3 [1930]: 872). There was a close correlation between income and family size. Fang (p. 873) found that families with annual incomes of under 300 yuan averaged only 2.7 members, whereas households with more than 900-yuan incomes averaged 7.5 members and those with incomes of over 1,100 yuan averaged 9 members.

[†]Fang Fuan, "Shanghai Labor," p. 876, found in his survey of 100 laboring families in Yangshupu a total of 235 men and 176 women, a ratio of 135.5 males per 100 females. By contrast, among postal workers there was virtually equal distribution of male and female family members and among printers women outnumbered men, with a ratio of only 94.2 males per 100 females (ibid., pp. 993, 1004).

graphical origins, most workers married spouses from their own locales.*

As might be expected of people who retained strong attachments
to their rural roots, marriages reflected traditional peasant practices.
"Commercial marriages" (*maimai hunyin*) were the norm. Initiated by a
matchmaker (who was often a factory Number One), the marital arrangements hinged upon agreement between parents of the bride and groom
on an acceptable bride price. This price might vary according to the age,
earning power, and looks of the prospective bride. Often the bride was as
young as fourteen or fifteen years of age, especially among silk filature
workers who had entered the factory at ages eight or nine. Once the price
had been decided on, a fortune teller was hired to ensure that the "eight
characters" of the bride and groom were properly matched. When the fit
was affirmed, the bride price was paid in cash or clothing, jewelry, furniture, and quilts, and the wedding could proceed. Marriage ceremonies
were usually modest in scale. The bride would be met with a sedan chair
or rickshaw and taken to her new abode. There a red cloth was hung over
the doorway of the room the new couple would occupy, incense and
candles were lit to honor heaven, earth, and the ancestors of the two
families, and a simple banquet was enjoyed with friends, relatives, and
matchmaker.[25]

Standard marriage and funeral practices and a common belief in folk
Buddhism, ancestor worship, and spirit mediums characterized most
working-class families in Shanghai. But popular customs could sometimes divide workers—generally along native-place lines. The different
modes of dress preferred by women cotton workers from Jiangnan and
Subei was one illustration of such divisions. Jiangnan women were partial to subdued colors of blue, black, and gray in fashions modeled after
the Shanghai student: a long dress, leather shoes, a down overcoat in
winter, and a fountain pen clipped to the outside of one's attire. Subei
women tended toward bright satins of red and green, embroidered shoes,
and pink socks.[26] Such distinctions in attire were outward manifesta-
tions of a deeper rift between women cotton workers from these two
areas. As Emily Honig observes, "Localism—expressed in dress style,
eating habits, marriage customs and dialects—was the basis of the most
important divisions and antagonisms among workers."[27]

The cultural gulf that separated workers from different native places,
most notably South and North China, was widened by the tendency for

---

*Yang Ximeng, *Shanghai gongren shenghuo chengdu de yige yanjiu*, p. 23, found
that in 95 percent of the households for which he had data (n = 174), spouses came
from the same province.

factory workshop assignments to follow native-place as well as gender lines. In the cotton mills, Jiangnan women could be found in the spinning and weaving departments, Subei women—allegedly because of their greater height and physical stamina—in the roving department, and men in the janitorial and machine rooms.[28] These workplace divisions were a product of labor recruitment patterns, mediated by contractor-foremen. In two of the Fuxin flour mills, for example, the polishing workshops were entirely peopled by workers from Ningbo and the packing workshops by laborers from Wuxi and Changzhou, while the outdoor wheat handling was done by Subei people. Each workshop was headed by a contractor-foreman from the same native place as his or her workers.[29]

Segregated according to the geographical origin and gender of its members, the factory workshop was often a world unto itself. Its boundaries delimited workers' social networks. Sisterhoods, which pledged small coteries of women workers to mutual aid, were formed along workshop (and thus native-place) lines.[30] The narrowness of workers' horizons was further ensured by the general illiteracy of unskilled laborers. A survey of women workers in the Yangshupu district revealed that fewer than 1 percent had received any education.[31] Similarly, at the Naigai Wata Number Seven mill in Caojiadu district only 50 or 60 of the more than 3,000 women workers were "literate." And just a few of these were actually literate enough to read a newspaper.[32]

Protest Patterns

The combined effect of workshop segregation and widespread illiteracy may have served to inhibit class consciousness, but it certainly did not prevent collective action among unskilled workers. Of the 33 recorded strikes in Shanghai between 1895 and 1910, 76 percent were launched by unskilled women workers.* In subsequent years, the frequency of their strikes increased, although the Republican Revolution brought a decline in the *proportion* of strikes they initiated. During the tumultuous period immediately following the revolution (1911–17), unskilled women workers participated in only 40 percent of the strikes in the city.[33] In 1918, on the eve of the May Fourth movement, the proportion dropped even further, to 33 percent.[34] This relative decline in militance (despite the increase in the ratio of women factory workers in the

*Zhongguo jindai gongyeshi ziliao 2: 1299–1301. At the turn of the century, Shanghai had approximately 30,000 cotton and silk filature workers, of whom some 20,000 were women and approximately 7,000 were children (ibid., 2: 1181).

Shanghai work force)* suggests the indifference of such workers to the politicization of the day. In a period when artisans were joining new political parties, launching coup attempts, establishing class-divided guilds, and presenting ambitious demands for higher wages and rights to organize, unskilled workers on the whole continued to engage in more limited forms of protest.

Appendix B shows that the great majority of work stoppages among unskilled laborers were reactions to a decline in income. In 74 percent of the cases, strikes were responses to a deterioration in conditions of labor, especially wages. To be sure, demands for a wage increase also occurred, becoming more frequent with the inflation that accompanied World War I. Yet these demands remained relatively uncommon, especially in comparison with those by skilled artisans. Artisan families were generally dependent on a single breadwinner, which helps to explain the greater willingness of skilled laborers to place demands for wage raises at the center of their protest agenda. Claiming responsibility for the welfare of an entire family, they were quick to argue aggressively for pay increases whenever inflationary pressures undermined their standard of living. For unskilled workers, whose individual wage constituted a relatively small percentage of total family income, the link between one's own pay and one's family welfare may have appeared somewhat less direct. In any case, though employers were usually receptive to demands by skilled workers for a wage sufficient to maintain a family, they did not extend the same consideration to their unskilled work force.

The differences in the demands of skilled and unskilled workers were obviously linked to their respective positions in the Shanghai labor market. Aware that they were irreplaceable, factory artisans felt free to challenge their employers. By contrast, unskilled workers' wage-related protests seldom went beyond a call for modest pay increases. Absent were the claims to organizational rights that marked artisan struggles in this same period.

The earliest reports of strikes among women textile workers show the defensive nature of these conflicts.[35] The most common cause of walkouts, particularly in Chinese-owned factories, was the reduction or withholding of wages. A defensive strike was not necessarily peaceful, however. Typically the confrontations involved violence, especially between

*The increased number of women workers is suggested by the rapid establishment of new textile mills in this period. Whereas during the sixteen years between 1895 and 1910 only 11 new mills were opened in Shanghai, in the seven years from 1911 to 1917, 43 were established. And in 1918–19 another 29 were opened. See Luo Zhiru, *Tongjibiaozhong zhi Shanghai* [Shanghai through statistical tables] (Nanjing, 1932), p. 63.

women workers and Indian factory guards. Violence among workers, along lines of native place or gender, also occurred with some regularity.[36] Often strikes were precipitated by a change in the payment system from a daily wage to a piecework scale.[37] This innovation became especially common when many Shanghai cotton mills were bought by Japanese at the end of World War I. The Japanese introduced a variety of other administrative reforms, modeled on prevailing practices in their own country, which met a less than friendly reception from Chinese workers. Among the major complaints was a "baby ban" that prohibited working mothers from taking their infants into the factories for nursing.[38]

Strikes to protest unwelcome changes were frequently led by Number Ones, especially when the issue was wages, a matter of mutual concern to labor recruiters and ordinary workers.[39] Protests to demand the ouster of a particularly cruel supervisor also sometimes occurred,[40] most commonly in foreign-owned mills. As an astute observer of Shanghai industrial conditions noted:

> There are causes of dissatisfaction in the foreign factories which do not arise in the Chinese factories and vice versa. The Chinese owners are sometimes apt to be in arrears with wages, which does not ever seem to occur in foreign factories. On the other hand, foreign owners . . . [face] demands for the removal of foreign overseers, foremen and watchmen, who are accused of bullying and assaulting the workers.
>
> The British owners for a century, the Japanese for a lesser period, have been accustomed to the factory system of mass production. The British factory owners in China sometimes, the Japanese generally, employ foreign foremen and overseers. Both employ Sikh watchmen and the police of the International Settlement. As in England or Japan or any other industrial country, the worker is a mere unit, a hand feeding a machine. But in addition, in China, the workers belong to a race alien to the foreign owner, which he has always regarded as inferior. Add to this that their names seem to the foreign owner or foremen all exactly alike, their faces indistinguishable one from the other, and the dehumanising process is complete.[41]

The pervasive racism in many of Shanghai's foreign-owned factories created a ready pretext for workers' resistance.[42] Widespread participation by women textile workers in the "patriotic" struggles of May Fourth and May Thirtieth is to some extent attributable to their smoldering resentment of maltreatment at the hands of Japanese and British supervisors. Rather than interpret such resistance only as the blooming of Chinese nationalism, however, we should also seek its roots in more mundane structural factors. When foreigners served as labor supervisors, workers were not bound by the patron-client ties that characterized relations with contractor-foremen from their own native places. As a result, they were more free to demand the removal of authority figures. This fact was, of course, not lost on foreign managers, who after the May Thirtieth Movement were increasingly inclined to implement contract labor systems in which gangster-foremen assumed the task of recruiting and supervising workers from their own native villages.[43] To be sure, such supervisors could and did often instigate protests among their subordinates. Still, a strike fomented by a factory foreman seeking higher income posed less of a threat than one launched by Marxist cadres calling for overthrow of the capitalist system.

Conclusion

For both skilled and unskilled workers, native-place origin helped to shape patterns of solidarity and conflict, but this politics of place operated quite differently in the two cases. Among artisans, who hailed overwhelmingly from the more affluent regions of South China, guilds served to mediate between place of origin, job opportunities, and styles of labor protest. The communitarian rituals of guild life encouraged a proclivity for unions, labor parties, and politicization in the form of nationalism and revolution. For unskilled workers, who originated predominantly (though certainly not exclusively) from disaster-prone areas of the North China countryside, the authoritarian gang offered an entrée to the forbidding world of Shanghai labor. The protests of this sector of the work force, often instigated by gangsters-cum-foremen, were typically defensive in character.

To be sure, these generalizations—like most such assertions in the social sciences—must admit to numerous refinements and exceptions. Among South China artisans were persons of Cantonese and Jiangnan origin who often put rivalry with one another before dedication to a wider political cause. The ranks of unskilled workers, moreover, held a substantial number from the Jiangnan area. Shanghai cotton weavers and Ningbo dock loaders are but two examples. On the whole, however, these Jiangnan recruits enjoyed somewhat more security and better compensation than did workers from villages in the North.

Gender differences further complicated a politics of place among unskilled laborers. Male workers were evidently more inclined toward active participation in gang networks than were women from the same areas. Perhaps viewed as more committed to urban life than their female counterparts, unskilled males were also more likely to receive factory training that promoted them to the ranks of the semiskilled. Over time, the association between semiskilled male workers and gangster politicians became increasingly important. Unskilled women, whose ties to the countryside remained firmer, played a less prominent role in this development.

In Part III, which presents detailed case studies of the labor movement in the tobacco, textile, and transport industries, I will elaborate on these distinctions. But to understand the growing gulf that would come to divide working-class supporters of Communist revolution from clients of gangsters working hand in glove with the GMD, we must first turn to the view from above. In Part II, the focus shifts to the politics of partisanship in the machinations of Party strategists engaged in a fierce battle for the allegiance of Shanghai labor. The struggles of partisans, however, were far from immune to the influence of preexisting social patterns.

Site of the *Siming gongsuo*, where Ningbo
sojourners and French colonialists clashed in
1874 and 1898. (From *Shanghai renmin
gemingshi huace* [Picture book of Shanghai
people's revolutionary history], Shanghai,
1988).

A shantytown dwelling in Shanghai at the turn of the century.
(From *Shanghai Picture Book.*)

A foreign-owned shipyard in Shanghai, 1853.
(From *Shanghai gongren yundongshi* [History
of the Shanghai labor movement], Shenyang,
1991.)

Earliest traffic department employees of the British-owned
Shanghai Tramway Company, established in 1908. (From
Shanghai Picture Book.)

Tramway mechanics at work, ca. 1920. (From *Shanghai Picture Book*.)

Child workers at the Japanese-owned Rihua cotton mill, ca. 1920. (From *Shanghai Picture Book*.)

Older women working in the leaf department of a tobacco factory, ca. 1921. (From *Nanyang Brothers*.)

Younger women working in the packing department of a tobacco factory, ca. 1921. (From *Nanyang xiongdi yancao gongsi shiliao* [Nanyang Brothers Tobacco Company historical materials], Shanghai, 1960.)

A 1957 painting by Meng Guang and Yang Zushu depicting the precipitant of Shanghai's historic May Thirtieth Movement of 1925: the fateful confrontation between cotton worker Gu Zhenghong (center) and the Japanese security guard (left) at the Naigai Wata mill. (From *Shanghai Picture Book*.)

The Shanghai workers' militia parades through the streets after the successful Third Workers' Armed Uprising, March 1927. (Courtesy UPI/Bettmann Archive.)

Strike in 1927 snarls the Shanghai waterway. (Courtesy UPI/Bettmann Archive.)

Celebrating the victory of the Third Workers' Armed Uprising, March 1927. Banner from the Shanghai Communist Party identifies the Shanghai General Labor Union as a "model for the national proletarian revolution." (From *Shanghai Picture Book*.)

British American Tobacco Company workers on strike in 1934 to protest the closing of the original BAT factory. Here workers engage in a standoff with police at the company wharf. (From *Shanghai Picture Book*.)

Shanghai women march in 1946 to commemorate the
first Women's Day celebrations after World War II. (From
Shanghai Picture Book.)

A communist labor organizer under arrest in 1948 for his
mobilization efforts at the Shanghai Power Company.
(From *Shanghai Picture Book*.)

PART TWO

View from above.

The Politics of Partisanship, 1919–49

ON THE EVE OF THE MAY FOURTH MOVEMENT in 1919, the city of Shanghai was home to a bifurcated labor movement that reflected the divergent origins and working conditions of its primary constituents. When the May Fourth activists burst onto the Shanghai labor scene in the 1920's, they found it necessary to revise their agenda to make it intelligible to either preexisting tradition. The inexperienced young labor organizers were not the only ones to be transformed by this interaction, however. Their initiatives served as a powerful catalyst for dramatic changes in the Shanghai labor movement.

In the three decades between the May Fourth Movement of 1919 and the establishment of the People's Republic in 1949 the Chinese labor movement came of age. Whether measured by Chinese or international standards, Shanghai was the scene of extraordinary labor unrest during this period. Its outlines are well known, having been carefully traced by previous scholars.[1] Chinese labor, receptive to Communist inspiration, was highly politicized by the mid-1920's, only to fall prey to Chiang Kai-shek's "white terror" in the coup of April 1927. A decade later the Japanese invasion breathed new life into radical mobilization efforts, and by the war's end Communist-instigated strikes were again a prominent feature of the urban scene.

As Figure 1 indicates, the incidence of strikes fluctuated markedly over the three-decade period for which we have reliable statistics. Strike waves typically occur in response to larger political and economic currents. As economists have shown, strikes generally increase in times of prosperity, a pattern that holds true across industries.[2] Edward Shorter and Charles Tilly have pointed to the political environment as a major precipitant of strike waves. Political crisis, like economic growth, tends to generate an across-the-board rise in the level of labor protest.[3] In

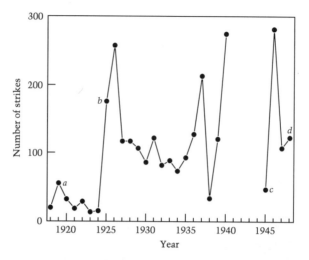

Fig. 1. Frequency of strikes in Shanghai, 1918–48. [a] In-
cludes 33 incidents in connection with the May Fourth
Movement. [b] Includes 100 incidents in connection with
the May Thirtieth Movement. [c] Includes only the period
August–December. [d] Includes only the period January–
July.

Shanghai, these economic and political triggers were often as much
international as domestic in origin. The city was divided into multinational sovereignties and fueled by the investment of foreign as well as
native capital, thereby drawing it into the vortex of global political and
economic forces.

The first noticeable rise in the frequency of Shanghai's strikes occurred in 1919 during the May Fourth Movement to protest Japanese
imperialism in China. In that year, 33 of the 56 strikes were staged in
conjunction with May Fourth. Six years later, a much larger jump in
strike frequency reflected the impact of the May Thirtieth Movement
against both British and Japanese imperialism. One hundred of the 175
work stoppages that year were part of the historic May Thirtieth general
strike. The following year, two more general strikes were held in Shanghai to support the workers' rebellions that paved the way for a Nationalist takeover of the city.

Despite the suppression that accompanied Chiang's April coup, strikes
continued to erupt throughout the decade of Guomindang rule, culmi-
nating in 1937 with a total of 213 incidents. The remarkable number of
worker protests that year can be attributed, in part, to the relative prosperity of the Shanghai economy on the eve of the Japanese invasion. The

Japanese attack in August 1937 (and the attendant rush of refugees into the International Settlement) wreaked havoc with the Shanghai economy, but by 1940 production was again equivalent to prewar levels.[4] This year of economic improvement was also a time of exceptional strike activity; 275 strikes occurred in Shanghai in 1940—more than in any previous year.

The strikes of the 1940's were not simply an indication of relative prosperity; they were also a protest against runaway inflation. From the 1911 Revolution until the Japanese invasion of 1937, consumer prices in Shanghai had risen gradually, with an annual inflation rate of around 2.5 percent.[5] After August 1937, however, the cost-of-living index skyrocketed—a trend that would continue and intensify after the war ended. The large number of strikes in 1940 and again during the Civil War years were obviously related to the rampant inflation then plaguing the Shanghai economy. That issue, more than any other, united the urban populace in opposition to the GMD.

Familiar as these strike waves are to the student of modern Chinese history, they are typically portrayed as the product of novel political strategies engineered by a recently aroused intelligentsia. Equating the fate of Chinese labor with that of the political party that claimed to be its vanguard, scholars of labor history have generally been content to elucidate the policies of the Communist Party. But Communists were not the only claimants to the spirit of May Fourth. Guomindang partisans also made serious efforts to enter the labor scene in the early 1920's. Under the aegis of the United Front, the mobilization activities of these two political parties were largely complementary. The rift surrounding Chiang Kai-shek's April coup, however, intensified their competition.

Whether pledging allegiance to Sun Yat-sen's Three Principles of the People or to Marxism-Leninism, leaders of both the CCP and the GMD felt compelled to assign the working class a high priority. Believing that industrialization was the hope of the future, both the Nationalists and the Communists made major efforts to enlist the labor movement under their own political banners. In the process, parties and states—as well as labor itself—underwent fundamental change.

To be sure, the ideological formulations of these rival parties were substantially different. Whereas Communist labor organizers emphasized the importance of class struggle (jieji douzheng) spearheaded by a united, class-conscious proletariat, the GMD stressed the necessity of class harmony (laozi hezuo), with labor and capital cooperating for the economic development of the nation.[6] Neither the Marxist logic of the CCP nor the modernization image of the GMD accorded well with the realities of Shanghai labor, however. Workers harbored genuine grievances that undermined the possibility of harmony, but their frequent struggles did not indicate a class-conscious unity. Deep divisions within the working class persisted, ensuring a fragmented constituency for both parties.

Which workers followed the lead of Communist revolutionaries? Which workers were hospitable to agents of the Guomindang regime? And which workers proved resistant to the overtures of outsiders and their political agendas? An educated guess might hypothesize that the Communists struck a responsive chord among the mass of poorly paid unskilled workers in large factories. Such workers, after all, came closest to meeting the classic definition of a proletariat and were thus a natural target for cadres inspired by a Marxist vision of social change. The Guomindang might be expected to have developed a constituency among white-collar workers who favored class harmony over the radical implications of a Communist labor movement. For the social base of the independent labor movement we might logically look to artisans, a group known across the globe for a capacity to take radical action on behalf of its own interests.

A superficial survey of Shanghai labor history lends some credibility to these hypotheses. The May Thirtieth Movement, a high point of Communist-inspired strike activity, began in the cotton mills—surely the quintessential proletarian industry (see Chapter 4). A hotbed of Guomindang-controlled labor was the white-collar Shanghai Post Office, where several top GMD–Green Gang leaders got their start as labor organizers (see Chapter 5). Finally, an independent labor movement did indeed exist among artisan ink workers, whose strikes in the 1920's and 1930's were notably free of outside political leadership.[7]

Yet when we probe beneath the surface, as we shall do for the remainder of this book, the hypothesized patterns appear much less evident. The ideology and strategy of party cadres was an imperfect guide to ultimate results. Part II, "The Politics of Partisanship," examines the contest between Communists and Nationalists as they battled for control of Chinese labor. Chapter 4, "Heyday of Radicalism," chronicles initial Communist activities in the city. Chapter 5, "Conservative Interregnum," focuses on the zenith of Guomindang strength during the Nanjing decade of 1927–37. Chapter 6, "Radical Resurgence," takes the story of Communist recovery from the Japanese invasion through the Civil War struggle.

CHAPTER FOUR

Heyday of Radicalism, 1919–27

THE YEARS FROM THE May Fourth Movement (1919) to the Three Workers' Armed Uprisings (1926–27) were tumultuous for Shanghai labor. Chinese urbanites' growing awareness of global events helped to link labor protest to both domestic and international political and economic currents. The dominant concerns of the day—national humiliation, warlordism, inflation—set the stage for unprecedented cooperation across lines that ordinarily divided workers. A critical catalyst in this politicization of labor strife was the activity of young partisans, mostly patriotic students educated in "modern" schools. And yet, as these activists would discover, workers were heir to a diverse repertoire of cultural traditions and protest experiences that were only partially susceptible to manipulation by outside cadres.

The May Fourth Movement

Communist, Guomindang, and Western scholars alike recognize that the May Fourth Movement constitutes a watershed in China's modern history.[1] On that fateful day in 1919, thousands of Chinese students poured into the streets of Beijing to express their outrage at the terms of the Versailles Peace Treaty ending World War I. Infuriated by provisions of the treaty that threatened to turn China's northern province of Shandong into a virtual colony of Japan, the demonstrators castigated their government for its capitulation to Japanese aggression and unleashed a torrent of nationalist fervor that spread quickly across the land.

Intellectuals were not the only group to be swept up in the patriotic sentiments. On June 5, the day after the news of mass arrests of students in Beijing reached Shanghai, the city was brought to a standstill by a shopkeepers' closure followed by a workers' strike involving some

60,000 participants. Japanese-owned cotton mills were the first to be affected, but soon the work stoppage spread to the shipyards, utilities, printing, tobacco, and transportation industries. This five-day shutdown of the country's largest industrial center forced the hand of Beijing in a way that the student protests of the preceding month had been unable to accomplish. The government offered a public apology, released arrested student demonstrators, discharged three officials involved in the Paris peace talks, and refused to affix its signature to the Versailles Treaty.[2]

Although politicians and intellectuals were stunned by the novel spectacle of working-class political protest, the May Fourth strike in Shanghai did not mark a sharp break with workers' ongoing traditions of action and organization. During the protest, familiar urban institutions played a key part in the rapid mobilization of the working class.

Among artisans, native-place associations, guilds, and proto-unions assumed the leadership role. The Ningbo native-place association was especially active in promoting a work and business stoppage among its members, appealing to patriotic inclinations that dated back to the Ningbo community's confrontation with the French half a century before.* Skilled mechanics in industries as diverse as railroads and waterworks joined the strike under the auspices of their metalworkers' guild. Printers also participated in large numbers, urged on by the Sincere Comrades Society at the Commercial Press.[3] Painters from Shanghai, Ningbo-Shaoxing, and Suzhou quickly added their support. Construction workers soon followed suit.[4] The guild for ginseng dealers, located on Salty Melon Street in the old Chinese city, was preparing its annual celebration for the birthday of its patron deity at the time the strike began. Funds collected for the banquet were donated to the patriotic cause instead.[5]

For less skilled workers, factory foremen were key intermediaries. More than ten foremen in foreign-owned cotton mills encouraged the strikers by forming an organization (with some 200 workers) to promote national products.† The Green and Red gangs played a crucial supportive

---

*Wusi aiguo yundong ziliao [Materials on the May Fourth patriotic movement] (Beijing, 1979), pp. 454, 458, 468, 473. To be sure, patriotic fervor was encouraged by economic interest. For example, several months before the general strike of May Fourth, Ningbo umbrella makers in the city had launched a protest against competition from the importation of Japanese umbrellas. See T. Furuya, "Goshiki Shanhai no shakai jōkyō to minshū" [Shanghai's social conditions and populace during May Fourth], in Goshi undō shizō no saikentō [A reexamination of the historical image of the May Fourth Movement], ed. Chūō Daigaku jimbun kagaku kenkyūjo, (Tokyo, 1986), pp. 226–27.

†Wusi aiguo yundong ziliao, p. 467. Gender apparently was a factor in determining whether factory workers participated in the strike. According to a British police report, two-thirds of the 20,000 cotton workers on strike in the International Settlement were males (although women composed the great majority of cotton workers). See Joseph Chen, The May Fourth Movement (Leiden, 1971), p. 150.

role. On June 5 chieftains of both gangs met and decided that all thieves and pickpockets under their control would join in the general work stoppage. Beggars were ordered to refrain from begging for the duration of the strike; food handouts from their beggar heads provided sustenance for the idled mendicants. Even some prostitutes were reported to be substituting patriotic songs for their usual nighttime solicitation routines.[6]

Differences between skilled and unskilled workers were reflected in their public demonstrations. On June 10, reports of two such events suggested the contrast. In eastern Shanghai, some 500 rank-and-file workers congregated at a small neighborhood temple to prepare for their march. Most participants arrived equipped with clubs and square pieces of cloth, as was the custom in rural protests. After someone in the temple had written a character on the cloth, it was tied around the club in the style of peasant warriors. But when the workers saw that police forces had grouped to prevent access to the International Settlement, their leaders suggested that everyone simply return home. The protesters hastily abandoned the banners they had prepared and rushed off in various directions behind their leaders.[7] In contrast, at a demonstration by artisans in the old Chinese city that same day, each participant carried a personally inscribed banner and paraded proudly down all the major streets. As a newspaper described the event with evident surprise, "Although they were craftsmen, their speeches were stirring and they maintained decorum and discipline."[8]

Such distinctions in protest style did not stand in the way of concerted action by skilled and unskilled workers during this time of national crisis. Furthermore, many workers showed some interest in developing sustained cooperation. On June 12, as the work stoppage was winding down, more than 2,000 mechanics, factory foremen, and ordinary laborers met at the *Siming gongsuo*, the main guild for Ningbo sojourners in Shanghai. There they drew up initial plans for a workers' organization to outlive the strike.[9]

Observers at the time may not have fully appreciated the deeper roots of this labor activism, but they were impressed by the political potential of an aroused working class. Li Lisan, an early Communist labor organizer, wrote soon after the outbreak of the strike, "Before the May Fourth Movement, there was almost no recognition of mass power, but since then progressive youths . . . realize that the future of the national revolution requires arousing the broad masses, especially the worker masses, to participate."[10]

In the aftermath of World War I, Shanghai's worker masses—like their counterparts elsewhere around the globe—were easily aroused. As James Cronin has remarked, "Paradoxically, the war that at its inception marked the dissolution of internationalism, ended with a strike wave of international dimensions."[11] As in Europe, the strike wave that rolled across China was in part a product of rampant inflation.[12] But workers in both places asked for more than a wage increase; they also made organizational and political demands.

The similarities between European and Chinese protest strategy were hardly accidental. More than 10,000 Chinese workers had been recruited by European factories during World War I to replace men who left for the battlefield. When the Chinese were displaced by militant Europeans after the war, they returned home well schooled in tactics of labor strife.[*]

The blending of old styles of protest with a new cosmopolitan consciousness was evident in the strikes of this period. When the city's painters walked off the job in October 1919, they first went through the time-honored ritual of gathering at their guild to burn incense and offer prayers before the patron deity of their trade and then issued a petition pointing out that "workers all over the world have been receiving wage hikes. Moreover, in many countries laborers work only eight hours a day, unlike Shanghai's painters, who toil from dawn to dusk."[13]

Growing awareness of labor movements elsewhere in the world inspired Shanghai artisans to undertake equally bold efforts. Increased unionization was one outcome of this process. In early 1920, after a general meeting convened at the temple of the god of healing, the city's 5,000 traditional medicine apothecaries launched a successful strike for a wage hike. Then, to safeguard their gains, the pharmacists founded a "friendly society" (youyi lianhehui) obviously modeled on foreign precedents.[14]

Birth of the Communist Party

Shanghai's postwar strike wave convinced leftist intellectuals of the need to reach out to the working class.[15] In keeping with this spirit, Chen Duxiu, future cofounder of the CCP, traveled to Shanghai in early 1920 to try his hand at labor organizing. By May of that year, Chen—under the tutelage of Comintern emissary Gregory Voitinsky—had published the

---

[*]In France alone, Chinese workers engaged in 25 strikes between November 1916 and July 1918. On at least two occasions they also acted as scabs to break strikes among French dockworkers and gas workers. See Chen Sanjing, *Huagong yu Ouzhan* [Chinese workers and the European war] (Taipei, 1986), pp. 142–44. When the returned workers arrived in Shanghai, they were usually greeted at the dock by French Concession police inspector and Green Gang patriarch Huang Jinrong. Authorized by the French to provide the returnees with resettlement subsidies, Huang may well have used the opportunity to recruit new members to his growing gang network. See *Minguo ribao*, Jan. 24, Feb. 12, May 4, 1921.

results of a comprehensive survey of working conditions in the city and founded a Marxism Study Society for a handful of young radicals committed to building a progressive labor movement.[16]

Students from the province of Zhejiang, whose native-place association had taken an active interest in the May Fourth strike in Shanghai, formed a mainstay of this forerunner of the Chinese Communist Party.[17] By the end of the year, the initiative of these energetic organizers had resulted in the establishment of two labor unions under Communist sponsorship. It was probably not coincidental that this breakthrough occurred in the trades of metalworking and printing, which were dominated by artisans from Zhejiang.[18] The new unions reflected long-standing concerns of Jiangnan craftsmen. The Shanghai Mechanics' Union, whose 70 or so initial members were drawn from industries as diverse as shipbuilding and cotton, pledged in its founding manifesto to uphold customary practices of apprenticeship and mutual aid.[19]

Shanghai, as industrial capital of China and home to a tradition of labor protest, seems in retrospect an obvious starting place for the new Chinese Communist Party. But to contemporaries the fit was far from perfect. As Chen Duxiu wrote in a series of essays on Shanghai society published less than a year before the first congress of the CCP was convened in the city:

> In analyzing Shanghai society [we find] a large portion are totally ignorant laborers who suffer privation and hardship. Another portion are traitorous businessmen who make a living directly or indirectly under foreign capitalism. Another portion are swindlers who sell fake Western medicines or lottery tickets. Another portion are prostitutes. Another portion are evil gangsters and police. Another portion are "black curtain" writers and booksellers dealing in promiscuous romances, superstitious formulas, and profitable new magazines. Another portion are gangster politicians. Committed young students are only a small portion, and situated in this sort of environment they have barely enough strength for self-protection, let alone for overcoming the environment. . . . Because of this, I believe that if a national congress can be convened, *it should not be held in Shanghai.* . . .
>
> What type of people are most powerful in Shanghai? A superficial look shows that major political and economic power is in the hands of the Westerners, but the internal social situation is quite different. The majority of factory laborers, all of the transport workers, and virtually all of the police . . . are under the control of the Green Gang. The great strike at the time of last year's student movement [i.e., May Fourth] already revealed their authority. . . . The commands of gang leaders are more effective than those of the Municipal Council. . . . The only way of eliminating them is to publicly establish legal unions in each industry. . . . Whether Shanghai unions are developed is thus not only an urgent matter for labor but is also a matter for Shanghai social order.[20]

Despite Chen Duxiu's reservations, Shanghai served as the setting for the opening congress of the Chinese Communist Party in July 1921. The first resolution promulgated by the new party began with the sentence, "The basic mission of this party is to establish trade unions."[21] The following month, to carry out its stated mission, the CCP founded the Chinese Labor Secretariat in Shanghai. The most active member of the secretariat, a young student named Li Qihan, had already shown considerable promise at labor organizing when he helped found the mechanics' and printers' unions the previous year. But these unions were built on the foundation of well-established artisan guilds. To move beyond the world of literate artisans and make common cause with the less skilled rank and file of the Shanghai proletariat was more challenging. As an early activist remembered:

> Our work met with many difficulties. . . . Hardest to handle were the Green and Red gangs. Finally we decided that several comrades should infiltrate their ranks. But at that time our comrades were all students. If we wanted them to jump up on a stage and deliver a speech or jump down and write an essay, there were always volunteers. But to enter the Green or Red Gang one had to knuckle down and learn their customs and regulations. Then, through various guises, one could begin work. Who had the patience for that?[22]

Fortunately for the development of the Communist labor movement, Li Qihan (who, perhaps significantly, came from the province of Hunan) had enough patience to work with gangsters. As a teacher in a Communist-sponsored school for workers, Li became close friends with a woman cotton worker, who was a gang member. She introduced the young Marxist to her Green Gang master, who welcomed Li Qihan as a disciple. The connection proved to be of enormous assistance in his gaining acceptance among workers in the cotton and tobacco industries. By the end of 1921, Li had convinced contacts in both industries to form leftist-leaning labor unions.[23]

The Conservative Challenge

The Communists were not alone in the quest to organize the Shanghai working class. Guomindang politicians and factory foremen were equally anxious to channel labor activism in directions favorable to their interests. In the year following May Fourth, such individuals sponsored the formation of more than a dozen labor associations in Shanghai.[24] Though these endeavors were limited, they point to the widespread interest in labor organization generated by the May Fourth general strike. Among the self-styled "unions" included in this reformist effort was the

Industrial Volunteer Society, founded by a cotton mill foreman and a school principal and directed by the owner of the Dasheng Ironworks. The group offered shares in a new textile factory, but only one loom was ever put into production.[25] Another such group, the Shanghai Staff and Workers' Association, intervened during a strike in October 1919 at the Sanxin cotton mill to demand a wage raise and a weekly holiday for the workers.[26] A third such group, the National Society for Industrial Progress, sponsored a weekly lecture series, a vernacular newspaper, and a part-time school for workers. Its inauguration ceremonies featured speeches of support by such GMD notables as Hu Hanmin, Dai Jitao, and Liao Zhongkai, and its director was a capitalist with close ties to Cantonese politicians. The more ambitious projects of this group—the establishment of a workers' clinic and credit bureau—were never realized.[27]

To some extent, the fledgling Communist movement in Shanghai was able to make common cause with these conservative initiatives. Chen Duxiu, for example, attended the inaugural ceremonies of several of the "signboard unions," as orthodox CCP historiography would later call them.[28] The Communists also supported the joint effort by conservative labor associations to sponsor Shanghai's first celebration of an international labor day on May 1, 1920. Although police closed the stadium where the event had been scheduled, some 5,000 workers gathered at a nearby park to shout "long live labor" and other slogans calling for a three-shift, eight-hour workday.[29]

Communist revolutionaries could benefit from reformist groups' promotion of labor interests, but the relationship was not without tension. At the behest of several signboard union leaders, a conference was convened in November 1921 to consider the possibility of uniting all of the city's labor unions—including those operating with CCP support—under a single umbrella organization. Although Li Qihan and another Communist representative attended the conference, they walked out in protest when several of their demands were rejected.[30]

The post–May Fourth Shanghai labor movement was characterized by shifting patterns of cooperation and conflict between radicals and conservatives. Even at this early stage, partisan rivalry elicited distinctive responses from different elements of the work force. In 1922, a strike wave, inspired to some extent by the efforts of outside organizers, swept the city. The unusual level of labor unrest, following closely on the heels of the establishment of the Labor Secretariat, has often been interpreted as evidence of growing Communist influence.[31] Indeed, there is ample evidence to support this contention. For example, the longest-lasting strike that year (which endured for 27 days) was by gold- and silversmiths demanding recognition of a recreation club that had been organized by Communist artisans within their trade.[32] A participant in this protest recalled that it was spearheaded by craftsmen (90 percent of whom hailed from Ningbo) who resented that they were treated less well than the white-collar clerks who sold their products.* Though this work stoppage by skilled artisans was the lengthiest strike of 1922, it was not the largest. That honor went to a protest by 10,000 unskilled women silk filature workers, which was promoted not by Communists but by gangsters with close ties to GMD politicians.

Vexing to the Communists as the conservative challenge was, warlord repression presented an even more serious obstacle to their supremacy over the labor movement. On February 7, 1923, the brutal suppression of a Labor Secretariat–inspired strike along the Beijing-Hankou railway seriously jeopardized the Communist enterprise throughout the country. As Deng Zhongxia, an activist in the secretariat, recalled:

> As soon as the Chinese Communist Party was founded, it promoted a labor movement in Shanghai. However, it was unable to make much headway. Small gains were quickly reversed. In the winter of 1922 . . . nothing remained except a tiny group of printers and mechanics joined by a handful of shop clerks. During the desolate days following the February Seventh defeat, there was simply no way to mobilize.[33]

Soon after the railway incident, in which 35 strikers were killed by the troops of warlord Wu Peifu and his allies in three major assaults, the Labor Secretariat ceased to operate. Once again the initiative was handed to conservative union leaders, many of whom enjoyed close relations with both gangsters and the Guomindang right wing.[34]

The United Front

The prevailing political atmosphere changed markedly with the declaration of a united front between the Guomindang and the Communists in early 1924. This momentous alliance permitted individual Communists to join the Guomindang and resume labor organizing under the sponsorship of a newly established GMD Labor Bureau. The formal partnership between these political contenders led to increased mobili-

---

*Yang Mengyan, Mar. 30, 1959, transcript of interview, Labor Movement Archives of the SASS Institute of History. Communist influence did not signal a fundamental break with customary protest patterns. The gold- and silversmiths' strike was eventually settled by the mediation of the Ningbo Native-Place Association, which insisted that workers apologize for their unruly behavior by lighting candles and setting off firecrackers at a shop that had been damaged by rioting during the course of the strike (*Minguo ribao*, Nov. 2, 1922).

zation of the Shanghai working class. Membership rosters for 4,448 GMD members in Shanghai during the years 1924–25 list "worker" as the occupation for nearly one-third of them (1,482 members). Among those with this designation, metalworkers, carpenters, mechanics, printers, and male cotton workers from Ningbo and other Jiangnan locations were especially numerous. Students, who made up the overwhelming majority of the GMD membership in Shanghai, included a high proportion of well-known Communist labor organizers.[35]

Much of the energy behind the new upsurge in the labor movement emanated from the campus of Shanghai University. Established in October 1922 under the direction of President Yu Youren, a Tongmeng Hui activist in the 1911 Revolution, and Vice-President Shao Lizi, a member of both the Guomindang and the Chinese Communist Party, Shanghai University was from its inception a joint GMD-CCP venture. The school quickly gained a reputation for activism, attracting socially committed youth from around the country. Students from Zhejiang were most numerous, and theirs was also the most politically radical of the many native-place associations that sprang up on campus.[36]

In the summer of 1923, when Shanghai's 43-member Communist Party divided into four small groups, one was located at Shanghai University. With eleven members, including Deng Zhongxia, Qu Qiubai, and several other influential members of the Party Central Committee, the Shanghai University small group took the lead in labor organizing. The official declaration of a united front in January 1924 offered greater support and protection for such activities. The small group accordingly instructed all Communist Party and Communist Youth League members to join the Guomindang, permitting the formation of a GMD district branch at the university.[37]

Under the aegis of this united front, teachers and students at Shanghai University turned their attention to the world of labor. As instructors in the newly established and very popular Sociology Department, Qu Qiubai and Deng Zhongxia taught their enthusiastic students—one of whom was Yang Zhihua, a young schoolteacher from Zhejiang, who soon married Qu and became a prominent figure in the Shanghai labor movement, to combine the classroom study of Marxian sociology with the practical experience of labor organizing. Part-time schools for workers were the initial conduit for these mobilization efforts. By the summer of 1924, the Shanghai University small group felt sufficiently encouraged by the workers' response to its schools to open the West Shanghai Workers' Recreation Club as a meeting place for particularly progressive worker-students.[38]

One of the earliest successes of Shanghai University's part-time schools was Liu Hua, a young printer at the Zhonghua Book Company. After completing his three-year apprenticeship at the printing house, Liu enrolled at a part-time school attached to Shanghai University. Within three months Deng Zhongxia and Qu Qiubai initiated him into Communist Party membership, and just a few months later, Liu Hua assumed direction of the West Shanghai Workers' Recreation Club. Located in the heart of the Xiaoshadu cotton mill district, the Recreation Club concentrated much of its attention on Japanese-owned mills in the area.

A pivotal figure in the Communist effort to organize cotton workers was Tao Jingxuan, a mill worker at the Naigai Wata Company, who was both a Recreation Club activist and a CCP member. Unlike most Communist organizers, Tao had substantial experience as an unskilled laborer—he was a former dockworker from Hubei. Tao set to work organizing leaders of the five native-place gangs (representing Anhui, Hubei, Subei, Shandong, and Shaoxing) at his mill and eventually persuaded them to pledge brotherhood in a ceremony at a small temple behind the factory. After exchanging cards and drinking wine with chicken blood, the five men declared Tao their "elder brother."[39] The value of such inroads was soon proven when in February 1925 a strike broke out at Naigai Wata to protest the replacement of 50 adult males, several of whom were active at the Recreation Club, by girl workers.[40] Its contacts at other cotton mills enabled the Recreation Club to extend the work stoppage to 22 Japanese-owned factories, taking the lead in forming a central strike committee, organizing pickets, and distributing strike pay to idled workers.[41]

 Tao Jingxuan, like Li Qihan before him, found that effective mobilization of the proletariat required recourse to familiar forms of solidarity, even when these included such "feudal" practices as brotherhoods and secret oaths. As outsiders to the Jiangnan region, both men were apparently able to take advantage of the native-place allegiances of unskilled workers, relatively few of whom could claim a southern pedigree.

Significantly, however, these mobilizational inroads made far greater headway among men than women. Even in an industry dominated by female labor such as cotton, male workers were evidently much more inclined to join CCP organizers than were their female colleagues. As Emily Honig has noted, "Few women joined the radical labor unions formed during this period; even fewer joined the Chinese Communist Party."[42] Recently Chinese scholars have acknowledged the difficulties that early Communist organizers faced in attracting women to their cause, explaining that "women workers, restricted by the ethics of feudal tradition, were generally compliant and lacking in fighting spirit."[43] Such an explanation seems inadequate, however, in view of the tradition of militance among women textile workers that stretched back into the nineteenth century (see Chapter 3). And many women did participate in the strike waves of the 1920's, though the tune to which they danced was seldom called by Communist cadres. Only when attention was devoted to the special conditions and concerns of women, such as Yang Zhihua's initiatives toward female laborers in the tobacco industry (see Chapter 7), did unskilled women workers show much enthusiasm for the CCP.

Thus, crucial as the United Front was in facilitating Communist gains within the labor movement, major shortcomings remained. Furthermore, the alliance had not erased all animosity between the Communists and at least one section of the Guomindang. "Right-wingers" hostile to any accommodation between the two parties continued to resist the growth of a radical labor movement. This resistance often took the form of direct involvement in labor affairs, usually through support for conservative unions. Gangster-dominated labor associations such as existed at the Nanyang Tobacco Company or among women silk filature workers were the most promising entrée. The formation in August 1923 of the Shanghai Federation of Labor brought together 32 of these conservative labor groups in an institutional framework closely tied to the right wing of the Guomindang.[44] That such an organization could present problems for the radical labor movement was shown during the February cotton strike, when a leader of the federation shared information about the protest with Japanese authorities.*

The threat from rightist elements within the GMD was a major concern of Communist leaders at the time. In January 1925, at the fourth national congress of the CCP, a resolution on the labor movement noted:

> One can easily find all sorts of reactionaries even in ordinary labor unions. The Guomindang right is now plotting to amalgamate these anti-Communist elements under its own control. . . . To advance the class struggle, it is necessary to smash all types of labor union reactionaries, especially the Guomindang right. . . . We must exert every effort to work within the Guomindang Labor Bureau, taking advantage of this chance to transform

---

*The archives of the Japanese Foreign Ministry (#S-350) reveal that Wang Guanghui, a leader of the Nanyang Tobacco Union and a central figure in the Shanghai Federation of Labor, took the opportunity during a trip to Beijing in February 1925 to confer with Japanese officials about the strike in Shanghai's Japanese-owned cotton mills. See Shanghai Academy of Social Sciences Institute of History, ed., *Wusa yundong shiliao*, [Historical materials on the May Thirtieth Movement] (Shanghai, 1981 and 1986), 2 volumes, 1: 394–95. A former activist in the Hunan labor movement, Wang was co-opted by conservative elements when he fled to Shanghai to escape persecution following a cotton mill strike in Changsha in early 1923. Another federation leader, Mu Zhiying, a female gangster who headed the women silk filature workers' union, also intervened in the February cotton strike to caution workers against being used by outside parties (*Shen bao*, Feb. 24, 1925).

the Guomindang unions into unions for class struggle, thereby developing a unified labor movement.[45]

Some headway was made in this direction on May 1, 1925, at the second National Labor Congress. In contrast to the first such convocation three years earlier, the second congress was boycotted by the GMD right. The absence of the conservatives (and the disarray of the GMD following the death of its leader, Sun Yat-sen) gave the Communists a virtually free hand in shaping the agenda. As a consequence, the meeting sanctioned the establishment of a National General Labor Union. Ostensibly an organ of the GMD, the new national union was in fact a Communist creation.[46]

The strengthening of the United Front under tighter CCP control naturally enhanced the capacity of Marxist organizers to lead the labor movement in directions amenable to their political designs. The results were soon evident in the Shanghai cotton industry. Immediately after the February 1925 strike had ended, the Recreation Club was renamed the Japanese Cotton Mills Union, with Liu Hua as its chairman. This organization took charge of the historic strikes that broke out in the mills once again in May 1925. On May 15, shortly after the new round of strikes began, Gu Zhenghong, a male cotton worker and an activist in the Recreation Club during the February strike, was killed by a Japanese foreman in a melee at his factory. The incident was well publicized by Communist cadres and generated an outpouring of sympathy for the labor martyr. On May 24, Liu Hua chaired a memorial service for Gu Zhenghong attended by thousands of workers.[47] A reporter who estimated the crowd at more than 10,000 commented: "I dare say that this sort of grand proletarian gathering is unprecedented in Shanghai. Nine out of ten participants were workers."[48] On May 30, throngs of sympathizers—mostly workers and university students—joined in a solidarity demonstration. As a postal worker who was also a member of the Communist Party remembered that fateful day:

> Our group had more than 30 people, almost all of whom were workers. There were postal workers, wood carvers, railway workers, carpenters and other artisans, clerks in used clothing stores, and workers in foreign companies. In addition, there were some middle and elementary school teachers. Most of the group were "university" [i.e., Communist Party members], "middle school" [i.e., Communist Youth League members], and activists close to our Party. There were also some GMD members, but not a single one from the right wing. The right-wingers even fabricated a crisis atmosphere, saying, "It won't do to participate. Participation will surely lead to trouble. Let's not succumb to the tricks of the Communist Party." Quite a few of our comrades joked as they chewed on *dabing*, poking fun at those right-wingers

who spoke so nicely but were really engaged in destructive, shameful behavior. All of us were mentally prepared to be arrested, but we certainly never imagined anything worse than that.[49]

When, contrary to expectation, the British police fired on the demonstrators—leaving 10 dead and 50 wounded—the May Thirtieth Movement was born.*

The May Thirtieth Movement: A Fragile Alliance

The tragedy of May Thirtieth presented the Communists with an extraordinary opportunity for using new labor organizations to counter the power of their right-wing competitors. On May 31, the day after the bloody incident on Nanjing Road, the Shanghai General Labor Union (GLU) was hastily inaugurated as a branch of the National General Labor Union. Under the chairmanship of Li Lisan and the general management of Liu Shaoqi, the Shanghai GLU established ten command posts (later increased to 30) that undertook to provide direction to the city's restive workers.

First to enlist under the GLU banner was the Shanghai Printers' Federation, an outgrowth of the Zhejiang Printers' Union (so named because most of Shanghai's printers came from the province of Zhejiang), which had been established two years before with the assistance of Communists from Hangzhou.[50] Many others followed suit, and soon the Shanghai GLU boasted a membership of 117 unions with more than 200,000 workers.[51] While Liu Shaoqi labored quietly behind the scenes to handle bureaucratic problems, Li Lisan cut a more flamboyant figure. A tall, heavy-set man, Li traveled about the city by car, surrounded by several bodyguards of similarly imposing stature. Among those impressed by Li's display of proletarian prowess was a bathhouse owner and Green Gang master who invited the union leader to become his disciple. With Party approval, Li Lisan—who, like Li Qihan before him, came from Hunan Province—was duly inducted into Green Gang membership.[52] Once again, gangster ties proved instrumental in gaining important allies for the Communist labor movement. A British police report noted at the time, "Red and Green Gangs have joined forces with labor agitators . . . and given allegiance to Li Lisan."[53]

At least to some extent because of such gangster connections, the GLU was able to turn the May Thirtieth movement into a strike of unprece-

---

*In all, thirteen died from the bullet wounds inflicted by British police. Nine of the thirteen were workers, one a Cantonese cook and the other eight all of Jiangnan origin. See *Wusa yundong shiliao,* 1: 720–21.

dented scale.[54] In Shanghai alone, more than 200 enterprises with over 200,000 workers participated in the work stoppage.[55] Factory Number Ones, most of whom were gang members, were pivotal in sustaining the general strike. By July, Japanese cotton mill owners were offering full wages to foremen and forewomen if they would show up at the mill daily for two hours and stop helping to distribute strike pay. (Most of the strike fund had been donated by the city's Chinese Chamber of Commerce.) The Number Ones pleaded to be excused from the condition about strike pay, claiming that their lives would be endangered if they failed to oblige the General Labor Union.[56]

Gangster support was the sine qua non of a large-scale strike in Shanghai, but it did not always come easily. One particularly powerful Muslim gangster in western Shanghai continued to cause trouble even after he had enjoyed two porkless banquets at GLU expense. Only when no fewer than ten Communist labor leaders agreed to become his sworn brothers did the harassment subside. Even the May Thirtieth martyr Gu Zhenghong (originally from Subei) turned out to have a gangster relative who undercut the GLU's handling of the case by conducting his own negotiations for reparations from the Japanese authorities. The interference ceased only after 40 GLU pickets dragged the gangster out of bed one night, took him to a branch office of the union, and gave him a sound thrashing.[57]

Of more lasting concern to the Communists was the continuing presence of the gangster-dominated Shanghai Federation of Labor. Although the power of this conservative organization was substantially diminished by the May Thirtieth upsurge, it was not eliminated. Throughout the summer, the federation issued a series of acerbic press releases portraying the GLU and its leadership as illegitimate and corrupt upstarts on the Shanghai labor scene. Li Lisan, despite his own gang connections, was a favorite target for these attacks: "When the strike started, a rickshaw ride was a luxury for Li but he now has acquired a motor car, two concubines and several gangster bodyguards." The GLU was also taken to task for high-handed tactics in dealing with its opponents: "A labor union is a people's organization, not a yamen. . . . Should it make arrests as it pleases?"[58] On August 22, the tension came to a head. Nearly 100 gangsters armed with iron bars and knives raided the offices of the General Labor Union. Li Lisan managed to escape by rushing out the back door in the nick of time, but eight other union officers were stabbed by the intruders. It was quickly established that the assault was the work of the Federation of Labor.[59]

Gangsters and their right-wing unions were not the only problem faced by Li Lisan and his GLU. Unhappy workers also created serious difficulties during the May Thirtieth strike. As the primary disbursing stations for the strike funds that sustained the work stoppage, GLU offices were a magnet for the hungry. It was soon discovered that more than a few workers were queuing up repeatedly in hopes of garnering more than their fair share of strike pay. To curb the abuses, the GLU began to require that workers present certificates from their labor contractors or Number Ones to qualify for a weekly subsidy. This was fine for workers who labored in relatively secure jobs under sympathetic foremen, but it was impossible for the many—such as "wild chicken" dockworkers—whose employment was temporary at best. As the strike dragged on, disgruntled dockworkers became violent toward the GLU and its financial backers. On August 12, some 2,000 longshoremen disrupted a Chamber of Commerce meeting to protest the suspension of support for the strike fund. They quickly consumed the food that had been prepared for a Chamber banquet and then proceeded to smash dishes and chairs. Joined by beggars and other members of Shanghai's rowdy underclass, dockworkers staged similar raids on GLU offices.[60]

Even ordinary cotton workers, despite their reputation as the quintessential proletarian revolutionaries, did not always participate with the same mind-set as the Communist instigators. As one such worker remembered the May Thirtieth Movement:

> Some students came to our factory. We didn't know they were Communists. All we knew was that they had come to help us workers. They told us to strike and promised they'd provide enough money for us to survive during the work stoppage. We were delighted by this news so we went on strike. Every two weeks we could pick up our pay. . . . I was arrested and held by the police for a while. At that time people were superstitious and believed that you'd have bad luck when you got out of jail. So I went and took a bath, shaved my head, and burned incense to expel the evil vapors.[61]

Under pressure from both gangsters and disgruntled or uncommitted workers, the General Labor Union decided to seek a settlement. Negotiations with the Japanese consul-general resulted in compensation for the family of martyr Gu Zhenghong and a guarantee of better working conditions in Japanese-owned factories. Paltry as the concessions were, the GLU felt compelled to call an end to the strike. By late August, some three months after it had begun, the historic work stoppage was over.

The enormity and longevity of the May Thirtieth strike is obvious evidence of the strength of the Communist labor movement at this time, yet the radicals had not gone unchallenged. It was hardly the case, as has often been argued, that

> The May Thirtieth Movement brought to an end the fierce struggle to gain influence among the Shanghai proletariat that had been waged for several years between the militant Communists and the . . . groups fostered by the

local employers and the right wing of the Kuomintang [Guomindang]. . . .
During these mass struggles, the entire working class had rallied to the
support of the General Union, which remained in control of the economic
and political struggles of the Shanghai proletariat until April 1927.[62]

Rather than interpreting May Thirtieth as a complete victory for the
Communist side, it is perhaps more apt to characterize it as the product
of an uneasy and fragile alliance. To the extent that the Communists
were able to make common cause with gangsters and other power brokers in the world of labor, they could fashion a formidable protest movement with substantial political clout.* This coalition served them well
in May Thirtieth and it would again during the Three Armed Uprisings.
But the tensions inherent in such a partnership were very real, as the
coup of April 1927 would reveal.

In the meantime, the Shanghai GLU was subjected to relentless pressure from the local warlord authorities. In October, the union's headquarters were sealed and labor leader Liu Hua was arrested. On December 17,
1925, the former printer who had done so much to mobilize the city's
workers was executed.[63] When another printer from the Commercial
Press was chosen to head the GLU, he was jailed in April 1926.[64]

The Three Armed Uprisings

Despite such setbacks, the radical labor movement in Shanghai was
soon to be rescued by more distant political forces. When the Northern
Expeditionary troops of Chiang Kai-shek won a series of military victories, the balance of power began to tip against Sun Chuanfang's warlord
regime. Cheered by the prospect of a GMD takeover, Communist labor
leaders renewed their efforts to mobilize the Shanghai working class. In
spite of its clandestine status, the GLU—in concert with the Jiangsu-
Zhejiang Communist Party—took the lead in organizing popular resistance to the Sun Chuanfang regime. Following an abortive uprising in
October 1926, Zhou Enlai was dispatched to Shanghai to provide overall
direction to the growing struggle. In February 1927 a second uprising was

*One small yet enduring product of the alliance was a "dog-beating brigade" (dagou
dui) led by a Communist printer at the Commercial Press, two other workers, and a
Red Gang master. This armed brigade dealt harshly with scabs and other opponents of
the radical labor movement. According to one of its leaders, it remained active until
1936 (Xu Meikun, "Yi qiyi qianhou" [Remembering before and after the uprising],
Shanghai gongyun shiliao, 1987, no. 2, p. 1). The British police reported in 1933 on the
organization by Shanghai Communists of "Dog Beating Groups" to attack their enemies with axes and iron bars and to foment factory disputes with the aim of bringing
about a general strike in the city (Shanghai Municipal Police Files [in the U.S. National Archives, Washington, D.C.], D-2554/36).

launched on the heels of a massive strike involving 350,000 workers. Partly because of failure to coordinate the work stoppage with the insurrection, however, this attempt was suppressed by Sun's forces. Over the objections of Chen Duxiu, who argued in a report to Party Central that "the time for strikes has been superseded by the time for organization," Zhou Enlai approved yet a third attempt. On March 21 the simultaneous launching of a general strike (with an estimated 800,000 participants) and an armed uprising finally routed the warlord troops and welcomed the Northern Expeditionary army to Shanghai.[65]

During the third and successful uprising, workers at the Commercial Press assumed a leading role in the fighting. This activism reflected the radical leanings of the educated Jiangnan artisans who worked in Shanghai's largest printing house. As early as the May Thirtieth Movement, Commercial Press employees included some 170 Communist Party members, heavily concentrated in the editorial and translation departments.[66] Such notables as Chen Yun, later to become a leading economic planner in the People's Republic, and Mao Dun, the leftist writer, were active in Commercial Press unionization and strike efforts at this time.[67] By October 1926, the number of Party and Youth League members had risen to some 400, constituting about 10 percent of the enterprise's employees. More than 100 of the workers' pickets that spearheaded the third uprising were recruited from the Commercial Press, and the headquarters of workers' pickets for the entire city was located at its Recreation Club.[68] The militance of workers at the press was undoubtedly a product of their literacy and cosmopolitan outlook. As a former worker recalled, "Our Commercial Press served the scholarly community. There were quite a few intellectuals among us, many of whom could speak English. . . . Some of our comrades made contacts with foreigners while others of us organized pickets."[69]

Second only to the Commercial Press in the size and activism of its armed pickets was the Shanghai Post Office, another employer of well-educated and well-paid workers from the Jiangnan region. Here too the tradition of radicalism ran deep. A leader of the postal pickets remembered: "I had fought in the 1911 Revolution and thus had some military knowledge. Seeing that the other workers didn't know much about fighting, I put them in order one by one."[70]

Mechanics also contributed greatly to the successful uprising. An important example was Yang Peisheng, a highly skilled copper fitter. Born in the Shanghai suburb of Chuansha to a lower-gentry family, Yang had apprenticed for many years at a Shanghai machine factory before entering the Xiangsheng Ironworks in 1914. Five years later, in the May Fourth strike, he helped to found a machinists' union. Despite his political activism, Yang Peisheng's exceptional work skills earned him promotion to supervisor of the fitters' department in 1921. Known to his fellow workers as "Master Yang" (*Yang shifu*), he joined the Ningbo native-place association in 1923 and the Communist Party two years later. In February 1927—wearing a mandarin jacket and satin skullcap that revealed his identification with the educated elite—Yang presided over the inauguration of a new metallurgical union. The following month he directed armed workers' pickets in the Pudong district, relying heavily on fellow mechanics for support. With the victory of the third uprising, Yang Peisheng was named vice-chairman of the Shanghai General Labor Union. He assumed the chairmanship the next month.[71]

Important as committed printers, postal workers, and mechanics were to the success of the armed uprising, the general strike required much wider participation. Once again, gangster cooperation was an important factor in the Communists' ability to reach out to a broad working-class constituency. Shortly before the first armed uprising, Wang Shouhua (then chairman of the Shanghai General Labor Union) learned from Shanghai business leader Yu Xiaqing that "negotiations have already been undertaken with Frenchtown's Smallpox Jinrong [i.e., Green Gang patriarch Huang Jinrong] and other major gangsters, who are very supportive." In a secret planning meeting of the Shanghai District Committee of the Communist Party just two days before the third uprising, Wang Shouhua reported to Zhou Enlai that "[gangster chieftain and opium czar] Du Yuesheng has asked us to help him. . . . He requests that we not raise the opium issue. Meanwhile, he hopes to reorganize all the Green and Red gangs in Shanghai under our command."[72] Huang Jinrong and Du Yuesheng provided substantial assistance; confidential Communist records reveal that the gangsters supplied money for Communist-sponsored unions, arranged the release of arrested workers, passed along intelligence on the activities of the warlord authorities, and offered protection to CCP cadres operating out of the foreign concessions.[73]

Thanks in part to this aid from gangster leaders, the Communists were able to direct an armed insurrection that within two days handed them control of the country's largest city. By March 22, the 5,000 workers' pickets—several hundred of whom were armed—had occupied the police stations, railway stations, Jiangnan Arsenal, and the courts and prisons. In most cases, warlord troops simply abandoned their posts, but in Zhabei District heavy fighting claimed the lives of nearly 200 workers. One week later, a new municipal government was installed, with representation from the CCP, GMD, Green Gang, and business interests.[74] Just as the antiforeignism of May Thirtieth had brought together radicals and conservatives in a powerful, albeit conflictual, partnership, so the antiwarlordism of the Northern Expedition reunited these unlikely allies. Political crisis—whether prompted by a sense of national peril or an urge for national unity—made for strange bedfellows.*

The "heyday of radicalism" from the May Fourth Movement to the Northern Expedition thus did not represent an unqualified victory for the young Chinese Communist Party. The working class remained embedded in preexisting forms of solidarity despite its growing cosmopolitanism. Only by activating such bonds—often via agreements with unsavory intermediaries—could the CCP harness labor militance to its own agenda. The rhetoric of revolutionary class struggle notwithstanding, successful labor organizing required enlisting the aid of "feudal" associations. Although artisan guilds offered the initial and most dependable entrée for Communist efforts, large-scale mobilization of labor required the cooperation of Guomindang and gangsters as well. This was a period of stunning successes for the CCP, but each advance involved the complicity of some notoriously fickle allies. Just how shaky this coalition actually was became tragically clear within weeks of the victory of the third armed uprising.† Gangsters Huang Jinrong and Du Yuesheng, as it turned out, had found a more reliable backer for their illicit opium interests.

*Antagonism toward foreigners did not disappear during the Three Armed Uprisings, of course. Anecdotal evidence of lingering xenophobia is provided in the memoir of a cotton worker who recalls that during the third uprising he and his friends seized a young man with a mustache, mistaking him for a Japanese. When, after some roughing up, the detainee's identity as a Chinese was finally established, the workers rebuked him: "Since you're really a Chinese, you shouldn't be imitating the Japanese with that mustache of yours." Replied the hapless victim: "Actually, I was imitating Sun Yatsen" (Wu Shunlin, May 5, 1958, transcript of interview, Labor Movement Archives of the SASS Institute of History).

†The assassination of General Labor Union chairman Wang Shouhua by agents of Du Yuesheng in April 1927 showed the gangster's capacity for turning against his former allies.

CHAPTER FIVE

Conservative Interregnum, 1927–37

THE ALLIANCE THAT HAD sustained the dramatic strike waves of the mid-1920's was shattered by Chiang Kai-shek's coup of April 12, 1927. This momentous turning point, which devastated the Communist labor movement and forced the radicals out of the cities and into a twenty-year exile in the countryside, was executed by the Shanghai gangsters.[1] It resulted in a markedly changed configuration of partisan politics in the labor movement. Grateful for the crucial assistance of gang leaders, the new Nationalist regime returned the favor by providing state positions and perquisites to its helpful henchmen. The resulting patronage system, in which opium czars mediated between working-class clients and top-level politicians, became the hallmark of labor relations under the Guomindang.

Gangsters and the Rise of Chiang Kai-shek

The role of gangsters as purveyors of social forces and state resources can be traced to the very apex of the GMD political system. It may well be, as was widely rumored, that Chiang Kai-shek himself had entered the Green Gang as a disciple of the Tongmeng Hui revolutionary, Chen Qimei.[2] In any case, by the early 1920's Chiang had pledged allegiance to the powerful Shanghai gangster Huang Jinrong.* When the Generalis-

---

*Chiang Kai-shek was introduced to Huang by business magnate Yu Xiaqing and later turned to these two when he and Chen Guofu (nephew of Chen Qimei) found themselves in serious economic trouble as a result of dealings on the Shanghai commodities exchange. A loan from Huang and Yu enabled Chiang to leave Shanghai for Guangzhou in 1921 to join Sun Yat-sen's revolutionary enterprise (Cheng Xiwen, "Wo dang Huang Jinrong guanjia de jianwen" [What I saw and heard as Huang Jinrong's butler], in *Jiu Shanghai de banghui* [The gangs of old Shanghai] [Shanghai, 1986], p. 157).

simo returned to the city as commander of the Northern Expeditionary forces on March 26, 1927, the first to greet him was his old mentor, "Smallpox Jinrong."[3]

Although long-standing personal connections were a key element in Chiang's dealings with gangsters, his reliance on men like Huang Jinrong was prompted by more than friendship. As even Communist organizers had been forced to acknowledge, these colorful local strong men were the effective rulers of early twentieth-century Shanghai society. Not to win their cooperation was to ensure defeat for either radical or conservative partisan enterprises.

Though the sponsorship of the Nationalist regime would offer unprecedented opportunities for the gangsters, their involvement with state authorities was not a new phenomenon. Huang Jinrong, the "godfather" of the Shanghai Green Gang, had come to the city in 1900. After living as a petty gangster for several years, he was recruited into the French police force as a plainclothes criminal detective. Police work in Shanghai's French Concession did not require severing ties with the underworld, and Huang kept a foot in each camp. His big break came a few years later, when Huang succeeded in obtaining the release of a French bishop who had been kidnapped while on a trip to North China. The bishop was a close friend of both the French consul and the French chief of police in Shanghai, and Huang was handsomely rewarded for his service with a newly created post as chief inspector for the Frenchtown police. Promotion to this powerful position greatly enhanced Huang Jinrong's standing as a gang master in the Shanghai underworld; as many as 20,000 of the city's residents (including Chiang Kai-shek) subsequently pledged their discipleship to him.[4]

Among those who took Huang as a mentor was Du Yuesheng. Born into a poor family in Pudong and orphaned at an early age, Du worked for several years at his uncle's fruit stand along the wharf by the old Chinese city. The boy's penchant for throwing rotten fruit at well-dressed rickshaw passengers did not endear Du to his uncle, however, and eventually he was fired for having stolen money for gambling. While jobless, Du made the acquaintance of the powerful Huang Jinrong. Huang's paramour, a former brothel madame, took an immediate liking to "Fruit Yuesheng," as he was then known, and saw that Du was given work in Huang's criminal empire. Like generations of secret society chieftains before him, Du Yuesheng rose to fame and fortune through Shanghai's lucrative opium trade. First assigned as an assistant in a Cantonese-owned opium den in Hongkou, Du was soon promoted to manage one of Huang's large dens in the French Concession. More entrepreneurial than his mentor, Du quickly saw the possibilities for turning Huang's Frenchtown connections to maximum advantage. With his master's sanction, Du established the "Black Stuff Company" to extract a monthly fee from every opium hong in the French Concession in return for a guarantee of freedom to sell openly without police interference. The system was maintained by substantial monthly payoffs to the French authorities.[5]

Soon Du's ambitions reached beyond the boundaries of Frenchtown. To expand the scale of opium operations, he made contact with another gangster and opium magnate in the city, Zhang Xiaolin. Zhang's close relations with the Shanghai garrison command had allowed him to gain control of the opium trade at the critical point where the Yangzi and Huangpu rivers joined. In 1920, Zhang agreed to cooperate formally with Du Yuesheng and Huang Jinrong. Henceforth Zhang would rely on the garrison command to transport opium downriver to the wharf of the old Chinese city, whereupon Du's men would shepherd it into the French Concession. Huang's connections with the French police ensured lucrative disposal of it there. The close relationship among Huang, Du, and Zhang—sealed by a sworn brotherhood ceremony—was further solidified in 1924, when Huang allocated some of his extensive landholdings in the French Concession to build adjoining residences for his two right-hand men.[6]

By challenging the political status quo in the Yangzi valley, Chiang Kai-shek's Northern Expedition threatened to undermine the opium business. Thus it was more than revolutionary spirit or personal goodwill that inspired the opium triumvirate of Shanghai to offer their services to the Generalissimo in the spring of 1927. The maintenance of their profitable trade was their major consideration. Chiang's willingness to work out a mutually agreeable modus operandi ensured the support of these powerful gangsters.

In late March 1927, Chiang Kai-shek's close associates Yang Hu, Chen Qun, and Wang Boling—all of whom had underworld ties—had been dispatched to Shanghai to establish contact with gangster leaders. There they met secretly with the opium triumvirate of Huang Jinrong, Du Yuesheng, and Zhang Xiaolin to lay plans for the anti-Communist offensive that was soon to follow.[7] Together they formed a Mutual Advancement Society (*gongjin hui*), charged with carrying out an assault against radical forces in the city.* On April 3, a confidential report by the British

---

*The title "Mutual Advancement Society" connoted a distinctive pedigree, having been the name of the political party sponsored by veteran revolutionary and Green Gang patron Chen Qimei when he assumed the military governorship of Shanghai following the 1911 Revolution (see Chapter 2). Chiang was a great admirer of Chen Qimei, whom he first met in Japan in 1906 and served under as regiment commander in 1911–12 when Chen was military governor of Shanghai. Even after Chen's assassination by agents of Yuan Shikai in 1916, Chiang retained close ties with the

police noted that "Zhang Xiaolin and others are reorganizing the Mutual Advancement Society. The members of this society are followers of the Green Gang. Its purpose is to oppose the Shanghai General Labor Union and radical elements among the workers. This movement has the full and energetic support of Chiang Kai-shek." On April 5, a week before Chiang's coup, the police foretold the coming event: "The Mutual Advancement Society is now preparing a surprise attack on the headquarters of the Shanghai General Labor Union to disarm the personnel there. The surprise attack will be carried out by Green Gang members, with assistance from plainclothes soldiers."[8]

The advance knowledge of the British police was not testimony to their expertise in intelligence work. Rather, the foreign authorities were themselves directly involved in the anti-Communist operation. Du Yuesheng had already met secretly with International Settlement and French Concession officials to communicate the gangsters' price for participation in the assault: 5,000 rifles and sufficient ammunition from the French, coupled with a guarantee of safe passage through the International Settlement for gangster participants. Both conditions were readily agreed to by the foreign authorities, who were anxious to purge their factories of radical influence.[9]

On the night of April 11, only hours before the fateful attack began, the opium triumvirate met with Chiang's trusted lieutenants Yang Hu, Chen Qun, and Wang Boling to drink wine and swear loyalty in front of a picture of the famous Peach Garden Oath.[10] At two o'clock in the morning of April 12 the offensive commenced. Hundreds of mobsters wearing armbands marked with the character for "labor" (*gong*) fanned out from the concessions into the neighboring Chinese areas to wrest control from the workers' pickets of the GLU. The battles were brief, as the Mutual Advancement Society—reinforced by Northern Expedition soldiers—quickly took command of picket stations and union offices. Al-

---

family of his former mentor. The subsequent rise of Chen Qimei's nephews, Chen Guofu and Chen Lifu, attested to this continuing association. The Chen brothers' powerful "CC Clique" was organized among conservative GMD elements only a few weeks after Chiang had revived historical memories by reactivating the Mutual Advancement Society for his April coup. See Fan Songfu, "Shanghai banghui de neimu" [Inside the gangs of Shanghai], *Wenshi ziliao xuanji*, 1980, no. 3, p. 155; Hu Shengwu, "Minchu huidang wenti" [The question of gangs in the early Republican period], in *Huidangshi yanjiu* (Shanghai, 1987), pp. 227–30; Hung-Mao Tien, *Government and Politics in Kuomintang China, 1927–1937* (Stanford, Calif., 1972), pp. 47–57. Mutual advancement societies had been active elsewhere in China around the time of the 1911 Revolution. For Hubei, see Joseph W. Esherick, *Reform and Revolution: The 1911 Revolution in Hunan and Hubei* (Berkeley, Calif., 1976), pp. 153–58, 229–31. In 1920, a gang-based Mutual Advancement Party had enrolled many male cotton workers in Shanghai (see Chapter 3).

though 200,000 workers went on strike the following day to protest the suppression, they were unable to resist the combined gangster-military forces. Hundreds of workers and labor organizers lost their lives in the ensuing bloodbath.[11]

The Nationalist Order: Labor Organization from the Top Down

Having crushed the Communist-controlled GLU, Chiang's men immediately undertook to impose their own organizational framework on the Shanghai labor movement.[12] The objective, in classic corporatist fashion, was to create a network of tamed labor unions under government direction.[13] On April 13, Yang Hu and Chen Qun presided over the formation of the Unification Committee for Shanghai Union Organization (*Shanghai gonghui zuzhi tongyi weiyuanhui*). A thinly veiled metamorphosis of the Mutual Advancement Society, the Unification Committee was a gangster-staffed operation that quickly developed a reputation for ruthlessness. Workers coined the phrase "tigers and wolves abound" (*hulang chengqun*), a pun on the given names of Yang Hu and Chen Qun, to describe the cruelty with which the Unification Committee carried out its task of reorganizing the Shanghai labor movement. Communists and others suspected of harboring leftist sympathies were summarily rounded up and put to death.[14]

The brutality of the Unification Committee generated overt resistance from some sectors of labor. Most vocal in leading the popular opposition was the gold- and silversmiths' union, a leftist-leaning association of skilled craftsmen.[15] It quickly became apparent, however, that workers' protests were hopelessly ineffective in the face of such heavy-handed suppression tactics.

The draconian methods of the Unification Committee proved unpalatable even to some members of the Guomindang. Exasperated by the committee's alienation of labor, Zhou Zhiyuan, director of the Office of Agriculture and Industry under the Shanghai GMD Party Branch, instructed one of his trusted subordinates to engage in separate and secret efforts at union reorganization. The Party staff member was, however, soon detected and tortured to death by the Unification Committee. In mid-November, with the encouragement of Zhou Zhiyuan and national Labor Bureau director Ma Chaojun, representatives of more than 120 Shanghai unions established the Shanghai Workers' General Association (*Shanghai gongren zonghui*) to counter the power of the Unification Committee. Promoted by the Shanghai GMD as a Party-sponsored alternative to the military-controlled Unification Committee, the General Association openly competed for the allegiance of the city's labor unions.[16]

The factional battles that wracked the Shanghai labor scene in this early period were but a harbinger of the endless intragovernment disputes that would eventually sap the Nationalist state of its capacity to rule. After almost half a year of internecine warfare between the two umbrella organizations, GMD Party Central stepped in during the spring of 1928 to order their dissolution and replacement by the new Reorganization Committee for Shanghai Unions (*Shanghai gonghui zhengli weiyuanhui*).[17]

The Reorganization Committee was investigating, ordering, and registering all of the city's unions according to Party principles but immediately ran into difficulties. The biggest problem was dissension among the nine leaders of the committee. Only one of the nine, a former printer at the Commercial Press, could lay claim to any working-class credentials, and he was assassinated, allegedly by underground Communists, shortly after assuming office.[18] The other eight committee members represented a variety of state agencies including the Shanghai GMD, Public Security Bureau, Bureau of Agriculture, Industry, and Commerce, and Garrison Command. The committee members considered themselves representatives of these rival agencies rather than spokesmen for the interests of labor, and they fought bitterly among themselves. A secret investigation conducted by GMD Party Central in the summer of 1928 concluded that the Reorganization Committee had made no headway in its appointed task of union work and by its ineptitude was inadvertently contributing to a resurgence of the Communist labor movement.[19] In October, only six months after its inception, the Reorganization Committee was dissolved by Nanjing. Henceforth responsibility for Shanghai labor was to rest with the People's Discipline Committee of the Shanghai GMD Party Branch and the newly established Bureau of Social Affairs of the Shanghai municipal government.[20]

Over the next several years, a stream of labor legislation issued forth. Covering the gamut from factory inspection to strike resolution, the laws, though still corporatist in intent, bespoke a more positive attitude toward labor on the part of the Nationalist regime.[21] Co-optation was to replace coercion as the main instrument of domination. Rules and regulations were promulgated, but in spite of the good intentions of many of the newly appointed staff members dealing with labor affairs at the Shanghai Party Branch and Bureau of Social Affairs, the city's complicated administrative structure doomed most reform efforts to failure. Shanghai's factories were heavily concentrated in the International Settlement so any attempt to impose Chinese laws was bound to provoke the foreign authorities. As the *Municipal Gazette,* voice of the International Settlement's Municipal Council, complained in the winter of 1928:

> The Social Bureau of the Greater Shanghai Municipality continues to interfere in labor disputes in the Settlement and French Concession and its impudence in this connection was manifest during the month. . . . This policy of usurping the authority of the Settlement administration is obviously in accord with an order jointly issued by the Social Bureau and the People's Training Committee of the local KMT [GMD] headquarters which requires all labor disputes to be mediated by the Social Bureau.

A few months later, the *Gazette* complained of "another attempt by the Social Bureau to usurp the judicial functions of the Provisional Court and turn them to political ends" in trying to register all labor unions in the International Settlement.[22] The resistance of the foreign authorities took a toll on the initiatives of the new Chinese regime. In 1930, the director of the Bureau of Social Affairs, Pan Gongzhan, reported that only 157 unions had registered with his bureau. This was a far cry from the more than 500 unions that had been active in Shanghai on the eve of the Guomindang takeover, though it did indicate the government's interest in labor organization. Pan complained that his bureau faced two formidable obstacles in carrying out its responsibilities in the area of labor control. First was the continued existence of the foreign enclaves—the International Settlement and the French Concession—where foreign residents (backed by foreign powers) governed with their own councils, courts, police, and public utility companies. To play its assigned role in union registration and dispute mediation, the Bureau of Social Affairs needed the cooperation of the foreign authorities, which it seldom got. The second impediment to the proper functioning of his bureau that Pan identified was "people who instigate labor unrest for their own profit."[23] No doubt Pan was here referring in part to remnant underground Communist organizers trying to resuscitate their radical labor movement, but he was also probably alluding to elements within his own Guomindang Party.

One source of intraparty dissension was the left wing of the GMD, which, although seriously weakened by the coup of April 1927, continued for several years to play a significant role in efforts at mass mobilization.[24] Under the Reorganization Faction (*gaizu pai*) of Wang Jingwei, the left wing established a Shanghai Labor Movement Committee to encourage strikes for higher wages and stimulate opposition to the corruption of Chiang's Nanjing regime. With the active participation of several prominent anarchists, the Labor Movement Committee managed to recruit workers to join a series of abortive anti-Chiang coup attempts.[25] Vexing to the Nanjing regime as such lingering leftism within the GMD was, it declined markedly when Wang Jingwei was elected as president of the Executive Yuan in late 1931.

A more lasting source of intraparty dissension came from the very group to which Chiang had turned in mounting his April coup: the Green Gang. The dissolution of the high-handed Unification Committee had already brought to an ignominious close the first experiment in gangster-dominated labor control under the new Nationalist regime. Soon to follow, however, was another—more subtle and successful— form of intervention.

Gangsters in Command

Having witnessed the failure of the Unification Committee and its successors, the ambitious Green Gang chieftain Du Yuesheng decided to try his own hand at organizing Shanghai labor. An obvious starting point was the unskilled work force, most of whose members were already under the thumb of gangster overseers. On the docks, for example, countless labor contractors had sworn allegiance to one or another of the opium triumvirate.[26] Du Yuesheng made skillful use of such contacts in a successful bid to take over several of the city's shipping companies.[27] But to cultivate laborers as committed clients would demand more than a convenient understanding with their foremen. It would also require serious attention to the interests of workers themselves. For this purpose, the unskilled occupations, with their long-standing tradition of authoritarian management, were not a promising entrée. Wharf contractors adamantly opposed any proposals that would reduce their share of the workers' paychecks, and resorted to arms to block government-sponsored reforms.[28] If Du Yuesheng were to win over the workers of Shanghai, he would have to find more progressive allies.

Communist labor organizers had been silenced, and the most vocal and articulate spokesmen for the rights of Shanghai workers were the leaders of a group of unions known as the Big Seven (*qida gonghui*). These unions included the publishing and printing unions of the Commercial Press, the postal union, the British American Tobacco Company (BAT) and Nanyang Brothers tobacco unions, the newspaper union, and the Chinese Electric union. All seven had been mainstays of labor radicalism during the Three Armed Uprisings, and in several of these unions, undercover Communists remained active.[29] Stimulated by the leftism of the Reorganization Faction, in 1928 the unions, "on behalf of those workers filled with revolutionary spirit," petitioned the central authorities to protest Nanjing's dwindling support for the labor movement. By the following year, when it became clear that the policies of the central government were unlikely to improve, the disheartened reformist union leaders were receptive to advances from a more aggressive player.[30]

First among the unionists to ally with Du Yuesheng were Lu Jingshi and Zhu Xuefan of the Shanghai Post Office. A Chinese government agency that was directed by a foreigner, the Post Office was targeted by Du as an institution with sufficient social and political clout to serve as an ideal entry to the unions.[31] The employees of the Shanghai Post Office, 40 percent of whom held staff-level positions, had been a focus of partisan attention for some time. On the eve of the May Thirtieth Movement in 1925, the first Communist Party branch at the Post Office included seven members, six of whom were staff-level employees who had previously worked as teachers. Only one was an ordinary worker, although 60 percent of postal employees were rank-and-file workers, including semiskilled mail sorters and carriers (who needed a modicum of literacy to perform their jobs) as well as unskilled coolies.[32] (By contrast, a Post Office branch of the Social Democratic Party, which, despite its misleading name, enjoyed close relations with the warlord authorities, was twice the size of the Communist branch and drew its membership heavily from ordinary mail carriers.)[33]

Under the terms of the United Front, members of the CCP branch were also registered with the Guomindang. Superficial cooperation between the two parties was undermined by deeper disagreements, however. The rift widened during a postal strike in August 1925, when Guomindang activist Lu Jingshi advocated negotiations rather than the immediate work stoppage initiated by the Communists. Although Lu Jingshi's go-slow approach was rejected in the heady atmosphere prevailing at that time, his restraint became an advantage under the changed circumstances following the April 12 coup. Competition between Communists and moderates continued for several years, but by the end of 1928 Lu Jingshi and his colleagues had gained the upper hand.[34]

It was to this tamed postal union that Du Yuesheng made overtures that would soon prove highly profitable both for himself and for his newfound allies among the union leadership. Under the patronage of the opium czar, Lu Jingshi quickly rose to become a member of the executive committee of the Shanghai Guomindang and director of the martial law division of the Shanghai Garrison Command. His fellow postal unionist Zhu Xuefan soon assumed the chairmanship of the newly created Shanghai General Labor Union, established to provide overall direction to the city's labor movement.[35] A foreigner who later came to know Zhu as representative of Chinese labor to the International Labor Organization (ILO) in Geneva recalled: "Chu [Zhu] had been down-and-out, as poor as only a Chinese worker can be. He dreamed of organizing labor unions that would fight for improving the lot of the workers. And he had all the qualities to make a labor leader, but not the ghost of a chance to succeed. Then Tu [Du] heard of him, took him on as his student, and he made good."[36]

But it was Du Yuesheng whose star rose most spectacularly. In 1933 an English-language "Who's Who" of China described the opium magnate as "one of the leading financiers, bankers and industrial leaders of China," with "a long and honourable record of important achievements in public and civic service, having on many occasions rendered invaluable aid to his country." Among Du's many official positions were listed those of "advisor to the Military Commission of the Nationalist government, member of the Legislative Body of the Municipality of Greater Shanghai, member of the Supervisory Committee of the Chamber of Commerce of Shanghai, and chairman of the Executive Committee of the China Merchants Steam Navigation Company, which is government controlled."[37] As a foreign contemporary remarked, Du "was a combination of Al Capone and Rockefeller."[38]

The mutually advantageous partnership between Du Yuesheng and his followers from the Post Office was built on the foundation of labor control. "Yellow unions" operating under government approval and dominated by officials with gang connections were the chief instrument through which Du and his associates exercised influence over the world of labor.[39]

Although yellow unionism is often dismissed as a sham, devoid of any positive benefit for its working-class members, the situation was actually very complicated. As in corporatist systems elsewhere in the world, groups that submitted to state direction were rewarded with official funds and favors.[40] The postal union is a good example. Shortly after the April 12 coup, this erstwhile bastion of radicalism was reorganized under GMD auspices. The new union was allocated office space on the fourth floor of the central post office building and was granted one thousand yuan in operating expenses by the postal authorities. This sum had been agreed upon as part of a strike settlement five years earlier, but only with the change in political regime was it actually disbursed. The cozy relationship between the new leaders of the postal union and the new government did not preclude union activism on behalf of workers' interests. An early test came when the director of the Shanghai Post Office rejected the union's demand for a standardized annual bonus for mail carriers. Although the request was opposed by leaders of the upper-level staff (who were largely factions from the southern provinces of Guangdong and Fujian), union representatives quickly set off to Nanjing for discussions with the Ministry of Communications—which approved the union's demand. These dramatic demonstrations of union activism were accompanied by an ongoing interest in the welfare of ordinary (semiskilled) workers. A unionist of the time recalled:

> There was a mail carrier by the name of Chen Mingdao then working in the registered-mail division. His family of four depended entirely upon his wages for their livelihood. Once when he had completed his route and was returning home, his bicycle ran into a ditch. His foot was injured, preventing him from going to work. After more than six weeks on sick leave, although he was not fired his wage payments were terminated. When we learned of this situation, we made an investigation. Establishing that Chen really was bedridden and that his family of four had no means of support . . . our union conducted several rounds of negotiations with the deputy director of the Post Office. . . . Finally the postal authorities felt compelled to arrange for Chen Mingdao to be sent to Renji Hospital for treatment, with all medical expenses covered by the Post Office. His wages were paid as usual and it was agreed that if his foot did not heal properly he would be reassigned to work indoors.[41]

Yellow unionists built up allegiance among the Shanghai labor force by obtaining such concrete benefits for workers. As a result, gang membership grew, so that by the end of the Nanjing decade, one out of five postal workers had sworn loyalty to a gang master.[42]

Du Yuesheng recognized the importance of attending to labor's demands. Through the introduction of postal unionists Lu Jingshi and Zhu Xuefan, their patron was invited to intervene in virtually every major strike that broke out in the city. Du's services as labor negotiator par excellence were employed—often to the benefit of labor—in industries as diverse as cotton, printing, silk weaving, jewelry, journalism, and rickshaw transport. On more than one occasion Du drew on his personal bank account first to subsidize the strike committee and then to augment the financial settlement that management was willing to grant.* Such displays of benevolence earned the gangster the gratitude of workers, employers, and the general public and often netted him a significant share of the company stock as well. As the British police observed, "The old French opium gang seems to be supplementing its income from smuggling by promoting racketeering in Chinese industrial enterprises." The financial rewards for Du's services were substantial, but the British police offered another, equally important explanation of the opium czar's

---

*This was Du's mode of operation during the French Tramway strikes of 1928 and 1930, the Nandao Tramway strike of 1932, the Nanyang Brothers Tobacco Company strike of 1933, the Shanghai Power Company strike of 1933, and the Shanghai Electric Construction Company strike of 1937. See *Shanghai Municipal Police Files*, D-5310.

appetite for labor mediation: "His desire to settle labour disputes aims at winning the confidence of the public and especially the government authorities."[43]

Zhu Xuefan recalls in a recent memoir how Du's intervention in strikes helped the gangster chieftain shed his unsavory reputation and become a celebrity in Shanghai. Each time Du Yuesheng negotiated a settlement, Shanghai's four major Chinese-language newspapers (whose board of directors was chaired by Du) printed glowing reports of the occasion. Coverage of these events was facilitated by the Labor News Agency, which Zhu Xuefan established specifically for the purpose of publicizing his patron's exploits.[44] Du Yuesheng's biographer on Taiwan has argued that these activities were directly responsible for the opium czar's rapid rise to fame:

> Regardless of whether it was Du Yuesheng or Lu Jingshi who sallied forth to settle labor disputes, their actions were perfectly coordinated into the smoothest of operations. Several years later, Du Yuesheng and the Shanghai municipal party branch joined forces in leading the labor movement. Shanghai industrialists and labor leaders in both the Chinese areas and the foreign concessions, regardless of trade or occupation, rushed to enter Du's gate. The confluence of these forces gave Du Yuesheng enormous power. The ease with which he subsequently launched his monumental undertakings can be traced back to the firm foundations laid during this period.[45]

Though Du Yuesheng's ascent was certainly attributable to the support of both government and big business, labor was also a critical pillar in the power base of the gangster chieftain and his henchmen. As a result, the gangsters were eager to champion the cause of labor—and even to promote labor strife—when such a strategy promised greater payoff. Zhu Xuefan could justifiably boast to a foreign visitor to his Labor News Agency that "we are the only people who defend the Shanghai workers against exploitation."[46] Zhu and several other Green Gang labor organizers even founded a small printing house in which they surreptitiously printed strike handbills which regular presses, subject to tight government censorship, dared not handle.[47]

The targets of gang-directed strikes were various. As early as the autumn of 1927, Green Gang union leaders in the British American Tobacco Company launched a strike for higher wages which quickly became linked to a Guomindang effort to extract increased taxes from the multinational giant (see Chapter 7). The Ministry of Finance of the Nationalist government secretly supplied strike pay to keep the workers off the job until BAT agreed to an acceptable settlement.[48] But governments as well as corporations could fall victim to Du's labor stratagems. In 1932, the Green Gang instigated a strike at the French Tramway

Company to protest the unfriendly policies of a new French consul and police chief who threatened to curtail opium and gambling in the French Concession.[49] That same year, Du's followers in the Shanghai Post Office launched a politically motivated strike that spread rapidly to postal workers in Beiping, Tianjin, and Nanjing. Although the strikers complained that recent increases in the price of stamps had not been accompanied by commensurate wage hikes, the real target of the protest was the leadership of the Ministry of Communications. At the time, the ministry was controlled by Wang Jingwei's Reorganization Faction, a rival to the CC Clique with which Du Yuesheng was more closely connected.[50]

These examples suggest the range of concerns that motivated Du Yuesheng's promotion of labor unrest. Sometimes, as in the BAT strike of 1927, Du's objectives coincided with those of the Nationalist government. At other times, as in the 1932 postal strike, protest was directed against an agency of the government. By deputing the Green Gang as its chief labor organizer, the fragmented state had created a powerful challenge to its own hegemony. The outcome was identical to the situation found in so many Third World countries whose leaders feel compelled to reach an accommodation with local strong men. Joel Migdal writes, "The paradox . . . is: while the strongmen have become evermore dependent on state resources to shore up their social control, state leaders have become evermore dependent on strongmen, who employ those resources in a manner inimical to state rules and laws."[51]

The fascinating interplay among state, gangsters, capitalists, workers, and foreigners, all of whom suffered from internal divisions, defined Shanghai politics under the Nationalists. When the Shanghai branch of the Guomindang first authorized the formation of a General Labor Union headed by Zhu Xuefan, the Bureau of Social Affairs (BSA)—which was a government, rather than a Party, institution—refused to recognize its authority. Not until three years later, when Nanjing intervened in the dispute, did the BSA agree to accept the new umbrella union. By that time the GLU's standing committee of five labor organizers consisted entirely of Green Gang members. Eventually the BSA was forced to open its doors to the gang. By 1936, three of the four departments at the bureau were headed by disciples of Du Yuesheng. Needless to say, the Labor Dispute Department and its subordinate Mediation Office were among the agencies that fell under Du's command.[52]

Du Yuesheng was not content merely to reap the economic rewards which his control over labor made possible. He was also determined to gain social respectability. In June 1931, all of Shanghai came to a standstill for several days to celebrate the founding of Du Yuesheng's ancestral temple. In honor of the special occasion, Lu Jingshi and Zhu Xuefan arranged for the local post office to dispense a special postmark.[53] The lavish festivities (complete with colorful parade, three days of operatic performances, a worship ceremony presided over by the mayor of Shanghai, and banquets for 50,000 guests per meal) reflected Du Yuesheng's desire to translate his substantial economic and political capital into commensurate cultural and social standing.[54] An eyewitness noted:

> Shanghai was an interesting place on June 9 when Tu [Du] opened his ancestral temple. A parade in which thousands of gangsters, business men and government officials took part, passed from Tu's home on Rue Wagner and made its way through the city while extra reserves of police guarded the streets enroute. In the van of the procession marched men carrying congratulatory scrolls from Chiang Kai-shek, Chang Hsueh-liang, Mayor Chang Chun of Shanghai, Dr. C. T. Wang, then foreign minister, M. Koechlin, then French Consul-General . . . and from other Kuomintang officials and personalities in various parts of the country.
>
> Tu had special launches plying back and forth between Shanghai and Pootung, carrying thousands of guests who paid tribute at his ancestral tablets. Among these guests were secretaries or representatives of all ministers and officials in the Nanking Government as well as from the Municipality of Greater Shanghai and the Gendarmerie Headquarters. Many high officials were present in person, Mayor Chang Chun came as the delegated representative of Chiang Kai-shek. A fortune in gifts was given Tu and the Chinese press reported that he distributed to followers and servants the sum of $70,000.[55]

The ancestral temple was an effort to invent the proper pedigree absent in Du's actual family history. Further to foster a genteel image, Du began to don long mandarin robes and to write his name with a studied calligraphic flair that belied his lack of formal education. An institutional expression of Du Yuesheng's acquired respectability was the formation in 1932 of the Constant Club, an association of some 1,500 of Du's more prestigious followers.[56]

By the mid-1930's Du Yuesheng was a cornerstone of Shanghai high society. A typical day would see him entertaining anywhere from one to two hundred guests, many of them top officials and wealthy businessmen, at his posh Frenchtown residence.[57] No less a personage than Sun Fo, president of the Legislative Yuan, turned to "Mister Du Yuesheng," as he was respectfully addressed, for a happy resolution of his complicated love affairs.[58]

Du won an ironic victory in his struggle for respectability in 1934 when Chiang Kai-shek appointed him director of opium suppression in the city of Shanghai. In actuality, the post facilitated Du's monopoly of the opium trade because the Chinese Maritime Customs was under orders to hand over any drug seizures to the Shanghai Opium Suppression Bureau, which Du now headed. Publicly, however, Du made a show of great piety. In October 1936, when Madame Chiang suggested that the most fitting birthday present for her husband would be airplanes with which to fight the Japanese, Du Yuesheng rushed to comply. His generous gift of a plane named Opium Suppression of Shanghai was duly celebrated in all the newspapers.*

The meteoric ascent of Du Yuesheng was telling testimony to the efficacy of gang connections in promoting upward mobility in Republican Shanghai. Du's obsession with social acceptance underscored the distance the parvenu had traveled on his journey from orphaned fruit seller to power broker. The thousands of followers who flocked to Du's fold in the 1930's were motivated by a similar desire for promotion and prestige. Lacking the head start of a comfortable family background, these disadvantaged yet ambitious elements of Shanghai society were attracted to Du Yuesheng's gangster network as an alternative path to fame and fortune. As one of Du's former followers recalled, the great majority of his fellow clients were "people with a certain ability and potential who faced formidable obstacles in fulfilling their aspirations."[59] Affiliation with Du Yuesheng was a calculated strategy for getting ahead in an otherwise inhospitable environment.

Such recruits, although evident in virtually every industry, were especially numerous among semiskilled laborers. Mail carriers at the Shanghai Post Office, drivers and conductors at the French Tramway Company (see Chapter 9), and cigarette rolling machine operators at the British American Tobacco Company (see Chapter 7) were typical of the yellow union constituency. Lacking the remuneration and job security enjoyed by factory artisans, yet more committed to urban life than transient unskilled workers, semiskilled laborers were easily persuaded of the advantages to be gained by an accommodation with labor racketeers. Under the combined sponsorship of gangsters and government, the middle portion of the Shanghai labor force gained a new political importance.

This political trend reinforced developments in the structure of production that had substantially increased the size of the semiskilled sector. By the Nanjing decade, the "second industrial revolution," which

---

*The irony was not lost on Du himself. As a foreign crusader against opium recounted her meeting with the gangster chieftain at this time: "Tu [Du] looked at me attentively. 'Yes, I am the head of China's Opium Merchants,' he acknowledged moodily. I appreciated his frankness, and described to him how the whole of Geneva was in uproar when Generalissimo had appointed the Opium Tsar head of the Shanghai Suppression Bureau! A fleeting smile made Tu's face quite human. He himself must have considered the appointment a huge joke" (Ilona Ralf Sues, *Shark's Fins and Millet* [Boston, 1944], p. 92).

had swept European and American industries around the time of World War I, was in full swing in Shanghai. Less skilled, employer-trained male operatives could be found in increasing numbers in both Chinese and foreign-owned factories.[60] Obsessed with efficiency and profitability, industrial managers began to replace their older employees with less expensive workers. An unemployed laborer laid off by the closure of a British American Tobacco Company factory explained bitterly, "BAT closed its gates last year [1934] . . . because workers' wages at the old factory were all at least one or two yuan higher than elsewhere. They shut down the factory to eliminate the older workers and hire new workers at lower wages. . . . They paid no heed to how much money we had made for them in the past; they regarded our lives as their own playthings."[61] The beneficiaries of such changes were of course the newer, less skilled entrants to the labor force.

Although the dovetailing of political and economic trends afforded semiskilled workers an unprecedented prominence in the labor movement of the 1930's, artisans and unskilled laborers were not invisible during this period. The yellow unions made inroads among both of these sectors.* On the whole, however, artisans retained radical inclinations and unskilled workers an unruly independence that fit uneasily if at all with the designs of government and employer-affiliated racketeers. The widespread introduction of scientific management techniques in this period heightened artisans' animosities toward their employers,[62] and insecurity of employment among unskilled laborers militated against their involvement in unionization. As the corrupt practices of gangster unionists became evident over the course of the Nanjing decade, these other sectors of the work force were increasingly disposed to go their own ways.

Communist "Leftism"

Disillusionment with the Guomindang regime would eventually be a major reason for the resurgence of a revolutionary labor movement in Shanghai, but it translated only gradually into direct support for the Communists largely because of the repressive character of the Nationalist state. The dangers of association with "Reds" were obvious enough to deter all but the most fearless and committed. Nationalist repression

*Among unskilled workers, the dockers' long-standing tradition of gangsterism made them periodically receptive to GMD overtures. Among skilled craftsmen, the construction workers' union was captured for a time by labor racketeers. See Number Two History Archives, #720-33; #722: 4-233; #722: 4-501; #722: 4-502; #722: 4-503; #722: 4-226.

was not, however, the sole cause of limited worker support for the Communists during this period. The actions of the Communist Party were also to blame.

Although orthodox Party historiography has for political reasons exaggerated the mistakes of the period, it is certainly true that the dominant policy emphasized an aggressive labor activism that was unrealistic in the repressive climate of the time.* In what was subsequently dubbed the "first leftist error" of the Chinese Communist Party, a secret politburo meeting in November 1927 advocated open opposition to Guomindang-sponsored yellow unions and continued emphasis on armed urban revolts.[63] Later that month an abortive fourth workers' uprising was attempted in Shanghai. Its brutal suppression impressed many Communists with the futility of persisting in "Qu Qiubai's adventurism," and the leftist line was roundly criticized at the Sixth Party Congress in July 1928.

The following year, however, the CCP under the advice of the Comintern returned to a platform that repudiated any cooperation with yellow unions and recommended the formation of independent red unions under direct CCP control. Aggressive street actions were also encouraged. The ineffectiveness of such tactics was suggested by a British police report: "A mob of about 100 Chinese quickly assembled at the corner of North Szechuan and Woosung Roads and on a signal of the firing of a cracker commenced shouting communist slogans and throwing pamphlets of a like nature into the air. . . . Eleven Chinese and one Formosan were arrested and a considerable quantity of 'Red' literature was seized."[64] By the spring of 1930, Party membership in Shanghai had declined by nearly 60 percent from the preceding year. Of the 500 or so remaining members, only 35 percent were factory workers and a paltry 3 percent were women.[65]

Still this aggressive mode of operations continued. The British police observed:

On the morning July 16, 1930, a demonstration was attempted on Nanking [Nanjing] Road when about 300 students and labourers congregated at the

---

*See Lawrence R. Sullivan, "Reconstruction and Rectification of the Communist Party in the Shanghai Underground, 1931–34," *China Quarterly*, 1985, no. 105, pp. 78–97, for an effort to rescue the Russian Returned Students who controlled the Jiangsu Provincial Committee in the early 1930's from charges of reckless leftism. As Sullivan shows by an examination of the journal *Liening shenghuo*, the stated policies of the Jiangsu Provincial Committee were a good deal more moderate than they have been portrayed in subsequent Party historiography. Nevertheless, stated policy and actual behavior were often at variance. See Shen Yixing, *Gongyunshi mingbianlu* [Controversies in labor movement history] (Shanghai, 1987), pp. 136–44, 156–65, for a discussion of leftist excesses in the Shanghai labor movement of the 1930's.

corner of Nanking and Thibet [Tibet] Roads and after shouting slogans and throwing pamphlets in the air proceeded east along Nanking Road until intercepted by the Police. A few minutes later a similar crowd of about 200 adopted the same tactics at the corner of Nanking and Fokien [Fujian] Roads. Proceeding east they stoned a passing tramcar breaking two windows and a private owned motor car breaking one window. In breaking up the different assemblies of demonstrators, the Police made 32 arrests.[66]

A few months later, at the Third Plenum of the Sixth Party Congress in September 1930, the "second leftist error of Li Lisan" was criticized for a policy of political strikes and worker insurrections that had alienated the vast majority of the working class. Still, there were those who promoted overt opposition to yellow unions through aggressive action—a program associated with Wang Ming at the Fourth Plenum of the Sixth Congress in January 1931 and later designated the "third leftist error" of the Communist Party.[67] A British police report of May 1, 1933, noted: "Documents captured recently show that the local branches of the Chinese Communist Party arranged to make the incidence of the new year, the Spring Festival and the anniversary of the Sino-Japanese conflict excuses for starting public demonstrations, disturbances and strikes. Nothing, however has come of these planes [sic] beyond two ineffectual attempts to create street-demonstrations on January 24 and 28 respectively, which were dispersed quietly by the Police."[68]

Not for several more years would the pendulum swing decisively in the direction of a more moderate approach. A recent history of the Chinese labor movement summarizes the period: "From the defeat of the Great Revolution [i.e., April 1927] until 1936 was an eight- or nine-year period in which the labor movement was dominated by leftist errors. This was the major cause of the failure of the labor movement in the white areas [under enemy control]."[69]

Through the early 1930's remnant Communists in Shanghai engaged in a variety of militant actions aimed at undermining the GMD regime. Such activism led to a steady stream of arrests. The toll on the CCP labor movement was costly: in 1930, some 2,000 Shanghai workers belonged to Communist-sponsored red unions, dropping to 500 in 1932 and to a mere handful by 1934.[70] Many of those incarcerated were high-level cadres who had been promoted rapidly from the ranks of workers.[71] Unfortunately for the progress of the revolution, a remarkably large number of these people—including the general secretary of the Party, the Party secretary of Jiangsu, the head of the Organization Department in the Jiangsu Party, and the general commander of the workers' pickets during the third uprising—defected to the Guomindang side.[72]

Conclusion

Over the course of the Nanjing decade, racketeers replaced radicals as the major strategists of partisan politics in the Shanghai labor arena. The remarkable rise of Green Gang chieftain Du Yuesheng was dramatic evidence of the importance of secret society gangs in the new Nationalist order. As a confidential Office of Strategic Services report on the GMD concluded, "The Kuomintang, which was born as a secret society and rose to power with the aid of another, found it necessary to create yet other secret societies for the double purpose of opposing its enemies, both internal and external, and bolstering its position under Chiang Kai-shek's leadership."[73]

In conception, the Nationalists' approach was corporatist.* The goal was to promote economic development free from the debilitating effects of class conflict. To this end, the state would reorganize society in such fashion that national growth and social order, rather than narrow sectarian interest, would be served.[74] Philippe Schmitter has defined corporatism as "a system of interest representation in which the constituent units are organized into a limited number of singular, compulsory, non-competitive hierarchically ordered and functionally differentiated categories, recognized or licensed (if not created) by the state and granted a deliberate representational monopoly within their respective categories in exchange for observing certain controls on their selection of leaders and articulation of demands and supports."[75] Schmitter points out that his definition is an "ideal-type description" from which real systems may depart substantially.† Clearly, as evidenced by its heavy reliance on gangs, the GMD never succeeded in its effort to install a hierarchically articulated system subject to stringent central controls.

---

*See Joseph Fewsmith, *Party, State and Local Elites in Republican China: Merchant Organizations and Politics in China, 1890–1930* (Honolulu, 1985), pp. 164–66, for an analysis of state corporatism under the Nationalists. Fewsmith argues that such policies emasculated Party authority (in favor of state power) and proved beneficial to the Shanghai merchant elite (at the expense of the merchant middle class). One outcome, he claims, was "the destruction of the labor movement" (p. 139). The Nationalists clearly pursued a corporatist project, but I would contend that this effort did not result in a complete demobilization of labor.

†Mexico, for example, though considered one of the most fully corporatist regimes in Latin America, in the area of urban labor allegedly falls short on four out of nine of Schmitter's criteria. See Alfred Stepan, *The State and Society: Peru in Comparative Perspective* (Princeton, N.J., 1978), p. 68. As David and Ruth Collier have observed, corporatism should be conceived not as "either present or absent," but as a "series of traits that may be present or absent to varying degrees" ("Who Does What, to Whom, and How: Toward a Comparative Analysis of Latin American Corporatism," in *Authoritarianism and Corporatism in Latin America*, ed. James M. Malloy [Pittsburgh, Pa., 1977], pp. 489–512).

The Nationalists' gang-based regime was not the mere hireling of China's upper classes,[76] yet neither was it an entirely "autonomous" entity that "was never accountable to political groups or institutions outside the regime."[77] The controversy that has developed in the China field over the character of the Nationalist regime mirrors a larger debate among general theorists about the nature of the state. While a Marxist scholarly tradition has seen the modern state as the "executive committee of the bourgeoisie," a Weberian tradition pictures the state as a "rational" entity operating according to rules of its own making. Faced with these alternative views of state-society relations, the challenge—as Charles Bright and Susan Harding have summarized it—is to arrive at "a conception of the state that accords it neither too much, nor too little, autonomy from social forces."[78] But what *are* the relevant social forces with which we should be concerned? Perhaps a case can be made that in an "advanced capitalist society" the domestic capitalist class is the critical social force with which the regime must interact in the statemaking process. Yet can the same be said for Republican China, where industry was still in its infancy?

China during the Nanjing decade was a fragmented society over which no single class could exercise hegemony. If we turn to the Marxist tradition for inspiration, the appropriate locus classicus would not be *Das Kapital*, which analyzes advanced capitalism, but *The Eighteenth Brumaire*, in which Louis Napoleon's rise to power is interpreted against the background of a divided France in the throes of transition from an agrarian to an industrial economy. Marx's characterization of Napoleon applies with equal force to Chiang Kai-shek: "The contradictory task of the man explains the contradictions of his government, the confused groping about which seeks now to win, now to humiliate first one class and then another."[79]

The Nationalists had to deal not only with the old and new elites of landlords and capitalists but with a recently politicized working class as well. Those, like Du Yuesheng, who could manage this valuable resource, were amply rewarded by a grateful regime. State support, in turn, bolstered the gangster's ability to draw yet more clients into his patronage network. Semiskilled immigrants from North China (as we will see in Part III) provided an especially receptive audience for this mobilization effort. The scenario matched that which encouraged the rise of Boss William Tweed in nineteenth-century New York or the Democratic machine in early twentieth-century Chicago: "The rapid influx of new populations for whom family and ethnicity were the central identifications, when coupled with the award of valuable opportunities for profit and an expanding public payroll, provided the ideal soil for the growth of party machines."[80] Patronage politics, whether in New York, Chicago, or Shanghai, could bring palpable benefits to workers, gangsters, and state officials alike. Ultimately, however, the very operation of this system also contributed to a politicization of labor that would eventually help to unravel the bonds of patronage.

Semiskilled workers - who were they? ←
Find out before going on.

CHAPTER SIX

← Radical Resurgence, 1937–49

LABOR RACKETEERING THRIVES on state sponsorship and wanes when government support is withdrawn. In wartime Shanghai the decline of gangster domination and its replacement by a radical labor movement was thus closely linked to the fading fortunes of the Guomindang regime. The Nationalist retreat following the Japanese invasion in the summer of 1937 reduced state patronage for gangsters and afforded Communist revolutionaries an opportunity to rebuild a working-class base.[1]

Taking full advantage of the nationalistic sentiments of the day, radicals once again reached out to racketeers in a bid for the allegiance of Shanghai labor. Bereft of their bureaucratic backers, gang chieftains were increasingly inclined toward "patriotic" cooperation with Communists, thereby contributing to an expansion of the social base of the revolution. Equally important to the growth in Communist support was a new policy on the part of the CCP itself. The changed strategy of the wartime period facilitated renewed contact with what would once again turn out to be the Communists' most reliable constituency among the working class.

The War of Resistance: Worker Nationalism

The Japanese attack on Shanghai in August 1937 followed years of aggression toward China. Beginning with the assault on Manchuria in September 1931, the Japanese military had made its intentions painfully clear to concerned Chinese. Many Shanghai workers, true to the patriotic legacy of May Fourth and May Thirtieth, were quick to join the cry for resistance to the invaders.[2] As early as October 1, 1931, a delegation of workers led by a postal unionist went to Nanjing to demand greater government opposition to the Japanese. The next month more than 70 Shanghai labor unions, under the direction of the postal and public utilities unions, sent a follow-up delegation to reiterate the demand. When the Japanese turned their guns on Shanghai in early 1932, workers at more than 30 Japanese-owned cotton mills walked off the job. The strike was supported by separate proclamations issued in the names of both the old Shanghai General Labor Union, now managed by a few remnant members of the Communist underground, and the new Shanghai General Labor Union, chaired by Green Gang labor leader Zhu Xuefan.*

When the Japanese threat loomed again in August 1936, the National Salvation Association (NSA) was formed to coordinate labor's opposition to Japanese imperialism. The new organization showed its strength three months later when it played a leadership role in another major strike at Japanese-owned cotton mills in the city. The strike was settled only after the intervention of Green Gang strong men Du Yuesheng and Zhu Xuefan and resulted in a modest wage hike for cotton workers.[3] Although its gains were meager in this time of galloping inflation, the strike is portrayed in standard CCP histories as a turning point for the labor movement. At the time, Mao Zedong described it as a "momentous incident in the new stage of the Chinese revolution." More recently, Chinese historians have hailed it as "the first successful large-scale strike in Shanghai since the defeat of the Great Revolution [i.e., April 12, 1927]."[4]

Although the Communist Party played a minimal part in the November 1936 cotton strike, it has been seen in retrospect as a vindication of the Party's new, antileftist labor policy.[5] The new line, announced by Liu Shaoqi in his April 1936 "Outline for Labor Movement Work in the White Areas," advised:

> Now is not the time for a decisive battle between revolution and counter-revolution.... Comrades and revolutionary workers must all join the yellow unions, participating in their various activities.... In those factories and enterprises without yellow unions ... we should use native-place associa-

---

*Jiu yiba—yi erba Shanghai junmin kangri yundong shiliao [Historical materials on the resist-Japan movement of Shanghai soldiers and citizens from September 18 to January 28] (Shanghai, 1986), pp. 104–9, 288–96. Liu Shaoqi, stationed in Shanghai at the time, helped provide a strike fund and soup kitchens to support the January 1932 cotton strike. Criticized as economistic "rightist opportunism" by Kang Sheng, these activities earned Liu demotion from his post as head of the CCP's Central Labor Bureau. Not until his appointment as director of the North China Bureau in the spring of 1936 was Liu Shaoqi again in a position to provide direction to the labor movement of the white areas. Over the next two years Liu took advantage of his new post to pen a series of essays which advocated attention to the economic needs of workers, in effect vindicating his earlier approach. See Shen Yixing, Gongyunshi mingbianlu [Controversies in labor movement history] (Shanghai, 1987), pp. 174–75.

tions, mutual aid societies, abstinence societies, and other old-style and new-style groups. . . . We must temporarily abandon the task of independently organizing red unions. Those clandestine red unions of past days must be quickly dissolved. . . . We must encourage and promote yellow union participation in anti-Japanese national salvation associations and movements, calling on all parties and factions within the entire nation to unite in resisting Japan and rescuing our country.[6]

Liu Shaoqi's "Outline" was welcomed by underground Communists engaged in the difficult and dangerous mission of labor organizing behind enemy lines, for it afforded a good deal of leeway in dealing with the complicated realities of their work. With the outbreak of open warfare following Japan's attack on Shanghai on August 13, 1937, the new liberal policy was eagerly—and often successfully—implemented.

The man charged with carrying out this fundamental change in the direction of the Shanghai labor movement was an outside cadre by the name of Liu Changsheng. From autumn of 1937 through the first years of the People's Republic, Liu assumed a central role in shaping Communist labor policy in the country's largest industrial city. A trained leather craftsman and shoemaker from Shandong, Liu was an artisan with a northern native-place identity. The mixture, unusual in Shanghai circles, was instrumental in enabling Liu to develop a labor strategy that appealed to both Jiangnan artisans and less skilled northerners.

Multifaceted as Liu Changsheng's approach was, the key to his success lay in the special attention he devoted to the more experienced and better-educated sector of the labor force. Liu personally headed the "staff committee" (*zhiwei*), a group of Party members made up entirely of well-paid, upper-echelon workers. Skilled craftsmen, technicians, engineers, and other white-collar professionals were primary targets for Communist Party recruitment drives under Liu's leadership.[7] The strategy bore results. As one of Liu's closest co-workers observed on the eve of Pearl Harbor, the Party's backbone membership in Shanghai "consists increasingly of seasoned, skilled workers."[8]

The initial focus of Party rebuilding during the wartime period was the National Salvation Association, which, because its labor network was dominated by the elite of the Shanghai work force, provided a hospitable opening for Communist mobilization efforts.[9] Particularly active in the NSA network was the Ant Society (*yishe*), a group of predominantly white-collar workers that was involved in patriotic causes in Shanghai from its establishment in February 1928 until its prohibition a decade later.[10] The Ant Society was also a major constituent of the Helpful Friend Society (*yiyoushe*), formed with Party support as a mutual aid association for printers, pharmacists, bankers, store clerks, and other relatively well-off workers. During its twelve-year existence, the Helpful Friend Society recruited more than 500 new Party members.[11]

Over time, CCP cadres began to employ other vehicles of Party recruitment as well. Nearly half of Shanghai's more than 5,000 Chinese-owned factories were destroyed in the Japanese attack, turning tens of thousands of workers into wartime refugees. Thanks to the financial assistance of several Green Gang leaders, some 40 to 50 refugee shelters opened to provide services for these victims.[12] Underground Communist cadres—many of whom had also lost factory jobs—offered their services as volunteers. In most shelters "little teahouses" (xiao chaguan) managed by Communist cadres soon opened as meeting places for refugees to enjoy singing, storytelling, newspaper reading, and discussion of current events. These centers yielded a large number of Party recruits; those of northern origin usually returned home to link up with the New Fourth Army, while Jiangnan natives typically remained with the labor movement. When overtly anti-Japanese associations were banned in early 1938, these labor organizers helped to convert the little teahouses and NSA groups into recreation clubs and mutual aid societies reminiscent of the artisan guild tradition of many Jiangnan workers.[13]

Nationalism was arguably the major issue around which the Communists built their wartime following, but it was not the only one. Inflation was also of great concern to Shanghai workers. As Table 3 indicates, their cost of living skyrocketed during the war years. Key to this inflationary spiral was the price of rice. Although surrounded by some of the best rice-growing areas in China, Shanghai became dependent on foreign rice after 1937. The Japanese military reserved Jiangnan rice for its army in China as well as for export to Japan, forcing Shanghai to purchase rice from Saigon just when Chinese currency was suffering a severe decline in exchange value. Rice riots became commonplace; 75 occurred in Shanghai during December 1939. Eleanor Hinder, chief of the Social and Industrial Division of the Shanghai Municipal Council, described the crisis:

> The distressing effects of high prices are illustrated by the practice of "rice sweeping" (and, indeed, the snatching of other commodities such as raw cotton) which has become a frequent sight in the city as a consequence of the rising prices. When a truckload of rice halts at a traffic intersection, a dozen waifs, adult and adolescent, appear from nowhere, moving like lightning. In a twinkling one or more rice bags are pierced with knives, and as the precious grain begins to run out, it is scooped swiftly with the dust of the roadway into a receptacle. The "sweeper" will often disappear before any police can act.

The deterioration in living standards was dramatically illustrated in that most grisly of statistics: the number of exposed corpses collected in the

TABLE 3

Cost-of-Living Index for Shanghai Workers, 1936–45

Year	Index	Year	Index
1936	100	1941	827
1937	119	1942	1,994
1938	151	1943	7,226
1939	198	1944	47,750
1940	428	1945	6,058,103

SOURCE: *Jiefangqian de Shanghai wujia* [Commodity prices in pre-liberation Shanghai] (Shanghai, 1961), p. 330.

streets of Shanghai. Shortly before the war, the annual figure had averaged 5,500. In 1937 it rose to 20,746, in 1938 to 101,047, and in 1939 to 110,173.[14]

The war was disastrous for those at the margins of survival. Conversely, those with some measure of security were best equipped to strike back. Recognition of this reality permitted the CCP to make significant inroads during these years of duress.

The continuing importance of the privileged stratum of Shanghai labor to the growth of the Communist movement was revealed in the case of the Commercial Press, targeted by Liu Changsheng as a promising site for recruitment efforts because of the high educational level of its workers as well as its record of revolutionary involvement. In April 1938 a Party branch was reestablished at the publishing house according to Liu's instructions. Party members quickly set about expanding their ranks by holding a variety of cultural activities tailored to the preferences of literate workers: a book drive that netted some 3,000 volumes for an employees' reading room, an in-house journal containing headline news and patriotic commentary, a current events discussion group intended to stimulate greater nationalism, sports teams, and drama and song groups. The greatest interest in these projects was found in the circulation department (*faxing suo*), where highly educated white-collar workers had long resisted the initiatives of gangster yellow unionists. In 1939, as inflationary trends aroused dissatisfaction over wages, workers in the circulation department decided to engage in a sit-down strike to bring attention to their plight. Disavowed by the yellow union at the press, the protest proceeded on schedule, timed for the period when schools were just about to open and textbook sales were brisk. Doors to Commercial Press book outlets remained open, but clerks refused to make any sales. The fourteen-day protest won a victory for the strikers, undermining the authority of yellow unionists and clearing the way for further Communist mobilization. By the time of Pearl Harbor, more than three dozen CCP members had been recruited at the Commercial Press.[15]

Although many of the Guomindang officials responsible for labor fled the city within a few months of the Japanese attack, the Communists could hardly exercise a free hand in reaching out to Shanghai's workers. The new Japanese overlords not only wielded a mighty espionage and military apparatus capable of identifying and suppressing their antagonists, they also had serious ambitions of harnessing Shanghai labor in service to their own political agenda. They sought out potential allies within the labor movement, concentrating on those who had felt slighted during the Nanjing decade. A diverse array of collaborators—from petty gangsters, to members of the Reorganization Faction of the GMD, to Trotskyites and other former Communists—was assembled in the Chinese Republic Workers' League. Sponsored by the Special Service Section of the Japanese Naval Landing Party, the Workers' League fomented labor disputes in non-Japanese factories.*

The Japanese takeover of the foreign enclaves in the aftermath of Pearl Harbor brought to an end these Workers' League activities. For several years the Shanghai labor scene was remarkably quiet, quelled both by the new political situation and by the disastrous economic plight that befell many of the city's factories.[16] In this intensely hostile environment, Communist cadres were forced to assume a very low profile, mobiliz-

---

*Most notable among these work stoppages was a six-month strike at the British-owned Chinese Printing and Finishing Company. The settlement, which provided for a generous 20 percent wage hike, also spelled the demise of the Workers' League, however. Insisting that the league was Communist-tainted, conservative elements within the Special Service Section replaced it with the Chinese Workers' Welfare Association led by a Taiwanese with close Japanese connections. The new group was less leftist in its composition but continued to launch costly work stoppages at non-Japanese (especially British, American, and Swiss) enterprises. After about a year of operation, the Welfare Association was dissolved and replaced by a new Shanghai General Labor Union under the direct control of Wang Jingwei's puppet regime. Within a few weeks of its inauguration the new union had gained control of 54 unions representing 211,482 workers. This umbrella organization directed a crippling transportation and utilities strike in the International Settlement and French Concession during the fall of 1940. See Robert W. Barnett, *Economic Shanghai: Hostage to Politics, 1937–1941* (New York, 1941), pp. 65–69; *Shanghai tebieshi zonggonghui gaikuang* [General condition of the General Labor Union of Shanghai Municipality] (Shanghai, 1941), pp. 121–25; Ma Chungu, *Shanghai gongyun de xianzhuang baogao* [Report on the current condition of the Shanghai labor movement] (Yenan, 1941), pp. 14–21; Wang Jianchu and Sun Maosheng, *Zhongguo gongren yundongshi* [A history of the Chinese labor movement] (Shenyang, 1987), pp. 234–35; Li Xun, "'Gudao' shiqi hanjian gonghui xingxing sese" [Various forms of traitorous labor unions during the 'isolated island' period], *Shanghai gongyun shiliao*, 1986, no. 3, pp. 21–25. British police reports credited the Japanese with a surprising degree of success in fomenting labor disputes during the years 1939–41; most of these were apparently settled to the benefit of the workers. See *Shanghai Municipal Police Files*, D-6449 and D-9601(c).

ing labor on an individual rather than organized basis. Personal friend-
ships, native-place ties, brotherhoods, sisterhoods, and secret societies
replaced unions as the principal means of establishing contact with
rank-and-file workers. Slowdowns and sabotage supplanted strikes as
the favored form of protest. Those strikes that did occur under CCP
sponsorship strived toward spontaneity in line with the policy of the
"three withouts": without leadership, organization, or mass momen-
tum.[17]

The low-key manner of the Communists in this period helped win
them new friends within the Shanghai working class, in part with the
assistance of gangsters. Although many gang leaders collaborated wholeheartedly with the puppet regime,* others were receptive to the patriotic
appeals of Communist cadres. Several friendly Green and Red Gang
chieftains supplied the CCP with critical intelligence about the plans of
the Japanese and their puppets. Another used his contacts on the docks
to disseminate Communist propaganda.[18]

Gangster contacts allowed the CCP to enlarge its following, but the
core of support for Communist initiatives throughout the war years
came from the more fortunate sectors of the working class. Some of the
most enthusiastic new recruits even occupied high-level management
positions. An example was Hu Yongqi, chair of the Shanghai Insurance
Employers' Association. The son of a silk weaver in rural Zhejiang, Hu
was educated at a missionary school in Hangzhou. Eventually he was
sent abroad on a church scholarship to study business at Columbia
University. Upon completing an internship with an insurance company
in New York, Hu returned to Shanghai. In 1931 he founded the Ningshao
Life Insurance Company, assuming the position of general manager. Like
many educated young Chinese, Hu grew increasingly distraught over the
Japanese threat to his country. As an active participant in the profes-
sional wing of Shanghai's National Salvation Association, he was introduced to Edgar Snow's *Red Star over China* and other materials about
the Communist revolution. In 1938 the young businessman applied for
membership in the CCP. Because of his high socioeconomic position,
Hu's request required the approval of Party Central in Yenan. Early the
following year, his application was accepted.[19]

Hu Yongqi played a central role in furthering Communist inroads

---

*A notorious example was gangster Chang Yuqing, who headed the Yellow Way
Society. A 315-pound former bathhouse proprietor, Chang directed his 700 followers to
combat Guomindang and Communist influences alike. Headquartered in the Hongkou district, his society specialized in extortion, kidnapping, and assassinations.
Yellow Way members were also responsible, at Japanese instigation, for fomenting
strikes in British-owned enterprises. See Li Xun, "'Gudao' shiqi hanjian gonghui
xingxing sese," p. 21; *Shanghai Municipal Police Files*, D-8458.

among workers in the Shanghai insurance business by helping to establish the Insurance Federation, a CCP-backed organization that promoted cultural, educational, and welfare activities among insurance company employees. The inaugural meeting of the federation, held at the Ningbo Native-Place Association on July 1, 1938, was attended by more than 400 insurance workers. The activities of the Insurance Federation closely paralleled those of CCP organizers at the Commercial Press. A reading room was opened with contributions gathered during a successful book drive; a monthly journal boasting Hu's calligraphy on its title page was published; a current events lecture series by progressive speakers was launched; a *pingtan* operatic group, classical Chinese music group, and harmonica group (which played songs like "The Happy Coppersmith") were formed; athletic competitions were held. The most dynamic of the Insurance Federation's organizations was the drama troupe. Inaugurated in the fall of 1938 with some 20 participants, it soon grew to number more than 80 members, many of whom subsequently joined the Communist Party. Its first performance was a modest event held at the Ningbo Native-Place Association in December 1938, but by the following year the drama troupe was attracting sizable audiences. Hu Yongqi arranged for most of the proceeds from these performances to go directly into the coffers of the New Fourth Army.[20] The Insurance Federation delivered people as well as money to the Communist cause; some 60 CCP members were recruited from the ranks of insurance employees in Shanghai.[21]

Advances among insurance workers were symptomatic of the general receptivity of white-collar labor to the Communists' wartime message. Department store employees showed further evidence of this pattern. For example, workers at Yong'an Department Store clandestinely circulated several of Mao Zedong's speeches by hand copying them into small notebooks. Known collectively as "Little Grasses" (*xiaocao*), these notebooks also included short stories, poems, cartoons, and songs written by the workers. Many of the worker-authored contributions displayed a mentality well attuned to the Communist perspective. One such essay, which appeared in an April 1944 edition of "Little Grasses," contained the lines: "Nature blessed mankind with warmth and cold, but mankind created class society—causing warmth to be the exclusive preserve of the fortunate, while cold envelopes the unfortunate. . . . Why can't mankind overcome class differences?"[22] These notebooks naturally attracted the attention of CCP organizers. Relying on links established through the National Salvation Association, the Communists enlisted a substantial number of department store workers for Party membership.[23]

Although white-collar workers were a critical source of new adherents

to the revolutionary enterprise, the Party did not neglect its more familiar constituency of factory artisans. Renewed CCP organizational efforts
in shipyards and machine works resulted in the recruitment of a sizable
number of mechanics and carpenters. When the Japanese occupied these
factories after Pearl Harbor, they initially placed their own nationals
in supervisory positions over the unruly factory artisans. As the war
dragged on, many of the Japanese foremen were transferred elsewhere
and skilled Chinese workers were appointed to replace them. More than
a few of these new foremen were Communists. These strategically
placed cadres enabled the Party to launch a series of successful strikes in
the heavy industrial sector in 1942–44.[24]

The Shanghai Communist Party grew rapidly during the war with
Japan. From only 130 in November 1937, membership burgeoned to
more than 2,000 by the time the Japanese surrendered in August 1945.[25]

Civil War: Communist Artisans

In Shanghai as elsewhere across occupied China, the Japanese surrender precipitated a scramble between Communists and Nationalists
for control of abandoned territory. Initially the Communists hoped that
with the support of labor they might claim the country's largest industrial city. A year before the war's end, in anticipation of the internecine
struggle that lay ahead, Party Central had ordered the establishment of
a Shanghai workers' underground army (*Shanghai gongren dixiajun*).
Charged with the formidable task of recruiting for this army, labor cadres
in Shanghai fell into old habits, turning first to gangster elements. Several petty hoodlums, some of whom had been active twenty years earlier
during the May Thirtieth Movement, supplied the original manpower for
the workers' army. Sustaining the allegiance of gangster mercenaries,
however, required substantial payoffs. Strapped for funds, the Party returned to a more reliable source of recruits: skilled workers, especially
Jiangnan machinists.[26]

On August 23, 1945, more than 7,000 of these committed fighters—
many of whom were Party members—assembled at the Xinyi machine
works in preparation for an armed uprising aimed at seizing weapons
from nearby police stations and then marching to the city center to assist
the New Fourth Army in the liberation of Shanghai. That same afternoon, however, the rebellion was canceled on orders from Party Central.
After having approved the uprising three days earlier, Party Central had
received a cable from the USSR calling for peaceful coexistence with the
GMD in keeping with a new treaty of friendship between the Soviet
Union and the Republic of China. The workers' army was dissolved a few

days later and members whose identities had been revealed were transferred north to join the New Fourth Army in Shandong.[27]

Ill-fated as the workers' army was, its development illustrated the degree to which Party organizers in Shanghai were compelled in times of crisis to resort to their staunchest ally among the Shanghai working class. Although gangster elements could be instrumental in launching militant engagements, ultimately it was the skilled workers who proved willing to sacrifice for higher political goals. Happily for the Party, this sector of the working class grew substantially in the postwar period. Thousands of copper fitters, ironsmiths, and mechanics returned to Shanghai from the interior after the Japanese surrender.[28] In addition, more than 30,000 Chinese workers—largely educated, skilled workers from Jiangnan—were repatriated from Japan.[29]

The Party's increased attention to such workers was seen in 1946 with the founding in Shanghai of the China Technical Association (Zhongguo jishu xiehui). Its membership of well-educated engineers and other technicians in fields ranging from machine building to textiles grew from an initial coterie of 400 to some 3,000 by 1949. More than 100 of its members joined the Communist Party and served as guardians of Party interests during the transition to Communist rule.[30]

Support for the Communists was bolstered by the continuing scourge of inflation. The cost-of-living index for Shanghai workers jumped from 406,476 in 1946 to 3,015,669 the following year.[31] Again it was the relatively well-off workers who proved best able to protest the deterioration in living standards. In 1946–47 a series of innovative slowdowns in the Shanghai service sector reflected the influence of Communist leadership. First, personnel at the four major department stores launched a "sluggishness" (langong) movement in which workers feigned exhaustion so great that they were unable to wait on customers. On each counter was placed a sign explaining that management's refusal to grant an annual bonus had sapped workers of their energy; customers were requested to go elsewhere to make their purchases. Not to be outdone, grocery store workers soon followed with a "diligence" (qingong) movement in which service personnel were too busy swabbing down floors and polishing counters to attend to customers. Shortly thereafter another Shanghai department store was hit by a "frowning" (chougong) movement; customers were met with big frowns and complaints about inflation and the lack of an annual bonus by workers too preoccupied with their own troubles to make any sales.[32]

Liu Changsheng's wartime policy of targeting skilled and white-collar workers was yielding handsome payoffs in the postwar era. The division of labor among members of the CCP's Shanghai Labor Committee (gong-

wei) during the Civil War period reflected this special interest in the privileged sector of the work force. Mao Qihua, a printer, was assigned to the publishing industry with responsibility for producing propaganda for the workers' movement as well as organizing among fellow printers. He also handled some hospitals, movie theaters, and other service enterprises. Zhang Qi, secretary of the Labor Committee and a skilled silk weaver, was put in charge of railroads, shipping, and cotton (with special attention to mechanics). Chen Gongqi, a worker at the Shanghai Power Company, organized in water and electricity plants as well as the machine industry. Wang Zhongyi, a staff worker at the French Tramway Company, was in charge of efforts in that company, the silk-weaving industry, and some of the bus companies.[33]

Liu Changsheng's postwar program called for a further reorientation of the Party's focus, away from industries with a highly concentrated proletarian work force such as textiles and toward public utilities.[34] In November 1945 a CCP-backed federation of labor unions was established to encompass the city's six major utilities: the Shanghai Power Company, the Shanghai Telephone Company, the French Tramway Company, the British Tramway Company, the gas company, and the waterworks.[35] The logic was that utilities were the city's lifeblood; a strike in them would have immediate and serious repercussions for factory production and ordinary residential life alike. Moreover, because utilities employed a disproportionately large number of well-trained mechanics and engineers, the work force at such enterprises might be more inclined toward revolutionary initiatives. As a police report noted at the time, Communist methods of mobilizing utilities workers built on customary forms of artisan organization. More than 100 workers had been recruited into a Guandi Society, which met for periodic banquets and discussion of labor affairs. In addition, a Communist-sponsored Buddhist vegetarian society convened on the first and fifteenth days of each month for meatless meals and to plan militant activities.[36]

The Shanghai Power Company (SPC) proved especially fertile ground for these mobilization efforts. Its workers, predominantly older, well-paid, skilled artisans who had participated actively in the May Thirtieth Movement, claimed a record of unusual militance. Even during the height of gangster unionism during the Nanjing decade, SPC employees had distanced themselves from the prevailing trend. A British police report in 1934 noted that the majority of SPC workers refused to pay dues to the yellow union on grounds that it had not secured any real benefits for them during a strike the previous year: "A certain portion of the workers are influenced by Communist elements and are forming an organ with the object of overthrowing the union sponsored by the KMT."[37] Not until the Civil War period could this objective be accomplished. In January 1946 workers at the power company struck for an increased annual bonus. Supported by the newly founded federation of public utilities unions, they secured their demands. Thereafter the SPC union (whose twelve-person executive committee now included four Communists and four CCP sympathizers) took a leadership role in organizing workers to participate in public demonstrations critical of the Nationalist regime. The union also published its own journal, *Electrical Workers' Monthly*, with progressive articles authored by the workers themselves.[38]

The rapid expansion of the Communists' base of support was attributable in large part to the failings of the postwar Guomindang regime. Hamstrung by disastrous inflation and severe factional struggle, the GMD was unable to replicate the control over the labor movement that it had enjoyed during its heyday. The decline of the Nationalists was paced by the growth of the CCP. The Communist Party in Shanghai numbered 2,000 members at the time of the Japanese surrender and claimed more than four times that figure by April 1949.[39]

Guomindang Factionalism

Certainly the GMD did not underestimate the importance of Shanghai labor. Many of the same individuals who had promoted the system of yellow unions after Chiang's April coup were reassigned to positions of influence in the postwar period. Most notable among the returnees was Lu Jingshi, the former post office worker whose discipleship under Green Gang master Du Yuesheng had won him a series of prominent posts in the Nationalist regime. After the Japanese occupation of Shanghai, Lu followed the Nationalist government westward to its wartime capital in Chongqing. There he formed a close friendship with Dai Li, head of the GMD's secret police. In 1945, when Lu was ordered back to Shanghai to wrest control of the labor movement from Communist competitors, his connections with the secret police proved immensely helpful. A generous supply of weapons from Dai Li enabled Lu Jingshi to arm a group of faithful followers among the work force.

Dubbed the Shanghai Municipal Workers' Loyal National Salvation Army (*Shanghaishi gongren zhongyi jiuguojun*), Lu Jingshi's group set about raiding suspected Communist strongholds and unilaterally arbitrating labor disputes in much the same manner as the gangster-dominated Unification Committee nearly twenty years earlier. Ironically, the once reform-minded postal unionist now commandeered labor racketeering activities. Having successfully parlayed his union credentials and his Green Gang membership to attain high government office and gain the confidence of brokers of violence like Dai Li, Lu now viewed the labor movement purely as an instrument. To maximize labor's political potential it had to be directed against Communist opponents in service to the Guomindang state. Though the Loyal Army was dissolved after the reestablishment of regular government institutions in Shanghai, Lu subsequently founded the Workers' Welfare Society (*gongren fulihui*) and subsidiary Industrial Protection Brigade (*hugong dui*), which continued the practice of using secret service weaponry and training camps to develop an armed cadre of workers poised for struggle against the Communist threat.*

As influential as Lu Jingshi was in the postwar labor scene, his power did not go unchallenged. And the opposition came not only from underground Communists. Though Lu publicly named Communism as his principal foe, he actually faced more insidious adversaries within his own Guomindang Party. During the war years a serious rivalry had developed between the Military Statistical Bureau (*juntong*), controlled by Dai Li's Blue Shirts, and the Central Statistical Bureau (*zhongtong*), operated by the CC Clique of Chen Lifu and Chen Guofu.[40] These parallel intelligence networks, ostensibly directed against the Japanese and Communist threats, were devoting more energy by the war's end to fighting one another than to combating their common enemies. Having placed himself firmly within Dai Li's camp, Lu Jingshi now found himself at odds with rival GMD factions. The Central Statistical Bureau, for example, established a Labor Assistance Society (*laogong xiejinshe*) based in eastern Shanghai cotton mills and dockers' unions, which competed openly with Lu Jingshi's Workers' Welfare Association. Other prominent Guomindang labor leaders with whom Lu had cooperated in the past—Yang Hu, Ma Chaojun, and Zhu Xuefan—now cultivated their own labor constituencies so as to diminish Lu Jingshi's control.[41]

Thus although the number of officially registered unions mushroomed in the postwar years—from 295 unions with 227,949 members in late 1945 to 453 unions with 527,499 members in early 1947—these organi-

---

*Mao Qihua, "Lüetan jiefang zhanzheng shiqi Shanghai gongren yundong de yixie qingkuang" [A summary discussion of conditions in the Shanghai labor movement during the war of liberation], *Shanghai gongyunshi yanjiu ziliao*, 1982, no. 2, pp. 2–3; Shao Xinshi and Deng Ziba, eds., *Shanghai laogong nianjian* [Shanghai labor yearbook] (Shanghai, 1948), pp. 117–18. As paramount labor specialist under the reconstituted Nationalist regime, Lu Jingshi placed many of his closest colleagues in subordinate positions of power over the labor movement. Shui Xiangyun, who had risen through the ranks of the Shanghai Post Office as a faithful follower of Lu Jingshi, was given the chairmanship of the Shanghai General Labor Union. Other trusted friends headed the powerful tobacco and telephone unions. Within the Bureau of Social Affairs, Lu's associates held key positions with responsibility for labor affairs.

zations by ~KMT unions~ no means represented a solid base of support for the government.[42] Various groups of unions were beholden to rival officials, for whom links with labor were a means of undermining their opponents. Communist influence was certainly an important factor in the unionization movement, but competition among Guomindang functionaries— especially in anticipation of the National Assembly elections of 1947– 48—was evidently the major impetus for the hasty efforts at labor organization in this period.*

The CC clique, once closely allied with Green Gang chieftain Du Yuesheng and his protégé Lu Jingshi, now challenged their role in Shanghai politics. Its most dramatic confrontation was with Wu Shaoshu, one of Du Yuesheng's former disciples, who had linked up with CC clique leader Chen Lifu during the war. As head of the Shanghai GMD and vice-mayor of the city in the postwar period, Wu made a public show of withdrawing from his relationship with Du Yuesheng. Requesting that his name card acknowledging Du as teacher be returned to him, Wu published an open attack on Du in a newspaper he controlled. This was the first time in 30 years that a Shanghai paper had dared to print a derogatory statement about the powerful Du Yuesheng. Although Lu Jingshi tried to defend his patron by printing laudatory articles in one of his own newspapers, the damage to Du's reputation was irreversible. No longer would the opium czar be immune to public criticism.[43] The conflict was, moreover, no mere war of words. When Lu Jingshi volunteered his services as a delegate to the sixth national GMD Party Congress, Wu Shaoshu blocked the nomination. Later the insult was repaid in an assassination attempt on Wu by agents of Dai Li; although Wu's bullet-proof automobile withstood seven shots and saved him from harm, the rift was irreparable.[44]

Wu Shaoshu's power base lay in the Party and the Three People's Principles Youth Corps (sanqingtuan), both of whose Shanghai branches he headed in the immediate postwar period. But to gain hegemony over Shanghai politics he required a footing in labor as well. Though Wu, as director of the Shanghai Bureau of Social Affairs, placed several of his

---

*Wang Jianchu and Sun Maosheng, Zhongguo gongren yundongshi, p. 291, estimate that by late 1946 the Communists controlled 324 legal unions in Shanghai with a membership of more than 280,000. By their account, another 100 unrecognized unions were also under CCP direction. Although this estimate may exaggerate Communist influence, it is certain that the CCP had again become a factor of major significance in the Shanghai labor movement. Seemingly endless reports of union corruption and violence bore testimony to the instrumental and callous fashion in which many of the organizations had been established. Typical was a lengthy dispute at the China Textile Company in June 1947 that stemmed from the union director's effort to force the rehiring of a forewoman who happened to be his concubine. See Shanghai Municipal Archives #20-1-122. Several disputes in this period resulted in workers' deaths at the hands of government agents. See Number Two Archives, #2:2-1993.

trusted friends in positions of labor leadership,* it was clear that Lu Jingshi's armed Labor Protection Brigade retained the upper hand. One of Lu's favorite tactics was to encourage disgruntled workers to take their protests directly to BSA or GMD headquarters so as to embarrass Bureau and Party chief Wu Shaoshu. The strategy paid off: in early 1946, Wu was relieved of his directorship of the Bureau of Social Affairs; later that year, he lost the Party chairmanship.[45] Humiliated by these demotions, Wu was determined to expand the reach of his one remaining institutional base, the Shanghai *sanqingtuan*. In the summer of 1946, the Youth Corps was instructed to infiltrate the Shanghai labor movement. Over the next year, open conflict raged between Wu's Youth Corps and the Bureau of Social Affairs (now headed by his rival Wu Kaixian, a disciple of Du Yuesheng with close ties to Lu Jingshi). Exasperated by this aggressive competition from the Youth Corps, Wu Kaixian and Lu Jingshi lodged a formal protest with GMD Central. Party Central, for its part, was deeply concerned about the unruly student movement in Shanghai, which it attributed to the Youth Corps's abdication of its proper on-campus responsibilities in favor of labor organizing. In the summer of 1947 the mayor of Shanghai, acting on instructions from Party Central, succeeded in drawing up a "July gentleman's agreement" between the two factions; henceforth the Youth Corps would refrain from involvement in the labor movement and would in return enjoy a monopoly over student affairs.[†]

Anti-Communist Initiatives

The truce between its warring factions, albeit temporary, allowed the Guomindang to devote greater attention to the Communists. Aware that

---

*Ge Kexin, a member of the CC clique with close relations to Wu Shaoshu, was named deputy director of the Bureau of Social Affairs with primary responsibility for labor—a post Lu Jingshi himself had eyed. Chen Lifu's cousin was selected by Wu as Party secretary in the Bureau of Social Affairs. Wu also appointed several other close associates to the Shanghai General Labor Union and the Workers' Movement Leading Committee of the Party branch. See Jiang Menglin and Mao Zipei, "Kangzhan shenglihou Shanghai Guomindang neibu de paixi douzheng" [Factional struggles within the Shanghai Guomindang after the victory of the War of Resistance], *Wenshi ziliao xuanji*, 1979, no. 3, pp. 180–81.

†Fan Xipin, "Shanghai wuchaoan qinliji" [A personal record of the Shanghai dancers' upsurge], *Wenshi ziliao xuanji*, 1979, no. 3, pp. 193–94. The United Association for Security (*zhian lianhehui*) was established at this time with participation by military, government, and Party cadres. Lu Jingshi was named to head the association, with Wu Shaoshu as deputy director. The Shanghai Bureau of the Central Statistical Bureau, which had been competing with the Bureau of Social Affairs in organizing unions, agreed to limit its activities to gathering intelligence, which it would share with BSA officials at weekly conferences. See *Shanghai gongchao yu gongyun* [The Shanghai labor upsurge and labor movement], 1947, in Bureau of Investigation archives, Taipei, #556.89/7432. (This informative document was prepared as a confidential report by the Shanghai branch of the Central Statistical Bureau.)

the CCP had been concentrating its energies on public utilities, Lu Jingshi ordered his Workers' Welfare Society to step up surveillance in that sector.[46] At just the same time, the Shanghai branch of the Central Statistical Bureau came across a secretly printed Communist handbill that was traced to the Futong Publishing House. A few days later a team of secret agents raided the print works, seized a cache of sensitive documents, and arrested six Communists from the Shanghai Power Company who were on the premises to oversee publication of their union journal, *Electrical Workers' Monthly.* Soon an additional 21 radical unionists were picked up by the authorities.[47] Realizing now precisely where the heart of the leftist labor movement was located, the government closed down the unions of the Shanghai Power Company, the French Tramway Company, and the department stores—all of which had been under CCP leadership.[48]

For the moment, it seemed that the Guomindang might have dealt a fatal blow to the Communist labor movement. But the moment was fleeting. Within days, workers at the British Tramway Company, the French Tramway Company, and a score of silk-weaving and machinery factories walked off the job to protest the "Futong Incident."

The Futong sympathy strikes were Communist-inspired, conducted by skilled workers in enterprises with firm CCP roots. A few months later, however, a different segment of the Shanghai work force also made known its displeasure with GMD rule. On January 31, 1948, more than 5,000 cabaret girls marched on the Bureau of Social Affairs in protest against a government decision to shut down the city's 29 dance halls. When bureau director Wu Kaixian refused to meet with the demonstrators, they forced their way into the building. Doors, windows, and furniture were smashed and mounds of documents destroyed. After police arrived to subdue the rioters, a battle ensued, leaving more than 70 casualties.

Furious at this costly disruption of government routine, BSA Director Wu ordered a full-scale investigation into what he suspected was a Communist-instigated incident. For several months, an investigation team labored in vain to uncover evidence of Communist involvement. Special efforts were made to locate a "woman in red dress" (*hongyi nülang*), who was described by journalists as having demonstrated an exceptional command of martial arts during the assault on the BSA. No such woman could be found among the more than 700 who were arrested, however, and the many participants who were brought to trial vehemently denied any radical connections. The only links to outside parties that could be established were with the Three People's Principles Youth Corps, under whose jurisdiction the dance girls' union had operated.[49]

Two days after the dancers' riot, another confrontation with women protesters commanded the attention of the city's authorities. On January 30, a major strike erupted at the Shen Xin Number Nine cotton mill. Although Communists were involved in this protest, it was largely spontaneous. As one worker activist recalled, "Even if the Communist Party had not come forth to offer leadership in the struggle, we workers would have fought on our own."[50] The limited Communist leadership that did exist was centered in the machine room, among male mechanics (see Chapter 8). Nevertheless, the authorities were convinced that the predominantly female strikers were acting under Communist instruction. On the morning of February 2, more than a thousand military police descended on the factory to force out the workers. Three women were killed and more than a hundred injured in the battle that followed. The government, imagining a link with the dancers' riot, once again launched a determined but fruitless search for a "woman in red dress" who had allegedly directed the workers' offensive.[*]

Stymied in their attempt to prove Communist involvement in these protests by unskilled workers, the authorities turned their attention once again to the more skilled sector of the labor force. The reorientation paid off. In March, Wang Zhongyi—the cadre in charge of Communist organizing in the transport industry—was arrested. A name list discovered at Wang's home led to the roundup of hundreds of other CCP members, most of whom were mechanics.[†]

The Unraveling of GMD Power

As the government busied itself with efforts to smash Communist influence in the labor movement, its internal problems intensified.[**]

---

[*]In this case, the Communist-inspired "woman in red dress" may have actually existed. One reminiscence states that CCP member Qi Huaiqiong was wearing a red wool dress while battling the police. Once it was known that the authorities were searching for a woman in red, other workers helped her change clothes and escape detection. See Zhang Qi, "Huiyi Shenjiu erer douzheng" [Recalling the struggle of February 2 at Shenxin Number Nine], *Shanghai gongyun shiliao*, 1986, no. 1, p. 26. Other accounts, however, state that the culprit in red was actually a man (Shang Yiren, "Shenxin jiuchang erer douzheng jiyao" [Notes on the February 2 struggle at Shenxin Number 9], *Wenshi ziliao xuanji*, 1979, no. 3, p. 22).

[†]Shanghai zonggonghui, "Shanghai gongren zhandou zai diertiao zhanxian" [Shanghai workers struggling in the second line of battle], unpublished paper, 1984, pp. 32–33. Lu Jingshi himself was well aware of where Communist power was concentrated. In September 1947 he had established a special small group of his Workers' Welfare Society to take charge of anti-Communist operations. The small group focused primarily on the utility industry—especially the Shanghai Power Company and the French Tramway Company, and secondarily on the machine industry (ibid., p. 29).

[**]Even Lu Jingshi's own Workers' Welfare Society, which had grown to include 20,000 cadres as well as 10,000 armed workers in its Industrial Protection Brigade, was riddled with dissension. A "Shanghai faction," made up of long-standing friends of Lu

Many of the individuals who had served as bulwarks of government strength in the Nanjing decade now found themselves increasingly estranged from the Guomindang regime. Lu Jingshi's patron Du Yuesheng had returned to Shanghai after the war hoping to be named mayor of the city. Instead, perhaps to deflect attention from his own gang connections, Chiang Kai-shek named Qian Dajun to head the municipal government.* When the Shanghai legislature was established some months later, Du again hoped to assume the leading post. This time the CC clique saw that former BSA director Pan Gongzhan was given the honor. But the biggest wound to Du Yuesheng's pride came in the fall of 1948, when his son was arrested by Chiang Ching-kuo, son of Chiang Kai-shek, for illegal dealings on the Shanghai stock exchange. Seeing a picture of his handcuffed son on the front page of *Central Daily* was unbearable for Du Yuesheng. For more than a month the distraught father refused either to venture outdoors or to entertain guests. It was probably this incident more than any other that made Du leave for Hong Kong, rather than Taiwan, at the time of Shanghai's takeover by the Communists.[51]

Some former gang notables chose not to leave at all but to throw in their lot with the new regime. Wu Shaoshu, who had contacted the Communist underground after losing official government and Party posts under the GMD, remained and is now buried in the revolutionary cemetery of Babaoshan.[52] Gu Zhuxuan, Subei rickshaw magnate and Green Gang chieftain, agreed to cooperate with his nephew, a Communist cadre responsible for liaison with Shanghai gangsters. A second floor office in one of Uncle Gu's dance halls became the meeting place for Communist-gangster rendezvous in the early postwar period. Gu Zhuxuan was rewarded for his cooperation by being made special delegate to the first Shanghai people's congress convened by the Communist regime.[53]

By far the most significant defection to the Communist side by a Shanghai labor leader-cum-gangster was that of erstwhile postal unionist Zhu Xuefan. As China's delegate to the ILO in June 1936, Zhu was contacted by CCP agents while attending the meetings in Geneva. In-

---

Jingshi and Wu Kaixian, competed with a "Nanjing faction," whose cadres had attended the Ministry of Social Affairs' training institute and who adopted heavy-handed tactics in dealing with the more than 100 unions under their direction. In addition, a faction loyal to Zhu Xuefan and a "fence-sitting faction" harbored little personal loyalty to Lu Jingshi (*Shanghai gongchao yu gongyun*).

*The reasons for Chiang Kai-shek's disavowal of Du Yuesheng are not entirely clear. It may be that changes in the industrial structure reduced the need for reliance on Du as a labor mediator. Following the Japanese surrender, the Nationalist state took over numerous factories in the city, and government agents exercised direct management responsibilities. On the Nationalists' growing control over the industrial system, see William Kirby's forthcoming book on the National Resources Commission.

trigued by their invitation, he embarked on a secret journey to Moscow right after the Geneva conference for a meeting with Li Lisan and Kang Sheng, then stationed with the Comintern as representatives of the CCP. The discussions convinced the Shanghai labor leader of the need to work in concert with the CCP in fighting the Japanese threat. Back in China, Zhu took advantage of the spirit of cooperation induced by the second united front to meet periodically with Eighth Route Army representatives. He proposed using the newly founded China Labor Association (*Zhongguo laodong xiehui*), a GMD-initiated national labor union, to register and arm workers from across the country to join the effort against the Japanese. In April 1938 Zhu was named an honorary member of the steering committee at the first labor conference of the Communists' Shen-Gan-Ning border region in Yenan.* When Zhu Xuefan assumed leadership of the GMD-backed China Labor Association (CLA) in 1939, it admitted the general labor union of the Shen-Gan-Ning base area as one of its member unions. The CLA also recruited thousands of workers from Shanghai, Tianjin, and Hong Kong to contribute their services to the war effort behind enemy lines.[54]

The urbane Zhu Xuefan took advantage of his role as ILO representative to engage in fund-raising for the Chinese war effort during his many trips abroad. He was most successful in the United States, where the American Federation of Labor agreed to provide an annual contribution of $666,000 starting in 1943. The sudden wealth of the CLA aroused the interest of other GMD officials, and in 1945 Zhu was forced to fight off an effort by Ma Chaojun and Chen Lifu to found a rival labor organization which they hoped might gain access to the American funding. Having weathered that storm, Zhu soon faced another. In September 1946 Lu Jingshi, with the concurrence of other leading GMD officials, demanded that unions from the Communist liberated areas be expelled from the China Labor Association. When Zhu refused to accept this provision, his enemies reported to Party Central that Zhu had been secretly transporting weapons as part of a coup plot.[55]

Rather than respond to the subpoena served him by the Chongqing

---

*Zhou Enlai's address at the conference noted that there were two types of labor organizations in GMD-controlled areas. One, represented by Zhu Xuefan's China Labor Association, was patriotic and progressive. The other, controlled by officials such as Lu Jingshi, was part of the GMD secret service network, aimed at the Communists. Zhou Enlai's remarks, though not entirely accurate at the time, were prophetic. Actually, Lu Jingshi was then chairing the China Labor Association. By late 1939, however, Lu had been forced out and replaced by Zhu Xuefan. Because the GMD had approved the association as its legal representative to the ILO, Zhu argued that, according to ILO regulations, Lu's standing as a government official disqualified him from serving as union chairman (Lu Xiangxian, *Zhongguo laodong xiehui jianshi* [Brief history of the China Labor Association] [Shanghai, 1987], pp. 5–18).

high court, Zhu fled China for Hong Kong on November 12.* His departure spelled an end to the generous assistance the Chinese labor movement had been receiving from its American backers. Perhaps it was anger over the loss of revenue that accounted for an assassination attempt on Zhu by GMD agents only two weeks after he arrived in Hong Kong. In any event, the CCP made good use of the incident to cement its ties with the injured labor leader. Zhou Enlai dispatched Liu Ningyi, a May Thirtieth activist who had served for many years as a Communist labor organizer, to Zhu's Hong Kong hospital room to convey the Party's concern for his speedy return to health. On June 1, 1947, a fully recovered Zhu Xuefan set off with Liu Ningyi to attend a meeting of the World Federation of Trade Unions in Prague. After trips to New York and Geneva, Zhu met Liu Ningyi in Paris. At Liu's urging, Zhu agreed to return to China to visit liberated territory. Together the two men flew from Moscow to Harbin in early 1948 and were met by Li Lisan, who invited Zhu to participate in a labor movement congress then still in the planning stages. On the day following his arrival in Harbin, Zhu cabled Mao Zedong and Zhou Enlai to offer his wholehearted support for their revolution. He then set about helping to plan the forthcoming labor congress. On August 1, the sixth national labor congress, cosponsored by the Workers' Committee of the liberated zones and Zhu's China Labor Association, opened in Harbin. At the congress, the decision was made to reestablish an all-China General Labor Union. Chen Yun, the former Commercial Press worker, was chosen to chair the new GLU; Zhu Xuefan, Liu Ningyi, and Li Lisan were appointed vice-chairmen.[56] Although the China Labor Association was formally disbanded shortly after the establishment of the People's Republic, its leader was not forgotten. Zhu Xuefan, the former gangster and postal unionist, became first minister of post and telecommunications in the new Communist government.

Conclusion

The cooperation of turncoat gangsters was of major assistance to the Communists in their efforts to gain leverage over Shanghai labor. Unreli-

---

*According to Lu Jingshi's own account, he made every effort to retain Zhu Xuefan's loyalty, visiting on the night before his departure to plead: "We Chinese have our own Chinese principles. Other people can betray the GMD, but you and I cannot" (*Wushinianlai Zhonghua minguo yougong yundong* [Fifty years of the Chinese postal workers' movement] [Taipei, 1980], p. 58). A People's Republic source reveals that Lu Jingshi paid the living expenses of Zhu's family in Shanghai until the Communist takeover. According to this knowledgeable informant, Zhu wrote to Lu Jingshi shortly after his arrival in Hong Kong to say that he still did not understand why the GMD had been so hard on him (Li Jianhua, Sept. 8, 1962, transcript of interview, Labor Movement Archives of the SASS Institute of History).

able as allies, gang leaders proved willing to switch allegiances once the decline of the GMD rendered the CCP a more attractive alternative. With the help of these yellow unionists, the Communists were able to broaden their base of support within the Shanghai work force, especially among the less skilled. Still, the backbone of committed constituents for the revolutionary labor movement remained the more favored workers—white-collar employees and factory artisans in particular.

Literate and moderately well off, these more fortunate workers belonged to the category of "petty urbanites" (*xiao shimin*) of whom Perry Link has written so perceptively. According to Link, however, the *xiao shimin* of early twentieth-century Shanghai evidenced a basically conservative mentality. By contrast, Yeh Wen-hsin points out that many CCP revolutionaries were drawn from this petty urbanite sector. The apparent contradiction between these two observations—one stressing the conservative mentality, the other the revolutionary behavior of the Shanghai petty urbanite—can perhaps be resolved by noting that radical activism is often conservative in motivation. As E. P. Thompson discovered in the case of England, artisans clinging to traditional values occupied the front ranks of labor militants.[57]

Such workers made up a disproportionate share of the most dedicated enthusiasts for the Communist labor movement in Shanghai, as will be detailed in Part III of this volume. The changed policies of the wartime period and the concomitant crumbling of the Nationalist regime made it easier for CCP organizers to find common ground with their natural constituency within the working class. This stress on the alliance between Communist partisans and skilled laborers, however, does not explain the ultimate victory of the revolution. That outcome was more dependent on events in the countryside than on the direction of the Shanghai labor movement.[58] Nevertheless, the partnership between revolutionaries and artisans was hardly inconsequential. Just as the Nationalists were deeply affected by their ties to gangster-led semiskilled workers, so the CCP labor movement's foundation (contrary to most previous interpretations) on artisan—rather than proletarian—support would have profound implications for the subsequent character of Chinese communism.[59]

PART THREE

The Politics of Production

THE THREE DECADES LEADING UP to the founding of the People's Republic of China (PRC) were momentous times for Chinese labor. Events of that period were not, however, entirely unanticipated. Previous protest experience prepared disparate segments of the working class to respond quite differently to the challenges presented by modern political parties.

How do we explain the varying political proclivities of Shanghai workers? In part, the differences can be attributed to native-place origins: workers from diverse regions of the country brought with them to the city contrasting experiences and expectations. In part, the variation was owing to the programs of competing political parties: Communists and Nationalists presented different approaches to labor, and workers' responses were similarly divided. But the politics of place and partisanship were not the only forces at work on the Shanghai labor movement. The production process itself helped to segment the working class into distinctive political elements. Having dealt in Parts I and II of this book with the first two factors, we now consider the third. Again the aim is not to portray these as discrete independent variables but rather to insist upon their interrelatedness. Only by appreciating the links among culture, society, economics, and politics can we approach a comprehensive understanding of the modern Chinese labor movement.

Part III presents case studies of labor unrest in three Shanghai industries: tobacco (Chapter 7), textiles (Chapter 8), and transport (Chapter 9). These three were selected for their importance to the city's economy, for their illumination of certain key variables (e.g., foreign versus Chinese ownership, gender composition, and skill differentiation among the work force), and for the availability of relevant source materials. The argument is that the conditions of labor within each industry gave rise to segmented patterns of militance. In making this assertion, I am building on a growing body of scholarship linking labor process to labor politics.[1] As this literature demonstrates, market position and shop floor experiences can promote competition as well as solidarity among workers.[2] An intensive examination of particular industries and firms is thus necessary to establish why and how workers located at different points in the production process resorted to different political strategies.*

As was shown in the discussion of the politics of place and partisanship, skill was a critical variable in accounting for divisions within the working class. Here that issue is explored more intensively, tracing the lines along which skilled, unskilled, and semiskilled workers differed systematically in their political orientations and actions. Particular firms and industries displayed particular mixtures of skill levels. In the case of the British American Tobacco Company, we encounter divisions among unskilled leaf pullers and packers, semiskilled cigarette rollers, and skilled mechanics. In the silk industry, we find a clear demarcation between unskilled spinners and skilled weavers as well as among weavers employed at different types of enterprises. In the transport industry, skilled tramway mechanics occupied a political space almost as distant from those of semiskilled drivers and conductors as from unskilled rickshaw pullers and wharf coolies.

Skill levels were not the only source of workplace distinctions. Gender made a further contribution to on-the-job differentiation. The tendency to segregate men and women in separate workshops discouraged unified collective action. In many industries, unskilled women workers were initially considerably more strike-prone than their male counterparts. As labor protest grew increasingly politicized over the course of the Republican period, however, the skilled and semiskilled male workers proved more responsive to the unionization efforts of party organizers.†

* As Charles Tilly has noted, "The well-known correlations among skill, worker organization, strike capacity, and success in strikes rest on characteristics of the firms, industries, and labor markets within which they appear" ("Solidary Logics: Conclusion," *Theory and Society*, no. 17 [1988]: 455).

† An argument that male unionists are often unsympathetic to the concerns of women laborers is made in Heidi Hartmann, "Capitalism, Patriarchy, and Job Segregation by Sex," in *Women and the Workplace*, ed. Martha Blaxall and Barbara Reagan (Chicago, 1976), pp. 137–69. Hartmann holds that male workers tend to side with employers in perpetuating sex segregation because it enforces low wages for women and keeps them subordinate to men both at work and at home. Consequently, according to Hartmann, male-dominated labor unions frequently exhibit hostility toward women workers. As research by Ruth Milkman has established, however, the interests of male workers can work for or against women, depending on the characteristics of the industrial setting. In the American automobile industry, which employed few women, male workers colluded with employers to oppose women's efforts to defend

Much of the explanation for this phenomenon rests with the outside cadres, most of whom were men and few of whom evidenced much understanding of either the importance or the appropriate strategies for mobilizing women.* When unskilled women did join partisan projects, their involvement was often mediated by the handful of women organizers working for either the CCP or GMD. Even then, their politicization was usually temporary.

The major exception to the tendency for women workers to remain outside the partisan labor movement was in the silk-weaving industry. There, thanks to the innovations of the Meiya Company, women were welcomed to the ranks of the skilled. Large numbers of women operatives from Zhejiang, many of whom were literate, were employed at high wages. Quite a few of them became Communist activists. In other words, when women were not relegated to the lower rungs of the production hierarchy, they proved as interested in political involvement as male workers in comparable positions.

The politics of place (divided by the cultures of South and North China) and of partisanship (defined by rivalry between the Chinese Communist Party and the Guomindang) may—at least on first glance—appear peculiar to the Chinese case. By contrast, the politics of production (differentiated by skilled and less skilled workers) are immediately recognizable to students of labor around the globe. In the case studies that follow, I attempt to demonstrate that familiar differences in skill level were intimately linked both to popular culture (or place) and to political allegiance (or partisanship). Although the specific content is unique to China—indeed to Shanghai—the general relationships are, I believe, more widely applicable.

---

wartime job rights. In electrical manufacturing, however, men supported elimination of wage discrimination against women so as to reduce the likelihood of female substitution. See Milkman, *Gender at Work* (Urbana, Ill., 1987).

*The tendency to associate labor with masculinity was as prevalent in Chinese political circles as in the West. This symbolic representation of labor as masculine has, as Joan Scott points out, distorted labor history as well as labor politics. See Scott, *Gender and the Politics of History* (New York, 1988), chaps. 3 and 4.

CHAPTER SEVEN

Tobacco

CIGARETTE PRODUCTION, although a twentieth-century newcomer to the Chinese industrial scene, quickly became a major component of the national economy. By midcentury, rolled tobacco was China's third largest light industry, employing more than 80,000 workers. In tax revenues, it stood second to none, accounting for approximately half of all taxes on industrial production.[1]

The cigarette industry was introduced to China in 1902 by the British American Tobacco Company. Tobacco itself was nothing novel to the Chinese; it had been widely cultivated as a cash crop by peasants since the late Ming dynasty. But BAT's enormously productive rolling machines, buttressed by an ingenious advertising campaign, helped to create an unprecedented demand for tobacco. Seeing the profits to be made, Chinese-owned factories soon sprang up in imitation of the BAT model. Only three months after the launching of BAT's operations in Shanghai, a Chinese company was established for cigar production. The following year, a domestically owned cigarette factory opened, but it could not compete with either the quality or quantity of BAT's products and soon shut down.[2]

Not until World War I, when the exigencies of warfare diverted Western commercial interests, did a large number of domestic cigarette factories appear on the scene. In 1917, the Chinese-owned Nanyang Brothers Tobacco Company opened a factory in Shanghai. Although competition from BAT was severe, the Nanyang Company managed to garner a respectable share of the market. Nanyang's success reached a climax during the devastating boycott and strike against its multinational rival in the May Thirtieth Movement of 1925—sustained, not coincidentally, by a huge contribution from Nanyang to the strike fund. As Sherman Cochran has shown, however, Guomindang policies were not kind to the

Chinese tobacco industry. The GMD regime, despite its professed nationalism (and the backing it had received from the Chinese owners of Nanyang), formulated a tax program that effectively undermined domestic competitiveness. Driven by the short-term objective of maximizing tax revenue rather than a long-term goal of promoting native industry, the Nationalist state sapped the profitability of Chinese-owned enterprises and thereby ensured the prosperity of the British American Tobacco Company.[3]

A host of studies link economic prosperity to strike activity.[4] Thus it is not surprising that the enormous financial success of BAT was accompanied by extraordinary labor unrest. For this reason (and the further consideration that rich archival materials on the company are available), my discussion of protest in the Shanghai tobacco industry will focus on the case of the British American Tobacco Company.

No firm in China was more subject to strikes than BAT. In the 23 years between 1918 and 1940, BAT's Shanghai factories experienced 56 strikes. The inordinate amount of strife was not simply a function of either size or foreign ownership, for BAT had fewer than half as many employees as the next most strike-prone company, the Japanese-owned cotton conglomerate of Naigai Wata.[5] Founded in 1902 by a merger of Duke's American Tobacco Company and the Imperial Tobacco Company of England, BAT's susceptibility to protest surely reflected its economic success. Despite serious setbacks of war and political turmoil, the company's production figures reveal an impressive capacity for growth and recovery (see Table 4).

The earliest strikes at BAT, known popularly as *yaoban* or "rocking the shift," were short-lived affairs launched by women workers in the stemmery and foil-wrapping rooms. In the early 1920's, however, the first Communist labor organizer in Shanghai, Li Qihan, focused on mechanics as a prime target of mobilization efforts. In response, Green Gang leaders organized a following among male workers in the rolling department. These basic divisions among BAT laborers, although bridged in several momentous all-factory strikes, persisted for decades.

Labor Conditions

To understand the sources of divisions in the workplace, it is necessary to know something about the background of the workers and their place in the structure of production. As in most tobacco factories, production at BAT was divided into three major departments: leaf, rolling, and packing. The leaf department (*yanye bu*) was primarily composed of women workers in the stemmery (*yezi jian*) who removed the tobacco

TABLE 4
BAT Production in China
(measured in 50,000-cigarette units)

Year	Output	Year	Output
1912	102,700	1925	489,160
1913	114,460	1931	661,081
1914	77,620	1932	560,687
1915	92,100	1936	895,756
1916	109,260	1937	1,124,554
1917	115,020	1938	858,523
1918	153,720	1939	857,297
1919	240,440	1940	869,165
1920	267,320	1941	819,853
1921	277,940	1946	77,524
1922	307,880	1947	302,392
1923	399,880	1948	246,108
1924	557,640	1949	178,919

SOURCE: *Yingmei yangongsi zaihua qiye ziliao huibian* [Collected materials on BAT business activities in China] (Beijing, 1983), p. 212.

leaves by hand. A few male workers were employed in other workshops of the leaf department to operate the machines that steamed, cut, dried, and perfumed the leaves. The rolling department (*juanyan bu*) was a largely male division responsible for the machine work of rolling into cigarettes the dried tobacco silk processed by the leaf department. The packing department (*baozhuang bu*) handled the simplest stage in the production process—placing the cigarettes in boxes and cartons. This work was done by women in the foil-wrapping room (*xibao jian*), although some men were also employed in the department on machines that produced the containers. In addition, there was a machine shop where skilled male mechanics (known popularly as *tongjiang*, or coppersmiths) repaired the factory machinery.[6]

Each department, and each workshop within a department, differed in the size, skill level, wages, gender, and social background of its work force. Although the number of employees fluctuated greatly from year to year, the basic divisions remained stable. Women consistently outnumbered men in the cigarette factory by a margin of about 10 percent.[7] These women worked almost exclusively in the packing department (where 68 percent of factory employees labored) or in the stemmery of the leaf department (where 15 percent worked). Men monopolized the cutting machines (which claimed 6 percent of the employees) and the rolling machines (where another 11 percent worked).[8] In addition, some 350 men were employed as skilled craftsmen in the machine shop.[9]

Interactions among workers in different divisions were constrained both by the natural lines of production and by artificial factory regulations. As one former BAT employee recalled, "We workers couldn't roam about. If you worked in one department but went over to another you'd be beaten by the guards if they saw you. . . . There were separate gates for men and women to enter the factory. If someone went through the wrong gate, she or he would be beaten."[10]

At least until the May Thirtieth Movement, contacts among laborers in different BAT workshops were rare.[11] And when the excitement of May Thirtieth and the Three Armed Uprisings gave way to Guomindang repression, management again tightened the reins. In 1932, lavatory permission tags were issued—two to a workshop—in an effort to restrict interaction among workers during their breaks.[12] In 1938, distinctive uniforms (paid for by the workers) were required; women in the leaf department were issued matching blue jackets and aprons, and women in the packing department were outfitted with blue jackets and white aprons.[13]

The nature of production and the imposition of factory rules thus acted together to limit the likelihood of worker solidarity. But the structure of employment itself provided an even more insidious source of fragmentation. Workers at BAT, as in most other large Shanghai enterprises, were hired by workshop foremen or Number Ones. The hiring process began when the prospective employee was introduced to the Number One by a mutual friend, sometimes a relative and almost invariably from the same native place. Only after the new worker paid the Number One a handsome recruitment fee or hosted a lavish banquet at one of Shanghai's finer restaurants would she or he be permitted to begin work. Hiring was just the first stage in a long-term personal relationship between workers and foremen. To retain a job, a worker had to provide periodic gifts of money and goods and demonstrate an acceptable level of fealty to the Number One.[14] An employee in BAT's leaf department remembered: "Our Number One had an elder brother who ran a biscuit [dabing] shop. He expected us workers to buy his brother's biscuits. These biscuits were the leftovers that hadn't sold that morning so they were very hard and we didn't want to buy them. But anyone caught not buying them would immediately lose her job."[15] The feudal aspect of workshop relations was reinforced by the practice of passing jobs from parent to child (pending the Number One's approval, of course) in a replacement (dingti) system not unlike that adopted for a time in some present-day Chinese factories.[16]

Workshops were to a certain extent semi-independent fiefdoms over which central management could exercise only limited control. In his report of 1932, BAT General Manager I. G. Riddick bemoaned the lack of uniformity, noting that the different departments had their own, often contradictory, standards of record-keeping, wage increases, punishments, and the like. On a few occasions workers dismissed on grounds of incompetence from one workshop had been rehired by another.[17] Yet however much top-level management may have deplored this diversity, it was not inclined to revamp an employment structure that in other respects served it well. Empowering Chinese Number Ones to hire and fire workers within their units freed British executives from some of the messier aspects of labor control but at the cost that each department within the factory operated almost as a world unto itself.

Probably no part of the factory offered a less pleasant work environment than the leaf department. As one former employee recalled, "Life in the leaf department was like the life of an adopted daughter-in-law. Only the Number Ones were allowed to talk. We were barely allowed to breathe."[18] The temperature was kept hot and humid to prevent leaf breakage. In winter, the contrast between the cold weather outside and indoor temperatures in the high eighties caused many workers to suffer from chronic bronchitis. Dust particles filled the air as tobacco leaves were ripped from their stems and shredded into tiny pieces. Yellow steam permeated the workshop, lending workers' sweat and phlegm a sallow hue. Handling the hot, wet leaves left more than a few workers with sopping clothes and blistered hands.[19] As a consequence of the cluttered, unsanitary conditions under which they labored, leaf department employees—who hailed predominantly from the Subei and Pudong areas—commonly referred to theirs as "garbage work" (*laji shenghuo*).[20]

The working conditions in the leaf department created a physical environment that was ripe for protest. As a worker remembered, "It was rather easy to start struggles in our workshop because the air was so filled with dust that you couldn't see clearly. The foreign overseers never ventured in and the Chinese staff would always wear gauze masks if they came in."[21] Indeed, more than a few BAT strikes were launched in the leaf department, where women's piece-rate wages were lower than those of women workers elsewhere in the factory.[22]

The rolling department, generally considered to be the "most important workshop in the factory," offered a marked contrast to the situation in the leaf department. Most rollers had at least ten years of on-the-job experience before being allowed to operate the machines by themselves, for their efforts largely determined the quality of BAT products. The rolling department consisted of semiskilled male workers, assisted by adolescent apprentices, who labored for daily, rather than piece-rate, wages.[23] Having acquired their job training in the factory itself, rollers evidenced far more loyalty to management than did other workers. Rolling-machine operators were often tied to their foremen by bonds of fictive kinship and secret society discipleship.* As in the leaf department, a large number of rolling department workers were from Subei (especially Yangzhou and Nantong) or Pudong.[24]

The packing department was made up largely of female workers who wrapped the cigarettes in tin foil and placed them in packs, cartons, or cans. Many of the workers had been recruited from the Shaoxing area through the recommendation of a Number One from their native place.[25] Although the work of these southern women in the packing department was less onerous than that of their Subei counterparts in the leaf department, wages were slightly higher in the packing department, probably a reflection of the differential market values of their native-place origins.†

Separate from these three departments of the cigarette factories was the machine shop, where the most skilled laborers were employed to service factory equipment. More than one-quarter of the workers in this division were fitters (qiangong); the rest were ironsmiths, woodworkers, cement masons, and the like. All were trained artisans, able to read construction blueprints. Their level of skill, we are told, was far higher than that of workers in most machine works around the city.[26] As a result, their services were in great demand.** It was among the factory artisans from Jiangnan that Communist labor organizers would discover their most receptive and steadfast audience among the BAT work force. The machine shop was well situated logistically to act as a catalyst for labor protest. It was at the very rear of the BAT compound in Pudong, and the mechanics had to pass by all the other factory workshops whenever they engaged in a walkout.[27]

---

*In BAT's Thorburn Road factory, the rolling department foreman organized both a Guandi Society and a Boxing Association among his subordinates (Yingmei yangongsi zaihua qiye ziliao huibian [Collected materials on BAT business activities in China] [Beijing, 1983], p. 1116). At BAT's Huaqi factory, the Number One was a gangster with close connections both to Green Gang labor leader Lu Jingshi and to bandits in Pudong. Acting as "adoptive father" to the rollers under his supervision, he invested their gift money in a gambling house and in the Empress movie theater (July 18, 1963, transcript of interview, archives of the SASS Institute of Economics).

†The suspicion that higher wages in the BAT packing room were related to native-place origins is reinforced by wage statistics from the Nanyang Tobacco Company. In 1930, workers in Nanyang's leaf department received a maximum daily wage of $1.00 while workers in the packing department received a maximum of only 85 cents (Nanyang xiongdi yancao gongsi shiliao [Historical materials on the Nanyang Brothers Tobacco Company] [Shanghai, 1958], p. 301). Native-place origins being equal, work in the leaf department apparently commanded a higher wage.

**When Nanyang Brothers opened a new factory in 1925, they offered jobs to BAT's mechanics. To retain skilled workers, BAT felt compelled to counter with a 50 percent raise in wages (Nov. 21, 1963, transcript of interview with mechanic at BAT's new factory in Pudong, archives of the SASS Institute of Economics).

Divisions among the work force were reflected in their wages. By the mid-1920's, concessions to workers during a series of successful strikes had given BAT a reputation as a "golden rice bowl" because of the high wages and good treatment afforded its workers, especially compared with other industrial laborers in the city.[28] A Communist report, remarking on the fortunate circumstances of BAT workers, observed with evident disapproval that "on holidays these workers go downtown to amuse themselves or stay home to play mahjong. Only a few enlightened workers engage in proper [*zhengdang*] pastimes."[29] Despite this generally comfortable situation, conditions differed for workers in various divisions of the factory. In 1926, the average monthly wage of a mechanic was over 30 yuan and that of a rolling machine operator over 20 yuan, whereas women in the packing department averaged only 13 yuan and in the leaf department a mere 10 yuan per month. According to factory estimates of the cost of living for a family of five in Shanghai, a mechanic's wage could supply 125 percent of family needs, semiskilled rollers could cover 92 percent, and ordinary women workers only 57 percent of the family budget.[30] Such wage discrepancies were exacerbated by the practice of paying women according to a piece rate (calculated in the leaf department by the weight of the leftover stems and in the packing department by the number of filled containers) while men were paid by a daily time rate. Symbolically as well, women were shabbily treated. Whereas male workers traditionally were granted 50 to 100 complimentary cigarettes a week, women received a mere 50 free cigarettes a year.[31]

Native-Place Divisions

Wages in the Shanghai tobacco industry reflected differences in skill level, gender, and native-place origin. The latter mirrored the sources of capital in the industry. A myriad of tiny tobacco factories that sprang up in Shanghai during the Republican period were founded for the most part by small businessmen from Zhejiang, who naturally hired their fellow provincials as workers. Accordingly, some 45 percent of Shanghai tobacco workers came from the Ningbo-Shaoxing area. Nanyang Brothers, Shanghai's second largest tobacco producer, was owned and operated by Cantonese, who recruited workers from their hometown. About 5 percent of Shanghai's tobacco workers hailed from the Canton area. BAT, which by 1925 employed more than one-quarter of the city's tobacco workers and represented over 70 percent of British investment in Shanghai, proved more eclectic in its hiring practices. Many of its workers (e.g., the "Shaoxing gang") came from Zhejiang, an even larger number were from Jiangsu, helping to account for the 45 percent of Shanghai's tobacco workers who claimed the province as home, whether from Pudong (25 percent), Subei (15 percent), or Wuxi and Changzhou (5 percent).[32]

Native-place origins were reflected in demeanor:

> Workers in tobacco factories, being mostly from Jiangnan, dress in fashionable and clean clothes. Because of this, a superficial look suggests that tobacco workers lead a rather comfortable life. Inside the factory, the average backward worker looks down on anyone wearing old clothes. So those workers who have no money borrow from others in order to have a couple of outfits made. Especially at New Year's and other festivals, or at the wedding of one of the workers, they'll borrow money at high interest or join a loan association so as to have new clothes made. . . . Many workers are really very poor, yet for fear of ridicule they are forced to dress well.[33]

The concern for outward appearance suggested a sense of personal pride that probably also contributed to the unusual level of protest activity among tobacco workers. Such activism was closely related to native-place origins.

Because workers from the same geographical areas tended to congregate in particular workshops, local cultures overlapped with work experiences to create a powerful potential for labor activism. Shared lifestyles, dialects, and entertainment choices prepared subgroups of laborers for collective action. Management was not unaware of the dangers of concentrating workers from the same native place in the same work unit. But the perils of integration may have seemed even more problematic. A former worker from the Nanyang Brothers Tobacco Company recalled:

> Most Nanyang workers were from Ningbo or Canton and had a very parochial mentality. When a worker in the rolling department was once stepped on by a worker from Canton, a feud erupted. The Ningbo worker beat up his Cantonese opponent, in violation of factory regulations. So the other Cantonese workers pressed for dismissal of the Ningbo worker. But we workers from Ningbo resisted. At mealtime we smashed our rice bowls over the heads of the Cantonese workers. Production was brought to a standstill. The head of the rolling department at that time was from Ningbo, while the general manager of the factory was from Canton. So each gang of workers had its patron. Finally we were separated into two work groups.[34]

The tendency of tobacco factories—and most other factories in Shanghai—to segregate workers from the same native place helps to explain the small-scale, fragmented character of the early labor movement.*

---

*The first union at Nanyang was promoted by the general manager and chief inspector, both of whom were Cantonese. Nineteen of the 21 workers on the steering committee were also Cantonese (*Shanghai Municipal Police Files*, I.O.-4831).

Early Strikes

The first recorded strike in the history of the Shanghai tobacco industry occurred at BAT in 1906 and was quickly suppressed when Chinese authorities arrested the leaders. The dismal failure of this initial protest attempt persuaded workers to refrain from similar endeavors for nearly a decade. But when the company recovered from an economic slump coincident with the onset of World War I, it experienced renewed labor strife. In early 1915, women in the leaf department struck to demand higher wages, although they quickly accepted management's promise of negotiations and returned to work. A year later, about a hundred temporary laborers at BAT engaged in a brief work stoppage to protest a cut in wages.[35]

Subsequent strikes at BAT were less easily resolved. In the summer of 1917, women in the packing department walked out to protest a reduction in their piece rate. The more than 1,000 strikers destroyed production materials, forcibly prevented other workers from entering the factory, and attacked the police with umbrellas. The strike continued for three weeks until management agreed to a compromise. The following spring, women in the packing department again walked off the job, but this time only workers in the boxing room participated. They were protesting management's plan to equalize wages in the department by reducing piece rates for the boxing room. Women in the foil-wrapping room, who had traditionally received a lower rate, were conspicuously absent from the protest.[36]

A few months later, more than 300 child apprentices in the rolling department struck to protest the longer work hours instituted by the new general manager. The youths gathered at a nearby temple and swore a solemn oath, pledging not to resume work until their demands were met. After a week had elapsed, however, the foreman of the rolling department hired two gangsters to impose order. These two had numerous followers in the department and were able to break the strike and enforce an immediate return to work. Impressed with this speedy resolution, BAT's general manager put both gangsters on the company payroll to ensure against any future labor protest in the critical rolling department.[37]

Leaf department women, some 500 strong, struck in October 1919 to express displeasure over the company's decision to add a night shift.[38] The following month, women workers in the leaf department again failed to show up for work. This time they demanded, and received, a wage hike. A few days later, male workers in the same department refused to work until they were granted an equivalent increase.[39]

In the spring of 1920, women in the packing department struck to protest a reorganization scheme but resumed work after management "explained the benefits" of the new system. The following year women in the leaf department were again off the job, expressing dissatisfaction with a change in piece-rate calculations. Women were transferred from the packing department to replace them. Three months later, yet another strike was undertaken by women in the leaf department in a fruitless effort to raise wages. The protest collapsed when several forewomen were replaced.[40]

Although the surviving accounts of these early strikes are too brief to permit detailed analysis, a general pattern is clear. Of the twelve strikes in BAT cigarette factories during the decade and a half before Communist cadres arrived on the scene, ten were launched by women. The other two involved child apprentices and males following the lead of women in their department.

The activism of women tobacco workers resonates with the findings of researchers focusing on very different societies. In a study of Russian factory women around the turn of the century, Rose Glickman notes that "women workers in the tobacco industry were remarkably volatile, militant, and tenacious." The explanation she proposes is that this activism, exceeding that of women in other industries, was most likely owing to "some combination of greater urban experience and literacy, longer work life, and the predominance of women under one roof."[41] Louise Tilly, building on the findings of Michelle Perrot, also points to a surprisingly high level of protest activity by women tobacco workers in France. She notes that "working conditions and wages were superior to those of most female jobs. Apprenticeship, parent-to-child continuity in the same occupation, and lifetime commitment to one job provided opportunities for the development of solidarity and association among women tobacco workers."[42]

Glickman and Tilly present illuminating comparisons between women in the tobacco industry and other women workers, but they do not compare men and women workers within the same industry. If early strikes in the British American Tobacco Company are any indication, the intraindustry comparison provides even more compelling evidence for the activism of women tobacco workers. Significantly, however, these early strikes were largely defensive in motivation. Despite the affluence of their employer, women workers at BAT were subjected to repeated cost-cutting initiatives, and they protested a deterioration in livelihood. The BAT case also cautions against interpreting this activism on the part of women workers as indicative of a budding feminist consciousness. Women in different departments of the factory did not engage in joint protests and on occasion served as scabs when another department was on strike. Even within the same department, women laborers were sometimes divided by workroom.

Communist Inroads

If women's activism, fragmented by workplace, was the dominant form of early strikes at BAT, this pattern was complicated in the summer of 1921 by the appearance of Communist organizers. That July, BAT mechanics gathered to grumble about a new British manager who had been assigned to their division. The new overseer proved to be a much harder taskmaster than his predecessor. Outraged by what he saw as a lack of discipline in the machine shop, the new director reduced each mechanic's wages by five cents and imposed fines on any craftsman who persisted in the customary practice of chewing pilfered tobacco. To protest this breach of tradition, mechanics declared a strike.[43]

The protest by skilled BAT machinists (unlike the strikes of unskilled women workers just a few months earlier) attracted the attention of the young Communists whose recently established party was committed to the development of a militant labor movement. Interest in mechanics as a promising base of support had been foreshadowed in earlier mobilization initiatives. The city's first Marxist-inspired union was the Shanghai Mechanics' Union. It was thus natural that the strike by BAT machinists (possibly inspired by the recent establishment of the Shanghai Mechanics' Union as well as a successful strike by mechanics in Canton a month earlier) should have elicited Communist attention. Within two days, Li Qihan, the young Marxist labor organizer, was dispatched to the temple where BAT strikers had congregated. Li took along some monetary contributions which, although modest, enabled the workers to rent an office near the temple to serve as headquarters for a strike that would eventually include much of the BAT work force. Under Li's tutelage, the workers chose representatives and drafted a set of demands, which were approved by a mass meeting convened at the temple grounds. Their slogans indicated partisan inspiration: "Labor is sacred!" "Redeem our blood and sweat!" "Reclaim our humanity!"[44]

When the strike had gone on for two weeks, BAT management decided to pay off one of its less savory foremen—a gangster by the name of Wang Fengshan—in exchange for an agreement to hire scabs. The strikers were inclined to deal with Wang's betrayal of their cause by force, but Li Qihan persuaded them to adopt a more moderate attitude. The happy outcome of this restraint (perhaps bolstered by a competitive payoff from the workers' side) was a change of heart on the part of foreman Wang. The conversion was celebrated by Li Qihan in an article in *Labor Weekly*, the journal of the Communist-controlled Chinese Labor Secretariat, then headquartered in Shanghai. In this often-cited article, Li expressed sympathy for the plight of factory foremen, noting that they worked long hours for low pay. Pointing out that many foremen were Green Gang leaders, bound by a pledge of mutual aid to fellow gang members among the ordinary laborers, Li pleaded with these "foremen-gentlemen" to follow the lead of Wang Fengshan in walking hand in hand with the workers.[45]

Thanks to the defection of key personnel among lower-level staff and the intransigence of the strikers, the protest ended in victory on August 10, more than twenty days after it had begun, with management acquiescing to all demands. Later that month, Li Qihan helped the workers solidify their gains by forming a BAT union in another mass meeting held at the local temple. At Li's suggestion, the new union was housed in the office of the Chinese Labor Secretariat.[46]

Li Qihan's success in leading the workers of BAT was not entirely attributable to his Marxist zeal. His membership in the Green Gang, a status that predated the 1921 strike, was equally important. Presumably Li's involvement in the gang made it easier for him to persuade BAT foreman and Green Gang leader Wang Fengshan to throw in his lot with the striking workers. But when the BAT union was organized in the aftermath of the strike, Li Qihan did not permit the gangster foremen to participate. As Zhang Guotao, then director of the Labor Secretariat (of which Li Qihan was secretary), remembered:

> Enormously stimulating to Communist Party members, the victorious strike of the Putung [Pudong] tobacco workers was an important factor contributing to the rapid passage of the work plan for the Secretariat. It excited Li Ch'i-han [Li Qihan] especially. . . . He had thought it necessary to be conciliatory in dealing with the "old men" [i.e., gang leaders]. It was for this reason, in fact, that he had joined the secret society. . . . Using a new policy of struggling against the "old men," however, we had hit our mark with the first shot we fired. In the future, therefore, Li announced that we should stick to this new policy.[47]

Li Qihan's exclusivity carried a high price, however.* In June 1922, Li was arrested by gangster-connected policemen, and the BAT union was forced to cease operations. Although the union soon relocated at the Pudong textile union under the new name of the Tobacco Workers' Recreation Club, in September the textile union was closed down as well.[48] Shanghai's leading English-language newspaper expressed the au-

---

*That foremen retained considerable power over their subordinates was shown in April 1922 when two feuding foremen gathered dozens of BAT workers to fight with iron poles on their behalf (*Minguo ribao*, Apr. 19, 1922).

thorities' reasoning in taking action against the unions: "That agitation [by labor unions] is occasionally connected rather with some conspiracy of internal politics than with the ordinary causes of labour unrest appears unquestionable. It is, perhaps, too much to say definitely that the labouring classes are being used by politicians for their own ends, but signs are visible here and there which distinctly point to some association between the two."[49]

The Gangster Factor

Fear of politicized unions did not prevent the British from resorting to alternative, gangster-sponsored labor organizations as they did in November 1922, when a Communist-aided protest at BAT demanded the reopening of the textile union and recognition of the workers' recreation club. Faced with the likelihood of another debilitating work stoppage, BAT management enlisted the assistance of local mobster Shao Bingsheng and his newly formed Society for the Advancement of Virtue in Industry, a Green Gang organization in Pudong. Promising his followers a better settlement than any that could be negotiated by the CCP-backed union, Shao managed to recruit more than 300 rolling-machine operators and persuade them to cross picket lines and return to work.[50]

Suspecting that BAT compradore Wang Weizhou was behind Shao's scabbing effort, hundreds of workers forced their way into Wang's home, ripping up bedding and clothing and smashing dishes and furniture. The display of violence only hardened the attitude of BAT management, which responded by summarily dismissing several hundred strikers, nearly all of whom were employed in the machine shop. The next day all remaining workers were back on the job. Although the strike ended without achieving any of its initial demands, management was eventually forced to grant concessions to the more than 300 rolling-machine operators who had returned to work early. Claiming, through the Advancement of Virtue Society, that their display of loyalty qualified them for strike pay, these workers engaged in a two-day sit-down protest of their own. Only after management assured them of back pay for the duration of the strike did they restart their motors.[51]

As we have seen, an uneasy relationship between would-be labor organizers from the Communist and Green Gang camps was already in evidence by the early 1920's. Operating in totally unfamiliar territory, young Communists found it necessary to join the Green Gang and extend olive branches to factory gangsters simply to gain a foothold in the Shanghai labor movement. But then it was the gangsters' turn to mimic Communist mobilization methods. The successful formation of Marxist-inspired labor unions prompted Green Gang leaders to organize their own advancement societies. This development of parallel tactics would characterize Communist–Green Gang activities for decades to come. Each learned from the other as both became increasingly sophisticated in dealing with Shanghai labor. But as the case of BAT suggests, similar tactics on the part of Communists and gang leaders did not evoke identical responses from workers. Communist initiatives were most successful among the skilled mechanics from Jiangnan, whereas the Green Gang constituency was concentrated among rolling-machine operators, men who performed less skilled work for lower wages and who hailed predominantly from less prestigious regions of the country. Relatively insecure in their jobs, rollers were less inclined to challenge the status quo. As one rolling-machine worker remembered, "At that time we had no consciousness to speak of."[52]

Although unlikely to launch a politicized protest on their own, semi-skilled and unskilled workers were essential participants in any large-scale labor movement. To link such workers in common struggle with the more radical factory artisans required, in 1920's Shanghai, an accommodation between gangsters and Communists. Such an alliance was responsible in part for the startling size and longevity of the May Thirtieth strike wave that swept across the city in June 1925.

The May Thirtieth Strike

The four-month May Thirtieth strike at BAT has the distinction of being the longest work stoppage in the history of the Shanghai labor movement. Weekly strike pay from a fund managed by their reestablished union enabled the laborers to maintain solidarity for a remarkable period of time. The protest ended only after management agreed to raise wages, improve the treatment of workers, and refrain from dismissing employees without just cause.

One of the more interesting features of this important strike was the prominent role of women workers in the packing department. The strike began on June 4, when several skilled male workers in the print shop of BAT's Number Three Factory west of the Huangpu crossed the river to tell their fellow workers in Pudong about the dramatic events taking place in the city proper. Reaching the Pudong compound just at noon, the excited messengers leaped onto stools and shouted out their news to the lunchtime crowd gathered outside the factory buildings. The first to show interest were women in the packing department of the Number Two Factory, who declared an immediate work stoppage. Soon the strike spread to the machine shop and then to all the rest of the BAT work force—some 15,000 in number.[53]

Women in the packing department were not only the first to declare a strike, they were also especially active in the BAT propaganda teams that traveled about the city and surrounding countryside to promote public understanding of the strike and to solicit monetary contributions for its continuation. For women in the packing department to go on strike was certainly not unusual, but their active participation in an all-factory struggle that was more political than economic was a new phenomenon. Much of the credit must go to Yang Zhihua, a leading member of the newly established Shanghai General Labor Union. Born twenty-five years earlier in a declining landlord family in Zhejiang, Yang had taught for two years in her village school before moving to Shanghai in 1923 to study sociology at Shanghai University. There she met and married Qu Qiubai, then chairman of the Sociology Department, joined the Communist Party, and embarked on a career of organizing women workers. As another student at Shanghai University recalled, "Because I was from the same native place as [Qu] Qiubai, I often visited at his home. There I saw Yang Zhihua, dressed just like a mill worker. . . . She was thoroughly immersed in the women workers' way of life, taking a personal interest in their livelihood, marriage, children, housing conditions, and the like."[54] Yang focused on women's mundane routines as a means of building support for the revolution. To camouflage her radicalism, she regularly scheduled meetings with other labor activists at the Jade Buddha Temple. Dressed as pilgrims, the women easily escaped detection by the authorities. When male cadres joked that all these temple visits suggested that Yang herself was a believer (*xintu*), she retorted, "Isn't it a good thing to be a rebel believer?"[55]

Despite Yang's efforts, however, her April 1925 work report noted that she had no connections with "backbone elements" at BAT. To facilitate her work, Communist Party officials introduced Yang to the head of the Xiangsheng Ironworks union in Pudong. Located not far from the BAT compound, the ironworks was one of Shanghai's oldest shipbuilding yards. The skilled mechanics who worked there came predominantly from Zhejiang, and the wife of the union leader was close friends with many of the workers at BAT. Accordingly, she was able to introduce Yang Zhihua to two of her fellow provincials in the packing department. Becoming sworn sisters with these two women workers gave Yang an entrée to the BAT work force.[56] The young cadre, known popularly as "Elder Sister Yang," convinced several women in the packing department to work actively on behalf of the strike. One such recruit recalled:

> When Yang Zhihua came to the factory to lecture about male-female equality, I realized just how unfair my own family situation was. We three sisters were all working so that our one brother could attend school. Both men and

women students came to our factory, but I didn't go near the men for fear of gossip. I thought, "These students all come from very rich families—especially the women students must be from really rich families to be able to go to school. Why are they so kind?"[57]

Moved by Yang Zhihua's altruistic example, many women in the packing department became involved in the May Thirtieth Movement. Organized into teams of a dozen or so people, the women recruits traveled around the Shanghai countryside in an effort to arouse public sympathy and support. More than a few shopkeepers and students were persuaded to drop coins into the baskets carried by the women as they worked their way across the city. Out in the countryside, however, the reception was less enthusiastic. As one worker remembered: "Yang Zhihua organized us women in the packing department to go to the countryside to propagandize about May Thirtieth. We took along our bamboo baskets and stood up on stools to lecture the villagers. But when the peasants saw this they'd curse us and shout out, 'You little so and sos. You eat well and yet have nothing better to do.' "*

The gap between the peasants and the tobacco workers, the latter dressed fashionably in advertisement of their Zhejiang origins, was substantial. Yet shared native-place backgrounds must have made it relatively easy for women tobacco workers to accept the leadership of the young intellectual from Zhejiang. Women in the BAT packing department who were tied to Yang Zhihua by bonds of geographical origin and sworn sisterhood were willing to plunge wholeheartedly into the May Thirtieth maelstrom.

That these women did not necessarily join the movement out of conscious commitment to the Communist cause is borne out by an interview conducted in 1958 with Zhu Quanfa, a workers' representative to the strike committee from the packing department during the May Thirtieth upsurge. Zhu expressed considerable surprise at her interviewers' questions about Communist involvement in the strike and replied, "Only because of what you've said do I realize that the Communist Party was leading us . . . at that time we just followed along because it seemed like the right thing to do."[58] One of Zhu's co-workers in the packing department put the matter even more bluntly: "I didn't understand much about strikes. . . . When people marched I just followed

*Zhao Shengying and Zhao Yinying, Feb. 21, 1957, transcript of interview, Labor Movement Archives of the SASS Institute of History. The lion's share of the strike fund came from Chinese businessmen who welcomed the work stoppage in rival enterprises. Nanyang Brothers Tobacco Company, anxious to profit from BAT's misfortune, contributed 100,000 yuan to the general strike fund. This sum represented about 12 percent of all monies received (Sherman Cochran, *Big Business in China* [Cambridge, Mass., 1980], p. 178).

them. . . . During the four-month strike, we received quite a bit of strike pay. We thought: 'Here we are getting money without even working.' We didn't understand anything else. Then the factory reopened and everyone went back to work."[59]

The strike pay may have been ample incentive for some workers, but for others—particularly those with dependents to support—it could not compensate for the loss of regular wages.* Another striker remembered, "The women from Subei, leading their hungry children by the hand, would seek out the workers' representatives to ask when the strike would finally end."[60] Even the activism of workers' representative Zhu Quanfa waned quickly. As she explained her exit from the labor movement: "After I got married and had responsibilities I was less gutsy. I couldn't participate in struggles because I had a child and major expenses."[61] Although there is no doubt that Communist cadres played a leading role in Shanghai's historic May Thirtieth Movement, it is equally clear that old-fashioned ties of native place, fictive kinship, and gang membership were often the building blocks of mobilization efforts. Familiar pragmatism rather than a new ideological fervor explained the participation of many workers.

Despite the rather modest aspirations on the part of most strikers, the May Thirtieth walkout at BAT elicited some major gains for labor. Wages were raised, working conditions improved, and back pay was issued for the strike period. Acutely aware that a prolonged shutdown would allow its competitors to capture a larger share of the ever-growing cigarette market, BAT was anxious to settle. Within weeks of its reopening, the multinational had easily reclaimed its paramount place in the market.[62]

Small-scale labor disputes to protest oppressive foremen or to demand further wage hikes occurred frequently in the months following the conclusion of the May Thirtieth strike at BAT. But these were brief affairs, usually resolved by minor concessions within a day or two.[63] Not until the Three Armed Uprisings of 1926–27 did the factory again witness major upheaval.

The Three Armed Uprisings

In the Three Armed Uprisings, BAT workers again stood at the forefront of the action. Even more than during May Thirtieth, different

---

*Most sources state that workers received 2 yuan each week in strike pay, which was about 80 percent of the regular wage of a woman worker in the leaf department. As such, it would have covered only about 40 percent of the cost of living for a family of five (*Yingmei yangongsi zaihua qiye ziliao huibian* [Collected materials on BAT business activities in China] [Beijing, 1983], pp. 1042, 1173).

workshops acted in concert.[64] A few days before the third uprising, BAT militants had received a shipment of weapons concealed in a coffin and transported across the Huangpu River by sampan in the dead of night. At noon on March 21, machines were stopped simultaneously in the leaf, rolling, and packing departments. Following the directions of some 70 preappointed leaders (many of them members of the Communist Party), workers streamed out of the factory and prepared for armed struggle.[65] The workers were equipped with a small supply of hatchets, staves, knives, pistols, hand grenades, and firecrackers (which were detonated inside kerosene drums to enhance the martial atmosphere of the procession). They quickly joined other workers in Pudong, marching together to the local police office, where they frightened off the constabulary and seized stockpiled weapons. As one BAT worker recalled the events of that historic moment:

> On the night before the third uprising a meeting was held where it was announced that we would rise up at two o'clock the following afternoon. At 1:35 P.M. the next day, we shut off our machines. Shortly thereafter, workers from the Rihua cotton mill, the Xiangsheng Ironworks, and the Little Nanyang tobacco factory rushed into our workshop shouting, "Comrades, those of you with badges, please show them." Our badges were pieces of white cloth, about the size of a slice of dried bean curd, on which was stamped some character or other in red. These badges had been issued one or two months earlier, and we had been instructed not to show them to anyone, not even family members. They were to be treated as a life and death matter and were to be stored in the box in the factory where we kept our clothes—not at home. Now I pulled out my badge, pinned it on, and followed everyone out. Exiting by the gate for male workers, we came to the third district police office. Greatly frightened, the police handed over their guns to us. Then we proceeded to the fourth district police office and found that the officers had all fled, leaving behind their weapons. After arming ourselves, we marched in rows—just like soldiers. We took shifts standing guard, replacing the police in maintaining the public order.[66]

Panicked by the workers' militance, warlord troops quickly abandoned the Pudong area to the rule of labor. The success of the Third Armed Uprising generated immense excitement. Having routed Sun Chuanfang's regime and assumed effective control of the city, workers prepared to welcome the Northern Expeditionary forces, holding out almost millennarian expectations for their arrival. A former BAT worker remembered: "We were overjoyed because the warlords had been defeated. The revolution had been won. We wouldn't have to suffer oppression from imperialism any more. Some even said prices would go down."[67]

Workers' representative Zhu Quanfa recalled, "I knew the Guomindang was on its way and I dreamed that after they arrived we workers would have our patron."[68] On March 22, more than 1,000 BAT workers participated in ceremonies establishing the new Shanghai provisional government. For their own governance, BAT laborers organized a new union chaired by Li Changgui, a Communist with Green Gang connections. Ironically, the new union was headquartered at the former house of compradore Wang Weizhou, who had moved to the safety of the International Settlement after his home was raided by workers in the strike of 1922. Operating out of their new union office, several hundred BAT employees served as "workers' pickets" (*gongren jiuchadui*) to maintain order in the vicinity of the Pudong compound.[69]

BAT Under the Nationalist Regime

This workers' world would not endure. In what Harold Isaacs termed "the tragedy of the Chinese revolution," the Guomindang shattered the united front that had brought together Nationalists, Communists, gangsters, and workers in common opposition to the warlord regime.[70] Most Communist cadres who survived the massacre fled to the countryside, thereby transforming the Chinese revolution from a proletarian into a peasant struggle. But the forced exodus of radical organizers did not mean the end of the Shanghai labor movement. For many factories, with BAT again heading the list, the Nanjing decade was a period of intense conflict.

The legacy of unionization contributed to the persistence of strikes. Communist cadres had hastily inaugurated labor unions in the heady days following May Thirtieth and the Three Armed Uprisings, and these institutions did not entirely crumble in the White Terror of April 1927. The BAT union that had been founded one month before the April coup was reorganized on June 5 under GMD direction "to improve workers' living conditions, develop the tobacco industry, and further the national revolution under the Three Principles of the People."[71] Li Changgui remained director of the union but was joined on the standing committee by two Green Gang leaders in the factory: Gu Ruofeng and Chen Peide.

The reorganized union found ample opportunity for action under the changed circumstances introduced by Nationalist rule. As Parks Coble and Sherman Cochran have shown, the early relationship between the Shanghai bourgeoisie and the Guomindang was less cozy than previous scholarship suggested.[72] The new regime leaned hard on Shanghai's industrialists to extract the financial resources needed to bolster its rule. In the case of the tobacco industry, extraction came in the form of a new tobacco tax of 50 percent *ad valorem*, declared in July 1927.

The British American Tobacco Company, accustomed to favorable terms under the previous warlord regimes, refused to pay the new impost and closed down one of its Pudong factories on July 26, idling 8,000 workers. Management explained that the closure was necessitated by the unfavorable economic climate, an obvious reference to the tax. The company's corporatist union responded by enlisting the support of Nanjing in announcing a boycott of BAT products. Threatened with serious economic difficulties if it persisted in its protest, BAT decided to reopen its factory on August 15. Moreover, it agreed to recognize the negotiating authority of the union as well as to compensate the idled workers with two days' pay.[73]

The issue of the tobacco tax remained unsettled, however. Its importance was evident in a strike that began on September 30 when leaf department workers demanded a general wage hike and a guaranteed eight-hour workday. The yellow union intervened, and the protest expanded rapidly. Within a week, the rest of the company's work force had joined, bringing the number of strikers to more than 9,000.

Although the September walkout had been prompted solely by work-related concerns, it was soon politicized, when, following an agreement between Guomindang officials and Gu Ruofeng and Chen Peide of the BAT union, the union called upon the company to pay the tax. In exchange for publicizing the tax issue, union leaders were promised financial support from the state coffers. A student of Egyptian labor has argued that "what counts in determining the political orientations of workers and their organizations is not simply the organization of the productive process itself or the attitude of the state toward 'workers' as a category. Rather what counts is the orientation of the state to the particular industry or even firm."[74] The hostile orientation of the new Guomindang regime toward BAT would prove to be a critical factor in sustaining the strike of 1927 for nearly four months, rendering it the longest industrial dispute of the Nanjing decade.

To undermine the multinational tobacco giant, the Nationalist government found several ways to assist the strikers financially. First, Chinese tobacco companies—most notably Nanyang Brothers and Huacheng—were persuaded to contribute to the BAT strike fund. Zhang Tinghao, then head of the section of the Shanghai Bureau of Social Affairs responsible for workers' affairs, recalled his involvement in developing this strategy:

> I went to see the head of the Bureau of Agriculture and Industry of the Shanghai Guomindang, Zhou Zhiyuan, to discuss my plan of talking with some of the Chinese-owned tobacco factories to encourage them to contribute to a support fund for BAT strikers. With BAT on strike, Chinese com-

panies could produce more, and eventually take over the BAT market. As the Chinese firms made more profit, they could contribute a percentage to the strike fund to ensure that BAT remained shut down. This way they could destroy BAT.[75]

Zhang's plan was quickly implemented. According to British police reports, Nanyang contributed 20,000 yuan and Huacheng 10,000 yuan to the BAT strike fund.[76] These generous gifts were not simply the result of Zhang Tinghao's powers of persuasion. A special government program of perquisites for the two Chinese tobacco companies was introduced to encourage their support of the strike. Nanyang and Huacheng were permitted to purchase tax stamps at 70 percent of face value and then resell them (to smaller firms) at a 15 percent discount. Two-thirds of the profits generated by this scheme were to be deposited with the BAT union.[77]

Guomindang support for the strike was not limited to such indirect methods. Its Unification Committee announced in early October that it was providing financial support for a range of union activities, including the printing of some 15,000 handbills and posters.[78] In a confidential memo of November 14, 1927, Ma Chaojun, director of the Guomindang Labor Bureau, revealed that he had personally contributed 20,000 yuan to the strike fund and Wang Xiaolai (a prominent Green Gang leader who also headed the Shanghai Tobacco Bureau) had given another 8,000 yuan. Noting that the BAT union still lacked sufficient funds to pay the strikers, Ma instructed the Ministry of Finance to allocate an additional 20,000 yuan for that purpose. Ma pointed out that BAT should pay millions of yuan each year in tobacco taxes. For that reason alone, it seemed worth financing strikers in a protest that promised to force the company to abide by the new tax laws. As Ma saw it, "BAT's oppression of its workers is a minor matter, but its refusal to pay the national tax is a major concern."[79]

The BAT union, cheered by this support from the Nationalist regime, waged an escalating propaganda war against the company. Proclamations were issued frequently and immediately reprinted in all the major newspapers. In one such declaration the union pronounced: "We have progressed from economic struggle to political struggle, from a labor dispute to an international issue. Having tasted the bitter oppression of international capitalism, we fight as vanguards in the struggle against it."[80] When the British stationed naval forces at the factory, the union charged that Chinese territorial integrity had been violated and characterized the strike as a "diplomatic measure" whose purpose was to defend Chinese sovereignty, resist foreign products, develop Chinese industry, and assist the workers.[81]

The relegation of the workers' welfare to last place in the list of strike goals suited the politically ambitious union leaders Chen Peide and Gu Ruofeng, who were anxious to curry favor with the new Nationalist regime. Even the Communist who chaired the BAT union, Li Changgui, was inclined to accept the terms of Guomindang support. A former worker recalled, "Originally Li Changgui was one of us, but later he was mobilized by them. They offered monthly stipends."[82]

Despite his apparent sellout, however, Li continued to argue for the importance of work-related demands. To silence him, Chen and Gu accused Li of Communist connections. On November 30 a police raid on Li's home netted four packets of Communist pamphlets. The young union leader was immediately arrested and sentenced to two years behind bars.*

With Li out of the picture, Chen Peide and Gu Ruofeng exercised free rein in promoting the union's accommodation with the Guomindang. But a strike sustained by government funds could be squelched by government fiat. In early 1928, the Guomindang, through negotiations conducted by its urbane finance minister, T. V. Soong, came to an understanding with BAT. In the resulting agreement, signed during a dinner party at Soong's posh Shanghai residence and sealed by a three-million-yuan payment from BAT, the company pledged to remit taxes, to recognize the authority of the union, and to improve workers' livelihood.[83] To sweeten the settlement, the BAT union was promised a handsome monthly subsidy to be paid from tax bureau proceeds.[84] Each worker was offered ten yuan in strike pay, and by January 18 the factory was back in operation.

Gu Ruofeng and Chen Peide now set about the task of consolidating their power base. As a former worker described it, "Chen and Gu had cooperated in having Li Changgui arrested. But then the two couldn't get along and each cultivated his own faction."[85] Gu Ruofeng's strength was based in the Number Two Factory, where he had once held a minor staff position. Chen Peide, who had previously worked in the BAT warehouse, drew most of his supporters from the Number One Factory. Before elections, the two leaders hosted lavish banquets and handed out towels and other gifts in an effort to win votes.[86]

The competition between Gu Ruofeng and Chen Peide mirrored a more serious rift between their respective mentors in the Green Gang,

*"Shangyan yichang gongchangshi" [Shanghai Number One Tobacco Factory's factory history], n.d., SASS Institute of Economics. The political allegiance of Li Changgui remains obscure. According to his own testimony, Li joined the CCP shortly before the April 12 coup and remained loyal to its directives (Li Changgui, Aug. 12, 1958, transcript of interview, Labor Movement Archives of the SASS Institute of History). But his interviewers found "many doubtful statements" in Li's testimony, and concluded that "this person's political status is still unclear."

Du Yuesheng and Huang Jinrong. Although the two gangsters had cooperated in the April 12 coup, the new opportunities presented by Guomindang rule whetted the appetite of the ambitious Du Yuesheng. To expand
his power, Du was even prepared to move against his erstwhile patron,
Huang Jinrong. Accordingly, Du's top lieutenant, Lu Jingshi, now head of
the martial law division of the Shanghai Garrison, arrested Huang's
favorite disciple, Chen Peide, on trumped-up charges of Communist
sympathies. Chen was released only after Huang went in person to plead
his case with the director of the garrison, Yang Hu.* Huang Jinrong
looked back on the conflict with evident resentment:

> Originally Du Yuesheng called me "Uncle Huang." Not long after the
> April 12th Party Purification, Chiang Kai-shek came to Shanghai and I
> personally introduced Du Yuesheng to him at Longhua airfield. . . . Later my
> follower Chen Peide and Du's followers Lu Jingshi and Zhou Xuexiang
> became bosses in the Shanghai labor unions. But Chen's ability fell short of
> Lu's . . . and Du's prestige outstripped my own. From this point on, when Du
> spoke with me on the phone he no longer called me "Uncle Huang," but
> changed the term of address to "Elder Brother Jinrong." This left a bad taste
> in my mouth.[87]

Though Huang Jinrong was losing his grip on the Green Gang, he was
able to rescue his disciple Chen Peide through an appeal to friends in the
Shanghai Guomindang.

The local authorities were willing to sanction and even encourage
factionalism within the Green Gang. At BAT, the rivalry soon crystal-
lized into an officially subsidized system. According to a confidential
memo by BAT's general manager, I. G. Riddick, the Shanghai Guomindang received some 1,750 yuan a month from tobacco tax revenues, of
which it kept 550 yuan for its own purposes and divided the remainder
among three factions at the BAT union: 500 yuan for Chen Peide's group,
500 yuan for Gu Ruofeng's "Shaoxing gang," and 200 yuan for a third,

---

*Huang Zhenshi, "Wo suo zhidao de Huang Jinrong" [The Huang Jinrong whom I
knew], in *Jiu Shanghai de banghui* [The gangsters of old Shanghai] (Shanghai, 1986),
p. 177; Cheng Xiwen, "Wo dang Huang Jinrong guanjia de jianwen" [What I saw and
heard as Huang Jinrong's butler], ibid., p. 164. The timing of this incident is unclear.
Based on Taiwan sources, Brian Martin and Edward Hammond date the incident in late
1927 and do not mention Lu Jingshi's involvement (Brian Martin, "Tu Yueh-sheng and
Labour Control in Shanghai," *Papers on Far Eastern History*, no. 32 [1985]: 99–137;
Edward Hammond, "Organized Labor in Shanghai" [Ph.D. dissertation, University of
California, 1978]). Recent memoir materials from China, however, argue persuasively
that Lu Jingshi, as head of the martial law division, played a central role. Since Lu did
not assume the post until 1932, it seems likely that the incident occurred around that
time (*Da liumang Du Yuesheng* [Big gangster Du Yuesheng] [Beijing, 1965], p. 56). The
following year Huang and Du again locked horns over the settlement of a labor dispute
at the Nanyang Brothers Tobacco Company. See *Shanghai Municipal Police Files*,
D-4611.

smaller faction. This symbiotic relationship between local politicians and labor union leaders reminded Riddick of Tammany Hall.[88]

Government backing bolstered the union leaders' confidence in challenging BAT management. Chen Peide in particular seems to have played a catalytic role in a series of work stoppages at the Number One Factory. With a loyal following among workers in the rolling department, Chen initiated strikes in that workshop. As a woman in the adjacent packing department recalled:

> There were many strikes in those days, but I didn't understand them. All I knew was to follow the lead of the Number Two Workshop [the rolling department]. We could hear the sound of their motors from our workshop. When they went on strike the sound stopped. Then they'd shout to us, "We've already turned off our motors. Anyone who wants a wage raise should join us at once." We'd stop work and the strike would spread to other workshops. We women in the tinfoil wrapping room would bang our cigarette tins, clamoring for a raise.[89]

Chen Peide's involvement in these protests triggered the ire of the company, which tried to have him discharged in early 1931 on grounds of having forced workers to go on strike. Investigations by the Bureau of Social Affairs and the Public Security Bureau of the Shanghai government found Chen innocent of all such charges.[90]

Despite their cordial relationship with Chen Peide and other union leaders, the local authorities were not entirely at ease with developments in the BAT labor movement. By the end of 1931 the former union director Li Changgui, released from prison, was again organizing among the BAT workers. On one occasion Li led a hundred workers, armed with iron bars, to take over the union. The *North China Herald* described the incident as "a direct result of efforts by Communists to regain their control of local labor." Once more Li Changgui was arrested and sentenced to prison.[91]

The authorities intervened in BAT union affairs again when a serious dispute over union elections developed between workers in the leaf and packing departments. The elections were halted by the Shanghai Guomindang, which ordered the Public Security Bureau to guard against "counterrevolutionary activities" (a euphemism for Communist involvement) in the union.[92] Shortly thereafter the Public Security Bureau arrested four Communists who worked as mechanics in BAT's Thorburn Road factory. The four had led more than a hundred followers in an abortive attack on the local police station, hoping to seize weapons to arm a workers' uprising.[93]

Fear of a resurgence of Communist influence at BAT only reinforced the bonds between the Guomindang authorities and their partners among the union leadership. To BAT management, however, labor unrest instigated by Guomindang minions was almost as unwelcome as Communist-inspired unrest. To reduce the likelihood of either, BAT decided to take a drastic step. On the morning of May 12, 1934, a brief sign was posted at the gate of the compound announcing that the Number One Factory would be closed permanently. Management noted that the building and equipment were obsolete, but the Number One Factory had served both as a center of Communist mobilization efforts in 1925–27 and more recently as the power base of Chen Peide. A former worker expressed the common view of the motives behind BAT's action: "Workers at the Pudong Old Factory were very militant. One year there were as many as 83 slow-downs and strikes. Because of this the foreigners connived to shut down the factory."*

Interpreting BAT's move as an effort to crush their union, Chen Peide and Gu Ruofeng temporarily joined forces in calling for a sympathetic strike at the Number Two Factory. On May 21, the entire work force walked off the job. Once again the Nanjing regime secretly authorized the disbursement of funds for BAT strike pay.[94] This six-week strike ended on July 4 without achieving its goal of reopening the Number One Factory, although the company was required to provide the unemployed workers with severance pay. The union accepted the settlement only after Chen Peide received a hefty payoff from the company.[95]

The dispute of 1934 ultimately marked a major downturn in Chen Peide's union organizing career. Having seen the conflict as an opportunity to mount what turned out to be an unsuccessful attempt to wrest control of the General Labor Union from Du Yuesheng's disciple Zhu Xuefan, Chen now found himself out of favor with the Shanghai GMD, staffed by Du Yuesheng's men. When an October 28 union election resulted in a landslide victory for Chen Peide and his Subei sidekicks, the result was declared illegal by the local party branch. Two months later a new election, convened under orders from the Shanghai Guomindang, deprived Chen Peide of the union position he had held for the previous seven years.[96]

Communist Gains

Disillusioned with their labor union's limited success in restraining BAT management and disgusted with its growing factionalism and cor-

---

*Ma Zhulan, July 18, 1963, transcript of interview, Archives of the SASS Institute of Economics. The *Shanghai Times*, June 18, 1927, reported that the closure was because the plant had become unprofitable; the *China Press*, May 28, 1927, attributed the closure to the "alleged insubordination of workers."

ruption, some workers began to search for alternatives.* In 1934, a few women workers in the packing department were radicalized through night classes at the Pudong YWCA. Influenced by young Communist instructors (including Jiang Qing, then known as Lan Ping, who taught songs at the Pudong YWCA twice a week), two of the packing department women enlisted in the Communist Youth League.† But one of the new recruits left BAT shortly thereafter to join the New Fourth Army, and most of the instructors at the YWCA school (including Jiang Qing) were arrested for their subversive activities.

Communist mobilization efforts in the packing department were stymied, but the BAT machine shop proved more receptive. A young mechanic named Shan Genbao was introduced to the National Salvation Association by one of his neighbors, a postal worker. Soon thereafter Shan organized a newspaper reading group at BAT to promote patriotism among his co-workers. In the summer of 1938, Shan joined the Communist Party and within a year had recruited two fellow mechanics. In early 1940 a Party branch was established, with Shan as secretary. The new Party branch sponsored a savings and loan association joined by more than 60 workers in the machine shop (20 percent of its total work force).[97]

After Pearl Harbor, BAT fell under Japanese control. The BAT machine shop was one of Shanghai's premier machine works, and the Japanese were determined to convert it to military production. Shan Genbao fomented a slowdown to delay the conversion process. The following autumn the machine shop was again at the forefront of worker activism, this time initiating a strike for rice rations to offset inflation. The stoppage spread to other workshops through the efforts of women in the packing department. The rolling department was the slowest to respond. A former rolling-machine operator observed: "I remember very clearly that when women from the Number Three Workshop [the packing de-

---

*A letter from unemployed BAT workers to Party Central in Nanjing charged that the union was embezzling government subsidies for the unemployed. According to the complainants, union leaders had been systematically siphoning off the funding allocated for workers' welfare in T. V. Soong's settlement of early 1928 (Number Two History Archives, #722: 4-232).

†*Zhandou de wushi nian*, pp. 109–13; Roxane Witke, *Comrade Chiang Ch'ing* (Boston, 1977), p. 84; Xu Peiling, Sept. 3, 1958, transcript of interview, Labor Movement Archives of the SASS Institute of History. That year women workers at ten Shanghai tobacco factories formed a Resist Japan Society. A contemporary CCP report observed, "Unfortunately at that time only women participated; not a single male joined. Of course, this is not to say that male workers were more backward than females" (Zhu Bangxing et al., *Shanghai chanye*, p. 597). In March 1941, six BAT workers were dismissed for underground anti-Japanese activities. Although my source does not reveal their gender, one was from the leaf department and the other five from the packing department, which suggests that most—if not all—were women (*Yingmei zaihua*, p. 1071).

partment] came in we were still working at our machines. They shut off the motors and we stopped work."[98] After a four-day factory shutdown, the Japanese manager agreed to issue rice rations.[99]

On the whole, however, labor unrest during the years of Japanese management was severely limited. Military repression and economic duress operated in tandem to dampen the spirit of militance at BAT. Only after the war's end did the company's workers reclaim their reputation for unruly behavior.

The Civil War Struggle

Following the Japanese surrender in the summer of 1945, Shan Genbao and his comrades were determined to reestablish a leftist union at BAT. Their first planning meeting was held at the home of a metalworker; Communist strength was largely confined to the machine shop.[100] The rolling department, by contrast, was controlled by Hong Meiquan, a Green Gang and Guomindang member who had worked closely with Gu Ruofeng and Chen Peide a decade earlier. Hong, a longtime rolling-machine operator, led a powerful sworn brotherhood society in the rolling department. After the war, with Gu and Chen appointed to the preparatory committee for the Guomindang's Shanghai Labor Federation, Hong Meiquan's star was on the rise. Decked out in a new wardrobe of flashy Western suits and leather shoes, Hong frequented Shanghai's most expensive dance halls. Following an introduction to Green Gang labor leader Lu Jingshi, Hong joined Lu's Workers' Welfare Society and, with his approval, was appointed director of a newly established, government-approved BAT union in March 1946. Two of the other three members of the union's standing committee were Communist or Communist-inclined metalworkers.*

The pressing problem for the Communists was their confinement to a limited segment of the work force. As an intra-Party report on the BAT situation confided, "All our foundation is in the copper fitters' room (*tongjiang jian*). We don't have enough contact with other workshops. Although a few of our people work in other departments, we have been unable to develop a mass following there." At the end of 1946, CCP membership at BAT was distributed as shown in Table 5. None of these cadres were women.[101]

Zhandou de wushi nian, pp. 165–75; Archives of the Bureau of Investigation, Taipei, #556.282/810. The war years had not blunted the rivalry between Chen Peide and Gu Ruofeng, which remained as intense as ever. But now Gu, who was closely allied with Lu Jingshi, held the upper hand. Hong Meiquan was clearly in the Gu-Lu camp.

TABLE 5

Communist Party Members at BAT,
Late 1946

Work site	CCP members
Machine room	12
Leaf department	5
Rolling department	4
Office	1
Print shop	1
School (teachers)	2
TOTAL	25

SOURCE: Archives of the Bureau of Investigation, Taipei, #556.282/810.

To be sure, the mechanics were an active group. In June 1946, Shan Genbao led more than twenty of them to participate in a demonstration protesting the Civil War. The following spring he organized them for a citywide protest against the cost-of-living index freeze. These activities attracted considerable attention, however, and mechanics were subjected to increased surveillance. If worker militance were to continue at BAT, it would have to shift its base of operations to a less closely monitored workshop.[102]

In the summer of 1947, as demand for a Sunday wage began to sweep the BAT work force, Shan Genbao and other Communist organizers made a bold decision to relinquish leadership of the struggle to a few trusted allies in the rolling department. A leader of the strike recalled: "At that time the reactionary union was watching the copper fitters closely. Since the fitters were already very 'red,' we tobacco rollers were charged with this struggle. I was a sworn brother of Hong Meiquan, the head of the yellow union. The chief of the rolling department was also Hong's sworn brother. So Hong harbored no suspicions about our workshop and hadn't blacklisted any of our workers."[103]

The success of this strike eroded Hong Meiquan's strength, a development that was intensified in the struggle for an annual bonus later that year. In the latter protest, the general manager's refusal to consider the workers' demand for a three-month bonus prompted a group of copper fitters to lay siege to his office. All the top-level management of the company were barricaded until rescued by Guomindang troops many hours later.[104] Despite this display of militance, the workers were unsuccessful in attaining their demands. When union leader Hong Meiquan returned from a meeting at the Bureau of Social Affairs in the company of Gu Ruofeng (now head of the bureau's Labor Dispute Mediation Section), the flushed faces of both men bore testimony to the fine food and drink they had just enjoyed. Their slurred words, reporting the intransigence of BAT management, were not warmly received by the assembled workers, who had been anxiously awaiting better news on the eve of the lunar new year holidays.[105]

Despite the discrediting of Guomindang labor leaders, it was not all smooth sailing for the revolutionary side in the months leading up to Communist victory. During the spring of 1948, CCP initiatives received a serious setback with the arrest of Shan Genbao by Guomindang secret agents.[106] The following year another ten BAT workers—six from the machine shop and its subsidiary repair shop, two from the rolling department, and two from the leaf department—were arrested.[107] The few Communist-inspired protests that occurred at this time were launched in the packing department, under the direction of the two women who had joined the Youth League some fifteen years earlier (one of whom had recently returned to BAT from the New Fourth Army).[108]

Not until the Guomindang's flight from Shanghai in the spring of 1949 did Communists attain unchallenged control of the BAT labor movement. Shan Genbao was released from prison to serve as chairman of a new union at the factory. His nemesis Hong Meiquan, although granted an indefinite leave of absence with pay by the British management, eventually returned to Shanghai to make peace with the new unionists. Shielded for some time by friends within the Public Security Bureau, Hong was finally arrested on April 30, 1951, during the campaign to suppress counterrevolutionaries.[109]

Conclusion

By the time the British American Tobacco Company fell under Communist control, its workers had compiled an impressive history of labor protest spanning nearly half a century. It is hardly surprising, then, that labor historians in China have devoted a good deal of attention to the workers of BAT, praising them as exemplary proletarian fighters. Although the pattern of labor protest at BAT was not qualitatively different from that in other Shanghai tobacco factories, it was more pronounced. To explain the exceptional level of strife at the multinational, Chinese scholars have pointed to its foreign ownership, suggesting that imperialist exploitation stimulated fierce resistance on the part of patriotic workers. In a similar vein, Sherman Cochran has analyzed the difference in level of labor unrest between BAT and its Chinese-owned rival: "The commitment of workers in the cigarette industry to . . . economic nationalism was reflected in their willingness to go on strike more often against BAT than Nanyang even though wages were sometimes higher and never lower at the Western company." I would suggest, however, that the higher wages at BAT are actually a clue to its greater strike propensity. Higher wages, reflecting a firm's prosperity, are commonly correlated with higher strike frequencies. In 1925, at the zenith of the competition between the two tobacco companies, BAT's paid-up capital in China amounted to U.S. $99,385,000 whereas Nanyang's came to only $4,916,000.[110] In light of these figures suggesting that BAT was considerably more affluent than its Chinese rival, their respective strike rates (56 strikes at BAT and 8 at Nanyang in the period between 1918 and 1940) seem less out of line. The company's prosperity rather than foreign ownership per se would appear to account for much of the discrepancy.*

It is important to recognize that the BAT case is not primarily the story of a patriotic, revolutionary working class united in the struggle to seize power on behalf of its own interests. It is instead a story shaped in important ways by the competing agendas of outside partisans: gangsters and state authorities as well as young Communist intellectuals. Most important, it is a story that reveals the complexity of the workers themselves. Although sometimes capable of united action, the workers of BAT were divided by differences in skill, wages, gender, and native-place origins. Such divisions complicated the labor movement, some of whose participants became enthusiastic advocates of Communist revolution, some of whom threw support to the Guomindang and its Green Gang henchmen, and some of whom remained outside the reach of would-be organizers.

That BAT was not unique in this regard is demonstrated by a comparison with the Chinese-owned Nanyang Brothers Tobacco Company. As a former Nanyang worker described the situation in his factory:

> The rolling department had two sections: a "new workshop" whose workers were mostly from Shanghai and an "old workshop" comprised entirely of Cantonese. In 1922 a union was started at the factory and we demanded a bonus and wage hike. But as soon as negotiations got under way, management gave each of the workers' representatives 300 yuan, packed in a cigarette carton. When they received the bribe, the Cantonese representatives from the old workshop stopped negotiating on our behalf. So we decided to

---

*Foreign-owned firms typically were profitable and therefore strike-prone. Moreover, in the case of the BAT strike of 1927, foreign ownership meant important financial support from both the Nanyang Company and the GMD government over the "nationalist" issue of taxes. Nevertheless, workers' memoirs do not suggest that nationalism was a motivating factor in most strikes at BAT. Resentment against profits more than against foreign ownership appears to have been of primary concern. Only during the highly politicized strike waves of May Fourth, May Thirtieth, and the Civil War years did nationalism play a major role in labor mobilization.

form a new union, replacing [GMD member] Guang Gongyao with Tang Yuan, a coppersmith [*tongjiang*], as director of the union.*

Two years later another coppersmith raised the demands that led to the most costly strike in Nanyang's history. In September 1924, mechanic (*tongjiang*) Yao Baofu protested new factory regulations and called for the reinstatement of two women workers who had been dismissed. When management refused to comply with these demands, the entire factory—more than 5,000 strong—went out on strike. Although unsuccessful, the protest elicited vocal support from the Communist Party, which used the Nanyang strike as an opportunity to vent its disgust with the Guomindang right wing.†

If mechanics were the instigators of "radical" protest, rolling-machine operators provided a constituency for Green Gang labor leaders. Such was the case at BAT, Nanyang, and other tobacco companies as well. Although Green Gang–directed rollers sometimes went out on strike against factory owners, they usually did so at the behest of disaffected gangster-foremen.** The close relations between these labor barons and the Nationalist Party rendered semiskilled workers an important reservoir of support for the GMD.

Unskilled women workers, though initially at the forefront of labor protest in the tobacco industry, were generally loath to become involved in sustained political commitments, partly because of the insecurity of unskilled labor, partly the burden of family pressures, and partly the inattention or insensitivity of outside cadres. When labor organizers (such as Yang Zhihua during the May Thirtieth Movement) did consider their concerns, women workers were not unreceptive. Such connections were rare, however, and for the most part women leaf and packing workers remained free from both CCP and GMD affiliations.

*Li Lin, Apr. 17, 1958, transcript of interview, Labor Movement Archives of the SASS Institute of History. Tang Yuan was dismissed from Nanyang during the 1924 strike, arrested, and sentenced to six months in prison. After his release, he became a mechanic at the Jiangnan Shipyard and was soon promoted to the position of division chief of the machine department. His untimely death in an industrial accident precluded further union activism.

†*Nanyang xiongdi yancao gongsi shiliao* [Historical materials on the Nanyang Brothers Tobacco Company] (Shanghai, 1960), pp. 328–47; Cochran, *Big Business in China*, pp. 172–76. In hagiographic accounts, Communist cadre Xiang Jingyu is credited with having provided CCP leadership to the strike. See Li Ming, "Dao Xiang Jingyu tongzhi," [Mourning Comrade Xiang Jingyu], in *Lieshi zhuan* (Nanjing, 1949), p. 231. Although the exact nature of Xiang's involvement in the tobacco strike (as in the silk filature strike that same year) is unclear, the public attention the CCP devoted to the strike is undeniable. See the following issues of *Xiang dao*: no. 83, Sept. 17, 1924, no. 84, Sept. 24, 1924, no. 85, Oct. 1, 1924, no. 96, Dec. 24, 1924.

**This was the case in labor disputes at Nanyang in 1933–34 (*Shanghai Municipal Police Files*, D-4611) and at the Fuxin Tobacco Company in 1935 (ibid., D-7107).

Each factory setting was unique in its particular mix of native-place origins, gender ratio, and skill levels, but the general design was clear. The interaction of popular culture and workplace experiences generated distinctive political orientations on the part of workers in different workshops within the same factory. These distinctions, moreover, were not entirely idiosyncratic but tended to coalesce in regular patterns that are identifiable across industrial divisions. In many respects, the BAT copper fitter had more in common with a skilled silk weaver than with the unskilled laborer in the leaf room or packing department of his own factory. Intraenterprise fragmentation did not, however, incapacitate the Chinese working class. Instead, it created solid bases of support for different, and sometimes fiercely competitive, forms of labor politics.

CHAPTER EIGHT

Textiles

SINCE THE LATE NINETEENTH century, textiles have formed the mainstay of Shanghai industry. In 1861 a Britisher founded the city's first mechanized silk filature. Although a failure, the venture inspired imitative efforts by French and American businessmen a few years later. Soon Chinese entrepreneurs adopted the idea with even greater success. By the turn of the century, Shanghai boasted a prosperous silk-reeling industry, buoyed by strong and steady demand from overseas weavers. As a luxury commodity, however, silk had a limited market; eventually cotton overtook it as Shanghai's principal industry. Nevertheless, silk remained an important component of the city's economy. Moreover, unlike cotton, which was dominated by Japanese and British investment, silk factories were by the turn of the century almost exclusively owned and operated by Chinese. This remained true even after mechanized silk weaving was introduced in 1915. Filatures, which employed unskilled women workers in low-paying jobs, and weaving factories, where skilled males and females worked for much higher wages, were virtually all in the hands of Chinese entrepreneurs.[1]

Inasmuch as the well-known activism of Shanghai cotton workers is often attributed to their resentment of foreign management, it is instructive to compare protest patterns in the cotton mills with the case of an indigenous textile industry. The statistics on strikes in Shanghai compiled by the Bureau of Social Affairs show that from 1918 to 1940, cotton workers did indeed strike more frequently than silk workers. But when strike frequencies are standardized by the number of workers in the industries (averaged over the 22-year period), cotton workers turn out to have been a good deal less strike-prone. Instead, the highly skilled and well-paid silk weavers produced the greatest number of strikes per worker. Cotton production, a much less skilled and less well-compen-

TABLE 6

Strikes Among Shanghai Textile Workers, 1918–40

Industry	Hourly wage (1932)	No. of workers	No. of strikes	No. of strikes per 1,000 workers
Silk weaving	.112	12,000	249	20.8
Cotton	.044	135,000	370	2.7
Silk reeling	.034	52,000	102	2.0

SOURCE: *Shanghai Strike Statistics, 1918–1940*; Zhu Bangxing et al., *Shanghai chanye.*

sated line of work, gave rise to far fewer strikes per worker.[*] And silk reeling, the least skilled and worst paid occupation, generated even fewer strikes (see Table 6).

These data suggest that the skill level of the workers (which correlates closely with their wage level)[†] may have been more critical than the nationality of ownership in accounting for labor activism. Such statistics tell us little, however, about the politics of labor protest. Did skilled and unskilled workers participate in different forms of activism with contrary political implications? To explore this question, the silk industry, bifurcated as it was between the unskilled job of spinning and the skilled occupation of weaving, offers a revealing case study.

Silk Spinning

As Table 7 indicates, the Shanghai silk reeling industry grew from modest beginnings in the late nineteenth century to a respectable position in the 1920's and early 1930's before its subsequent depression and wartime collapse. Most factories employed two to four workers per loom, and the average filature was a large enterprise of 500 to 1,000 workers. Women and children made up 95 percent of the employees. Most were from impoverished families in which the husband's wages were insufficient to cover household expenses. Filature workers labored under wretched conditions to augment family income. Rock-bottom wages,

---

[*]Because of the huge number of cotton workers in Shanghai, their protests were usually large-scale affairs. Cotton strikes averaged 2,286 participants, whereas silk-weaving strikes averaged only 212 participants. When standardized by the number of workers in the two industries (135,000 in cotton and 12,000 in silk weaving), however, silk weaving turns out to have had a somewhat higher participation rate. Many silk-weaving enterprises were extremely small, employing only a few dozen workers, so the participation rate in the industry is impressive.

[†]As the authors of a 1932 survey of industrial wages in Shanghai note, "The one essential factor determining the rate of wages for different groups of workers is the skill required of different jobs. Higher degree of skill commands higher rate of pay." See Shanghai Bureau of Social Affairs, *Wage Rates in Shanghai* (Shanghai, 1935), p. 54.

long hours, frequent punishments, and seasonal layoffs combined to make silk reeling one of the least desirable jobs a woman could find. Filature owners, primarily Jiangnan entrepreneurs, were notoriously unresponsive to the complaints of workers, most of whom hailed from Subei. With little prospect of improving the conditions of labor, silk workers were ready to abandon this line of work for any more promising alternative that might appear. As a consequence, the industry suffered an exceptionally high turnover rate among its employees. Still, there were always enough illiterate, untrained young women to replenish the ranks.[2]

In contrast to tobacco, cotton, or silk weaving, the engine room was not usually one of the regular departments in silk spinning factories. Instead, the work was contracted out to a skilled mechanic (nicknamed an "old devil" or *laogui*) who hired his own assistants, bought most of his

TABLE 7

Shanghai Silk Reeling Industry

Year	No. of filatures	No. of looms
1890	5	–
1901	28	–
1911	48	13,737
1915	56	–
1916	61	–
1917	70	18,386
1918	68	18,800
1919	65	18,306
1920	63	18,146
1921	58	15,770
1922	65	17,260
1923	74	18,546
1924	72	17,774
1925	75	18,298
1926	81	18,664
1927	93	22,168
1928	95	23,534
1929	104	23,582
1930	105	25,066
1931	105	25,394
1932	112	25,300
1934	20	–
1935	24	5,000
1937	2	–

SOURCES: "Shanghai zhi siye" [The silk industry of Shanghai], *Shehui banyuekan* 1, no. 19 (1935), pp. 46–48; Eleanor Hinder, *Social and Industrial Problems of Shanghai* (New York, 1942), p. 18; Robert Y. Eng, *Economic Imperialism in China: Silk Production and Exports, 1861–1932* (Berkeley, Calif., 1986), p. 45.

own equipment, and agreed to supply enough power to run the looms for a fixed monthly sum.[3] The absence of skilled mechanics from the factory roster surely contributed to the difficulties Communists encountered when trying to mobilize filature workers.

Silk spinning involved an eight-step production process: cocoon drying, peeling, selection and boiling, silk reeling, stretching, inspection, and packaging. Adult women handled the more complicated tasks, and children did the unpleasant work of beating the cocoons to free the filament for reeling. This operation (known as *dapen*, or "beating the basins") was performed over basins of nearly boiling water, with which the youngsters' hands came into frequent and painful contact. The inhumane treatment of child workers aroused the attention of the foreign community, whose moralistic outcry was undoubtedly made easier by the absence of foreign capital in the silk industry. As one observer reported on her inspection of a Shanghai filature: "Tiny children stood for an eleven-hour day, soaked to the skin in a steamy atmosphere, their fingers blanched to the knuckles and their bodies swaying from one tired foot to the other, kept at their task by a stern overseer who did not hesitate to beat those whose attention wandered."[4]

Early Strikes and Organizations

It was natural that workers would seize an opportunity to escape the terrible conditions inside the filatures. Strikes, when workers poured out of the factory for the freedom of the streets and parks, provided just such an opportunity. Rarely did filature workers occupy their own factories in the course of a work stoppage. The high incidence of chain reaction strikes, in which women and children in neighboring factories stopped work simply to "get in on the excitement" (*kan renao*) without raising any demands of their own, is perhaps best explained by the desire to flee the hated factory routine.* The success rate of filature strikes was not high. During the years 1895–1913, of the 24 strikes for which data exist, only four were victorious.[5] The success rate improved in later years, with 37 of the 102 strikes between 1918 and 1940 resulting in a complete victory for the workers,[6] but it was still low enough to suggest that strikers may have been prompted by motives other than the hope of satisfying their stated demands.

---

*Similarly, Michelle Perrot describes the early French factory as an "industrial 'penal colony,' where the 'convicts' labor under the surveillance of the 'guards.'" The strike was thus the equivalent of a jailbreak, "a mass exit toward the open, the village, the street, the community restored" ("The French Working Class," in *Working-Class Formation*, ed. Ira Katznelson and Aristide R. Zolberg [Princeton, N.J., 1986], p. 18).

The festive atmosphere of many silk filature strikes was more reminiscent of a rural fair than of a calculated strategy for material gain and made it difficult to incorporate silk workers' struggles into the programs of political organizers. It was certainly not for lack of effort that outsiders had such difficulty in mobilizing the silk reeling industry. As one of the largest groups of industrial workers in the city (second in size only to cotton), silk filature workers attracted a good deal of attention from labor cadres. Periodically these overtures bore results, but the membership of such organizations was far from stable or committed.

The first proto-union for Shanghai filature workers was founded in May 1912, in the politicized days following the Republican Revolution. This Shanghai Women Silk Workers' Benevolent Association proposed to upgrade the skills of its members by operating a training institute. According to the founding manifesto of the association, a more skilled work force would elicit fewer punishments for sloppy work and therefore be less strike-prone. The training institute never materialized, however, and silk workers continued to stage feisty walkouts to protest mistreatment by management. Charging that the association was a threat to industrial harmony, the powerful Cocoon Guild of Jiangnan filature owners filed a protest with the governor of Jiangsu, demanding that it be banned. Even more damaging to the survival of the proto-union was the unwillingness of its members to pay regular dues. Within months of its inauguration, the association was dissolved.[7]

Gangster Inroads

When well-intentioned republicans failed to establish a lasting foothold among silk spinners, the door was open for gangsters. By the early 1920's, it was reported that the Green and Red gangs had made substantial inroads among women in both the cotton and silk industries.[8] In the summer of 1922, an all-city silk filature strike erupted, promoted by the newly founded, gangster-connected Shanghai Women Workers' Association for the Advancement of Industrial Progress. The head of the association, a female silk worker and gang member named Mu Zhiying, petitioned the Jiangsu provincial government for assistance in gaining a guarantee of a shorter workday and protection against maltreatment. As the first well-organized strike in the history of Shanghai's silk industry, the protest captured public attention. Widespread publicity was given to the banners carried by striking workers, which read: "A Republican World" (*gonghe shijie*), "Advance Morality" (*zengjin daode*), "Equality of the Sexes" (*nannü pingdeng*), "Protect Human Rights" (*baozhang renquan*).[9]

It soon became clear that the advancement association was not a spontaneous creation of the silk workers. Three provincial assemblymen from Subei, hoping to enhance the position of their neglected part of Jiangsu Province, had encouraged the formation of a silk workers' association. The lucrative silk business was owned almost entirely by entrepreneurs from Jiangnan, and a workers' organization promised to afford the Subei advocates some leverage over their rich southern rivals. One of the assemblymen, a Yancheng representative named Wu Yibo, had made a special visit to Shanghai in June 1922 to recruit local leadership for the venture. There he made contact with gang member Mu Zhiying, who was also a Yancheng native, and two other women silk workers from Subei. The assemblyman provided money for the three women to rent an office and print handbills explaining the purpose of their new organization.[10]

Only a few weeks after the advancement association was established, some women workers went to its offices to seek help. They had been denied a day off, despite blistering temperatures that made work almost unbearable. The association leaders responded with a request to the Cocoon Guild to reduce hours during the hot weather. When the demand was rejected, the strike ensued. Two days after the conflict erupted, Mu Zhiying noted in a press interview that although a reduced workday was the stated demand of the strike, the real issue was the unwillingness of the Cocoon Guild to recognize her association. Her remarks were prescient: the following day Mu and five of her associates were arrested by the garrison command, acting on a tip from the Cocoon Guild. With its leadership behind bars and the advancement association prohibited, the silk strike ground to a halt.[*]

Once the strike had ended, however, the Cocoon Guild took the lead in pushing for Mu's release. Noting that she was "an ignorant girl who had surely been duped by outside agitators," the filature owners suggested that Mu be freed and put under close surveillance. The following day the

---

[*]*Minguo ribao*, Aug. 7, 9, 10, 15, 1922, May 1, 1923. An important feature of the strike was the cooperation between women from the two Subei counties of Yancheng and Taixing. Known commonly as "big feet" or "small feet," in reference to the practice or absence of bound feet in their home counties, women from the two areas had not always been on the best of terms. In this case, however, the long-standing antipathy was overcome. It seems likely that the cooperation was made possible by the mixed native-place origins of the strike leadership. Mu Zhiying was a Yancheng native, but at least one of the other women strike leaders (who are usually identified in the sources simply as "Jiangbei," i.e., Subei, in origin) was probably from Taixing. We know that the two women leaders arrested in the July 1920 strike were from Yancheng and Taixing and we know also that those involved in the 1920 strike were active in sponsoring the advancement association in 1922. See ibid., July 14, 1920, July 24, Aug. 8, 16, 1922.

woman gangster was released. As a further conciliatory measure, the owners agreed to reduce working hours during the summer months. Instead of beginning at 5:00 A.M., the workday would start at 6:00 A.M. and would finish at 5:30 P.M., rather than the usual 6:30 P.M.[11]

Conflict between owners and workers, underscored by their disparate native-place origins, continued to plague the silk industry. In January 1924, Subei women founded the Shanghai Silk and Cotton Women Workers' Association, headed by the redoubtable Mu Zhiying. Fearful that this development augured another strike wave, the Baokang silk filature (managed by an entrepreneur from the Jiangnan county of Wuxi) decided to fire all its Subei workers and replace them with Shanghai natives.[12] Walkouts at other factories soon followed. By June, a crisis was brewing. More than 14,000 silk workers at fourteen filatures struck, demanding a wage hike, reduction of working hours, and recognition of their union.*

In this tense situation, both Mu Zhiying and the Cocoon Guild saw an opportunity for compromise. Perhaps still grateful for its help in obtaining her release from jail a year and a half earlier, Mu now entered into negotiations with the Cocoon Guild for the purpose of establishing a workers' union that would meet with its approval. The agreement, hammered out in early July by provincial assemblymen Wu Yibo (Mu's Yancheng patron) and Chen Renhou (spokesman for the interests of Jiangnan filature owners), allowed the creation of a union attached to the Cocoon Guild, which would give it a monthly stipend of 300 yuan. In return for this sizable subsidy, the union would ensure the absence of strikes in the industry.[13]

The new system proved its effectiveness almost immediately. With her monthly stipend, Mu hired 48 unemployed women workers to moni-

---

Minguo ribao, Mar. 27, June 18, 20, 21, 25, 1924; "Lun Shanghai sichang bagong fengchao" [On the strike wave in Shanghai silk factories], *Funü zazhi* 10, no. 7 (1924): 1064. The Communist Party expressed sympathy for the June silk workers' strike and attempted to become centrally involved. At the time, Chen Duxiu wrote: "We recognize that the demands of the women strikers are all legitimate. We hope that society in general, and the GMD (which advocates improving workers' livelihood) in particular will come forth to publicly support these poor women" ("Shanghai sichang nügong dabagong" [The great strike of women workers in the Shanghai silk factories], *Xiangdao*, no. 71, June 16, 1924). Communist labor organizer Xiang Jingyu, who was also a leader of the GMD Women's Bureau and member of the GMD Peasants' and Workers' Bureau, offered her assistance to the strikers. It is not clear, however, that these efforts at involvement had any significant effect on the course of the strike. See Li Ming, "Dao Xiang Jingyu tongzhi" [Mourning Comrade Xiang Jingyu], *Lieshi zhuan* [Biographies of martyrs] (Nanjing, 1949), p. 231; Deng Zhongxia, *Zhongguo zhigong yundong jianshi* [A brief history of the Chinese labor movement] (Beijing, 1949), p. 136; *Shanghai gongren yundong lishi dashiji* [A chronology of the history of the Shanghai labor movement] (Shanghai, 1979), 1: 81–82. For a hagiographic, and evidently exaggerated, account of Xiang's success in bringing "Communist Party leadership" to the strike, see Dai Xugong, *Xiang Jingyu zhuan* [Biography of Xiang Jingyu] (Beijing, 1981), pp. 74–94.

tor the situation in every filature. Any signs of unrest were reported first to the workshop forewoman and then to union leader Mu Zhiying, who quickly intervened to prevent an escalation of grievances. Sometimes simple persuasion was enough to convince workers to remain on the job; sometimes a nominal wage hike was required. In either case, filature owners were delighted with the guarantee that production would continue uninterrupted by costly walkouts.[14]

Mu's carefully cultivated relationship with filature forewomen was the key to the enormous authority that she exercised over rank-and-file silk workers.* The system effectively precluded efforts by Communists to reorganize this sizable contingent of laborers under a union more responsive to revolutionary leadership. As Communist cadre Yang Zhihua, who had so successfully organized women tobacco workers, recalled of her visit to the silk union:

> Once I went to the home of several women workers who had participated in the [1924] strike. They took me to the "union" office. The place was very neat and tidy. Outside the main gate was an attractive sign which read "Shanghai Silk Factory Employers' Association." The table in the reception room was covered with a white tablecloth on which were set a lovely teapot and teacups. Seeing this display, I became suspicious: how could a union be so extravagant? Just then a rotund woman about 40 years of age sashayed in. She was wearing a silk dress, in striking contrast to the women workers who wore tattered garments. As soon as the women workers saw her, they arose timidly and addressed her as "Union Director Mu." This "union director," it turned out, was Mu Zhiying—a Shanghai woman gangster who was used by the capitalists as a scab. This union was not really an organization of the workers themselves. . . . I believed the immediate priority was for the workers to have their own organization, but . . . [Communist organizer Xiang] Jingyu cautioned: "At present we still lack a working base among the women workers and their consciousness remains quite low. We'd best use familiar techniques of forming friendships and sisterhoods to get our work under way. Then later we can gradually develop a union organization."[†]

During the May Thirtieth Movement, when most of the city's factories were brought to a standstill in the general work stoppage, silk filatures

---

*Mu's union gave the forewomen the right to represent the workers in their workshop, with the understanding that the forewomen were responsible for "educating" their subordinates and preventing any unrest among them (*Minguo ribao*, Sept. 13, 1925).

†Yang Zhihua, *Huiyi Qiubai* [Remembering Qiubai] (Beijing, 1984), pp. 8–9. At the same time, Xiang Jingyu went on record to denounce Mu Zhiying's union: "Its headquarters are located right inside the Cocoon Guild; it is already a behind-the-scenes guest of the capitalists!" ("Shanghai sijian nügonghui shi gongrende haishi zibenjiade?" [Is the Shanghai women silk workers' union the workers' or the capitalists'?], *Funü zhoubao*, no. 71 (1925), reprinted in Dai Xugong and Yao Weidou, eds., *Xiang Jingyu wenji* [Writings of Xiang Jingyu] (Changsha, 1985), p. 193).

were a notable exception. By stationing another 100 agents at filatures across the city and organizing "lecture teams" of filature forewomen, Mu Zhiying's union was able to prevent silk workers from participating in the massive strike wave.*

Communist Gains

Despite the impressive prowess demonstrated by the union during May Thirtieth, a rift began to take shape within the ranks of filature workers. Several of the women—most notably a worker named Zhu Yingru—who had cooperated closely with Mu Zhiying during the 1922 strike were expelled from the union in January 1925. Although the reason for their expulsion is not clear, it may have stemmed from an expression of dissatisfaction with Mu's dictatorial leadership style. At any rate, once outside Mu Zhiying's orbit, the women began to gravitate toward the Communist side.[15] Although this development had little effect during the May Thirtieth Movement, it became important soon afterward. In August 1925, the first silk filature strike since the formation of Mu's union broke out in the Hongkou district. Leadership of the strike was in the hands of Zhu Yingru and the other women who had earlier been ostracized by Mu Zhiying.[16] Although Mu and the Cocoon Guild were able to agree on a conciliatory settlement that brought a speedy end to the walkout, Mu's hegemonic control had begun to unravel.[17]

In June 1926, a major strike at some 46 filatures in Hongkou and Zhabei districts was aimed directly at the union. The precipitant was a demand by Mu that two cents per day (about 5 percent of the average daily wage) be deducted from workers' wages to support union activities. Claiming that her union was responsible for the steady increase in wages over the past several years, Mu argued that the deduction was only a token repayment for the union's invaluable assistance. Workers did not see the matter the same way, of course, and when the filatures were slow in issuing wages they feared that factory owners were withholding payment until Mu had received her desired cut. A work stoppage quickly spread, with strikers demanding that Mu Zhiying be relieved of administrative duties and her union closed. Although Mu tried to employ the

---

*The Cocoon Guild gave the union additional financial support to facilitate surveillance and propaganda activities during May Thirtieth. See Cocoon Guild Archives, file #516, in the SASS Institute of Economics. Filature owners were of course happy to see strikes affect industries other than their own; the guild exacted contributions from all member filatures, based on the number of looms, to donate to the general strike fund. See Cocoon Guild Archives, file #1191.

same tactics that had forestalled workers' participation during the May Thirtieth Movement, the situation had changed:

> Mu Zhiying, wearing a white silk dress and clutching a leather pocketbook, rode by automobile with several factory forewomen to all the districts of women workers to admonish the women to return to work unconditionally. At first the workers were very surprised by this sight, mistaking her for a factory owner's wife. But when they heard Mu Zhiying harshly demand to see the strike leaders, they realized she was the scab. In unison they replied, "We are all leaders! Down with the scab!"[18]

Embarrassed by the loss of authority, Mu wrote to the Cocoon Guild tendering her resignation. But an emergency meeting of the guild, attended by more than 100 filature owners and managers, decided that Mu's meritorious activities during the May Thirtieth Movement had earned her their continuing support.[19]

With Mu under fire, the Communist-led Shanghai General Labor Union saw an opportunity to enter the conflict.[*] In exchange for dismissing Mu Zhiying, the GLU offered to negotiate a return to work. Fearing a still wider conflagration if this demand were not met, the head of the Shanghai garrison command issued a notice announcing that Mu Zhiying's union was abolished.[†] More than six hundred military police were deployed to restore order, and both Mu Zhiying and her chief rival, Zhu Yingru, were arraigned for questioning.[20] Released soon thereafter, both women—in violation of police orders—quickly set to work trying to create unions that would obey their commands. Perhaps sensing that Zhu Yingru's Communist connections were something of an advantage at this historical juncture, Assemblyman Wu Yibo returned to Shanghai for a clandestine meeting with Zhu in which he offered to back a new silk workers' union under her direction.[21]

The Limited Radicalism of Silk Spinners

Even with such support, Zhu Yingru did not find it easy to organize many silk workers. For one thing, family pressures often militated

---

[*]The CCP journal *Xiang dao* welcomed the women silk workers as "a new armed force within the ranks of the Shanghai proletarian movement. Oppressed by the capitalists and government authorities and misled by the scab Mu Zhiying, they were living in the eighteenth level of hell and were unable to participate actively in last year's May Thirtieth Movement. But this year they are struggling courageously, starting to raise their own demands. Their battle is heroic, orderly, and deserving of great praise." See "Shanghai zuijin de bagongchao" [The recent strike wave in Shanghai], *Xiang dao*, no. 159, June 23, 1926.

[†]Cocoon Guild Archives, file #520. In her defense, Mu wrote to remind the Cocoon Guild of her loyalty over the years. Blaming the current problems on dissension within the ranks not only of the workers but also of the capitalists, Mu charged that outside agitators had directed the recent unrest.

against sustained activism. As Communist cadre Yang Zhihua described the aftermath of the June 1926 strike:

> Brave and enthusiastic young women workers who wanted to strive to maintain the strike could of course sever family bonds and march courageously forward. But sooner or later they had to return home. It was said that when they went home they were scolded, scorned, and beaten by parents, elder brothers, and sisters-in-law. Given nothing to eat, they were left to starve to death. The other family members said, "Not having come home for several days, you must have been shacking up with somebody. This kind of girl can go away and die." One worker's father gave her a length of rope and a knife, asking her to make her own choice.[22]

In addition to family restraints, would-be activists faced formidable deterrence from factory owners and forewomen. As a consequence, Zhu Yingru was forced to proceed cautiously. After organizing a Sisters Corps of women silk workers to participate in the Three Armed Uprisings, Zhu notified the Cocoon Guild in advance of the anticipated work stoppage so as to minimize economic losses. As it turned out, however, she mobilized only about 200 workers (out of some 75,000 in the industry at the time) to participate in the third uprising; no real interruption of production occurred.[23]

In an all-district meeting of the Shanghai CCP on April 1, shortly after the success of the third armed uprising, it was confidentially reported that organizing work in the silk filatures was "unimproved" (*wu qise*). Although a female cadre had been transferred to help out, "Zhu Yingru is again at loggerheads with her. Currently their work consists entirely of co-opting staff members. It's terrible."[24]

Although the April 12 coup destroyed much of the Communist labor movement in Shanghai, Zhu Yingru carried on as before. That May she asked the Cocoon Guild to inform all filatures in the city that they should close for one day to permit workers to attend the inaugural ceremonies for her new Unification Committee–approved union. The Cocoon Guild did not comply, however, and instead fired off a letter to the Unification Committee, demanding that Zhu's union be sealed and she herself arrested. By way of justification, the guild pointed out that Zhu had a long history of subversive activities. After being dismissed from her filature job five years earlier for bad behavior, Zhu had joined Mu Zhiying in organizing a union. Subsequently, she linked up with Communist Party member Yang Zhihua to organize a rival union under CCP control. Suggesting that Zhu was a Communist remnant liable to foment strikes, the Cocoon Guild called for an immediate halt to her activities.[25]

A series of filature strikes did ensue, though how instrumental a role Zhu Yingru played is unclear. Perhaps the relative health of the silk industry encouraged a wave of demands for higher wages. At any rate, the Unification Committee intervened repeatedly to secure wage increases for striking filature workers.*

A tragic incident that November triggered a dramatic change in political climate. When thousands of silk workers gathered at a Zhabei teahouse to discuss strategy for yet another round of strikes, the building collapsed from the sheer weight. More than 100 women died in the disaster. In the recriminations that followed the incident, Zhu Yingru was arrested.[26] For several months thereafter, the silk filatures were uncharacteristically quiet. Then in March 1928 four male mechanics were fired from one of the few filatures that operated its own engine room. Refusing to accept the dismissal, the men remained on the factory premises until a police contingent was called in to expel them forcibly. One of the mechanics, Jiang Axing of Shaoxing, died a few days later of wounds inflicted during the confrontation. With a new martyr to the cause, the pent-up frustrations of Shanghai silk workers exploded in fury. For the next several months, a series of general strikes to protest the handling of the Jiang Axing case paralyzed the silk industry. By year's end, filature workers had compiled an extraordinary annual strike record in which more than a million and a half worker-days were lost to walkouts. With the exception of the cotton industry in 1925, no other Shanghai industry before or after experienced as huge a loss.[27] The silk filature strike wave elicited a proclamation from the Big Seven unions (see Chapter 5), pledging their support to unionization efforts among the silk spinners.[28]

 In fact, however, the workers' enthusiasm for unions was limited. A stream of complaints from women workers revealed that unions were often seen more as the cause than the solution to their problems.[29] Few workers were anxious to become embroiled in union politics of either the Communist or Guomindang variety. To be sure, attempts to organize the silk workers continued on both sides.† In the summer of 1930, a Communist handbill confiscated at several of the city's filatures proclaimed: "The revolutionary climax lies just ahead: the fourth armed

---

*Minguo ribao, June 29, 30, July 1, 7, 8, 1927. Perhaps the Unification Committee was also intimidated by the unruly behavior of the silk workers. On one occasion women strikers seized pistols from a Labor Protection Brigade dispatched to their factory by the Unification Committee. A worker and a member of the brigade were injured in the crossfire (ibid., July 9, 1927).

†For several years before her arrest in 1930, for example, a forewoman accused variously of being in cahoots with capitalists or Communists had some success in organizing women workers in Hongkou. See Number Two History Archives, #722: 4-233; "Zhongguo xiandai zhengzhishi ziliao huibian" [Compilation of materials on contemporary Chinese political history] (Nanjing, n.d.), vol. 2, no. 43, document 5409.

workers' uprising is exploding. The imperialists, Guomindang, and capitalists are trembling for they will all be overthrown. The General Labor Union calls on all Shanghai silk workers to join with other Shanghai workers in a general strike."[30]

Unfortunately for such revolutionary dreams, however, radical sentiments on the part of would-be organizers were not buttressed by firm working-class support. Chen Xiuliang, a returned student from the Chinese Communist Workers' University in Moscow, was assigned in July 1930 to work in the Shanghai filatures. She recalled the situation:

I went to many factories to investigate the actual conditions. The silk filatures had no Party or League members, but how many union members? This was hard to figure out. Surely the women workers to whom I had been introduced were red unionists. I put it to them frankly: "Have you joined the union?" They replied: "We joined." But upon further inquiry I found that the union to which they were referring was the yellow union run by the Guomindang, not our so-called "red union." Had a red union ever actually been established? Not in the silk filatures, I'm afraid. The idea had gotten no further than the cadres' drawing boards; the workers knew nothing of any red union. . . . When I told them that the union platform stipulated an eight-hour workday and a month's maternity leave, they replied, "That's nice, but it won't happen."

As Chen discovered, silk spinners were inclined toward an independent form of protest not easily incorporated into the designs of outside organizers:

The strikers would move from one factory to another yelling, "Turn off the machines!" Some women workers, hearing the cry, would shut off their machines and rush out to see what was happening [kan renao]. In this way there would develop a kind of chain reaction, which we called a "general strike." This type of strike had reportedly been invented by silk filature workers. . . . One morning when I went to a silk filature I saw that it was already out on strike. But just as I was exulting in the thought that the great general strike had arrived, an old woman worker screamed, "The Communist Party has come to make trouble!" I was arrested, trundled into a police car, and jailed.

Although Chen concluded that a chain reaction strike "could be effective when the silk business was prosperous and capitalists could afford to make concessions,"[31] in the summer of 1930 the capitalists were not in a conciliatory mood. A worsening economic climate, the product of worldwide depression, was forcing massive factory closures.* Radical orga-

---

*By early September, more than 70 filatures had closed, leaving 28,000 workers unemployed (*Minguo ribao*, Sept. 28, 1930). By November, virtually every filature had

nizers were disappointed in the hope that unemployed workers would be grist for revolutionary mills. As a report on the silk industry noted: "Most silk filature workers are recruited from the fields and still have relatives back in the countryside. During this depression in the silk industry, many of them have gone home to their villages. Those without land have hired out their labor, causing a 20 percent drop in the wages of hired laborers."[32] The tendency for silk spinners to revert almost immediately to a rural existence made it virtually impossible to organize them into any sustained mode of proletarian politics. The issue was soon to become moot, in any event, for the Sino-Japanese War spelled the demise of Shanghai's silk reeling industry.[33]

Although women silk filature workers were one of the first groups of industrial workers in Shanghai to develop a pattern of strike activity, accounting for 24 of the 51 strikes that occurred in the city from 1895 to 1913,[34] their struggles did not prepare the way for subsequent mobilization efforts. As unskilled laborers more tied to the fields than the factories, silk spinners proved only marginally receptive to overtures from outside organizers of either the Communist or Guomindang persuasion.

Silk Weaving

A very different scenario developed among Shanghai's silk weavers. Occupying skilled jobs that paid well, these fortunate laborers were known popularly as "labor aristocrats" (guizu gongren). They were notably absent from the massive workers' strikes that swept through most of the city's factories in the 1920's. Over the ensuing two decades, however, weavers distinguished themselves as one of the most volatile and politicized elements in the labor force.

China's modern silk-weaving industry emerged rather late. Until World War I, silk weaving was a form of handicraft production centered in the Jiangnan artisan towns of Hangzhou, Huzhou, and Suzhou. Small workshops, equipped with two to five looms per shop, were owned by master craftsmen who personally oversaw the production process and then sold the products at gala tea parties to middlemen merchants. Despite the small scale of production, the industry was united by powerful guilds. That such institutions could serve the interests of artisans as well as merchants was shown by a string of guild-based silk weavers' strikes stretching back to the seventeenth century.[35]

The general prosperity that swept China's business community during

---

shut down, putting more than 100,000 workers on the streets (Shen bao, Nov. 15, 1930). Although the factories reopened the following year (accounting for the stable figures in Table 7), they did so for only brief periods.

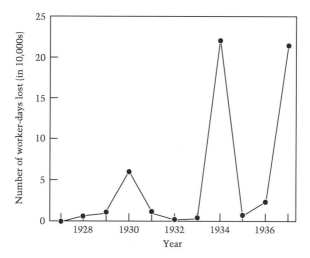

Fig. 2. Strikes Among Shanghai Silk Weavers, 1927–37.
From *Shanghai Strike Statistics, 1918–1940.*

World War I brought a change in the centuries-old silk-weaving system, as a few entrepreneurs began to invest in large-scale mechanized factories. In 1916, the Wuhua Silk-Weaving Company was opened in Shanghai with over 100 looms (modeled on a Japanese prototype) and several hundred weavers. Four years later, the Meiya Silk-Weaving Company— soon to become the giant of the industry—was established. The 1920's constituted a golden age for silk weaving. Dozens of master craftsmen fled the uncertainty of the countryside and opened small factories in Shanghai to share in the abundance of the newly mechanized industry.

By the end of the decade, however, the situation had changed. As producers of a luxury commodity tailored toward an international market, silk weavers were especially vulnerable to fluctuations in the world economy. That economy brought them prosperity in the 1920's, but a few years later—in the wake of the Great Depression, the Japanese invasion of Manchuria, the disastrous Yellow River flood, and the Sino-Japanese conflict in Shanghai—the picture was notably less bright. Scores of small silk-weaving enterprises suspended operations, putting thousands of skilled weavers out of work.[36]

The difficulties of the silk-weaving industry were apparently reflected in the strikes of its workers. As Figure 2 indicates, massive strike waves among Shanghai silk weavers occurred in 1930, 1934, and 1937. The pattern is very different from that which obtained in the city as a whole. For the majority of the city's workers, 1925–27 was the period of greatest labor unrest. In most Shanghai factories the level of strike activity de-

TABLE 8

Value of Chinese Silk Piece Goods Exported

Year	Value (in Chinese dollars)
1927	$28,223,472
1928	$25,987,270
1929	$20,484,285
1930	$17,827,441
1931	$17,695,349
1932	$14,754,601
1933	$15,648,269
1934	$11,289,794
1935	$6,987,582
1936	$6,217,958

SOURCE: D. K. Lieu, *The Silk Industry of China* (Shanghai, 1940), pp. 256–57.

creased in 1930 and 1934, and although 1937 was a year of increased strikes, the magnitude of that increase was far greater among silk weavers than in the city as a whole.[37]

The silk weavers' increased protest activity at first glance appears related to the hard times in the industry in the early 1930's. As Table 8 indicates, exports of finished silk products fell steadily during the Nanjing decade. But the relationship between economic hardship and labor unrest was not as straightforward as it initially seems. For the Depression years saw not only a general decline but also a fundamental restructuring of the silk-weaving industry. Smaller factories were forced to lay off substantial numbers of workers or even suspend operations altogether, but a few of the larger concerns continued to expand, thereby gaining a position of dominance in the industry. Strike activity was heavily concentrated in these more prosperous enterprises.

The Awakening of a Labor Aristocracy

The most successful survivor of the Depression years was the Meiya Company, founded in 1920 with comprador capital as a small factory of only twelve looms and 30 to 40 weavers. Business improved rapidly the following year when the comprador's son-in-law, Cai Shengbai, was hired as general manager. Recently returned to Shanghai from an educational stint at Lehigh University, Cai quickly put his American know-how to use by importing the latest-model U.S.-made looms and recruiting educated workers to operate them. Cai's two personnel managers, natives of eastern Zhejiang province, made frequent trips home to Shengxian and Dongyang counties to enlist bright young men and women as apprentice weavers. Only those who passed a difficult technical test were admitted as apprentices.

Thanks to the skill of its enthusiastic young workers, Meiya had by 1927 developed into the largest silk-weaving concern in all of China, with 408 looms and over 1,300 employees, more than half of whom were serving four- to five-year terms as apprentices. To encourage a high level of output among the young weavers, the company sponsored production contests, paid generous wages, and provided a variety of services: dormitories, cafeterias, clinic, library, night school, recreation club, sports teams, and the like. Aided by such forward-looking management, in the space of a decade Meiya grew into a ten-factory conglomerate with more than a thousand looms—nearly one-quarter of all the silk-weaving looms in Shanghai. Most silk-weaving establishments in the city had fewer than ten looms in operation.[38]

Both its source of materials and its market outlets were more diversified than other silk-weaving operations, putting Meiya in a better position to withstand the upheavals of the Depression years. As many of its less fortunate competitors fell by the wayside, the Meiya Company continued to enjoy hefty profit margins. By 1934, Meiya's 1,000 looms were half of all the silk-weaving looms in operation in Shanghai.[39]

Success bred problems for Meiya's managers, however. The highly skilled and productive young employees, aware of the company's prosperity, began to press for additional perquisites. In early 1927 a portion of the Meiya work force—inspired by the urgings of a Marxist student from eastern Zhejiang, He Datong—stopped work briefly to demand a wage increase, greater job security, and recognition of a labor union. Although General Manager Cai initially balked at these requests, he reversed his position when He Datong paid a visit to Meiya headquarters with a revolver in hand. The company agreed to a 40 percent wage hike, strike pay, no dismissals without just cause, and subsidy for a labor union. On March 21, 1927, the Meiya union was inaugurated. Shortly after Chiang Kai-shek's April coup, however, He Datong was put under surveillance by the Guomindang authorities. When police raided a clandestine meeting of Communist labor organizers, He Datong fled to the street below—only to slip on a watermelon rind. He was immediately apprehended and was executed shortly thereafter at the age of 24.[40]

With the demise of He Datong and the attendant dissolution of the Meiya labor union, the company—in an attempt to improve discipline among newly hired employees—reneged on its earlier collective agreement. In 1930 a worker was fired on grounds of incompetence and the remaining employees were required to sign an employment contract that substantially reduced their earlier rights. In protest, weavers at eight

Meiya factories (1,229 men and women) struck for two weeks. The outcome was only a partial victory for either side: in theory, the 1927 collective agreement would be honored, but workers would have to submit to an employment contract. Dissatisfied with the result, the weavers struck again two months later, in the summer of 1930. This time the protest lasted 35 days and ended with a settlement, negotiated by the Shanghai Bureau of Social Affairs, which was more favorable to the workers: the 1927 agreement was upheld, workers' bonuses were to be distributed, and recently hired temporary workers were to be given the status of permanent workers.[41]

The unrest of 1930 was the beginning of serious labor-management troubles for Meiya. A few years later, the sharp decline in the price of silk fabric (which dropped by some 50 percent from 1933 to 1934) precipitated another, more dramatic conflict. Because a large number of unemployed silk weavers were milling about the city, Meiya's profit-hungry managers decided this was a convenient time to cut labor costs. In 1933, the company reduced workers' wages by 10 percent. The following year, a second round of wage cuts, averaging 15 percent, was announced. This time, however, the employees were not so compliant. In the spring of 1934, workers at all ten of Meiya's factories—4,500 men, women, and children—went on strike.

Pointing out that the company had enjoyed record sales in 1933, the strikers demanded restoration of their pre-1933 wages. For more than 50 frenzied and often violent days, they pressed their case with management, city and Party officials, police, and the public. In the process the strikers forged links with outside allies, most notably the Communist Youth League. These connections would cost them dearly, for the strike ended with the abrupt dismissal of some 143 workers accused of radical sympathies. Government suspicions notwithstanding, the strike was not simply the brainchild of outside Communist agitators. Its impressive organization and articulate demands were features commonly found in the protest of factory artisans; Meiya weavers practiced a style of politics befitting their reputation as "labor aristocrats." The unsuccessful strike of 1934 marked the end of this particular type of protest, however. In subsequent years, as weavers forfeited many of their privileges, outside parties came to play a greater role in their political activities.

When Shanghai's textile industry began to recover in 1936–37, dozens of small silk-weaving enterprises reopened.* Officially sponsored unions

---

*Zhu Bangxing et al., *Shanghai chanye*, p. 135. In 1937, the city boasted more than 500 silk-weaving factories with over 7,000 looms. Approximately 40,000 workers were then employed in the industry.

found ready recruits among the recently rehired employees. The 1937 strike wave, which touched more than 200 of the city's silk-weaving factories, was testimony to the broad reach of the newly established unions. Thanks to government (and gangster) connections, the union-sponsored strikes proved somewhat more successful in attaining their demands, but not without a substantial decline in the workers' independence. By the time of the Japanese invasion in the summer of 1937, the weavers seemed to have lost many of the distinguishing features of a labor aristocracy: pride, control, and autonomy. More exploitative forms of management and increased political interference had left these once fortunate workers in a much less enviable position.

During the Sino-Japanese War and subsequent Civil War periods, however, worker activism grew in both frequency and political impact. Politicized by their experiences under the Nanjing regime and inspired increasingly by Communist revolutionaries returned from the countryside, silk weavers—especially those at larger, more prosperous enterprises—were to play a key role in the revival of the radical labor movement in Shanghai.

Social Composition and Popular Culture

Who were these silk weavers and how did they become such a significant political force? The numerical strength of Shanghai silk weavers fluctuated dramatically over the years: at the height of the Depression, employed silk weavers numbered under 10,000, but with the recovery of the industry in 1936–37 the figure more than quadrupled.[42] This sizable and shifting work force contained two different types of weavers. The most secure and most prestigiously employed group hailed from the eastern Zhejiang counties of Shengxian and Dongyang. These workers were educated young men and women who began their weaving careers with employment in the new mechanized factories of Meiya and other large companies.[43] For them the move to Shanghai was a form of upward mobility. The more than 2,500 job application forms that remain in the Meiya archives show that the great majority of new recruits came from peasant families. Yet these young weavers, most of whom were in their twenties when they entered the factory, were unusual peasant sons and daughters inasmuch as nearly all of them had received at least an elementary education.[44]

Workers from the traditional rural handicraft areas of Hangzhou, Huzhou, and Suzhou had been raised in families that had practiced small-scale silk weaving for generations and tended to be older and less well educated, driven out of their homes in the countryside by the decline of the rural handicraft industry. For them, the move to Shanghai was part of an unwelcome process of proletarianization in which they lost much of the freedom and control characteristic of traditional artisan production. Such weavers usually worked in small factories for lower wages and less job security than that enjoyed by their counterparts in the more mechanized sector of the industry.[45]

The contrast between the two groups of weavers is suggested by their literacy rates. A 1938 investigation of Shanghai silk weavers found that male weavers from eastern Zhejiang had an amazingly high literacy rate of 95 percent: 30 percent had a middle school education, 40 percent a primary school education, and an additional 25 percent at least minimal literacy. Among women weavers from eastern Zhejiang, the literacy rate was found to be 35 percent. In large part, this high literacy level was the result of Meiya's early hiring practices. By contrast, silk weavers from Hangzhou, Suzhou, and Huzhou, who made up the overwhelming majority of workers at smaller factories, had far lower rates: 20 to 30 percent literacy among males and lower levels for females.[46]

About half of the employees in the Shanghai silk-weaving industry were women. In the smaller factories, women tended to be confined to the preparation department (zhunbei bu) whereas men worked in the weaving department (jizhi bu), performing the skilled work of operating the looms. This division of labor by gender perpetuated customary practice in the Zhejiang countryside; silk weaving had usually been a male occupation in which weavers were responsible for the operation, maintenance, and repair of their looms. Women, it was widely believed, should not be engaged in the unseemly behavior of climbing about fixing complicated machinery. At the Meiya Company, Cai Shengbai's new management procedures led to a break with the traditional division of labor. Finding that women weavers were often as or more productive than men, Meiya hired large numbers of female weavers at wages that amounted to only 80 to 90 percent of the pay for males. The intention was to reduce costs as well as to create a more docile labor force because popular wisdom held that women workers were less demanding than men. Weavers at Meiya—whether male or female—were relieved of the burden of repairing machines by specialized mechanics trained at the Hangzhou Technical Institute.[47]

Differences in native place, educational level, and employment conditions were reflected in the distinctive popular cultures of these two groups of Shanghai silk weavers. The young, securely employed literates from eastern Zhejiang prided themselves on being sophisticated urbanites, fully attuned to the ways of the big city. When they had saved up some money, they spent it on the accoutrements of a "modern" life-style: Western clothing, leather shoes, trolley rides, movie tickets, foreign food.[48] As a clerk at the Commercial Press recalled of his encounter with employees at one of the city's larger silk-weaving enterprises: "Once my assistance was enlisted to help negotiate an end to a two-week strike at the nearby Wuhua silk-weaving factory. On my first visit to the factory, I wore old clothes, only to discover that the weavers refused to give me the time of day. The next day I showed up in a nice suit and overcoat and the negotiations made headway."[49] These fashion-conscious young weavers were seldom religious, and their friendship and mutual aid clubs were not of the traditional secret-society or sworn-brotherhood sort. Marriages among them were rarely arranged by family heads back in the countryside; instead they were often love matches with a simple wedding ceremony or no ceremony at all for those who preferred the cohabitation popular among the Shanghai students whose habits they so admired.[50]

Not all of their native eastern Zhejiang customs had been abandoned in the move to the big city, however. Many of the silk weavers were talented singers of Shaoxing opera, or *Yueju*, a skill they parlayed as guest performers in local teahouses.* At the Meiya Company, weavers formed a Shaoxing opera troupe which served as the organizational nucleus of the 1927 strike.[51] It was said that their stage experience and penchant for the dramatic made the young weavers effective public speakers; certainly the Meiya strike of 1934 offered ample evidence of their ability to inspire a crowd. Identification with native place was thus still salient among these "modern" labor aristocrats. The early Communist network at Meiya was actually organized along native-place lines.[52]

The largely illiterate workers from Hangzhou, Huzhou, and Suzhou adhered to a different set of norms. Country people by upbringing and instinct, these displaced weavers brought along much of their native heritage to soften the trauma of adjustment to life in Shanghai. Wearing the familiar clothing of the countryside (blue cotton jacket and trousers), they lived together in crowded, squalid conditions. For the most part, they were deeply religious: many were Buddhists, a few were Christian converts, and virtually all of them—according to a Communist study of 1938—believed in the unalterable power of fate. Marriages and funerals were an opportunity to rehearse customary rituals, complete with rau-

---

*Shaoxing opera, or *Yueju*, is said to have originated in the eastern Zhejiang county of Shengxian in 1906. Introduced to Shanghai in 1917, it was initially not a widely popular form of entertainment and was looked down on by fans of *Kunqu*, or Suzhou opera, which had originated in the more gentrified area of Jiangnan proper. After absorbing songs from Shaoxing and dances from Beijing opera, however, *Yueju* gained an immense following among Shanghai residents of the 1920s (Wu Guifang, *Shanghai fengwu zhi* [Gazetteer of Shanghai customs] [Shanghai, 1985], pp. 315–16).

cous drinking and feasting, which reinforced native solidarities. Kinship ties remained strong among such weavers, who often entered the factory in entire families. When these uneducated immigrants sought a Shanghai role model for emulation, they chose not the student but the gangster. Sworn brotherhoods, sisterhoods, and secret societies helped to provide some social identity for these uprooted workers.[53] As one woman weaver recalled:

> Ten of us in the preparation department of the Dacheng silk-weaving factory formed a sisterhood. Elder sisters one and two were from Hangzhou, as were sisters five and six. On our day off we met at a pavilion in a park and the one of us who could write scribbled all our names on a red piece of paper. She also wrote our group motto: "Share good fortune and troubles alike." The paper was kept by the eldest sister. After the ceremony we all went to an amusement center to enjoy ourselves.

Such groups could constitute an important informal support structure within the factory. The informant above remembered that she once avoided paying a hefty fine imposed by her supervisor only because her nine sisters threatened to engage in a slowdown unless she was pardoned.[54]

Differences in background and culture were reflected in political activities. To oversimplify somewhat, the literate, urbane workers from eastern Zhejiang (active in the strikes of 1930 and 1934) tended to undertake well-organized protests with clearly articulated demands, even claiming new rights and resources. Workers from rural weaving backgrounds (active in the 1936–37 strikes) tended, by contrast, to engage in briefer protests, which seldom went beyond an effort to reclaim lost ground. Yet despite this (often blurred) distinction, the gulf separating Shanghai's silk weavers was not so vast as to preclude cooperation. Unlike the situation in many of Shanghai's industries, among silk weavers fights between rival native-place associations were rare, at least until union organizers purposely stimulated such tensions. Sharing a sense of pride in their work as artisans, silk weavers were capable of uniting in pursuit of common goals. When Meiya's educated employees stood in 1934 at the forefront of agitation among Shanghai silk weavers, workers in smaller enterprises were quick to lend support.

The Meiya Strike of 1934

The Meiya strike of 1934 was probably the most publicized labor dispute of the Nanjing decade. Thanks to the literacy of the strikers, their demands gained a wide hearing. And thanks to the interests of both Communist cadres and Guomindang authorities, the strike became deeply embroiled in the political contest of the period.

The wage cut that precipitated the famous Meiya strike was prompted by anxiety over recent market trends. In 1928–31, buyers in India and Southeast Asia had accounted for more than half of the company's total sales. Over the next few years, however, Japanese competitors made significant gains in both markets; by 1934, Meiya's exports had dropped to 28 percent of total sales. Although 1933 had been a boom year for the company (with sales reaching a record high of over six million yuan), General Manager Cai Shengbai feared that the shift toward the domestic market spelled hard times ahead.[55] He therefore hoped to reduce operating expenses in anticipation of a business decline. According to company figures, wages at Meiya were an unusually high proportion of operating expenses, equivalent to 18 percent of sales. Thus Cai hoped to reduce the payroll sufficiently to ward off a feared drop in profits.[56]

The decision to cut wages was announced by management on March 2, the day after workers had returned from their new year's holiday. The following morning, weavers at the company's Number Six factory—the branch that housed Meiya's experimental laboratory and employed many of its most skilled craftsmen—did not show up for work.[57]

Protest was no stranger to the artisans at Number Six. Several months earlier, ten of the most skilled craftsmen at the factory (operators of the complicated five-tiered looms) had started a slowdown to demand higher wages. They were soon supported by others at Number Six: a small progressive reading group that predated the strike expanded into a larger friendly society (*youyi hui*) of 40 to 50 people, which also joined the work stoppage. After a month's agitation, the weavers succeeded in winning the wage hike for which they had struggled. Energized by this victory, the workers at Number Six inaugurated an all-company friendly society, with branches at each of the ten Meiya factories.[58]

Behind the scenes, a clandestine network of politicized workers buttressed the openly established friendly society. At Meiya Number Four, for example, some ten to fifteen weavers had joined the underground Communist Party during the initial years of Guomindang rule.[59] At Number Six, ten weavers had entered the Communist Youth League. Several of these league members elected to remain at their factory over the new year holiday in 1934, preparing for an anticipated additional round of wage cuts by Meiya management.[60]

Thus an organizational network was already in place when the strikers at Number Six dispatched deputies to the other branch factories in search of support.* Within a few days the rest of Meiya's workers, except

---

*Here I take issue with the otherwise generally valuable account of the Meiya strike by Edward Hammond, who asserts that "organization of the strike proceeded relatively slowly for several reasons, the most important being the lack of any pre-existing organization" ("Organized Labor in Shanghai, 1927–1937" [Ph.D. dissertation, Univer-

for the apprentices (numbering 500 youths), had also joined the protest.[61] Workers at each of the ten branch factories rapidly organized into small groups of about five to ten people. Each small group chose its own group leader, who thereby became a member of that branch factory's strike committee. The ten branch committees, in turn, selected three delegates to form the central strike committee, headquartered at Number Six and chaired by a Communist Youth League member from that factory. Under this central governing committee were established five functional units: general affairs, organization, propaganda, liaison, and security. The general affairs unit handled documents and accounts; the organization division was in charge of registration, investigation, and marshaling of strikers; the propaganda office, directed by another Communist Youth League member from Number Six, solicited monetary contributions and published a weekly newsletter about the strike; the liaison department was responsible for initiating negotiations and keeping in contact with outside parties; the security personnel were charged with maintaining order, protecting delegates at meetings, gathering intelligence, guarding factory machinery, provisioning food, and the like.[62]

These rapid organizational developments reflected preexisting informal networks among the workers. At Number Six, for example, the picket group in charge of security consisted of a twelve-man mutual aid association that predated the strike by five years.[63] Native-place bonds were also used in organizing workers. Zhang Qi, a skilled weaver at Number Six who hailed from the Zhejiang county of Pujiang, quickly succeeded in mobilizing the many women weavers at Number Seven who shared his native-place affiliation.[64] Probably because of such long-standing bonds, strikers were notably responsive to the directions of the strike leadership. As one participant recalled: "During the strike the workers were very disciplined. Every day we went to the factory to receive instructions. When we got to the factory, first we bowed three times in front of a portrait of Sun Yat-sen. Then we followed the instructions of the strike leaders. Some of us were assigned to guard duty, while others were sent out to collect contributions."[65]

Fortified by their remarkable organizational apparatus, the Meiya

---

sity of California, 1978], p. 222). The major sources for this case study—Zhu Bangxing et. al., *Shanghai chanye*, the *Shanghai Municipal Police Files*, interviews with workers, and government and factory archives—offer a much fuller, and quite different, picture of worker organization. None of these informative sources was available to Hammond. Still, Hammond is correct in pointing out that unions played next to no role in the 1934 strike. Although several Communists at Meiya Number Six had tried to form a red union shortly before the strike, not enough workers could be persuaded to participate and the organization never got off the ground. See Zhang Qi, Mar. 10, 1982, transcript of interview, archives of the Shanghai Number Four Silk-Weaving Factory.

TABLE 9
Wages in the Shanghai Silk Industry, 1930–34
(average hourly rates, in yuan)

Category	1930	1931	1932	1933	1934
Silk weaving	.096	.091	.112	.104	.087
Silk reeling	.044	.041	.034	.038	.029

SOURCE: *Wage Rates in Shanghai* (Shanghai, 1935), p. 54.

strikers proceeded to articulate their grievances. A week after the start of the strike, they issued a statement of their position, notable for its moralistic tone: "So long as we can survive [*shengcun*], so long as management sustains our survival, we will gladly suffer tribulation and oppression. . . . All we demand is survival. . . . Now wages have been cut again and survival cannot be sustained, so why must we continue to suffer day after day? Under such pressures, we have no choice but to resort to our ultimate weapon: strike!"[66]

By comparison with workers in other industries, the silk weavers' plight was not nearly as dismal as the Meiya manifesto suggested. In 1934, silk weavers were one of the most highly paid groups of workers in Shanghai, below only shipbuilders, printers, and mechanics. Their hourly wage rate was three times the amount workers in the unskilled silk reeling industry received, for example. Moreover, even among silk weavers the Meiya workers were especially fortunate, with wages averaging double those paid to weavers in smaller enterprises in the city.[67] Cai Shengbai's wage cuts were designed to bring the Meiya pay scale in line with prevailing wages in the industry, thereby increasing the competitiveness of his products.[68]

It was not *absolute* deprivation but rather the sharp *relative* decline in income that drove the weavers to protest. As Table 9 indicates, in 1934 wages in the Shanghai silk-weaving industry reached their lowest point in five years, a precipitous drop from the high pay that had obtained before the first round of Meiya cuts in 1933.

Meiya's silk weavers hoped to bring a halt to their recent reversals by appealing to the sympathy of their employer. They argued that the key issue was the "moral economy" question of whether wages were sufficient to maintain a decent livelihood for a worker's family, rather than the "rational" question of whether wages constituted too high a percentage of company expenses.[69] Having learned by experience that the Bureau of Social Affairs, the city's official agency for mediating labor disputes, was often ineffective, the strikers decided initially to negotiate directly with Meiya management. Accordingly, the central strike committee notified General Manager Cai Shengbai of its intention to open discussions on the afternoon of March 11 at the Number One factory on Rue Bremier de Montmorand in the French Concession.

On the agreed-upon day, some 40 workers' representatives, accompanied by more than 200 of their security personnel, arrived on schedule at the appointed location. The general manager did not show up, however; instead he sent word that the negotiation site should be changed to the company's head office, located in the International Settlement. Suspicious of the sudden alteration in arrangements, the workers' representatives refused to leave factory Number One. A party of French police soon arrived to try to disperse the crowd, which had grown to some 3,000 people. To separate the negotiators from their thousands of supporters amassing outside, an electric fence at the front gate of the factory was activated on orders from General Manager Cai. A battle then ensued between the police, equipped with tanks and machine guns, and the workers, armed only with stones. One woman worker was killed and many others were seriously injured in the two-hour fray. The fighting abated only when the workers retreated to a public recreation ground at the West Gate of the city. After an emotional mass meeting in which indignant spokesmen rebuked Meiya management for having betrayed their trust, the strikers decided to change strategy and petition the Bureau of Social Affairs for redress.[70]

Following a series of brainstorming sessions to agree on specific demands, in a couple of days the strikers were ready to submit a formal petition to the Bureau of Social Affairs. On March 13 more than 1,000 workers marched on the Civic Center to present their appeal, requesting that the Meiya management be held responsible for the medical expenses incurred by the injured and for compensation to the family of the deceased worker and also be instructed to issue pay for the strike period and restore the previous wage scale; and that the French authorities be ordered to bring the police officers responsible for the assault to justice, to compensate the strikers, and to print an apology in the press assuring that such incidents would not be repeated. The Bureau of Social Affairs promised only to give the requests due consideration.[71]

To spread their message as widely as possible and making good use of their literary skills, members of the Meiya central strike committee issued an open letter to the citizens of Shanghai. This manifesto, which was quickly reprinted in the major newspapers, blamed Meiya's General Manager Cai Shengbai for having ordered the police assault that left one worker dead and dozens more severely wounded and indicted him for failing to share the company's growing prosperity with its workers:

The Meiya Silk-Weaving Company is the giant of Shanghai's silk-weaving industry. Its business is flourishing, with enormous profits each year. Last year total sales were more than six million yuan, higher than in any previous year. But General Manager Cai Shengbai doesn't understand the meaning of cooperation between labor and management; he only knows how to increase company profits. He uses every possible scheme to exploit the workers. Recently he plotted to make further cuts in wages which are already at the bare minimum, leaving workers unable to maintain a livelihood and giving rise to this strike. Surprisingly, Cai Shengbai not only refused to seek an amicable solution; he has also used force to suppress the workers. . . . This violent use of foreign police power to murder our compatriots is comparable to the May Thirtieth tragedy. The workers are determined to carry on the struggle. We will not rest until we have expelled the violent, senseless capitalist running dog Cai Shengbai, have eliminated the irrational wage standard, and have avenged the death and injuries among the workers. People of all stations in life, having a sense of justice, must feel anger about this massacre. We hope you will advocate public morality in the form of punishment for the culprits. Moreover, we hope you will offer spiritual and material help to the starving workers.[72]

With this open letter, the strikers drew a sharp and visible line between themselves and management. No longer were China's labor aristocrats willing to undertake private negotiations in hopes of appealing to the moral sensibilities of their employer. Now the battle was a public one, which ordinary citizens as well as government agencies were invited to join. It was at this stage that outside Communist organizers, attracted by the apparent class consciousness of this once quiescent group of workers, became more actively involved in the silk weavers' strike.

Teahouses near the Meiya factories, where workers gathered to chat about the progress of their struggle, were a natural focus of Communist mobilization efforts. Under the pretext of looking for friends or relatives, young Communist activists sought out sympathetic teahouse patrons and made a few contacts among the strikers.[73] Over the next several weeks, resolutions exhorting the workers to more radical activities were issued by several Communist agencies: the Shanghai Western District Committee of the Communist Party, the Jiangsu Provincial Committee of the Communist Youth League, and even the Central Committee of the Communist Party (signed by Mao Zedong in Jiangxi).[74] A series of articles in Communist Youth League publications emphasized the need for the Jiangsu Communist Youth League to assume control of the Meiya struggle.[75] Yet despite this considerable attention, Communist agents enjoyed little success in their efforts to play a commanding role. An internal Party report, seized by the British police in early April, admitted that "although the attitude of the Meiya strikers is good, our own activities still remain outside the struggles." The report bemoaned a "lack of consolidated organization" and chided the workers' strike committee for being "unaware" of the division of responsibility between itself and the Communist Youth League.[76] Such "confusion" was obviously the product of a strike committee that operated independently of outside direction.

Communist agents may not have been fully effective in gaining control of strike leadership, but their efforts had important ramifications all the same. Fear of Communist direction hardened the position of Meiya's management and inclined the state authorities against the strikers. On March 15, the company issued an ultimatum: any worker who had not resumed work within two days would be considered to have resigned of his or her own volition, and new hands would be hired as replacements. The next day, representatives of the strikers were called to the Bureau of Social Affairs to meet with government and Party officials. The authorities strongly advised the strikers to resume work immediately, pending mediation by government and Party agencies.[77]

On the morning of March 17, the deadline set by management for a return to work, it was clear that government persuasion had failed to soften the militancy of the strikers. Accordingly, the authorities decided to adopt sterner measures. Plainclothesmen were sent to the various Meiya branch factories to seek out and apprehend suspected ringleaders. At Number Six, an attempted arrest was averted only because an alert member of the strikers' security force managed to sink her teeth into the hand of the policeman before he could complete his assignment. At Number Five, however, workers' pickets proved less effective. A woman weaver by the name of Liu Jinshui was apprehended on suspicion of being a Communist and was carted off to the local police station.[78]

The following day, more than 4,000 workers and supporters gathered at the West Gate police station to demand the release of Liu Jinshui. The officer in charge replied that he had no authority over the case, explaining that Liu had been arrested under direct orders from the Guomindang Central Executive Committee in Nanjing. Dissatisfied with this answer, the crowd refused to disperse. Instead, the protesters settled in for an all-night vigil, spreading themselves across the front gate of the station and into the surrounding streets so that all traffic in the vicinity was brought to a standstill. During the evening, several hundred workers from small silk-weaving factories in the French Concession and Nandao districts joined the sit-in. Merchants in the West Gate area sent food for the strikers, whose ranks were soon swelled by university students sympathetic to the cause. The next morning, dozens of silk weavers from factories located in more distant parts of the city also arrived to lend support.[79] At 10 A.M., the chief of Shanghai's Public Security Bureau, responding to intense public pressure, issued orders to release the prisoner.

Overjoyed by this outcome, the victorious protesters led their freed comrade away in a boisterous and triumphant firecracker parade. Flushed with success, the strikers quickly drew up a new and more ambitious set of demands to present to Shanghai authorities. In addition to the restoration of pre-1933 wages, the workers called for full pay during the strike period, a guarantee against dismissals without just cause, elimination of fines as a form of punishment, and equal pay for men and women.[80]

This last demand reflected the key role that women weavers were playing in the protest. Meiya's effort to create a more docile labor force by hiring female employees had evidently backfired. Women casualties in the March 11 incident, women activists in the strike security force, a woman prisoner—all pointed to the pronounced militance of female workers.[81]

The release of Liu Jinshui gave the weavers an important psychological boost, but unfortunately for them it did not augur a more accommodating attitude on the part of the authorities. To the contrary, public security agents actually stepped up surveillance and arrests among Meiya activists. On March 27, a confidential report by a Guomindang agent sent from Nanjing to investigate the strike concluded that Communist elements had infiltrated the movement. The agent advocated harsh reprisals.[82] Over the next few weeks, more than a dozen strikers were apprehended (and several of them sentenced to detention) for distributing strike literature and soliciting financial contributions.[83]

Once again, however, police intervention worked to expand the strikers' support group. To protest the police intimidation, Meiya's 500 young apprentices stopped work on April 5. The move came as a surprise to management because the traditional arrangement for apprentices relieved the company of any responsibility for the wages of these youngsters. At the start of their three- to five-year training period, apprentices were required to deposit a security payment of $30 to $50, nonrefundable should they leave the company before completion of the training period.[84] Although apprentices were surely the poorest of Meiya's workers, because they received no wages they would have seemed unlikely to participate in a protest against wage reductions. But the day after this group of workers joined the struggle, the strikers issued an updated set of demands which evidenced the concerns of their latest recruits. The new list called for the company to abolish the practice of requiring security money from apprentices, to protect apprentices from assault by foremen, and to provide every apprentice with a loom at the end of his or her training period.[85]

With all the employees now on strike, Meiya served as a magnet for other disgruntled workers in the area. Strikers in Shanghai's rubber factory sent delegates to Meiya's central strike committee for advice on how to organize effectively. Workers in Shanghai's pharmaceutical, to-bacco, and umbrella industries launched strikes. Even in the interior, in the traditional silk centers of Huzhou and Hangzhou, weavers followed the lead of their city cousins in striking for higher wages and improved working conditions. The Meiya strike was welcomed not only by other strike-prone workers but by some employers as well. Other silk-weaving concerns in Shanghai naturally profited from Meiya's work stoppage. Not surprisingly, these rival factories contributed heavily to the strike fund that sustained Meiya's militants during their lengthy protest.[86]

Seeing its market captured by competitors and without even any ap-prentices to carry on production, Meiya management tried to retaliate. Its first step was to reduce the quality of food still being served in workers' cafeterias. Meat was withdrawn from the already meager menu, and only the cheapest vegetables were provided. The decline in service was quickly met by heated protest. At Number Nine, 200 women work-ers engaged in a brief hunger strike.[87] Weavers at Number Four (led by the secretary of the underground Communist Party branch at the factory) barricaded the superintendent in his room. Police who tried to climb the factory fence in a rescue mission retreated hastily when workers un-leashed buckets of night soil from the roof. After two days and nights under siege, the factory superintendent signed a guarantee of improved meals and paid $100 in food subsidies.[88]

With tensions between workers and management running high, the Bureau of Social Affairs decided to attempt a more active role in settling the dispute. Green Gang leader Du Yuesheng was asked to intervene, but his efforts to talk the strikers into giving up their struggle proved fruit-less. Few of his own followers were among the Meiya work force, and Du was powerless to effect a solution. Pressed by an April 8 cable from Chiang Kai-shek ordering an immediate end to the strike, the bureau put together a formal mediation committee and scheduled an official meet-ing for the morning of April 10.[89]

Before 10 A.M. on the appointed date, hundreds of strikers converged on the Bureau of Social Affairs at the Civic Center. Marching two abreast and carrying portraits and statues of Sun Yat-sen, they distributed hand-bills proclaiming "Labor is sacred" (laogong shensheng). Once assembled outside the offices of the Bureau of Social Affairs, the weavers sang their strike theme song—"How sad, how sad, how terribly sad; Meiya work-ers' wages have been cut so bad"—and chanted in unison, "We want to work! We want to eat!" Much to their consternation, however, it soon became clear that no mediation could take place: Meiya's management had again failed to show. In place of negotiators, Meiya sent word that it had decided to shut down its factories. Since operations were being suspended, mediation was pointless. To demonstrate that the decision was more than idle talk, the company closed the doors of all its workers' cafeterias, leaving the strikers without a regular source of food.[90]

Meanwhile, the strikers, insisting that the Bureau of Social Affairs order a reopening of their cafeterias and enforce some acceptable settlement of the dispute, laid siege to the Civic Center. At about 6 P.M., when the staff of the Bureaus of Social Affairs, Education, and Public Health were preparing to go home for the night, the demonstrators sealed all doors and placed a tight cordon around the building. No one was to be permitted to leave until Meiya's representatives arrived to negotiate. As a cold rain began to fall, thousands of workers settled in to enforce their blockade. One intrepid young protester even delivered her baby in the dank, open air at the Civic Center that night.[91]

With the Meiya strikers now occupying the heart of Shanghai's municipal government, a large force of police and public security agents was called in. By the next morning, hundreds of policemen and six fire engines had reached the scene. In the midst of this confusion, Shanghai's mayor, Wu Tiecheng, arrived at the Civic Center and while making his way to his office was surrounded by strikers demanding his help in bringing about a settlement. Alarmed by this direct confrontation, the police decided to charge the workers. Brandishing batons and turning fire hoses on the crowd, they succeeded in dispersing the protesters, inflicting many injuries in the process.[92]

This April 11 incident marked a turning point in the Meiya strike.* Although the police assault generated public support for the strikers (workers at more than 100 small silk-weaving factories in the southern and eastern districts of Shanghai staged a brief sympathy strike soon after the April 11 affair), the state authorities had lost any empathy for

---

*Recent assessments of the Meiya strike by scholars in the People's Republic of China point to the April 11 protest as evidence of the disastrous effects of the "ultra-leftist" labor policies of the day. In this interpretation, the Meiya strike committee is blamed for having adopted a Wang Ming line of "blind adventurism" in a situation in which a moderate strategy of behind-the-scenes negotiation would have been more effective. The ultimate defeat of the Meiya strike, in this view, is attributable to misguided Party policy (Shen Yixing, *Gongyunshi mingbianlu* [Controversies in labor movement history] [Shanghai, 1987], pp. 140–42). Although it is certainly conceivable that the April 11 demonstration escalated tensions to the point at which compromise became impossible, it is less clear that the responsibility for this decision should rest with the "ultra-leftist" line in Communist Party labor strategy.

the workers' cause. Having experienced at first hand the disruptive effects of the strike, Shanghai officials were now more inclined than ever to identify with the position of Meiya's management.

Cooperation between capitalists and the state was also promoted by new tactics on the part of Meiya's general manager; during the course of the strike, Cai Shengbai compiled a clipping file of newspaper reports on successful efforts at suppressing textile strikes around the world.[93] Perhaps taking a cue from these materials, Cai decided to adopt a more aggressive role in putting an end to the strike. He reinforced ties of native-place origins with the director of the Bureau of Social Affairs by offering handsome compensation to the director and three of his underlings for their assistance in bringing the strike to a speedy conclusion.[94]

Government's hardened attitude was apparent in a series of public security moves intended to weaken the strike: a temporary martial law was declared in Shanghai, all public meetings were prohibited, and police were sent to every Meiya factory to round up activists. At Number Four, eleven strike leaders—including the Communist Party branch secretary—were arrested and sent to the Wusong-Shanghai garrison headquarters for detention.[95] On April 13, the Executive Committee of the Guomindang in Nanjing, which had also been contacted by Cai Shengbai, cabled the Shanghai Party branch with orders to take all necessary measures to break the Meiya strike immediately. Party Central expressed alarm over the involvement of "bad elements" (buliang fenzi)—a euphemism for Communist agents. By the next morning, the number of arrests at Meiya factories had risen to 40.[96]

Encouraged by these stiff government measures, Meiya management adopted a similarly hard line. Factory dormitories were locked up, forcing the workers to take refuge with friends or roam the streets in search of shelter. (Many workers resorted to sleeping in the public May Thirtieth martyrs' cemetery on the outskirts of town.) Homeless and leaderless, the silk weavers began to lose their fighting spirit.

The central strike committee, weakened by the loss of so many of its key members, found it difficult to retain control over the workers. Meiya's apprentices, enticed by the company's promise to provide them with their own looms if they returned to their jobs, were the first to resume work. Weavers then asked the strike committee to call off the walkout, threatening to resume work on their own if necessary. In a desperate attempt to salvage the situation, the strike committee announced a mass demonstration to petition city authorities on April 21. More than a thousand bedraggled workers showed up at the local Guomindang headquarters on the appointed day to demand the release of the arrested workers and the immediate reopening of workers' dormitories and cafeterias. The limited nature of the demands (which made no mention of wages) showed the sorry state to which the movement had sunk. Guomindang authorities, confident that they now held the upper hand, were firm in their answer: Meiya would be told to reopen the dormitories, but the workers must resume work at once. Tired and defeated, the silk weavers were back on the job the next morning, bringing to an end their 51-day walkout.

When they returned to work, the strikers found that changes had occurred in their absence. They were informed that the factories were being reorganized and that all workers must therefore reregister with the company. The process of reregistration, it soon became clear, entailed an investigation of one's involvement in the strike; as a consequence, 143 activists were dismissed.[97]

On April 27, Nanjing, responding to a direct appeal from Cai Shengbai, instructed the Shanghai authorities to deal harshly with "reactionary troublemakers" in the Meiya strike.[98] Three days later, the 40 previously arrested workers were sentenced to varying degrees of punishment: most received prison terms of 20 to 40 days; the Party secretary at Number Four, betrayed by two of his fellow cell members, was sentenced to five years behind bars.[99] This legal verdict brought the Meiya protest to an official conclusion.

What lessons were to be drawn from this long, and ultimately unsuccessful, exercise in workers' politics? For the Meiya strikers, the lesson was a bitter realization of the limitations of their own power. Theirs had been a classic "aristocratic" protest: organization was based on small, preexisting networks of workshop friendship; demands were moderate, articulate, and phrased in moral language with public appeal; outside assistance was welcomed, but leadership remained in the hands of the weavers themselves.[100] Yet clearly this style of protest was ineffective against an employer whose search for profits numbed the sense of respect and moral obligation he had once felt for his skilled work force.

A woman worker whose active participation in the 1934 strike was a turning point in her life, leading eventually to Communist Party membership, recalled: "When I joined the Meiya strike I was very young and naive. But after this strike I grasped the cruelty of class conflict and I realized that workers must struggle, must strike. It was an educational experience for me."[101]

If workers harbored any hope that the previously cordial relationship with management might be restored, they were quickly disillusioned. Cai Shengbai, proclaiming that "this dispute has left a scar not on a single person or a single enterprise, but on our entire national industry," proceeded to take retaliatory measures. In the months following the

strike, Meiya enforced a 30 percent wage cut, closed all workers' dormitories, and raised food prices in factory cafeterias.[102]

Even more disheartening to the defeated weavers was the implementation of a loom rental system, whereby the company leased out its looms
to members of the staff to manage on its behalf. With a guaranteed
annual rental income, Meiya gained a predictable source of revenue and
was relieved of the burden of dealing directly with the workers. Although
the company remained responsible for raw materials and sales outlets,
matters of hiring, training, and wages were entirely the personal responsibility of the staff members who leased the looms. Under this system,
operating expenses were reduced by about 15 percent and Cai Shengbai
solidified ties with his top staff at the same time that he put a comfortable distance between himself and the ordinary weavers. Among the
workers, the loom rental system exacerbated divisions along native-
place lines, inasmuch as staff foremen tended to exhibit favoritism toward workers with whom they shared such connections.[103]

In the aftermath of the strike, Meiya's once proud labor aristocrats lost
many of the privileges that had previously distinguished them from less
fortunate textile workers in the city. At the same time, other large silk-
weaving factories in Shanghai, pressed by the general depression in the
industry, reduced their scale of operations and adopted a loom rental
system similar to that of Meiya.[104] This step backward in the organization of the industry narrowed the gap between weavers employed at
larger factories with higher wages and better working conditions and
those who worked at smaller factories under less desirable terms.

The strike of 1934 had drawn attention to the heretofore unnoticed
political potential of Shanghai's silk weavers. Earlier labor organizers, of
either Communist or Guomindang affiliation, had tended to dismiss the
possibility of a major protest among this relatively skilled and well-paid
group of workers. The Meiya strike, however, generated considerable
enthusiasm for mobilizing silk weavers. As we have seen, Communist
agents attempted—albeit with limited success—to gain a deciding role
in the protest. Such efforts were instrumental in igniting the interest of
other outside parties as well. The Guomindang, for its part, sent agents
(under the guise of newspaper reporters) to try to dilute the wording of
strike petitions. Official unions also showed some interest in the conflict, although at the time just one of Meiya's factories was endowed
with such an organization. The lone union became active only after the
April 11 confrontation at the Civic Center, when it worked to persuade
weavers in that factory to withdraw support from the central strike
committee.[105]

As the dust from the Meiya strike gradually settled, some two to three years after the conclusion of the conflict, a new pattern of silk weavers' politics became visible—a pattern in which officially sponsored unions played a leading role. The weavers gained powerful allies among the authorities, but at considerable cost to their independence and integrity.

The All-City Strikes of 1936–37

The immediate aftermath of the Meiya strike saw a period of quiescence among Shanghai silk weavers. Sobered by the defeat of their "aristocratic" spokesmen and still suffering from severe economic depression, the city's weavers were loath to undertake another major protest. Those strikes that did occur were small in scale and limited in goals. In 1935, the average silk weavers' strike numbered only 55 participants, compared to an average of nearly 1,000 participants per strike the year before. Occurring in a time of acute depression, the strikes of 1935 were universally unsuccessful in forestalling wage reductions or worker dismissals.[106]

By late 1936, however, recovery in the silk-weaving industry brought an increase in both the frequency and success of protests. Improvement in the industry was attributable in large measure to illegally imported artificial silk from Japan. This cheap and plentiful contraband silk made it possible for small silk-weaving establishments to commence operations with very little capital. By the end of the year, some 480 silk-weaving factories were operating in Shanghai, most of them tiny workshops with only a few looms.[107] A total of 29 silk weavers' strikes occurred in 1936, by far the largest number of any year to date. The walkouts were brief in duration (averaging eight days) and modest in their goals but increasingly effective in bringing results. Located for the most part among workers in smaller factories that had only recently resumed operations, these protests were a good deal less bold than the Meiya strike two years earlier. Absent now were the demands for gender equality and better treatment for apprentices that had distinguished the 1934 movement. Also missing in 1936 were many women participants. In most cases, these were all-male strikes with limited wage demands.[108] The conservatism and gender segregation that characterized these protests reflected the social composition and structure of work in smaller silk-weaving enterprises. (The one notable exception to this pattern was another Meiya strike. For two weeks in the late summer of 1936, 150 women and 100 men at factory Number Two struck to demand a reduction in the control of labor contractors, abolition of the graded wage scale, and enforcement of better treatment by job foremen).[109]

The resurgence of widespread unrest among the silk-weaving community attracted the attention of Shanghai authorities, especially in the local Guomindang and Bureau of Social Affairs. Top-ranking officials in both agencies, embroiled in a bitter factional battle for power, saw the feisty silk weavers as a potential social base for their own ambitious designs. Accordingly, representatives of rival factions raced to found state-sponsored unions that would bring the silk weavers under their control.

In December, the first new silk weavers' union was inaugurated at a meeting attended by 600 people, including representatives of the Guomindang, the Bureau of Social Affairs, and the Guomindang-sponsored General Labor Union. Known as the District Four Silk-Weavers' Union, the new organization soon claimed 3,000 members in 120 factories. The chief force behind the union was an employee of the mediation section of the Bureau of Social Affairs. Making use of his native-place connections with weavers at several of the smaller silk factories in eastern Shanghai, he convinced his friends to unionize. The new union had an elaborate organizational structure (not unlike that of the Meiya strike committee), with sections in charge of general affairs, propaganda, mediation, security, organization, and liaison. Under the district union were some thirteen branch unions, controlling the more than 100 factory committees. Each factory was organized into small groups, numbering some 600 in all, of about five members each.[110]

Despite this impressive structure, the new union did not function altogether smoothly. According to police reports, at least two of the branch unions were actively plotting to usurp the leadership of the district union. The Ward Road branch (which included some 800 weavers at 40 factories) was closely associated with the District Four Tobacco Workers' Union, a Green Gang–controlled branch of the General Labor Union that hoped to wrest control over silk weavers from rivals in the Bureau of Social Affairs. A second branch union (which included some 350 weavers employed, for the most part, at the Meifeng factory) opposed the dictatorial manner of its parent union and identified closely with Meifeng management.[111]

District unions were formed elsewhere in Shanghai as well, involving politics no less complicated than in the fourth district. In January 1937 the District Three Silk-Weavers' Union was established in the western part of the city. The instigator, Wang Hao, was a member of the Peasant-Worker Section of the Shanghai Guomindang who had been sent to settle a five-factory strike in late 1936. A follower of Green Gang labor leaders Lu Jingshi and Zhu Xuefan, Wang was also a member of the Guomindang's paramilitary corps, the Blue Shirts. Since more than a few silk weavers in western Shanghai had received training from the Blue Shirts,

Wang Hao was able to draw on the connection to develop a following among the workers. With official approval from the Shanghai Guomindang, he settled the five-factory strike in a manner satisfactory to the protesters. Using the five factories as a base, Wang then proceeded to establish the District Three Union at a gala ceremony attended by Zhu Xuefan.[112]

One might not expect overtures from gangsters to have succeeded among a group of Jiangnan artisans, but the illiterate weavers at small enterprises, unsettled in their strange urban surroundings, shared much in common with the less skilled sector of the labor force. For them, gangster-led unions offered the possibility of securing a precarious livelihood.

Wang Hao's mission to organize the silk weavers was part of a concerted program by his backstage bosses, Lu Jingshi and Zhu Xuefan, to develop a base among labor in preparation for the upcoming National Assembly elections.[113] At the time, Lu Jingshi in particular was involved in an intense factional struggle with the director of the Bureau of Social Affairs (Pan Gongzhan), the head of the Shanghai Guomindang (Wu Kaixian), and the acting mayor of Shanghai (Yu Hongjun).[114] Each man had hopes of cultivating elements within the Shanghai labor movement to augment his position.

The workers welcomed unionization as a way to improve their situation. As one silk weaver recalled:

> We workers didn't realize at the time that unions were part of a Guomindang plot to drum up mass votes for its National Assembly. All we knew was that organization would give us strength. This fellow Wang, I understand, was a member of the Blue Shirts. But he had a "leftist" demeanor and was really trusted by the workers, who saw that he ate plain noodles, rode a bicycle, and lived in modest circumstances.[115]

Or, as another weaver put it, "When Wang Hao arrived, we were just pleased to have someone to speak up on our behalf."[116]

Intense government interest in silk weavers forced even the less amenable workers to respond. In February, the officially sanctioned District One Silk-Weavers' Union was inaugurated in the Nandao area, where six of the Meiya factories were located. It took considerable effort to convince the formerly independent workers at Meiya to join the unionization movement, however. Slowest to register in the new union were the craftsmen at factory Number Six, where the 1934 strike had originated.[117]

Once unions were in place across much of the city, Wang Hao moved to assume overall command by setting up a unified Shanghai Silk-Weavers' Committee for Improved Treatment. Immediately the cry for higher wages spread like wildfire throughout the silk-weaving community. On March 17, under the leadership of Wang Hao's committee, a mass meeting of more than 2,000 weavers was convened at an open field near St. John's University to draw up a unified set of demands. Requests for higher wages, shorter hours, and a general improvement in treatment were agreed upon and submitted to an official mediation committee. Arguing that their industry was recuperating from a depression and could afford to pay its workers better, the weavers demanded an across-the-board raise of 30 percent. After lengthy discussions, the employers consented to a 15 percent increase for workers earning less than 50 cents a day but refused to consider raises for those receiving more than this minimum amount. Since such poorly paid workers constituted only a small percentage of the silk-weaving community, the workers rejected the proposal and began to plan a citywide strike.[118]

Tensions mounted when various factories around the city received police protection, ostensibly to prevent the unions from intimidating workers who preferred to remain at their jobs. On March 29, 150 strikers at the Jinxin factory stormed the plant and attacked police who tried to bar them from entering the compound to meet with management. That same day, a crowd of 500 union members marched to the Yuanling silk-weaving factory to try to persuade workers there to unionize. Three of the agitators got into a scuffle with British police stationed at the factory. One of the three hurled a rock at the police sergeant and then tried to outsprint him, but as the English press explained, "Sergeant Lovell had represented the police in the athletic games in 1935 and had no difficulty catching up." The three activists were brought to trial a few days later, their heads swathed in bandages.[119]

Police efforts to slow the pace of unionization only intensified the resolve of union leaders. At midnight on March 30, a united strike of 220 mills (out of 354 total) and 11,944 workers (out of 23,000 total)[120]—by far the largest of the year's labor disputes—was set in motion by Wang Hao's Committee for Improved Treatment. As Table 10 indicates, the strike reached all areas of the city.

The rapid spread of the strike was encouraged by Wang Hao's policy of "factory-storming" (chongchang), in which Blue Shirt–trained workers' pickets rushed in and destroyed machinery in factories where workers were loath to strike.[121] Recent memoirs reveal that at the time underground Communist organizers opposed a general strike in the silk-weaving industry and advocated a more restrained strategy of separate struggles in factories with relatively "enlightened" management.[122] Although the Communists enjoyed some strength in the District Four Union, overall leadership of the striking silk weavers was firmly in the hands of Wang Hao.

TABLE 10

Spatial Distribution of Silk Weavers' Strike, March 1937

District	No. of strikers	No. of factories
International Settlement		
East district	4,000	169
West district	576	7
Other	838	6
French Concession	1,560	20
Nandao	3,000	10
Zhabei	2,000	8
TOTAL	11,974	220

SOURCE: *Shanghai Evening Post and Mercury*, Mar. 31, 1937.

Wang's tactics aroused criticism not only from underground Communists but also from his opponents within the Bureau of Social Affairs. Alarmed by this massive work stoppage in one of the city's key industries and hoping to undercut the power base of Wang and his backstage bosses, the Bureau of Social Affairs issued an emergency order declaring an end to the strike. In exchange for returning to their jobs, the strikers were promised an across-the-board wage increase of 10 percent, bonus payments, elimination of the loom rental system, and a new one-month paid maternity leave program. The offer was generous enough to erode the workers' enthusiasm for continuing the strike; by early April most weavers had resumed work.[123]

The bureau's order proved effective in convincing the workers to end their walkout, but it had far less impact on the managers, most of whom refused to honor the call for a 10 percent wage hike. During the course of the strike, Meiya's Cai Shengbai, who chaired the Silk-Weaving Employers' Association, had organized an ad hoc Committee to Counter the Strike Wave. The committee, funded by an assessment of two yuan per loom, used its resources to fight the compromise solution proposed by the Bureau of Social Affairs.[124] In mid-April Cai took his case to Guomindang headquarters in Nanjing, alleging that unionization efforts by local Shanghai officials were responsible for the rash of labor unrest in the city.[125]

Early the next month, when Chiang Kai-shek happened to be hospitalized in Shanghai, the Generalissimo took a personal interest in the struggles still rampant among the city's silk weavers. Perturbed by the daily newspaper accounts of strikes and slowdowns, Chiang called upon municipal authorities to bring a speedy halt to the disturbances. In response, on the evening of May 14 a large contingent of International Settlement police raided the District Four Silk-Weavers' Union on the pretext that the union had intimidated a worker at the Jinxin factory. Documents were seized, seals of office confiscated, and more than twenty workers detained at police headquarters for questioning.*

A few days later, representatives of the District Four Union (including the union secretary, an employee of the Shanghai Guomindang) went to the Bureau of Social Affairs at the Civic Center to request that the police return the stolen materials and release the union members being held in custody. The union leaders hoped that a prompt bureau response might forestall yet more strikes on the part of angry weavers in the eastern district.[126]

Authorities in the Bureau of Social Affairs were torn between loyalty to the union they had helped create and pressure from the central government in Nanjing. The intransigence of factory managers had undermined the bureau's strategy of using a unionized Shanghai labor movement for its own political purposes. Nanjing, for its part, shared with the International Settlement fear of a scenario in which the now heavily unionized silk, cotton, and tobacco workers would join hands to take charge of the city's economy. The Guomindang's corporatist dream would then become a Communist nightmare. As a local paper explained, "It is not the individual cases which bother the authorities seriously—it is the steady move toward union combination which undoubtedly will play a decisive part in labour relations of the future." The specter of Communist agents seizing control of a highly organized labor movement was never far from the imaginations of officials in Nanjing. As a pro-Guomindang paper described fears at the height of the all-city weavers' strike: "The bogey of Moscow is, perhaps, all too often trotted out by labour-scared employers, but definite evidence is in the hands of official circles to show that there is a direct link between current labour agitation and both financial and ideological inspiration from the Kremlin. . . . It is not only a question of wages which is being raised, but in whose hands is to rest the dominant political power."[127]

In fact, inspiration from the Kremlin played very little part in the silk weavers' spring offensive. The most active group of Communists (denounced as "Trotskyist" by their mainstream opponents in the Party underground) were at the Jinxin factory. There workers refused to accept the Bureau of Social Affairs compromise and continued a lengthy strike to demand a 30 percent wage increase.[128] Undoubtedly this radical connection helped precipitate the May 14 police raid on the District Four Union, for strikers at the Jinxin factory had been using union premises as

---

*Zhu Bangxing et. al., *Shanghai chanye*, p. 177; *Shanghai Municipal Police Files*, D-7744; Number Two History Archives, #2: 2-1054. The worker who tipped off the police complained that he had been locked up for four hours by the union and forced to kneel while wearing a placard that read "Jinxin factory running dog." Photos were taken of him in the humiliating pose.

a center for free food distribution. The union's president, moreover, was a former Jinxin worker with Communist leanings.[129] But on the whole, Communist involvement was not a major factor in the silk weavers' unrest.

Even without much Communist participation, however, the contest was most decidedly a political one in which factions within the Shanghai regime struggled for the upper hand. While state agencies jockeyed for power over the workers, previously submerged rivalries among the silk weavers rose to the surface. On May 24, a gang fight involving more than 500 unionized workers erupted at Meiya's Factory Number Ten. Workers from the same native-place association as their factory superintendent wanted to resume work, whereas other employees insisted on continuing to strike for better working conditions. From 11 P.M. until 6 A.M. the weavers fought a bloody battle in front of the mill.[130]

Authorities at the Bureau of Social Affairs realized they were losing control of the situation and decided that the silk weavers' unions must be destroyed. On June 3, the bureau ordered the closing of unions in districts one, three, and four. New unions, less likely to stir up trouble among the workers, were to be established.* On June 12, Wang Hao was arrested at the offices of his now defunct District Three Union. Released a month later, he was welcomed back with banners and firecrackers by weavers in the western part of the city.[131]

In the one month remaining before the Japanese invasion, ambitious Guomindang functionaries rushed forth to found new silk-weaving unions. Native-place attachments were used in the struggle to draw workers into the embrace of one or another rival union organizer. Repeated battles between these competing leaders and their fellow provincials indicated the fractionalized state into which the silk weavers had fallen by the summer of 1937.[132] When the Japanese seized control of Shanghai's silk industry that August, they found a once proud labor aristocracy in disarray.

The Communist Resurgence

The silk weavers' strikes of the Nanjing period shared certain features with artisan protests at other times and places under comparable social

---

Shanghai Times, June 3, 1937; Number Two History Archives, #722: 4-520. The last straw for the Bureau of Social Affairs was the unions' organization of a petition drive to take their case directly to Party Central. As one weaver recalled, "Everyone wanted to go to Nanjing to petition. Although we already saw through the Shanghai GMD, and knew that it could not represent the workers, we still harbored some illusions about Chiang Kai-shek" (Zhu Boqing, Aug. 22, 1961, transcript of interview, Labor Movement Archives, SASS Institute of History). Wang Hao's involvement in the petition drive precipitated his arrest (He Zhensheng, May 25–26, 1961, ibid.).

and economic circumstances. As Bernard Moss explains the workers' struggles of mid-nineteenth-century Paris: "Industrialization had advanced far enough with respect to labor and commercial competition to threaten the security, integrity and relative value of skilled craftsmen, enough to provoke resistance and protest, but not enough in terms of complete mechanization to destroy the craft and its capacities for resistance."[133] Even so, labor movements are not merely the product of industrial structure or market conditions. The larger political setting also acts as a critical force in shaping workers' protest. As Edward Shorter and Charles Tilly suggest, "We expect changes in the national political position of organized labor to cause strikes to increase. What is more, we expect the political dimension of the strike to expand over time, as the labor movement nationalizes."[134]

Shanghai silk weavers were no exception to this proposition. Outside organizers made silk weavers' strikes more frequent and more intertwined with political struggles on both local and national levels by the close of the Nanjing decade. In the short run, gangster-dominated unions threatened to rob the silk weavers' struggles of some of the defining characteristics of an artisan movement: craft pride, autonomy, moralism. But in the longer run, the politicization experienced during the Nanjing period would set the stage for even more momentous struggles by Shanghai silk weavers.

Within a year after the Japanese invasion, Communist Party branches had been reestablished at the two surviving Meiya factories. At Number Four, ten weavers joined the Party. At Number Nine, a three-member branch was set up.[135] Of the four Communist cadres who shared primary responsibility for rebuilding the Shanghai labor movement in 1938, two were former silk weavers.*

To be sure, the radicals were not without rivals during the wartime period. Wang Hao, the Blue Shirt instigator of the 1936–37 strike, collaborated with Japanese occupation forces. So too did some Trotskyite elements within the silk weavers' movement.[136] Nevertheless, it was clearly the Communists who scored major gains. On August 13, 1937—the day of the Japanese attack on Shanghai—young silk weavers formed the National Salvation Association with CCP sponsorship. The organization became an important recruitment vehicle for new Party members, drawn especially from the ranks of younger, better-educated weavers.[137]

---

*He Zhensheng, July 1982, transcript of interview, archives of the Shanghai Number Four Silk-Weaving Factory. Liu Changsheng, the leather worker, was secretary of the Party's work committee for Shanghai labor. Liu Ningyi served as deputy secretary. Silk weaver Zhang Qi was in charge of organization and silk weaver He Zhensheng handled general affairs.

After Pearl Harbor, when blatantly anti-Japanese activities were no longer possible even in the foreign concessions, the Party adopted less visible—and ultimately even more successful—mobilization methods. Chief among the changed tactics was an emphasis on "traditional" forms of worker association, most notably sisterhoods and brotherhoods. Although divided by gender and usually by workshop and native-place origin as well, the familiar groupings offered a comfortable mode of association. As was customary for these organizations, periodic banquets were held to celebrate group solidarity. In the midst of the drinking and jocularity of such occasions, Communist organizers injected a didactic tone: readings of Lu Xun's short stories and excerpts from Edgar Snow's *Red Star over China* were included to raise the political consciousness of the members. Based on the principle of mutual aid, the brotherhoods and sisterhoods became the organizational core of the many slowdowns and sit-down strikes that occurred during the latter years of the war.[138]

Following the Japanese surrender, silk weavers continued to play a prominent role in the social unrest that plagued the Guomindang regime during the Civil War period. Initially much of the organizational impetus for the protests came from the silk weavers' unions reestablished shortly after the war.[139] Three of the four district unions that reopened were led by members of the GMD, but two of these also had substantial underground Communist representation on their executive committees. Moreover, the District Three Union, which included two Meiya factories as well as three large Dacheng factories, was directed by a Communist: Tao Yunshan. A former Meiya worker who had been dismissed for his activism, Tao formed the union out of a long-standing sworn brotherhood association among his fellow workers. A relative employed in the GMD government enabled him to secure official approval for the undertaking. By early 1946, the District Three Union boasted a membership of more than 3,000 weavers at 115 factories. Although it faced competition from both Guomindang and remnant Trotskyite labor organizers, Tao's union played a leading role in the many protests by silk weavers that erupted after the war.[140]

In March 1946, more than 12,000 workers at some 300 Shanghai silk-weaving factories initiated a strike that persisted for nearly three months. The silk weavers were eventually granted a wage hike because of the personal mediation of Zhu Xuefan and the reduced influence of Meiya's general manager, Cai Shengbai. During the war Cai had quietly placed his two remaining factories in the hands of Italian and German businessmen so as to avoid a direct Japanese takeover. Although that decision proved financially beneficial, politically it opened Cai to the charge of having indirectly collaborated with the enemy. By threatening to publicize Cai's disreputable dealings, the District Three Union was able to exert a good deal of leverage over the once powerful capitalist.[141]

Further evidence of the silk weavers' activism was seen in the 1946 election of Pan Yueying as National Assembly representative. A skilled Meiya silk weaver, Pan was also an underground Communist Party member who earlier in the year had organized a demonstration by 50,000 female workers in Shanghai to celebrate International Women's Day.[142] The activism of Pan Yueying (and other skilled women weavers, especially among Meiya employees) harked back to the strike of 1934, when women had assumed a prominent role. Silent during the gangster-dominated years of 1936–37, these women militants reclaimed their voice in the struggles of the Civil War period.

In 1947 silk weavers were again at the forefront of protest in Shanghai. A proposal by GMD labor leader Lu Jingshi advocating establishment of a society to promote harmony between labor and capital in the Shanghai silk-weaving industry was roundly rejected by the workers.[143] Instead, on May 8, 1947, the four district unions mobilized more than 10,000 weavers in a march from the Bund to City Hall to demand that the cost-of-living index be unfrozen so as to keep pace with inflation. (In a desperate attempt to stem the runaway inflation of the day, Guomindang authorities had frozen the cost-of-living index so that wages would no longer rise along with prices.) The marching weavers distributed nearly 30,000 handbills with the message: "Prices travel like an airplane, but the index travels like an ant." At City Hall they delivered a stirring petition which opened with the words, "We want to live! We want to breathe! We want to continue to work for the good of the nation!"[144] This much publicized display of solidarity among the silk weavers inspired similar protests among other segments of the work force and helped convince the regime to reverse its policy.

The successful struggle to unfreeze the cost-of-living index had gained widespread support through public performances of a clever play about the evils of runaway inflation. The issues were vividly dramatized by women weavers cast in the roles of wages, prices, bonds, and so on. Playwright Wan Wenhua was a silk weaver and Communist Party member who had, according to her own recollection, become radicalized during a reading of Snow's *Red Star over China*.[145]

By late 1947, hundreds of such Communist Party members could be counted among the silk weavers of Shanghai. In November of that year, however, the revolutionaries suffered a major setback. When secret agents raided the Futong publishing house (see Chapter 6), among the Communists captured on the spot was Tao Yunshan, director of the

District Three silk weavers' union, who had gone to the publishing house to pay for the printing of *Silk Weavers' Bulletin*, a CCP-edited periodical. Unhappily for the fate of the silk weavers' movement, Tao made a full confession to the secret police, exposing many of his comrades.[146] The union was taken over by GMD agents (under the auspices of the Military Statistical Bureau) until turncoat Tao was deemed reliable enough to resume the directorship.[147] Stripped of their base at the District Three Union, Communist organizers lost a major foothold in the silk-weaving industry.

The stalwarts who remained were soon threatened by another Guomindang offensive. In March 1948 Communist labor leader Wang Zhongyi was arrested and CCP membership name lists in his possession were seized (see Chapter 6). The silk-weaving industry had been one of Wang's areas of primary responsibility, and the confiscated lists contained the names and addresses of most of the remnant Communist silk weavers. Thirty-two individuals were promptly arrested, 7 turned themselves in, and another 43 fled the factories for the New Fourth Army.[148] Although decimated by these government assaults, radicalism within the silk-weaving industry was not eliminated.[149] And at the time of Communist victory in 1949, the Party secretary of the underground Communist Labor Committee, Zhang Qi, was none other than a former Meiya worker (a skilled craftsman at Factory Number Six) who had been a leader in the strike of 1934.[150]

The key role weavers came to play in Shanghai's radical labor movement was very much the product of their experience during the Nanjing decade. Over the course of that difficult period, silk weavers lost many of their aristocratic privileges but gained solidarity with other industrial workers. As Michael Hanagan has described the process elsewhere: "The growth of a proletariat did not by itself produce mass strikes. . . . Instead, the growth of a proletariat *alongside* a mass of threatened artisans, artisans who acted as catalytic agents of working-class revolt, produced mass strike protest."[151]

Developments during the Guomindang era helped to make the silk weavers of Shanghai a "mass of threatened artisans" who would play a "catalytic" role in the Chinese labor movement. As recent scholarship on the British labor aristocracy has made clear, factory artisans are distinguished not merely by their higher wages but by a culture of solidarity that emphasizes mutual aid and inclines them toward efforts at unionization.[152] Labor aristocrats commonly engage in collective action to maintain their privileged status. Although such activity often bespeaks a fundamental conservatism on the part of this favored segment of the working class,[153] under certain economic and political circumstances the effort to preserve customary privilege can have radical repercussions.[154] For the silk weavers of Shanghai, the Nationalist period brought just such economic and political circumstances.

Initially in 1930, and then more dramatically in 1934, the battle was led by the privileged sector of the weaving community, concentrated in the relatively prosperous Meiya Company. These early strikes had much in common with classic artisan protests in other parts of the world. The *canuts* of Lyons, France—silk weavers who launched massive strikes in 1831 and 1834, described by Robert Bezucha—bear a resemblance to Shanghai strikers a century later. By Bezucha's account, these were highly educated workers (70 percent of the male weavers were literate) who enjoyed relative affluence and a distinct popular culture. Based on mutual aid societies, the weavers' strikes were "evidence not of dislocation, but of efforts at community organization. Far from being an uprooted, 'dangerous class,' they fought only when their future appeared gravely threatened."[155]

The threat facing Shanghai silk weavers in the early 1930s was the result of a drastic decline in the international market for their products. But global depression was certainly not the only precipitant. Changes in the Shanghai silk-weaving industry itself were another key ingredient. As the highly mechanized Meiya Company captured an ever greater share of a once competitive field, its search for profits (exacerbated, of course, by anxieties about the world depression) undermined earlier guarantees of worker welfare. Skilled workers then responded in what they considered an act of self-defense.

The utter failure of the Meiya strikes led to further change in the organization of the Shanghai silk-weaving industry. Most notably, a loom rental system reduced the artisans' autonomy and blurred differences between aristocratic Meiya employees and other weavers in the city. Under these conditions, unionization efforts by ambitious government agents gained headway in 1936–37. The result was a more acrimonious and politicized style of struggle which, although bereft of the "moral economy" flavor of earlier protests, helped to prepare the way for alliance with Communist revolutionaries in the wartime and postwar periods. In those years leading to the overthrow of the Guomindang regime, silk weavers reclaimed a radical voice, often speaking on behalf of the revolutionary cause.

Conclusion

Dominated as it was by domestic Chinese capital, Shanghai silk offers an instructive case of an industry whose strikes clearly did not arise from resentment against foreign control. Instead, location within the production process itself emerges as a critical variable.

By spotlighting several different categories of silk workers—unskilled reelers, "traditional" weavers at small enterprises, urbanized weavers at larger factories—this chapter has aimed to illuminate a range of working conditions and protest styles in a single sector of textile production. Filature workers, bound to the countryside by familial obligations and constrained by the dictates of powerful Number Ones, enjoyed relatively little latitude in the political arena. Chain reaction strikes to escape the monotony of the workplace were certainly within the realm of possibility, but a more sustained political commitment was unusual. For weavers, whose production skills ensured somewhat more secure urban employment and greater scope for protest, organized political action was more feasible. But even within the ranks of weavers, important differences can be discerned. Older workers, with long family histories of weaving in rural areas, whose recent exodus to the city was dictated by economic duress, gravitated toward forms of labor organization in which gangster involvement was often prominent. By contrast, the younger and better-educated workers at Meiya and other large-scale factories tended toward a more radical style of politics. Eventually these weavers became an important source of support for the Communist labor movement in Shanghai.

If differentiation among the workers was so pronounced in a domestically controlled industry like silk, can the same be said for the other wing of Shanghai textile production—cotton? Or did the greater involvement of foreign capital contribute to a more cohesive work force in the cotton mills? Cotton, though somewhat less dramatically divided by skill differences between spinners and weavers, nevertheless did contain important intraindustry variation. Most of the workers were unskilled or semiskilled women, but a small group of skilled male craftsmen commanded the highest wages and most secure working conditions. Again and again, we find this privileged segment of the work force standing at the forefront of Communist activities in the cotton industry. During 1925–27, for example, the important Party-sponsored textile union at the Rihua cotton mill in Pudong was chaired by a woodworker.[156] At the same time, CCP membership at the large Hengfeng factory was drawn predominantly from lower staff and copper fitters in the machine room.[157] The Party branch at the Dakang cotton mill, established in 1938, was organized by a former mechanic at the factory.[158]

In the famous February 2, 1948, strike at the Shenxin Number Nine cotton mill—often characterized as evidence of unskilled women workers' activism in the revolutionary struggle—Communist leadership was in the hands of a male metalworker, and strike headquarters were located in the machine shop. In fact, the Communist Party had targeted Shenxin Number Nine as a promising location for revolutionary activities precisely because it employed a higher proportion of male workers than most cotton mills. During the course of the strike, gender conflict threatened to sap the strength of the protest when male CCP members attacked the leader of the women workers. Accusing her of being on cozy terms with management and the Guomindang, they forced her into an unlit room and grabbed her by the throat in what may well have been a rape attempt. Although she was rescued by other women workers, her vocal chords were so severely injured in the assault that she could not speak for days.[159]

Gender was clearly an important basis of disunity among textile workers. Women tended to be employed as unskilled laborers, and men typically occupied the more advantaged artisanal jobs. Privileged (by native place and educational background as well as working conditions) vis-à-vis their female co-workers, male textile employees were apt to identify more easily with Communist student-cadres (who were overwhelming men from their same native regions) than with women in adjoining workshops.

The inability of Communist cadres to make substantial headway in the silk filatures was undoubtedly related to the dearth of mechanics (who in the Shanghai context were almost invariably men from Jiangnan) in these factories. Enduring attachments of women reelers to their rural roots further discouraged affiliation with a partisan cause. The organizational initiatives of gangster Mu Zhiying, backed first by assemblymen from Subei and then by filature owners themselves, relied on the cooperation of factory forewomen. Even so, they were short-lived. And less successful still were Communist overtures toward the women reelers.

That gender alone was not the issue, however, is dramatically illustrated by the example of silk weavers at Meiya and other mechanized companies. There educated young Jiangnan women, who had made a fundamental break with the countryside, showed themselves just as inclined as their male colleagues to engage in partisan activity. The situation was, however, quite different at the many smaller silk-weaving enterprises where women remained relegated to less skilled work. At those factories, displaced rural weavers became key constituents of the gangster-GMD unions established in 1936–37. Their strikes lacked the substantial female participation and demands for gender equality characteristic of the Meiya struggles.

The political propensities of different groups of textile workers thus bore a systematic (though never automatic) relationship to the underlying divisions of working-class life. It was not that gender, native place, or occupation in and of themselves caused a particular political disposition. Rather, these attributes were associated with different social networks (e.g., sisterhoods, brotherhoods, mutual aid societies, guilds, gangs), which in turn aligned variously with Communist, Guomindang, or independent movements. For this reason intraclass divisions did not immobilize the workers of Shanghai, who were instead well organized for distinctive, albeit often conflicting, styles of struggle.

CHAPTER NINE

Transport

FEW INDUSTRIES WERE MORE critical to the general health of the Shanghai economy than transport. A coordinated and efficient flow of products and people was essential for the city's commercial and industrial development. Perhaps no Shanghai industry was more obviously fragmented than transport, however. Electrically powered trains and tramways and human-powered wheelbarrows and rickshaws all conveyed large numbers of goods and residents from one part of the city to another, but they did so by very different means. Variation in technology was accompanied by differentiation in the composition of the work force and, in turn, by divided politics.

In contrast to tobacco and textiles, the transport industry was staffed almost entirely by male workers. Thus although native place and skill level appear once again as salient influences, gender was not a significant line of division in the workplace politics of this segment of the labor force. This chapter examines the political proclivities of Shanghai transport workers, focusing particularly on tramways and rickshaws.

The Tramway Industry

During the Republican period, Shanghai was served by three tramway companies, corresponding to the three governments that ruled the city. The French Tramway, Electric and Water Company was founded in 1905 to provide public utilities to residents of the French Concession. As BAT was the giant of British investment in Shanghai, so the French Tramway Company (FTC) was by far the largest repository of French capital in the city. In 1908 the Shanghai Tramway Company (STC) was established, initially as a joint venture with Chinese capitalists. But soon this company, which supplied public transportation to the International Settlement, was taken over by the British. Finally in 1912 the Chinese Tramway Company (CTC) was founded to provide service to the Chinese-controlled area of Nanshi.

Despite different nationalities of ownership, the three tramway companies operated in a remarkably similar manner.[1] Each was separated into a machine department (known officially as the *jiwu bu* and popularly as the *tongjiang jian,* or copper fitters' room) and a traffic department (or *chewu bu*). In each of the three companies, the majority of workers served as conductors or drivers in the traffic department, while a smaller number of more skilled laborers were employed as technicians in the machine department. No women workers could be found in either department. In addition, some 10 to 20 percent of the company's employees held staff positions. Most of the staff (who in the case of FTC had been educated in French Catholic schools and in the case of STC in Anglo-American Protestant schools) worked as accountants in the general office or as supervisors in the traffic department; very few were assigned to the machine department.

The geographical origins of workers in the two main sections of the company were rather different. Traffic department employees came mainly from the North; most drivers were recruited from Subei or the provinces of Hubei, Hebei, or Shandong. Machine department workers hailed from the more affluent areas of Shanghai and Ningbo. Work conditions in the two departments were also different. Drivers and conductors spent most of their workday isolated in separate trolley cars, under the supervision of a bevy of inspectors, which militated against worker solidarity. It also afforded an opportunity for graft on the part of the inspectors and their minions among the traffic crew, few of whom could resist the temptation to line their own pockets with a percentage of ticket sales.* By contrast, mechanics labored in close proximity to one another. As skilled technicians who were not easily replaced, they also received higher wages and averaged a longer work tenure with the company. The "elite" origins, concentrated working conditions, greater job security, and relative freedom from staff supervision fostered cohesion and militance on the part of the mechanics.†

*On corruption among traffic inspectors, see Zhu Bangxing, Hu Linge, and Xu Sheng, eds., *Shanghai chanye yu Shanghai Zhigong* [Shanghai industry and Shanghai workers] (Shanghai, 1984), p. 241. Passengers were routinely charged higher fares than the actual ticket value. The ticket value was duly remitted to the company, but the traffic crew would pocket the difference between it and the fare charged (*Shen bao,* Dec. 18, 1939). The traffic crew also colluded with pickpockets. See John Pal, *Shanghai Saga* (New York, 1963), pp. 191–92.

†*Shanghai Fadian gongren yundong lishi ziliao* [Historical materials on the labor movement at Shanghai's French Tramway Company] (Shanghai, 1957), 1: 1–15; Zhu Bangxing et al., *Shanghai chanye,* pp. 241–44, 265, 275–77, 369. At CTC, although the

In all of Shanghai's tramway companies, the split between the two departments had similar political repercussions. Mechanics were typically at the forefront of unionization activities and politically motivated strikes. (All three companies were subject to a fairly high level of strike activity, but foreign ownership was evidently not a major contributory factor. Of the 44 strikes that occurred between 1918 and 1940, 11 took place at the French Tramway Company, 15 at the Chinese Tramway Company, and 18 at the British-owned Shanghai Tramway Company.*) Drivers and conductors were subservient to the dictates of the gangster-inspectors under whose supervision they labored. Though far from quiescent,[2] the traffic crew was less likely to become embroiled in radical protest.

This difference was evident in the May Thirtieth Movement, when a sympathetic strike by mechanics at the British-owned Shanghai Tramway Company was undermined by recalcitrants within the traffic department.[3] Shortly thereafter three mechanics, members of the Communist Party, founded a union at the company. Their chief opposition came from an inspector in the traffic department, Ni Tiansheng. A former bathhouse masseur, Ni was a Green Gang member with numerous disciples among drivers and conductors from Subei. To discourage workers at STC from participating in the new union, Ni rewarded those who declined to join with gifts of phonographs and mahjong sets. Unionization proceeded rapidly only after Ni Tiansheng was assassinated by radicals in the machine department.[4] Antipathy between the two departments persisted, however. Prejudices growing out of their divergent native-place backgrounds prevented traffic crews and mechanics from cooperating in any sustained fashion, as was borne out during a 23-day strike in 1930 when drivers acted as scabs to force an early return to work.† A decade

---

minimum and maximum wage was the same in both departments, workers clustered at opposite ends of the scale. While 77 percent of mechanics received a monthly wage of more than 40 yuan in 1938, only 58 percent of drivers and 41 percent of conductors received this wage (Zhu Bangxing et al., *Shanghai chanye*, p. 373).

* *Shanghai Strike Statistics, 1918–1940.* These strikes, moreover, had a high success rate, with 84 percent resulting in either total or partial victories for the strikers. Strikes at the French Tramway Company showed the highest rate of success (91 percent), followed by the Chinese Tramway Company (87 percent), while the British-owned Shanghai Tramway Company was the least generous to strikers (61 percent success rate).

† Zhu Bangxing et al., *Shanghai chanye*, p. 267. A police report noted that the six principal leaders of the 1930 strike were employed in the machine department: four as fitters, one as a turner, and one as a carpenter. The general manager refused to negotiate with the strikers' delegation, arguing that they were unrepresentative of the workers. Instead he supplied the names of eighteen conductors whom he considered suitable representatives (*Shanghai Municipal Police Files*, D-1207). In 1937, when drivers and conductors had become more active in union affairs, Du Yuesheng played a central role in mediating disputes at STC, even paying 6,000 yuan from his personal account to settle a strike (ibid., D-4176/1).

later, conductors in the traffic department served as the core leadership of a collaborationist union established under Japanese auspices.[5]

At the Chinese Tramway Company, a parallel situation prevailed. After the April 12 coup, workers in the machine department constituted an "Old Faction" in conflict with the "New Faction" of drivers and conductors. Whereas the Old Faction remained loyal to the (now defunct) Communist-led General Labor Union, the New Faction pledged allegiance to Green Gang labor leaders Zhu Xuefan and Lu Jingshi. In one particularly acrimonious confrontation, members of the New Faction arrived equipped with revolvers, firecrackers, and red cloth. Allegedly they had planned to detonate firecrackers so as to muffle the sounds of gunfire, after which they would plant incriminating pieces of red cloth on the bodies of their victims among the Old Faction in hopes of placing them under posthumous political suspicion. The scheme was thwarted, but it further divided CTC's warring factions.[6]

Although a similar political bifurcation existed in all of the city's transport companies, the pattern was most pronounced at the French Tramway Company. Like the British American Tobacco Company, FTC became a hotbed of Communist organization during the Three Armed Uprisings and the site of intense Guomindang-Communist rivalry in the years immediately following the April 12 coup. (Again like BAT, the French Tramway Company was a highly profitable enterprise.*) In view of the important role the company played in the Shanghai labor movement, its story is worth detailed scrutiny.

The French Tramway Company

Considering the prominence that the French Tramway Company would come to attain in the designs of both Communist and Nationalist labor strategists, it is interesting that the company had little previous history of labor unrest. Aside from a brief show of sympathy during the May Fourth Movement of 1919, its first strike occurred in the spring of 1921 when employees of the traffic department demanded, and received, a 20 percent wage increase.[7] Not for another five years—this time under Communist supervision—did another strike take place.

Initial Communist efforts to organize at FTC met with little success. In the spring of 1923, the Party dispatched a member of the Socialist Youth League to work as a conductor. The brash young cadre alienated many of his fellow workers. A few months later, the Party sent another

---

*Edward Hammond estimates that the company saw a growth in capital value of over 10,000 percent during the first forty years of its existence ("Organized Labor in Shanghai, 1927–1937," [Ph.D. dissertation, University of California, 1978], p. 175).

organizer—a student returned from France. But this urbane intellectual, who could speak no Shanghai dialect, also failed to develop close relations with the workers.[8]

Communist overtures toward the French Tramway work force made little headway for several more years. In January 1926, Yu Maohuai, a Communist who had formerly been employed as a skilled worker at the Nanyang Tobacco Company, was hospitalized for an illness. In the hospital, Yu met two FTC conductors who were recuperating from traffic injuries. Discussions among them apparently convinced Yu of the potential for organizing at the company. Through the introduction of friends who worked as mechanics at the British Tramway Company, Yu obtained a temporary job in the machine department of FTC. There he got to know a young mechanic named Xu Amei, who would soon become the leader of Communist mobilization efforts at the company. Xu had been born twenty years earlier into a family of vegetable farmers whose land was located in the French Concession. The family holdings were later taken over by the French Tramway Company when it expanded its offices. At age seventeen, Xu Amei, after a four-year apprenticeship in the Jiangnan Shipyard, joined the machine department of FTC. Perhaps in part because of resentment toward the company over the loss of his family's land, Xu Amei was an immediate convert to the radical message delivered by Yu Maohuai when he entered the machine department three years later. Soon Xu became a member of the Communist Party branch that Yu established at FTC in October 1926. He was also a key participant in the inauguration of the French Tramway workers' union that December.[9]

Under the leadership of skilled workers in the machine department, the French Tramway Company was a major base of Communist operations during the Three Armed Uprisings. With more than 50 CCP members among them, the workers of FTC served as the main fighting force in the district of Nanshi.[10] Under the leadership of Yu Maohuai, pickets from FTC joined those from CTC and the Jiangnan Arsenal and, after occupying the local police station, took control of the arsenal.[11] Once the fighting had subsided, FTC workers—minus 46 pickets who remained stationed at workers' picket headquarters—marched triumphantly back to work accompanied by a hired military band and carrying banners that read: "The workers' revolution has succeeded! Down with imperialism! Liquidate the reactionaries!" The French general manager removed his hat in a respectful gesture of welcome to his emboldened workers.[12] Only two weeks later, however, the government crackdown of April 12 resulted in the dismissal of the 46 FTC pickets and prompted Yu Maohuai to flee the city, abandoning union activities at the company to Guomindang control. On October 4, 1928 a government-sponsored labor union was established at FTC. Although Xu Amei was a member of the union's standing committee, real power was held by Guomindang elements.[13]

In December 1928 the murder of an FTC driver by drunken French sailors precipitated a 24-day strike at the company. With committed participation by workers in the traffic division, this strike was settled only through the intervention of gangster Du Yuesheng. From his personal funds, Du provided 9,000 yuan in strike pay, promise of a monthly subsidy of 200 yuan for the union, and individual payoffs of 200 yuan to each of the workers' representatives.[14] The Communist Party made every effort to expose the corruption of Du Yuesheng and the GMD-controlled union, issuing a steady stream of handbills to this effect.[15] Xu Amei refused to accept the sellout, and his followers in the machine department briefly continued the strike. After being kidnapped and harassed by right-wing elements from the traffic department, however, Xu dropped out of the officially sponsored union and limited his organizational efforts to his fellow mechanics. Spending most of his spare time at teahouses frequented by his co-workers, Xu developed a reputation for recounting stories from popular novels such as *Water Margin* and *Romance of the Three Kingdoms*, relating these tales to contemporary labor struggles.[16]

Over the next year and a half, several successful strikes and slowdowns were launched by Xu's followers within the machine department. In May 1930, as the mechanics were gearing up for yet another walkout, Du Yuesheng intervened to warn Xu that a strike during the month of May would be construed as a Communist-inspired affair, liable to elicit the harshest repression. If only the workers would wait, promised Du, he would be able to help them attain their demands. After some deliberation, Xu Amei and his followers decided to follow the gangster's suggestion. This compromise earned Xu the wrath of the Jiangsu CCP, then under the influence of leftist adherents of the Li Lisan line. Charging that Xu Amei had sold out to yellow unionism, the Party expelled him from its ranks.[17]

Despite this setback, Xu remained active in labor organizing. The following month, 700 mechanics under his direction stopped work to demand a wage increase. To counter the militance of the mechanics, Li Linshu, an inspector in the traffic department and a follower of Du Yuesheng, organized a recreation club based on the Subei, Hubei, and Beiyang gangs among the traffic department workers. Under Li's instructions, conductors and drivers in the traffic department initially withheld support for the strike.* But when the strikers marched on the recreation club offices in an effort to win over members of the traffic department, police suppression left an innocent bystander dead. The result was an outburst of public sympathy for the strike,[18] which now expanded to include drivers, conductors, and even staff. The French were hopeful of ending the struggle before Bastille Day so that the Concession might be illuminated with decorative lights, as was customary for the occasion. But with the entire company (including electricians) still out on strike, the holiday came and went in darkness.

Mindful of the gangster's earlier promise, the strikers turned to Du Yuesheng for help in reaching a settlement.† Finally, after 57 days of intense negotiation in which Du played a key role, the strike was settled in an agreement that met all of the workers' demands.** A celebratory banquet, embellished by lights and other festive decorations, was convened at a local Ningbo restaurant. Then the strikers returned to work.[19]

Despite this seemingly amicable conclusion, the company retaliated by dismissing 40 workers who had been active in the conflict. Although those from the traffic department were soon reinstated, the 32 mechanics (including Xu Amei) were permitted to return to work only after a slowdown in the machine department forced management's hand. Welcomed back on the job with firecrackers and a company-provided car, Xu Amei quickly set about instigating another successful slowdown among the mechanics, this time over the issue of an annual bonus.[20]

The division between workers in the machine and traffic departments

---

*"Shanghai Fashang dianche," p. 10. At one point members of the traffic crew took a more aggressive tack in opposing the mechanics' strike. When machine department workers were walking back from a strike meeting in the Chinese district of Nanshi, an FTC tramcar suddenly drove right into the midst of the marchers to disperse them. One mechanic was seriously injured and others then proceeded to smash the tramcar in revenge. Finally the melee was quelled by Chinese police (Zhu Bangxing et al., *Shanghai chanye*, p. 330).

†The French were also anxious for Du to become involved, threatening him with a prohibition on gambling and opium dens in the Concession unless he negotiated an acceptable settlement. See Xue Gengshen, "Wo yu jiu Shanghai Fazujie" [The old French Concession of Shanghai and I], *Wenshi ziliao xuanji*, 1979, no. 6, p. 156; Xue Gengshen, "Wo jiechuguo de Shanghai ganghui renwu" [Shanghai gangsters I have known], in *Jiu Shanghai de banghui* [The gangsters of old Shanghai] (Shanghai, 1986), p. 92.

**Zhu Bangxing et al., *Shanghai chanye*, pp. 316–50; Jiang Along, "Wushiqitian dabagong" [The 57-day great strike], in *Zai jianku douzheng de suiyue li*, Shanghai, 1958), p. 13. Jiang Peinan, "Xu Amei," in *Zhongguo gongren yundong de xianqu* [Pioneers of the Chinese labor movement] (Beijing, 1984), 3:206–13. Leftist elements within the CCP remained hostile to Xu Amei's pragmatic methods. During the strike, handbills issued by his detractors accused the labor leader of being altogether too cozy with the GMD authorities and Du Yuesheng. See *Huangsegou Xu Amei gongkai chumai Fadian bagong xun* [Bulletin on yellow dog Xu Amei's open betrayal of the French Tramway strike], archives of the Bureau of Investigation, Taipei, #556.282/803.

had been bridged, but only temporarily, in the summer of 1930. A year later, the rift widened. When a mechanic who had been strolling along the Bund one morning bent down to pick up a coin he had inadvertently dropped, an approaching FTC trolley car was forced to slam on the brakes to avoid a collision. Indignant about the near accident, the driver and three conductors beat up the hapless mechanic. The injured mechanic reported the incident to his fellow workers in the machine department, who were furious at the violent treatment to which he had been subjected. Together they presented a set of demands to the company, proposing that the traffic department set off firecrackers in a gesture of apology to the machine department, the driver and conductors involved in the incident be dismissed and inspector Li Linshu be discharged for his complicity, the company guarantee that such incidents would not recur, and the company notify the traffic department that drivers and conductors were prohibited from assaulting people and ensure that the guilty driver and conductors be apprehended and held in custody in the machine department. After a morning of negotiations, the company agreed to pay 100 yuan for firecrackers, to discharge Li Linshu if he had been involved in the incident, and to guarantee that similar problems would not occur in the future. That same afternoon, however, Li Linshu stirred up some of his followers in the traffic department to exact revenge; a melee ensued in which several FTC workers were injured and hospitalized.[21]

Antagonism between the traffic and machine departments had reached the point of open warfare. At this juncture Li Linshu's backstage boss, Du Yuesheng, called on his friends in the French police force to have Xu Amei arrested on grounds of subversion. In September 1931, Xu was imprisoned. With the influential young mechanic out of the picture, Green Gang leaders found it easier to exercise control over the French Tramway union. Thus, it was under these changed circumstances that Du Yuesheng fomented a brief strike at FTC in the summer of 1932, a successful ploy to improve his bargaining position vis-à-vis the French authorities.[22]

When Xu Amei was released from prison in the spring of 1937, however, the tables were turned once again. Soon after Xu had resumed his old job at the company, he secretly organized a "brotherhood of ten," consisting of activists in the machine department. This group was the backbone of a successful slowdown launched by mechanics for higher wages in 1939. Under its flexible wartime policy, the Communist Party welcomed Xu Amei back into its ranks. At the same time, however, the mechanic's involvement in the National Salvation movement aroused the hostility of pro-Japanese forces in the city; in December 1939 he was assassinated by agents of Wang Jingwei.* Leadership of the Communist movement at FTC was passed along to Huang Fulin, a Shanghai-born mechanic who had apprenticed for several years at the Shenyang Arsenal before returning to his native city. In 1939 Huang entered the CCP, becoming secretary of a newly founded Party branch at FTC the following year. In 1941, he directed a strike in the machine department. His political identity was exposed in the course of the struggle, however, and Huang fled Shanghai to join the New Fourth Army.[23] The tragic demise of Xu Amei and the flight of Huang Fulin were a lesson to other Communist labor leaders at FTC, who now appreciated the need for some outside affiliation to camouflage their activities. Contacts were accordingly made with Red Gang leader Li Fang (ambassador to Germany under the Wang Jingwei regime), and by the war's end nearly 300 Red Gang members could be counted among the FTC work force. These gang members offered a base for Communist-inspired struggles in both the machine and traffic departments.[24]

Red Gang connections, though less salient after the war, left a legacy of improved relations between the machine and traffic departments. Building on this newfound harmony, workers at FTC organized the first union in postwar Shanghai. Cooperation between the two departments of the company was evident in a joint protest undertaken shortly after the Japanese surrender. When the Nationalists regained control of the city, strikes and slowdowns in public utilities were declared illegal. Mechanics at FTC, anxious to obtain guarantee of an annual bonus, came up with an innovative plan for getting around the prohibition. Workers in the traffic department were quick to implement the scheme, which called for drivers to continue driving on schedule while conductors simply stopped selling tickets. To the delight of the startled passengers, they were greeted upon boarding the trolley by a smiling conductor with a hospitable message: "Make yourselves at home. Today the ride is on us." Meanwhile, mechanics formed pickets to maintain order and decorated the trolleys with slogans explaining the workers' demand for higher compensation. For obvious reasons, this style of protest—known as the "grand invitational" (da qingke)—was immensely popular among ordinary citizens.† To the company, however, it was extremely costly. A nor-

*Jiang Peinan, "Xu Amei," pp. 220–22; "Shanghai Fashang dianche," p. 16. In 1950, Shanghai's Number Three Tramway Company (formerly the FTC) placed a tombstone commemorating Xu Amei in the Hongqiao public cemetery. During the Cultural Revolution, however, Xu was decried as a "traitor" by revolutionary rebels at the company and his tombstone was smashed.

†According to Chinese sources, the protest tactic was the invention of the FTC strikers. One source attributes the idea to the Communist leadership (Zhang Haopo, "Fadian gongren 'da qingke' zhuiji" [Remembered notes on the FTC workers' "grand

mal strike had the advantage of closing down operations altogether. In the invitational, however, there was no reduction in operating expenses to offset the loss of revenue. Under severe economic pressure, management acceded to the protesters' demands for an annual bonus and strike pay. Similar invitationals soon spread to workers in restaurants, bathhouses, and barbershops.[25]

As a direct result of the victory of the invitational, CCP membership at the French Tramway Company tripled, rising from 20 to 60. Active Party branches were established in both departments of the company.[26] The high priority which Party organizers placed on FTC helped catapult its workers to the forefront of labor militance in the postwar period. In the spring of 1947, all 2,400 employees marched on the Bureau of Social Affairs to register displeasure with the government's freezing of the cost-of-living index.* That fall, FTC workers joined with comrades in the British and Chinese tramway companies in a general strike to protest the Futong Incident (see Chapter 6).[27] In March 1948, radical organizing at the company suffered a serious setback when longtime CCP leader Wang Zhongyi was arrested. A search of Wang's residence uncovered a name list of more than 30 Communists in FTC's machine department, 14 of whom were promptly arrested. Nevertheless, by the following year Party membership at FTC had grown to an unprecedented 137.[28] As Red Army troops approached Shanghai in the spring of 1949, more than 700 workers at FTC joined a picket force to maintain order, patrolling the company to ensure that no matériel would be removed to Taiwan.[29] Two months after Shanghai fell under Communist rule, workers at French Tramway were the first in the city to form a new labor union.[30]

---

invitational"], in *Shanghai yishi* [Shanghai anecdotes] [Shanghai, 1987], p. 184). Another source attributes the invention to ordinary FTC workers (" 'Da qingke' douzheng chongpo bagong jinling de" [The grand invitational struggle's breach of the strike ban], *Shanghai gongyun shiliao*, 1987, no. 4, pp. 22, 28). It is probably more than coincidental, however, that just one month earlier workers on Tokyo's Keisei Electric Railway had engaged in exactly the same sort of protest—refusing to collect fares on cars that continued to operate. (Unlike Shanghai passengers, who were immediately enthusiastic about the invitational, in Japan "at the beginning the disciplined passengers felt uneasy about not paying.") See Theodore Cohen, *Remaking Japan: The American Occupation as New Deal* (New York, 1987), p. 219. I am grateful to Jeffrey Wasserstrom for suggesting this connection.

*Jiang Along and Chen Longxiang, "Fadian gongren yaoqiu jiedong shenghuo zhishu de douzheng," [The struggle of French Tramway workers demanding unfreezing of the cost-of-living index], *Shanghai gongyunshi yanjiu ziliao*, 1982, no. 3, p. 47. At that time, the police reported finding political slogans on the windows of FTC tramcars: "All businessmen are traitors!" "All bureaucrats are corrupt!" "Why has our wealthy mayor frozen the cost-of-living index?" Since the slogans were scratched with a hard implement through white paint, the police suspected that the deed had been committed by conductors using their ticket punch or door key (Shanghai Municipal Archives, #1-7-48).

Like the British American Tobacco Company, the French Tramway Company has figured prominently in studies of the Shanghai labor movement as an outstanding example of worker activism. Indeed, the workers at FTC did compile an impressive record of strikes and union organization over a three-decade period. But it is noteworthy that the company's history of labor strife began only with the May Fourth Movement. Lacking a "proletarian" work force such as was found in textile or tobacco factories, FTC was spared the "spontaneous struggles" that erupted at such enterprises in the first two decades of the century. Yet the skilled and semiskilled workers at FTC became exceptionally active under the influence of Communist and Green Gang labor leaders in the 1920's–1940's. As in other firms in which these outside political forces gained a solid footing, the reception varied along the lines of preexisting divisions within the work force.

It was not beyond the realm of possibility for tramway workers to act together in a manner celebrated by theorists of revolution, but the more common pattern was to divide along lines of skill and native place. Only when Communists compromised with secret society leaders were they able to build a united base of support among a work force whose internal contradictions often undermined its potential for solidarity.

Rickshaw Pullers

If tramway workers illustrate differences in background and political allegiances between skilled and semiskilled workers, the transport industry also had unskilled laborers. Rickshaw pullers, widely regarded as the consummate unskilled Chinese workers, made up a sizable group. Following its introduction to Shanghai in 1874 by a Frenchman, the rickshaw quickly became a popular mode of transportation around the city. Although their numbers fluctuated greatly according to the season, rickshaw pullers in Shanghai were estimated to average some 35,000 in 1920, 80,000 in 1934, and 100,000 in 1938.[31] Thus despite advances in mechanized forms of public transportation and strenuous efforts by government authorities to limit their numbers, rickshaw pullers were certainly not a dying breed in early twentieth-century Shanghai (see Appendix C).

The overwhelming majority of pullers came from peasant families in Subei. A survey of 100 Shanghai rickshaw pullers conducted in 1929 found that 85 percent were of peasant origin; of these, 92 percent still owned land back home.[32] Since most rickshaw companies in Shanghai were run by Subei people, particularly from the impoverished counties of Yancheng and Funing, it was natural that new arrivals from the region would find work in this trade.[33] As one aged rickshaw puller explained: "I'm sixty-two years of age, from Yancheng County. Our family has five or six mou of land, but it borders the sea and is now inundated by saltwater. Due to natural disaster in Subei, my wife, son, daughter, and I fled to Shanghai. Because of my age, I couldn't find a regular job so I went to see a rickshaw owner from my native place."[34] Bonds between employer and worker were further strengthened because most pullers (who typically came to Shanghai without their families) lived right at the rickshaw company, sleeping side by side on the floor of crudely constructed lofts above the office. Pullers with dependents tended to live in self-constructed shantytowns without benefit of running water, sewage, or insulation from the elements.[35]

Rickshaw pulling generated insufficient income to maintain a working-class family. In 1934, pullers averaged a monthly income of under nine yuan yet family expenses amounted to more than sixteen yuan. Even a bachelor could seldom make ends meet because the expenses of a single puller averaged more than ten yuan a month. As a consequence, many pullers fell deeply into debt.[36]

Considering the unhappy circumstances of their existence in Shanghai, it was perhaps not surprising that rickshaw pullers tended to maintain close ties with the rural areas from which they had come.* As a middle-aged puller described his situation:

> I'm thirty-six, from Yancheng. Two years ago I came to Shanghai because of natural calamity at home. I have four brothers; I'm Number Two. My eldest brother works in a lightbulb factory. Numbers Three and Five farm in Subei. Number Four also pulls a rickshaw in Shanghai. We five brothers have already divided the family property [fenjia], with each of us receiving thirteen mou of land. After I moved here, my landholdings were managed by my wife. But this year another natural disaster forced her and my six children to move to Shanghai. Now my land is being looked after by my younger brothers to help take care of our parents. After my parents die I'll reclaim the land.[37]

Even unmarried rickshaw pullers tended to maintain close contacts with relatives back in Subei. A nineteen-year-old bachelor from Funing remarked: "I haven't married because I'm not well off, but when I want to marry it will be easy because I have many relatives in Subei to help out. My uncle has no son so I've been made his heir. Now he's farming his

---

*Continuing native-place identification on the part of pullers and their families sometimes drew the Jiang-Huai Native Place Association into rickshaw affairs. This was the case in 1935 and again in 1936, when the association intervened on behalf of the families of pullers killed by foreigners in disputes over fare payment. See Number Two Archives, #722: 4-575.

more than twenty mou of land in Subei. If I have some extra money I send it back to him and if I run out of money my uncle sends me some."[38]

Many pullers went home each spring to help out with the farm work, returning to Shanghai after fall harvest.* These were true peasant-workers who kept one foot firmly planted in the countryside while the other ran through the city streets in search of a fare. When circumstances permitted, most pullers opted to return to Subei permanently. The result was an extremely high turnover rate among this sector of the Shanghai work force. A survey in 1940 showed that fewer than 30 percent of the city's rickshaw coolies had been pulling for three years, while a mere 2 percent had been pulling for as long as five years.[39]

Backbreaking though it was, the work of rickshaw pulling was easily enough learned to make it a natural occupation for peasant refugees in need of immediate employment. New pullers were instructed by more experienced colleagues in the techniques of pulling, the names and locations of city streets and landmarks, and the proper rates to charge. The apprenticeship period, known as "beating a wild chicken" (da yeji), lasted only a few days.[40] A steady stream of desperate Subei immigrants continuously replenished the ranks of Shanghai pullers. Unlike other Chinese cities, where a rickshaw was usually shared by two pullers working day and night shifts, in Shanghai the huge labor surplus meant that there were often as many as four pullers for every available rickshaw.

The intense competition among workers allowed owners to charge exorbitant rental fees mediated through an elaborate system of labor contracting. In 1919 the city's largest rickshaw enterprise, the French-owned Flying Star Company, retained sixteen major contractors to oversee the rental of its more than 2,000 rickshaws. Each major contractor, in turn, hired ten to twenty minor contractors responsible for dealing directly with the pullers. Major contractors rented the rickshaws from the company for 70 cents a day, subletting them (through minor contractors) to the pullers for a fee of 90 cents.[41] As a foreign observer remarked: "The rickshaw business, as with so many things in this wide-open town, had deteriorated into a racket. The licenses distributed each year by the Municipal Council were absorbed by a tight monopoly of rickshaw owners who, in turn, let their contractors handle the dirty work. The dirty work consisted of renting the rickshaws to the pullers."[42]

---

*Lei Jingdun, "Shanghai Yangshupu renlichefu diaocha" [Survey of rickshaw pullers in Shanghai's Yangshupu], graduation thesis, Pujiang University, Shanghai, 1930. A smaller number of pullers, from the areas of Chongming and Taizhou, engaged in peanut cultivation, putting them on an agricultural schedule opposite from that of Yancheng and Funing. These peasant-workers would go home in late fall and return to Shanghai the following spring.

As was true for most sources of easy money in Shanghai, the rickshaw trade attracted Green Gang involvement. Owners and pullers alike were drawn into the gangster orbit, in part as a method of keeping the authorities at bay. Although owners and contractors charged hefty rental fees to pullers under their employ, all parties faced a common enemy in the form of government interference. The British, French, and Chinese authorities enforced separate and expensive rickshaw licensing systems and imposed heavy fines for parking and traffic infractions. To cope with the constant police surveillance, employers as well as pullers found it necessary to enter secret society gangs. Gu Zhuxuan, the paramount Green Gang leader for Subei people in Shanghai, had joined the secret society to protect his rickshaw business from the predations of the Frenchtown police.* According to one estimate, 90 percent of pullers were also gang members.[43]

Although gangster connections helped soften the inherent tension between government authorities and rickshaw operators, hostilities still erupted periodically. As early as January 1897, more than 5,000 rickshaw and wheelbarrow pullers went on strike to register their opposition to an increase in license fees in the International Settlement.[44] In December 1915, thousands of pullers struck to protest higher rental fees in the wake of a decision by the Shanghai Municipal Council to limit the number of rickshaws in the district.[45] In April 1918, pullers rioted in response to a new Municipal Council traffic regulation prohibiting them from cruising along main thoroughfares or trolley tracks in search of passengers. Suspecting that the tramway companies were behind the new rule, the indignant rickshaw men—egged on by their contractors— threw rocks and mud on the trolley tracks and smashed tramcar windows. In the melee, one puller was shot and killed by a British policeman. Eventually, however, the protesters won a return to the status quo ante and rickshaws were again permitted to cruise the main streets of the city.[46]

Despite this feisty beginning, pullers did not become a mainstay of partisan-inspired protest during the Republican period. Although rickshaw coolies were certainly not absent from the labor strife that swept over Shanghai after the May Fourth Movement, they actually ranked

*Wang Delin, "Gu Zhuxuan zai Zhabei faji he kaishe Tianzhan wutai" [Gu Zhuxuan's rise to power in Zhabei and establishment of the Tianzhan dance hall], in *Jiu Shanghai de banghui*, p. 357. Gu had worked in the International Settlement police force, which was also very helpful to his business success; continuing connections with the British police shielded Gu's rickshaws from traffic and parking fines while operating in International Settlement territory (Huang Zhenshi, "Wo suo zhidao de Huang Jinrong" [The Huang Jinrong whom I knew], in *Jiu Shanghai de banghui*, p. 187).

TABLE II
Strikes in Shanghai's Transport Industry, 1918–40

Industry	No. of workers	No. of strikes	No. of strikes per 1,000 workers
Tramway	5,800	43	7.4
Longshore	50,000	25	0.5
Rickshaw	80,000	15	0.2

SOURCE: *Shanghai Strike Statistics, 1918–1940.*

among the least strike-prone components of the work force (see Table 11). Paternalistic relations with contractors and owners, buttressed by native-place bonds, tended to inhibit pullers from striking against their employers. Engaged in fierce competition for scarce job opportunities and working in isolation from each other, pullers lacked the employment security or on-the-job interaction that gave rise to higher levels of militance in more skilled lines of work. Widespread illiteracy also blunted awareness and interest in the larger political currents of the day. A survey of the Shanghai Bureau of Social Affairs found that only 9 percent of the rickshaw pullers could read all of the street signs in the city. The same survey noted that its interviewers had encountered great difficulty in carrying out their work not only because of the thick Subei dialect of the respondents but also because of the pullers' inability to understand "abstract" terms such as "livelihood" (*shenghuo*), "improvement" (*gailiang*), and "welfare" (*jiuji*).[47] Although this finding may tell us more about the elitist attitudes of the interviewers than about the allegedly benighted plight of their interviewees, it nevertheless indicates the substantial cultural gap that separated pullers from the city's petty urbanites. Furthermore, the rickshaw coolies' continuing attachment to a rural life-style did not incline them to devote much energy toward improving conditions of labor in a job from which they intended to escape as soon as possible.

The reluctance of rickshaw pullers to undertake sustained efforts at labor organization was reflected in their low level of unionization. A pullers' union was established after the victory of the third armed workers' uprising in 1927, but it enrolled only some 300 members and was dissolved in less than six months. In 1930, the Shanghai city government turned down a request for permission to organize a new union.[48] Not until three more years had passed was another union established with the concurrence of foreign authorities on the Shanghai Municipal Council. Known as the Pullers' Mutual Aid Association (PMAA), the new organization was supported by Chinese and foreign social reformers as well as by businessmen on the Municipal Council with interests in the city's tramway and bus companies. To reduce the profitability of the

rickshaw business while meeting the demands of reformers and pullers,*
the Municipal Council agreed to put a ceiling of 85 cents on daily rental
fees for rickshaws in the International Settlement. Moreover, 5 cents of
this rental fee was to be remitted by the owners to the PMAA to under-
write its welfare activities. Although rickshaw owners made strenuous
efforts to resist the new policy, even instigating a pullers' attack on
rickshaws operating in the Settlement in August 1934, they proved
powerless to alter the decision.[49]

The following year, the owners mounted a more forceful challenge to
new government policies in the form of a massive strike of some 40,000
pullers. The protest was prompted by a decision of the French Concession authorities to register (at a hefty fee) all rickshaws and rickshaw
pullers operating within their jurisdiction. Fearing that registration was
but the first step in an effort to restrict their business, the 250 rickshaw
owners in the Concession mobilized their contractors and coolies to
oppose the new policy. Gangsters were deployed to remove the air valves
of tires on any rickshaws that sported the new licenses, while owners
petitioned the authorities for a policy reversal. Fearful of registration and
pessimistic about the outcome of this protest, large numbers of pullers
elected to return to their homes in the Subei countryside rather than
persist in the struggle. As a reporter characterized their mentality,

> Hesitation on the part of the rickshaw coolies to come before the French
> authorities is attributed to a fear amongst some of them that the taking of
> their fingerprints will signify their adherence to the Catholic religion. Oth-
> ers labour under the belief that this measure implies that they would be
> taken to the Front in the event of another World War, while still a third party
> is under the misapprehension that it will mean leaving their wives.[50]

Whatever their motives, by one estimate as many as two-thirds of the
pullers in the French Concession had gone back home to their families in
Subei by mid-August. Desperate to keep up the pressure on the authorities, rickshaw owners began to issue food to striking coolies. Finally
gangster Du Yuesheng stepped in to negotiate a settlement whereby the
registration fee was reduced from 50 to 20 cents per rickshaw. Although
it did not satisfy either owners or pullers, the settlement was grudgingly
accepted and the struggle came to an end.[51]

The following year yet another owner-puller strike was launched, this
time in the International Settlement to demand the abolition of the

---

*As critics were quick to point out, rickshaw owners amassed hefty profits without
making any productive contribution. By 1933, the Flying Star Company was renting
out each of its 2,072 rickshaws for a daily fee of 1 yuan. Even when expenses for
licenses, repairs, and the like were deducted, the company netted 10 yuan per rickshaw per month. This added up to a net monthly income of 20,720 yuan or a yearly net
income of 248,640 yuan (Number Two Archives, #2: 2-1061).

PMAA and the registration of additional pullers. Arguing that the PMAA had provided few if any visible benefits for the more than 300,000 yuan it had collected, owners and pullers alike expressed their opposition to the association's call for further reductions in rental fees. Rather than meddling in the market, insisted its critics, the PMAA should publicly disburse its treasury to the pullers and close up shop. Needless to say, the Shanghai Municipal Council was not about to agree to the dissolution of the PMAA, but it did consent to add 5,000 pullers to the 40,000 already registered in the International Settlement.*

Sporadic strikes among rickshaw pullers continued through the Republican period, with equally lackluster results. An unpromising base of support for labor organizers of either the Communist or Nationalist persuasion, rickshaw pullers could not count on political patronage to promote their interests. Although pitied as the epitome of exploited labor, the rickshaw puller was also despised by young progressives as an uncomfortable reminder of the backward society they longed to leave behind.[52]

To be sure, radicals made occasional overtures to the rickshaw pullers, particularly during the ascendancy of the leftist line when Communist cadres in Shanghai were encouraged to reach out to the most downtrodden of the city's labor force. In September 1930, CCP labor organizers advocated a red union among Shanghai's rickshaw pullers whose numbers they estimated (probably with some exaggeration) at 120,000.[53] The following year, the GMD authorities expressed fear that "uneducated pullers" would be used by "reactionary elements"—an epithet for Communists.[54] In 1934, a Communist handbill enjoined rickshaw coolies to "Oppose the actions of the rickshaw owners!" and "Support the victories of the Red Army!"[55] During the 1935 strike in the French Concession, Communists issued a series of handbills calling on pullers to arm themselves in opposition to government, gangsters, and owners alike.[56] There is no evidence that such exhortations bore results, however. And by 1946, an order of the Administrative Yuan to phase out Shanghai's more than 20,000 rickshaws within three years made clear that this was indeed a moribund industry with limited prospects for long-term organizing.[57]

Unlike tramway workers, whose skilled and semiskilled members provided staunch support for Communist and Guomindang labor move-

---

*Xinwen yebao, Apr. 1, 1936; Li bao, Apr. 4, 1936; Da gongbao, Apr. 14, 15, 1936. Despite the public criticism, the PMAA did not markedly improve its welfare provisions. As Eleanor Hinder wrote of the association in 1944, "It is doubtful whether the authorities succeeded in ameliorating the puller's lot to any material extent. His standard of living was low in 1934 and apparently did not improve" (Life and Labour in Shanghai [New York, 1944], p. 131).

ments respectively, Shanghai's numerous rickshaw pullers allied with neither outside party.* Under the thumb of owners and contractors, rickshaw coolies enjoyed little scope for protest against their employers. Egged on by these same employers, pullers did mount periodic opposition to state regulations. But the prominent role of owners and contractors in such struggles ensured that any gains for pullers would be meager.

The relative quiescence of Shanghai's rickshaw men contrasts with the situation in Beijing, where David Strand characterizes the rickshaw pullers of 1929 as "among the most politically active groups in the city." The disparity is surely owing to the dissimilar socioeconomic circumstances of rickshaw workers in the two cities. Beijing pullers included a large percentage of urbanites—bannermen, former policemen, peddlers, unemployed craftsmen—in contrast to the overwhelmingly rural orientation of pullers in Shanghai. The Beijing rickshaw men also did not labor under a contract system, were much better off financially, and enjoyed higher levels of literacy and recreation than their Shanghai counterparts. As a result, Beijing rickshaw men "drew on the full repertoire of collective and public strategies available to city residents," whereas Shanghai pullers exemplified a much more restricted style of protest.[58]

The limited activism of Shanghai rickshaw pullers was similar to that of other unskilled workers in the transport industry who also faced a labor surplus problem. Wheelbarrow coolies and rice porters, for example, were more apt to battle one another for loading rights than to launch a united push for improved working conditions.[59] Dockworkers, as we have seen (Chapter 3), followed the lead of rival contractors in undertaking savagely competitive turf wars.

Dockworkers

Dockers were more drawn into the political conflicts of the day than most of their comrades within the unskilled sector of the transport industry largely because of the special attention that both Communists and Nationalists showered upon them. As the city's—indeed the nation's—link to the world economy, the shipping industry loomed large in the strategy of political organizers. Thus cadres of both parties went to great lengths to attract the pivotal dockworkers to their cause. It is noteworthy that their efforts yielded so few results.

Initially the Communists got off to a promising start by deploying

*In October 1937 "notorious rickshaw coolie agitator" and GMD member Chen Guoliang declared the formation of a national salvation association. According to police intelligence, however, Chen was working for his own ends with "no support from local labor unions" (*Shanghai Municipal Police Files*, D-8144).

several of their Hubei-born students to develop contacts with dock-workers from the same native place. One Party member from Hubei, Li Zian, volunteered to teach children of dockers in Pudong free of charge. The only compensation he asked was that the families of his students provide him meals at their homes. In this way, Li was able to spread his radical message among ordinary dockworking families. Such contacts became one source of dockers' participation in the May Thirtieth upris-ing.[60] Undoubtedly, however, most of the some 30,000 dockworkers who joined the three-month strike were motivated by other incentives. As an activist remembered, "We would find out who was still working and have a chat with them, telling them they would receive two dollars a week in strike pay as soon as they stopped working."[61]

The appeal of a steady income was especially great to the many tempo-rary workers, known as "wild chickens," who roamed the docks in search of employment. As another organizer recalled, "During the May Thirtieth strike, some permanent workers wanted to continue working, but we could more easily convince the wild chickens to strike. . . . After all, strikers and their dependents received twenty cents a day in strike pay."[62] Although a union of dockworkers was founded at the time of May Thirtieth, its influence did not endure much beyond the Three Workers' Armed Uprisings.*

As Party historians have pointed out, Communist inroads among dockers were inhibited by several factors. First, the mobility of wild chickens, who made up the majority of dockworkers, made it extremely difficult to assemble a stable following. Today's recruit would be gone tomorrow. Second, the more than 250 docks in the city were owned and operated by a variety of enterprises: shipping companies, cotton mills, tobacco factories, rice shops, and the like. This segmentation rendered coordinated political action a near impossibility, a problem exacerbated by the CCP's own mobilization strategy of dividing responsibilities along industrial lines. Dockers at the BAT wharves fell under a different revo-lutionary jurisdiction from their neighbors at the Rihua cotton mill, for example. Third, the power of labor contractors militated against outside organization among dockworkers in their employ. Controlling access to jobs on the wharf, contractors naturally wielded a good deal of influence over ordinary laborers. The ties were tightened by shared native-place identities, fictive kinship relations, and gang membership. These bonds

---

Shanghaigang shihua [Historical tales of the Port of Shanghai] (Shanghai, 1979), pp. 304–22. The dockers' union was organized in October 1926 by Tao Jingxuan, a Party member from Hubei who had worked on the docks and then at the Naigai Wata mills (see Chapter 4). Later that same month Tao was arrested and executed for his role in leading Pudong dockworkers' pickets during the unsuccessful first armed uprising. See Zhang Decheng, "Tao Jingxuan lieshi" [Martyr Tao Jingxuan], *Shanghai dangshi ziliao*, 1985, no. 5, pp. 39–44.

inclined dockers to follow the lead of their contractors in internecine feuds.[63]

The power of contractors also proved a barrier to Guomindang attempts to build a following among dockworkers. Offended by the unreasonable profits that contractors were extracting from workers' wages and hoping to win the gratitude of ordinary dockers, the government in 1928 passed a so-called "2-8 regulation" whereby the contractors' cut of wages would be limited to 20 percent, leaving 80 percent for the workers. This regulation aroused the immediate ire of the contractors, whose multiple layers of personnel had grown accustomed to a much larger piece of the pie. Drawing on their gangster connections, contractors throughout the 1930's prevailed upon gang members within the government to subvert implementation of the regulation. Rather than giving rise to a unified and loyal union, as lawmakers in Nanjing had imagined, the 2-8 regulation opened the door to a plethora of warring unions under the direction of rival contractors.[64]

During the War of Resistance period, returned Communist cadres tried to regain a footing among dockworkers, but results fell far short of expectations. By the war's end only fifteen CCP members could be counted among Shanghai's more than 60,000 dockworkers.[65] Workers' mobility, intraindustry segmentation, and the power of the contractors remained major stumbling blocks to revolutionary recruitment.*

Conclusion

The divisions within the Shanghai transport industry mirrored those of other industries and cities. The role of Xu Amei and his fellow mechanics in the development of a Communist labor movement at FTC paralleled the radicalism of their counterparts in tobacco production and textiles. Moreover, it resonated with the activism of mechanics in other parts of the world. As a journalist explained the participation of the skilled metalworkers of Petrograd at the time of the Russian Revolution:

> Workers in machine production are always in the forefront of every movement. . . . Turners, founders, blacksmiths, mechanics and machinists—all of these are developed people with a well formed sense of individuality and

---

*The steps the new regime took to reorganize the Shanghai wharves after 1949 reflected a recognition of these obstacles. First, in 1950–51 a campaign against labor contractors was launched. In 52 struggle sessions attended by more than 30,000 dockers, some 3,000 contractors were denounced and removed from positions of authority. Then a unified management for the Port of Shanghai was instituted, putting the city's 260 docks under central control. Finally, in 1953–54 large numbers of wild chickens were granted permanent worker status. See *Shanghaigang shihua*, pp. 336–38; Chen Gang, *Shanghaigang matou de bianqian* [Changes on the docks of the Port of Shanghai] (Shanghai, 1966), p. 66.

rather good wages. . . . The worker must think a great deal, reason in the very process of work. . . . In the form of their conversation and even their language, they are almost indistinguishable from our intellectuals. In my opinion, they are more interesting because their judgments are fresher and their convictions, once taken, are very firm.[66]

If skilled mechanics were typically in the vanguard of protests for political change, the opposite was generally the case for coolies. The difficulty of organizing a political movement among unskilled transport workers was not unique to Shanghai. Labor leaders in a port as distant as Manchester, England, faced similar obstacles in trying to unite dockers, who "were very often split into exclusive groups within the dockland community itself." As in Shanghai, the dockworkers of Manchester divided into foreman-led gangs along ethnic and religious lines: "There are, for example, Irish gangs, working for Irish foremen. . . . Catholics and Protestants are rarely found together in the same gang." Again as in Shanghai, more than half of the Manchester dockers were "floaters" or "drifters" without permanent jobs. The high level of casual employment led, in turn, to an unusually low level of interest in trade union affairs.[67]

In between these two categories of workers stood the semiskilled operatives. In the tramway traffic department, as in the tobacco rolling room, we find this intermediate sector of the working class, predominantly illiterate, employer-trained males from North China and Pudong, turning to gangster leadership. More wedded to urban life than the unskilled peasant-proletariat, this stratum of the working class was occasionally susceptible to political appeals. Yet pay, more than pride, motivated their partisan activities. The contrast with skilled mechanics was seen in December 1927 when a strike at the Shanghai Tramway Company was sparked by the death of a driver (or "motorman") who had succumbed to a stray bullet fired by a policeman. A Communist cadre active in the protest reported:

The mechanics on strike were highly indignant at the indifference of the motormen and conductors in joining the strike. . . . Explanations were given to the workers regarding the inadvisability of going to the company to receive their pay, but in vain. Their thirst for money was so strong that it was impossible for us to prevail against them on this question. . . . We found it very difficult to deal with workers who hail from Kompo [i.e., Subei]. They persisted in getting their pay and had no ears for anything else. . . . Our comrades at the old depot and among the mechanics were comparatively easy to manage.[68]

The absence of gender divisions in the Shanghai transport industry revealed the politics of place and production in especially stark fashion. Rifts along lines of native origin and skill level were particularly pro-

nounced, whether or not the enterprise was foreign or Chinese-owned.
Again it is worth reiterating that the relationship between native
place, job classification, and political behavior was indirect, mediated by
the mentality and associational habits of the workers. Moreover, this
mediation process was defined both by the peculiarities of the Shanghai
labor market and by the vagaries of partisan politics in the city. A surplus
of unskilled laborers and a dearth of skilled artisans combined to render
labor segmentation especially acute. But this phenomenon took on partisan significance only when outside organizers endeavored to attract a
working-class following. The success of their efforts was of course decided not only by workers' dispositions but also by the changing political
and economic context.

Conclusion

Most of this is a top-down study. Little about mentality.

DIFFERENT WORKERS ENGAGE in different politics. That, in a nutshell, is the argument of this book. In building the case for Shanghai, I have attempted to trace who these workers were, where they came from, what practices they brought with them to the workplace, what associations they developed there, and how such traditions and organizations shaped their patterns of collective action. Skill was found to be a key variable in differentiating among workers. Skilled, semiskilled, and unskilled workers differed in native-place origin, gender composition, and levels of education, literacy, and urbanization. Such differences were reflected not only in their mentality but also in their protests.

By linking working-class culture—mediated through workplace experience—to protest repertoires, I have tried to join the concerns of the "new labor history" (which emphasizes popular culture and shop-floor conditions) to a more conventional focus on strikes and other forms of labor militance. This connection has special historical importance for China because the divergent cultural and associational proclivities of the Shanghai working class became aligned with major political parties. Tracing the affinity of the guild-based Jiangnan artisan for the Communists or of the gang-based North China machine operator for the Guomindang reveals a good deal about the strengths and limitations of both parties. Each of these contending parties gave rise to its own state system (the Republic of China followed by the People's Republic of China) so that this study of the Shanghai labor movement is also to some extent a study of the social foundations of the modern Chinese state.

Of course, the way labor and the state have interacted in modern China is not precisely replicated elsewhere in the world. Indeed, a salutary trend in recent studies of labor is the move away from a universal model of working-class formation toward greater sensitivity to national variation.[1] But if every country's (and every city's) labor history is largely unique, the underlying variables are remarkably constant. In this chapter I review these commonalities, beginning with a look at other regions of China and then proceeding to a discussion of workers in more distant reaches of the globe.

The Chinese Comparison

Detailed studies of labor in other Chinese settings are not numerous, but the few that exist support my preoccupation with intraclass differentiation. An investigation of factory workers in the province of Yunnan during World War II highlighted the deep gulf that separated skilled workers, who hailed largely from the Jiangnan region, and unskilled workers from the interior:

> Worker #38, who came from Shanghai, is proud of his long connection with modern industry. His father was a motor repairman. His brother was also a skilled worker. They lived near a shop and during his childhood he often went there with his father and spent time playing with various gadgets. . . . He is, therefore, experienced in operating modern machines.
>
> Native laborers from the villages are familiar only with crops and the soil. . . . Chinese farmers have had no chance to acquire an elementary knowledge of mechanical tools. When they enter the factory they are completely lost. They seem to behave foolishly, because they have no industrial tradition.[2]

In Yunnan, as in Shanghai, skill and native-place origin went hand in hand. This close correlation, complained the author of the Yunnan study, led workers to overrate the importance of geographical background:

> This general belief, that promotion is related to place of origin and not to skill, is widespread. This is supported by the numerous complaints and rumors which I have gathered. . . . It is no doubt as a consequence of this that we find certain natives pretending to be of outside origin. To them the acquisition of skill has become a secondary consideration. Those who are too honest to make this pretense feel that skill is beyond their reach and become discouraged. It must be recognized that native workers are, in fact, unskilled. . . . I was surprised after interviewing them to find that many did not wish to become efficient workers. Their interest lay not there but in their homes on the land.[3]

Although the author of the Yunnan study expresses his hope that workers will rise above their obsession with native place to confront the more important issue of skill, the two factors were inextricably intertwined. This was not simply because unskilled workers remained tied to an agrarian countryside whereas skilled workers boasted a more urbanized and industrial background. It was also because the very definition of "skill" is subjective. As Charles Tilly has observed: "Skill is a social product, a negotiated identity. Although knowledge, experience, and cleverness all contribute to skill, ultimately skill lies not in characteristics of individual workers but in relations between workers and employers; a skilled worker is one who is hard to replace or do without, an unskilled worker one who is easily substitutable or dispensable."[4]

When most employers were of Jiangnan origin, geographical background was valued quite apart from on-the-job ability. Because skill is, as Tilly puts it, "a socially constructed relationship," its definition could be stretched in directions seemingly rather distant from the objective demands of the shop floor. This definitional process was not simply a product of employers' preference but reflected the stringent controls that skilled workers exercised over potential entrants to the trade. As holders of a monopoly over required knowledge and gatekeepers of the supply of labor to jobs demanding that knowledge, craftsmen played a pivotal role in shaping the criteria associated with their skills. Under such a system, native-place origin could easily be deemed an indispensable trait.

Experience with modern machinery notwithstanding, the skilled factory laborer operated in a world in some ways every bit as feudal as that of his unskilled counterpart from the countryside. It was not modernity, but a position of privilege that gave the factory artisan a vanguard role. Prosperity and status, buttressed by communal organizations and values, inclined the craftsman to radical protest.

The prominence of artisans in Shanghai's Communist labor movement was not an aberration. Lynda Shaffer found a comparable situation in Hunan Province. Based on her study of four strikes connected to the CCP-sponsored Hunan Labor Secretariat, Shaffer concludes that "artisans or other traditional workers played a leading role in the Communist-led Hunan labor movement, and, perhaps, in the labor movements of other provinces as well."[5] Significantly, in Tianjin, a city where labor was notably quiescent, Gail Hershatter discovered that craftsmen enjoyed few perquisites to distinguish them from unskilled workers. Artisans and factory workers alike remained closely tied to the North China villages which they all called home.[6] The lack of a labor aristocracy in Tianjin was probably more than coincidentally related to the absence of a lively labor movement in this important industrial metropolis.*

---

*During the years 1918–26, according to the calculations of Chinese scholar Chen Da, Tianjin experienced only 14 strikes, in contrast to the 638 that occurred in

The one major exception to the link between factory artisans and the Communist labor movement was in the Canton delta. There skilled workers were politically engaged but often on the side of the GMD rather than the CCP. For example, the Guangdong Mechanics' Association, which had enjoyed close ties to the Nationalists since the 1911 Revolution,[7] overtly opposed Communist mobilization efforts in the 1920's. As Ming Chan points out, during this period practically all of the Guomindang labor leaders were Cantonese, usually from the same county or township as the workers they sought to enlist. By contrast, the Communists were generally outsiders, unable to penetrate the artisan guilds that would prove hospitable territory for the formation of GMD-backed unions.[8] In this case the politics of place and partisanship (in the form of Cantonese labor organizers in service to the Guomindang) worked in concert to distance local craftsmen from the Communist cause. Comparative evidence suggests that this pattern was unusual, however.

Artisans and the European Labor Movement

The latest generation of scholarship on European labor has firmly established the critical role of the privileged artisan in the promotion and radicalization of working-class protest. Beginning with E. P. Thompson's *Making of the English Working Class*, a host of impressive studies have concurred that the skilled craftsman stood at the vanguard of the European labor movement.[9]

Various reasons are offered for this phenomenon. One explanation stresses the social networks of the artisans. Workers of the same trade often lived in homogeneous neighborhoods and gathered regularly at informal meeting places: the pub or music hall in England, the cafe or cabaret in France—the equivalent of the teahouse in China. Such spaces afforded an opportunity to air common grievances and an organizational center for protest.[10] In addition, by the mid-nineteenth century many artisans had developed formal mutual aid societies to promote their cause.[11] These associations carried out religious observances on patron saints' days and helped members at times of funerals, illness, and other personal crises. (The parallel to the *huiguan* and *gongsuo* of Shanghai is obvious.)

Shanghai in this same period ("Jin banian lai guonei bagong de fenxi" [Analysis of domestic strikes during the past eight years], *Qinghua xuebao*, June 1926). The discrepancy was nine times greater than the relative size of their work forces might lead one to expect. In 1928, the number of industrial employees in Shanghai was estimated at 222,670 and that of Tianjin at 47,519 (Maxwell S. Stewart and Fang Fu-an, "A Statistical Study of Industry and Labor in China," *Chinese Economic Journal* 7, no. 4, [1930]: 1083, 1087).

A second explanation highlights the affluence of skilled workers. The relative prosperity of artisans afforded resources to support mutual aid associations, which functioned as stepping-stones to full-blown trade unions. The funds invested in these institutions also supplied the wherewithal to sustain lengthy strikes.[12]

The concentrated working conditions of skilled laborers is cited as an additional factor inclining them toward political activism. This was as true for factory artisans as it had been for preindustrial craftsmen. As Eric Hobsbawm has noted, during World War I metalworkers "became in most countries of the world the characteristic leaders of militant labour movements." Michael Hanagan observes that "nowhere was artisanal survival inside the factory more clear than in metalworking. Although shut behind factory walls, metalworking artisans continued to behave as if they were in their own small shops."[13] Actually the phenomenon preceded World War I by more than half a century. In 1851, the Toulouse police, in an effort to explain why the factory metalworkers were "almost all socialist," pointed to the ease of spreading propaganda because of their concentration in *grands ateliers*.[14]

As a consequence of close on-the-job interaction, encouraged by the apprenticeship system, skilled workers took pride in their profession. Accustomed to steady employment and decent treatment, they held their employers to high standards. An awareness of their own economic value prompted such workers to press their advantage with management.[15] Jeffrey Haydu points out that "skilled workers typically enjoyed greater influence with employers by virtue of their central role in production and the greater difficulty in replacing them. Being fewer in number and enjoying greater freedom to move about the shop, they faced fewer problems than less skilled workers in discussing grievances, formulating demands, and coordinating action."[16] Though factory artisans were a privileged segment within the work force, they often saw themselves as spokesmen for the interests of labor as a whole. In their minds there was no necessary contradiction between what may be termed "craft consciousness"—awareness of the collective interests of one's particular skill group—and "class consciousness"—awareness of one's common interests with other working-class groups.[17]

Unlike unskilled laborers, whose attachment to the city was usually temporary and insecure, most skilled workers were committed to urban life. As permanent residents of urban society, they took an interest in public affairs beyond the horizons of the workplace. The high levels of literacy that characterized most artisan professions further contributed to their politicization.*

---

*A Moscow survey in 1908 showed that skilled workers, most notably metalworkers, had a literacy rate of about 90 percent and were considerably more urbanized

Artisan trades in which these traits of urbanization, job security, literacy, and pride in one's product were most pronounced were also trades that generated a disproportionate share of working-class militants. Natalie Davis points to the printing industry as an example. Robert Bezucha highlights the silk-weaving industry. Eric Hobsbawm and Joan Scott identify the shoemaking trade.[18] It may be worth remembering the background of several of Shanghai's most active Communist labor leaders. Chen Yun apprenticed at the Commercial Press, the city's largest printing house. Zhang Qi was a skilled craftsman at Meiya, Shanghai's premier silk-weaving enterprise. And Liu Changsheng, sent down from the North, had been a shoemaker.

But if artisans had all the organizational and cultural prerequisites for protest, what triggered their militance? Whereas an earlier generation of scholars stressed the unemployment and immiseration of craftsmen under the advance of mechanization, more recent studies dispute this view. For one thing, the introduction of machines did not always challenge artisanal skills. As William Sewell has shown, the growth of factories tended not to reduce but to multiply the demand for artisans and artisan-produced goods.[19] In addition, strike waves were seldom provoked by a declining or stagnating standard of living. On the contrary, upswings in the business cycle tended to generate higher levels of protest activity.[20]

Nevertheless, strikes did reflect important transformations ushered in by industrial development. According to many analysts, the primary precipitant of artisan radicalism was not the "first industrial revolution," which introduced large numbers of unskilled women and children to the urban work force, but rather the "second industrial revolution," which saw the entry of semiskilled, factory-trained male operatives. In this latter phase, challenges to the artisans' traditional monopoly on skill aroused their ire. Then came the introduction of Frederick Taylor's scientific management—an effort by employers to uproot the autonomous work processes that had been at the heart of artisanal strength. Such changes in the organization of production help to explain the targets of early artisan strikes: work discipline and factory foremen, rather than wages or machines.[21]

Although these authors do not extend their argument into an investigation of the competition between skilled and semiskilled workers, the present study of Shanghai suggests that such a path is worth pursuing.

(measured as the percentage born in the city) than textile workers (Diane Koenker, *Moscow Workers and the 1917 Revolution* [Princeton, N.J., 1981], p. 29). Such workers—skilled, well paid, literate, urbanized—led the Russian strike waves of the early twentieth century (ibid., pp. 76–78).

Much of the dynamics of labor politics in modern China can be traced to this inherent tension between the radicalism of once independent artisans and the conservatism of employer-trained operatives. That the Communists and Guomindang were able to tap this basic animosity helps to explain both the strengths and weaknesses of their contrasting labor programs.

Semiskilled Workers and the American Labor Movement

Although the European labor movement is usually held up as the standard for international comparison, in the case of Shanghai the parallels with American labor are at least as instructive. Behind this similarity lies a recruitment process that in both countries relegated workers from certain regions and backgrounds to certain lines of work. As John Cumbler has described the American pattern:

> Selective recruitment directed immigrants with various skills and experiences into particular occupations. Contacts with relatives and friends, often made before migration, steered newcomers into occupations and neighborhoods already identified with particular regions and origins. . . . Social and ethnic divisions channeled workers into worlds separated by traditions, customs and skills carried over from their past and reinforced by the experiences of their present life and work in ethnic groupings.[22]

Skill and native-place differences, in America as in Shanghai, were reflected in political orientations. In a study of the U.S. labor movement, Stanley Aronowitz has pointed out that initially the Socialists found their key base of support among skilled workers who were either native-born or of northern European origins. By contrast, the unskilled laborers, most of whom hailed from eastern and southern Europe, remained largely outside the radical labor movement.[23]

But there was, in both America and Shanghai, an intermediate group of semiskilled laborers who also played an important role in labor politics. Denied the security or status of the skilled worker, such individuals often resorted to gang networks in search of protection. Gangs helped rural immigrants make the difficult transition to urban life. They also served as brokers between workers and politicians. The case of Tammany Hall, the infamous Manhattan Democratic organization at the turn of the century, illustrates the linkage clearly.

In the United States, as in China, the 1920's witnessed a transformation of gangster operations to more sophisticated political activities. Prohibition in this country, like the ban on opium in China, served to tighten the link between politicians and gangsters.[24] In exchange for official protection for their illicit traffic, gangster leaders promised to deliver labor support to the politicians.[25] In 1923, the *New York Times* bemoaned the end of old gang methods, with their quaint emphasis on valor, and the advent of a new style that stressed calculated interference in labor issues.[26]

The involvement of organized crime in the U.S. Teamsters Union was symptomatic of this development. The union had been open to corruption ever since it was first formed to represent drivers of horse-drawn wagons (hence the name "Teamsters"). As a student of the mob has explained its hold over American transport workers: "Every worker was a little guy out on a limb, and therefore easy to intimidate." Racketeering and conservative politics were hallmarks of the union. In the early 1950's, suspicion of Communist sympathies was grounds for expulsion.[27]

The Teamsters' notoriety came to a head with the promotion of union activist Jimmy Hoffa by the Detroit Purple Gang and Chicago Mafia. The connection propelled Hoffa to political prominence, much as the combination of labor control and gang ties elevated Shanghai notables Du Yuesheng, Lu Jingshi, and Zhu Xuefan. For all of these men, gangs afforded an opportunity for rapid upward mobility. Hoffa's search for social respectability was made clear in one of his last speeches to the union faithful: "My daughter and my son finished college. It is the first generation for either a Hoffa or a Poszywak, my wife's family, on her mother's, her father's, my mother's and my father's side to have had an opportunity to finish college. It is a great American institution that permits men like myself to come from a warehouse to here, my wife from a laundry to where she stands here today."[28] That "great American institution" was in fact none other than the Mafia. It allowed upward mobility for Hoffa's family rather like that which Du Yuesheng's family enjoyed as a product of his Green Gang connection. Du's establishment of a family ancestral shrine and his concern with the higher education of his son showed a similar obsession with social respectability.[29]

For rank-and-file workers as well, patron-client gang ties were a means of getting ahead in an otherwise forbidding environment. As Hoffa recognized: "Personal contact is the key to service and giving the membership service is the only reason we are in the business. That political and social stuff—it's not important. I don't think the drivers expect me to be holding social gatherings for them or to go on the air and tell what's wrong in Germany or Italy. We're in the business of selling labor. We're going to get the best price we can."[30]

Gangsters succeeded in mobilizing semiskilled workers by publicly denying political interests, while at the same time their unions forged close links to powerholders. As Anton Blok has analyzed the Mafia, its key distinction from common banditry lies in its symbiosis with those who hold formal political office. The Mafiosi act as political middlemen or power brokers in patron-client networks that link politicians to the rank-and-file citizenry.[31] The insecure position of semiskilled workers, whose futures were tied to the city but who enjoyed few advantages in the struggle to stake out a permanent urban niche for themselves, made them especially receptive to this variety of organized crime. As employer-trained operatives who lacked the autonomous guild traditions of the skilled workers, they were easy recruits for yellow unions advocating economic gain rather than political resistance.

Unskilled Worker-Peasants and the Labor Movement

If artisans and semiskilled workers were predisposed to the appeals of radical and conservative labor leaders, respectively, unskilled workers were less likely to become attached to formal organizations of either political stripe. Retaining more allegiance to the countryside than to the city, such workers tended to engage in sudden but brief outbursts followed by swift retreats to old practices.[32] Seldom did their protests generate sustained political organization.

The rural attachments of unskilled laborers elicited the disdain of their urbanized co-workers. As a Russian metalworker remarked at the turn of the century:

> Everyone recognized the superiority of metalworkers, with all the advantages that that implied. . . . The oddness of textileworkers hit me in the eyes. Many of them still wore peasant clothes. They looked as though they had wandered into the town by mistake and tomorrow would find their way back to their native village. Women predominated among them and one never lost an opportunity to pour scorn on them. Alongside the textileworkers, the metalworkers appeared to be a race apart, accustomed to life in the capital and more independent.[33]

Lack of commitment to an urban future rendered these peasant-workers an unreliable base of support for unionists. As David Mandel has noted in the case of Russia, "the unskilled workers were the least active element of Petrograd's working class."[34]

When unskilled workers did take to the streets, their protests were often remarkably reminiscent of rural collective action. Charles Sabel describes a 1973 strike at the Ford plant in Cologne in which each factory gate was controlled by a group of peasant immigrants from a different town in Turkey. He notes, "The immigrants' style of struggle—dancing and fetes in an occupied factory, the participation of wives on picket lines—owes more to traditions of agrarian than of industrial conflict."[35]

Virtually all labor historians agree that cooperation between workers of different skill levels was not an automatic outcome of the process of industrialization.* In fact, to a great degree the history of labor is the history of conflict among workers.[36] Nonetheless, substantial as the gap between skilled and unskilled workers was in most urban settings, alliances were not impossible. Massive strike waves (e.g., May Fourth, May Thirtieth, or the struggles of the Civil War period in the case of Shanghai) depended upon just such cooperation. In the Russian Revolution, Diane Koenker observes, "the machine workers helped to catalyze, by their radicalism and their proximity, the less skilled textile workers into activism."[37] As Steve Smith explains:

> The two groups played different, but largely complementary roles in the revolutionary process. Those who built the labour movement were the "cadre" workers, especially metalworkers, for they had more time and money at their disposal, were at home in the factory, were more literate, had experience of informal shop-floor organization and a degree of job-control, and were thus better placed to participate in labour and political activities. The new workers, on the other hand, were often more turbulent than the "cadre" workers because they combined the manifold discontents of the low-paid worker with the grievances of the poor peasants and the specific oppressions of women and youth.[38]

The Significance of the Proletarian Strike

What enabled workers to bridge their differences and engage in common struggle? Many analysts have stressed the importance of a nascent class consciousness emerging to override previous divisions and draw skilled and unskilled workers together in concerted class action. For the early theorists of socialist revolution—Marx, Sorel, Lenin, and Trotsky—general strikes were a dramatic indication of the class-conscious potential of the working class.† Though it is currently fashion-

---

*Charles F. Sabel, *Work and Politics: The Division of Labor in Industry* (New York, 1982), points out that skilled and unskilled workers have a very different understanding of what constitutes a fair wage, for example. Peasant-workers typically repudiate the principles used to justify the wage hierarchy in industrial firms, arguing that pay should be proportional to the amount of a worker's effort rather than to its value. Skilled workers, whose labor enjoys a higher value, naturally see the issue differently.

†Karl Marx saw the strike as a key weapon in the arsenal of the proletariat as it progressed from economic to political struggle (*Karl Marx on Revolution*, ed. Saul K. Padover [New York, 1971], p. 61). For Georges Sorel, strikes expressed the proletariat's "noblest, deepest and most moving sentiments" (*Reflections on Violence* [New York, 1961], p. 127). V. I. Lenin, while emphasizing that true proletarian consciousness could

able for theorists to substitute some other term for "class consciousness," be it "subculture of opposition" or "culture of solidarity," the
argument remains familiar: only when workers transcend their differences through an awareness of their common plight as exploited laborers
can they take political action to further their own interests. *

old argument

   Do general strikes express a political activism born from shared understanding of exploitation in the workplace? To be sure, large-scale labor
protests reflect the wider economic and political world in which they
occur. Typically, national prosperity is highly correlated with strike
waves.[39] But national prosperity is not always experienced by workers as
an improvement in their own standard of living. In particular, the inflation that often accompanies economic growth may be seen as a cause for
alarm among well-paid and poorly paid workers alike. As James Cronin
points out, however, the issue of inflation unites workers by organizing
them at the point of consumption, rather than production. Whereas
labor at the workplace is divided by skill, gender, and ethnicity, at the
marketplace all workers are consumers who suffer in common the ill
effects of inflation.[40] Certainly the strike waves that occurred in Shanghai during World War I and the Civil War years were closely connected to
the inflationary trends of those periods.

   Political factors may also act to precipitate strike waves. As Edward
Shorter and Charles Tilly have found, political crisis—like economic
prosperity—tends to produce a rise in the level of strike activity across
industries.[41] In Russia of 1905, the tragedy of Bloody Sunday undermined
popular faith in the czar's paternalism and triggered a wave of urban
unrest among skilled and unskilled workers alike.[42] In China, the May
Thirtieth tragedy had a similarly catalytic effect. Significantly, political
crises in twentieth-century China have frequently involved an element
of nationalism. May Fourth was sparked by furor over Japanese incur-
sions after World War I, May Thirtieth was stimulated by hostility toward Japanese and British imperialism alike, and the Civil War protests
had an undercurrent of anti-Americanism. Like the issue of inflation in

---

be brought to the workers only by outside revolutionaries, nevertheless characterized
the strikes of nineteenth-century Russia as "class struggle in embryo" (*What Is to Be
Done?* [Beijing, 1975], p. 36). For Leon Trotsky, strikes were an indication of the
inherent radicalism of the proletariat and a vehicle by which less progressive workers
were drawn into the maelstrom of class conflict (*History of the Russian Revolution*
[London, 1967], 2:243).

   *Richard Jules Ostreicher, *Solidarity and Fragmentation* (Chicago, 1986), p. 60,
observes that "if there was to be an effective working-class presence, the separate
threads of different working-class cultures had to come together into a working-class
subculture of opposition which transcended ethnic identities." Rick Fantasia, *Cultures of Solidarity* (Berkeley, Calif., 1986), p. 238, argues that "cultures of solidarity . . .
can break down status hierarchies between workers in favor of a wider solidarity."

the economic arena, the issue of nationalism in the political arena mobilized urbanites in a fashion that transcended the divisions of the workplace. Men and women, northerners and southerners, skilled and unskilled—all could join in opposing foreign oppression. As a Shanghai cotton worker remembered the May Thirtieth Movement:

> At that time anti-imperialist sentiments were not only prevalent among workers; any Chinese who lived in Shanghai shared such feelings. During the strike even the police, the night-soil carriers, the servants at foreign residences, and the cooks all joined. This was definitely a mass movement. Certainly the Communist Party could never have been powerful enough to generate these sentiments. When people heard that the foreigners had killed one of us Chinese they were furious and felt that we must resist.[43]

It was not that workers usually engaged in strikes for patriotic purposes; as we have seen in the foregoing case studies, foreign ownership was a less salient factor in generating labor militance than the prosperity of an enterprise and the composition of its work force. Nor did workers require the duress of inflation to erupt in protest; dismissals of fellow workers or changes in management were more likely precipitants. In these more common cases of labor unrest, workers organized around workplace issues, often in a manner that bespoke a clear awareness of exploitation at the hands of their employers. But such awareness did not necessarily imply class solidarity. It was not simply, as Marx and Engels readily recognized, that "organisation of the proletarians into a class, and consequently into a political party, is continually being upset by competition between the workers themselves."[44] Rather, proletarian activism (in the form of both strikes and political parties) is often the *product* of just such competition among workers.

Rational choice theorists have forced us to confront the obstacles that lie in the path of collective action. Even when people share interests of which they are conscious, lack of trust may prevent concerted action.[45] Trust is more likely and free riders more easily overcome at the level of ethnic/gender/skill groups that divide the working class. The inclination of an industrial proletariat, it would seem, is to split along the lines of these (often competitive) intraclass groupings rather than to advance along some progressive road toward class cohesion. Most unions, strikes, and political parties are built on the foundations of one or another of these intraclass solidarities.*

---

*It may be, as Adam Przeworski and John Sprague argue in their important study of working-class politics, that "historical variations concerning the salience of class as a determinant of political behavior can be attributed to the strategies pursued by political parties" (*Paper Stones* [Chicago, 1986], p. 11). It is important to keep in mind, however, that successful political parties must to some extent tailor their strategies to

Labor militancy, in other words, is not tantamount to class consciousness. Indeed, the very awareness of substantial differences among workers often encourages labor activism. Depending upon their location in the job hierarchy, workers may be militant in trying to minimize, maintain, or magnify discrepancies in wages or working conditions between themselves and other workers.[46] Even in the important instances when workers at different skill and wage levels cooperate in joint struggles, the alliances do not necessarily reflect class consciousness.[47] In the case of Shanghai, as we have seen, inflation and nationalism precipitated many of the large-scale strikes. Such issues appealed to participants as *consumers* or *citizens*, rather than as members of a *class*. Moreover the mobilization that led to massive struggles was usually based on preexisting, smaller-scale groupings. Only when fictive kinship networks, native-place gangs, secret societies, and the like could be drawn into cooperation was a major upheaval possible. As David Strand notes of Beijing in the 1920's, "Mass politics was not a solvent capable of breaking down barriers based on status, native place or division of labor so much as it was an opportunity to display these divisions in public."[48]

"Traditional communities," observes Craig Calhoun, "give their members the social strength with which to wage protracted battles, the 'selective inducements' with which to ensure full collective participation, and a sense of what to fight for that is at once shared and radical."[49] Calhoun joins the currently fashionable trend of turning Marxism on its head to argue that traditional artisans and peasants were really more revolutionary (because of their preexisting communities) than modern factory workers, whose unions and parties inevitably become co-opted by the capitalist system. But is a line between the "traditional" artisan or peasant and the "modern" factory worker so easily drawn?[50] I would argue that much of the activism of the working class had roots in practices that long predated industrialization. As Herbert Gutman has noted, working-class worlds were still closely bound to preindustrial traditions: "Family, class, and ethnic ties did not dissolve easily."[51]

Skill is a powerful predictor of labor politics because as a "socially constructed relationship," it is usually closely linked to long-standing cultural and associational practices. Workers of differing skill levels often come from different places, are familiar with different forms of organization, attain different levels of literacy and education, and enjoy

---

the sentiments of their constituencies. Some sections of the working class, most notably the artisans, seem particularly responsive to class appeals. On the way communitarian traditions inclined artisans to class consciousness, see William H. Sewell, Jr., *Work and Revolution in France: The Language of Labor from the Old Regime to 1948* (New York, 1980), pp. 179–213.

different degrees of job security and urbanization. In the case of Shang-hai, the Jiangnan artisan was buttressed by a teahouse culture and guild organization that encouraged protest in defense of customary privilege. Relatively literate, well educated, and committed to city life, such work-ers were also susceptible to the appeals of radical student organizers, many of whom also hailed from Jiangnan. The unskilled laborer from North China, by contrast, had relatively little interest in the intellectual debates of the day. Uneducated and unattached to urban employment, such workers remained peasants in their attitudes and actions. Between these two groups stood the semiskilled workers. Although aliens to the "refined" culture of Jiangnan, these machine operatives from the North nevertheless intended to spend their lives in their adopted city. Because their origins severely limited opportunities for advancement, the semi-skilled turned to the secret societies.

That the divergent orientations of skilled, unskilled, and semiskilled workers reflected parochial underpinnings does not dilute their histor-ical importance. Even when workers were not expressing class con-sciousness, they could play a pivotal political role. Semiskilled workers, through their connections to gangsters and the Guomindang, helped to define the character of the Nationalist regime. Skilled workers, through their links to the Communist labor movement, were a key factor in the development of urban revolution. Unskilled workers, despite their com-parative disinterest in the two contending political parties, were critical participants in the massive protests that rewrote the course of modern Chinese history. Both the Nationalist and the Communist states were established on the heels of strikes joined by skilled, semiskilled, and unskilled workers alike.

The multifaceted militance of the Shanghai proletariat, rooted in the variegated lives and workplace experiences of its members, was at once more narrowly determined and more broadly influential than previous scholarship has suggested. Most scholars, Chinese and Western alike, have framed their studies of Chinese labor history (*gongyunshi*) within the confining category of Communist Party history (*dang shi*).[52] Jean Chesneaux, who interprets the modern Chinese labor movement as an advance toward class consciousness, assigns primary credit to the leader-ship of the Chinese Communist Party.[53] The making of the Chinese working class, in this view, is largely the product of outside direction. Andrew Walder, picking up the story of Chinese labor in the contempo-rary era, refers to a "remaking" of the working class under the policies of the socialist party/state.[54] These analyses stress the decisive role of the Communist Party in molding, and remolding, first a class-conscious and then a compliant working class.

This study of Shanghai labor raises questions about such interpretations. To the extent that Chinese workers were shaped by their culture of origin and workplace position, they were not clay in the hands of partisan potters to be fashioned according to their design. Previous experiences imposed limits and opened possibilities for different groups of workers to practice different forms of politics. Much of the dynamism of the Chinese labor movement, I would argue, is the product of interaction among these distinctive tendencies—only one of which proved to be a staunch ally of the Communist Party.

The Legacy of the Chinese Labor Movement

An examination of the history of the labor movement has important ramifications for our understanding of contemporary Chinese politics. As the second volume of this study will show, the Communists—like the GMD before them—quickly learned that a politicized labor force could not be ignored after the consolidation of state power. Instead, some workable accommodation would have to be reached.

Although it has been claimed that the Chinese working class was remade by the Communist state, it is important to keep in mind that many of the officials who developed PRC labor policies in the 1950's and 1960's were former activists in the labor movement. Chen Yun, chief architect of the socialist transformation of industry in the mid-1950's, had joined the Communist Party in the 1920's while apprenticing at Shanghai's Commercial Press. The radical union at the press, of which Chen was an active member, was an outgrowth of a printers' guild that predated the Communist movement by years.[55] A skilled worker from Jiangnan, Chen Yun was typical of many of the early adherents of the Communist labor movement in Shanghai. (When his policies were out of favor during the Great Leap Forward, Chen occupied himself by writing essays on the operatic tradition of his native Jiangnan region.[56]) Head of State Liu Shaoqi, who received his formative education in a work-study program geared toward factory labor, had undertaken his first political assignment as a labor organizer in Shanghai. Premier Zhou Enlai had directed the third—and successful—Shanghai workers' armed uprising in March 1927. Liu Changsheng, the leather worker in charge of Shanghai's Communist labor movement during the wartime and postwar periods, assumed the vice-chairmanship of the All-China Federation of Labor Unions after 1949. Zhang Qi, the skilled Jiangnan silk weaver who helped lead the Meiya strike of 1934 as a member of Shanghai's underground Communist Youth League, became director of the Shanghai Federation of Labor. Even Zhu Xuefan, the former gangster and Shanghai postal worker, had a hand in defining socialist policies as first minister of post and telecommunications in the PRC. As Du Yuesheng's chief lieutenant for labor affairs, Zhu had accumulated valuable experience in the area of industrial relations—experience he was ready to pass on to his new employers after 1949. (Today the aged Zhu occupies a prominent position in the National People's Political Consultative Conference as chair of the Revolutionary Committee of the Guomindang.)

The new Communist regime provided the opportunity for these former labor organizers to play key roles in the formulation of national policy. Considering the importance of skilled workers in the revolutionary movement, it is not surprising that the pattern put in place after 1949 strongly emphasized security and welfare[57]—issues dear to the hearts of craftsmen the world over.

Ironically, the artisan heritage was most visible in the sector of the industrial economy that most exemplified the new socialist system: state-owned enterprises. These organizations guaranteed permanent employment, high wages, and substantial welfare measures to their employees. Because of the perquisites it brought, a job in a state factory came to be known as an "iron rice bowl," in contrast to the less durable and less desirable "earthen rice bowl" of the collective sector.[58]

The exclusivity and paternalism of the Communist enterprise were reminiscent of the artisan guild. One needed an introduction from friends or relatives to join these selective organizations, which offered lifetime benefits to their privileged members. Like its guild forerunner, the socialist factory also stipulated certain behavioral norms for its membership.[59] But whereas the traditional guild had relied on the authority of its patron deity to enforce these values, the new state enterprise claimed legitimacy from the Communist Party.

In each province and city, the special prerogatives of workers at state factories were overseen by the local federation of labor unions, an arm of the state charged with responsibility for workers' welfare.* In the case of Shanghai, the city's federation of unions has been dominated by former activists in the Communist labor movement, most of whom rose from the ranks of South China artisans.

If the new Communist order embodied many of the priorities of skilled craftsmen, the same could not be said for excluded sectors of the labor force. Resentment against the benefits accruing to veteran workers at state enterprises was an important precipitant of the waves of labor unrest that have rolled across Chinese cities since 1949.

*In the early 1950's, the chair of Shanghai's municipal Trade Union Council was also the deputy secretary of the city's Communist Party Committee. See Paul F. Harper, "Trade Union Cultivation of Workers for Leadership," in *The City in Communist China*, ed. John Wilson Lewis (Stanford, Calif., 1971), p. 125.

As early as 1956–57, under the inspiration of the Hundred Flowers Campaign, strikes erupted at hundreds of factories. These labor protests were instigated for the most part by marginal workers: temporary and contract laborers, workers in the service sector, apprentices, and others who failed to share in the privileges bestowed upon skilled veteran employees at state enterprises.[60] Despite the vociferous protests of that period, the gap between permanent state workers and temporary or contract laborers widened in the years ahead.[61]

In 1966–67, during the Great Proletarian Cultural Revolution, serious struggles again broke out in factories across the country. In Shanghai, the ranks of so-called conservative Scarlet Guards were filled with older state workers, predominantly from the Jiangnan region, experienced in the pre-1949 labor movement. Their leaders were largely former underground Party labor organizers who hailed from the same region. The Revolutionary Rebels, by contrast, were mostly younger workers led in part by cadres sent down from the Subei area in the early 1950's. Among their constituents were more than a few unskilled contract and temporary workers.[62] Lynn White has explained the motivations of disprivileged workers:

> Unemployed and contract workers may not, at first, have been passionately excited about the errors of historians, the ideologies of novelists, or the philosophies of musicians—even though these issues concerned editorialists from the radical group that launched the Cultural Revolution in late 1965 and early 1966. Unemployed workers seem to have had some idea what political leaders they disliked, however. When men like Mayor Ts'ao Ti-ch'iu [of Shanghai], who had espoused the "worker-peasant system," were criticized for cultural policies, some enthusiasm was stirred within the lower proletariat.[63]

Factional strife was most intense at older factories, where pre-1949 activists were numerous and obviously privileged vis-à-vis younger workers. Such factories not only displayed glaring inequalities in labor treatment; they also boasted a glorious history of labor protest to which only the older workers could lay claim. As elder "revolutionary heroes" recounted their experiences at frequent factory history roundtables, resentment between the generations was bound to grow.

The indignation that veteran workers felt toward recent hirees was prefigured in interviews conducted by Chinese historians with former labor activists in the late 1950's. Again and again the interviewees concluded their statements with criticism of the younger generation. An elderly cotton worker declared: "Today's youth don't appreciate the difficult struggles which we undertook in the past. They complain that wages are low and treatment harsh. . . . If a young worker has picked up a bit of skill on the job he puts on airs and thinks he's hot stuff. . . . The youngsters boast that they are educated and charge us older workers with being uncultured."[64]

Subjected to repeated lectures by their elders about the revolutionary exploits of bygone days, younger workers longed for an opportunity to even the score. The Cultural Revolution offered them the chance. Interestingly enough, however, the methods which young Revolutionary Rebels employed in their own struggles bore an uncanny resemblance to the protest repertoires of the previous generation.[65] It was probably no coincidence that the Shanghai Number Seventeen Cotton Mill, where Wang Hongwen worked, had in the mid-1920's been the scene of labor violence strikingly similar to that of Cultural Revolution struggle sessions. In a 1925 incident at the factory, workers had tricked a hated foreman into attending a mass meeting at which he was publicly denounced. The hapless foreman was forced to kneel in front of the crowd with hands tied behind his back, dunce cap placed on his head, and a placard reading "Down with this traitor and running dog" hung across his chest. Photographs of the occasion were posted at the factory gate to serve as warning lest the unseated overseer ever tried to resume his post.[66]

When radical workers adopted similar tactics during the Cultural Revolution, their targets were the older generation and the institutions such as the Federation of Labor Unions that symbolized its privileged position in the new Communist order. In Shanghai, the year 1967 saw a string of attacks by Wang Hongwen's Revolutionary Rebels against the former Party underground labor organizers who then controlled the Shanghai Federation of Labor. Zhang Qi, director of the Shanghai federation and former secretary of the Shanghai Party underground, was subjected to repeated humiliation in public struggle sessions. His hands were forced behind his back in the painful "jet plane" position, a dunce cap adorned his head, and a placard across his chest announced him as a "running dog" who had committed "revisionist crimes." In December Zhang was imprisoned in the basement of the building of the federation he had helped to create.[67] Although Zhang Qi survived the Cultural Revolution in remarkably good health, many of his colleagues were less fortunate. A recent listing of fatalities in radical assaults on the Shanghai Federation of Labor illustrates the vulnerable position of former underground Party organizers, most of whom were skilled craftsmen from Jiangnan.[68]

The fissures of the Cultural Revolution are understandable only when interpreted against a labor history stretching back into the Guomindang past. But the importance of the Nationalist interregnum goes beyond the continuity in personalities and styles of protest. For in the Guomindang's handling of workers we can locate the beginning of a more intrusive pattern of state intervention in labor relations. Both the Nationalists and the Communists acceded to power with substantial working-class support. Both endeavored to rechannel labor activism into government-controlled institutions: the yellow unions under the Guomindang, the Federation of Labor Unions under the CCP. Both evidenced ambivalence toward the labor strife that persisted after their consolidation of state power.* And both sought, successfully, to co-opt labor leaders as state officials. (The meteoric rise of Wang Hongwen and his Revolutionary Rebels after the January power seizure of 1967 was more than a little reminiscent of the prominence enjoyed by Green Gang labor organizers in the aftermath of the coup of April 1927.) Moreover, the central leaders of both regimes felt compelled to emasculate new political institutions founded with workers' participation: the Shanghai provisional government established after the third armed workers' uprising in the spring of 1927 and the Shanghai people's commune created in the wake of the power seizure of January 1967. The latter institution prompted a strong protest from Chairman Mao: "With the establishment of a commune, a series of problems arises. . . . Communes are too weak when it comes to suppressing counterrevolutionaries. If everything was changed into a commune, then what about the Party? . . . There must be a party somehow! There must be a nucleus . . . be it called the Communist Party . . . or Guomindang . . . there must be a party."[69] For Mao Zedong, just as for Chiang Kai-shek, a politicized labor force could be a useful ally, but it also posed a potential threat to state control, regardless of whether the state in question was a Nationalist regime espousing support for the bourgeoisie or a socialist regime claiming to be a dictatorship of the proletariat.

Although the Communist regime is undoubtedly more powerful than its predecessor, the contemporary Chinese state is still not entirely autonomous vis-à-vis social forces. This is not to say that the current regime is a workers' state, any more than the Guomindang was a committee of the Shanghai bourgeoisie. But try as it may to exercise unbridled hegemony, the state is forced to deal with the possibility of opposition from societal interests. Among the forces with which the regime must come to terms, the working class—thanks to its impressive

---

*Mao Zedong's speech "On the Correct Handling of Contradictions Among the People" in February 1957 called for better education and improved leadership methods as an antidote to strikes that had broken out the previous year. In the spring of 1957, Liu Shaoqi proposed more boldly that union and Party officials should themselves participate in strikes to regain the confidence of the workers. See *Joint Publications Research Service* #41889, p. 58.

history of protest—rates a high priority. Having cut its political teeth in the process of mobilizing a labor movement, China's post-1949 leadership has been acutely aware of the clout of the working class. The perquisites state factory workers enjoy in China today can be explained, in part, by the regime's recognition of the latent economic and political power of this strategically situated group.*

No less than in the past, the working class remains fragmented.[70] And no less than in the past, its political orientations and activities are likely to follow the lines of this fragmentation.[71] The challenge to the student of Chinese politics is to trace the fault lines from their origins in the parochial practices of ordinary workers to their ramifications at the apex of the political system.

---

*In 1974–75, strikes and slowdowns were launched in many Chinese factories to demand bonuses and wage hikes, anathema as these were to the Maoist orthodoxy of the day. The most serious work stoppage, a series of strikes in the city of Hangzhou, was resolved only when Deng Xiaoping went in person to assure the restive workers of an impending wage reform. See Lowell Dittmer, *China's Continuous Revolution* (Berkeley, Calif., 1987), pp. 165–67.

Appendixes

Appendix A

Strikes by Artisans in Shanghai, 1902–19

Industry affected	Strike demand	Source
Shipyard (carpenters)	Wage raise	NCH, May 21, 1902
Foundry	Replace foreman	NCH, Jan. 29, 1904
Arsenal	Wage raise	Zhongwai ribao, June 6, 1904
Cotton (mechanics)	Replace foreman	SB, Apr. 30, 1905
Printing	Wage raise	SB, Nov. 10, 1905
Printing	Release of worker arrested for distributing anti-American handbills	SB, Dec. 5, 1905
Gas	Wage raise	NCH, Sept. 7, 1906
Water	Release withheld wages*	Shen bao, July 22, 1910
Bean curd	Wage raise	SB, June 17, 1911
Tailors	Against increased work hours*	SB, July 12, 1911
Printing	Wage raise	SB, July 27, 1911
Shipyard (carpenters)	Wage raise	NCH, Sept. 23, 1911
Foundry	Unionization	Taipingyang bao, July 15, 1912
Painting	Wage raise	SB, Nov. 6, 1912
Carpentry	Wage raise	SB, Nov. 26, 1912
Bean curd	Wage raise	SB, Dec. 2, 1912
Jewelry	Wage raise	SB, Dec. 11, 1912
Carpentry	Wage raise	SB, Jan. 5, 1913
Foundry	Control over hiring	SB, Feb. 16, 1913
Ink	Wage raise	SB, Mar. 8, 1913
Foundry	Replace foremen	SB, Mar. 20, 1913
Cloth dyeing	Control by artisan guild	SB, Mar. 18, 1914
Furniture	Wage raise	SB, June 3, 1914
Stone masonry	End purchase of Ningbo stone products	SB, June 19, 1914
Carpentry	Wage raise	SB, Aug. 20, 1914
Cloth dyeing	Change in guild leadership	SB, Sept. 29, 1914
Painting	Wage raise	SB, Oct. 26, 1914
Incense	Wage raise	SB, Nov. 6, 1914

Appendix A, cont.

Industry affected	Strike demand	Source
Carpentry	Wage raise	*SB*, Nov. 19, 1914
Tailors	Wage raise	*SB*, Nov. 30, 1914
Brassworking	Wage raise	*SB*, Jan. 17, 1915
Carpentry	Wage raise	*SB*, Feb. 1, 1915
Jewelry	Wage raise	*SB*, Apr. 2, 1915
Cloth dyeing	Wage raise	*SB*, May 7, 1915
Cloth dyeing	Wage raise	*SB*, July 20, 1915
Tailors	Wage raise	*SB*, Oct. 10, 1915
Butchers	Wage raise	*SB*, Dec. 14, 1915
Foundry	Wage raise	*SB*, May 26, 1916
Painting	Wage raise	*SB*, Aug. 25, 1916
Arsenal	Release withheld wages*	*SB*, Sept. 21, 1916
Arsenal	Abolish factory inspection	*MGRB*, Nov. 26, 1916
Printing	Unionization	*SB*, Mar. 31, 1917
Knife making	Wage raise	*SB*, Oct. 8, 1917
Ironworks	Dismissal of foreman	*SB*, Oct. 20, 1917
Barbers	Wage raise	*SB*, Jan. 1, 1918
Barbers	Wage raise	*MGRB*, Jan. 10, 1918
Ironworks	Maltreatment by factory guards*	*SB*, May 3, 1918
Carpentry	Wage raise	*Shishi xinbao*, May 7, 1918
Leather boxes	Wage raise	*SB*, May 12, 1918
Straw mats	Wage raise	*SB*, May 15, 1918
Wooden chests	Wage raise	*SB*, May 19, 1918
Bean curd	Wage raise	*SB*, June 29, 1918
Shipyards	Wage raise	*SB*, July 15, 1918
Wooden chests	Wage raise	*SB*, Sept. 18, 1918
Leather boxes	Wage raise	*SB*, Sept. 23, 1918
Silk dyeing	Wage raise	*SB*, Sept. 24, 1918
Scroll mounting	Wage raise	*SB*, Sept. 27, 1918
Metalworking	Wage raise	*MGRB*, Nov. 1, 1918
Paper lanterns	Wage raise	*MGRB*, Dec. 9, 1918
Umbrellas	Wage raise	*MGRB*, Mar. 13, 1919
Bookbinding	Wage raise	*SB*, Mar. 17, 1919
Machinery	Rehiring of dismissed apprentices*	*SB*, Mar. 22, 1919
Printing	Wage raise	*MGRB*, Apr. 5, 1919
Leather boxes	Artisan guilds' control of treasury	*SB*, Apr. 28, 1919
Knife making	Adherence to guild hiring rules*	*SB*, Apr. 29, 1919

NOTE: *NCH* = *North China Herald*; *SB* = *Shi bao* [Shanghai times]; *MGRB* = *Minguo ribao* [Republican daily].
* "Defensive" demand.

Appendix B

Strikes by Unskilled Workers in Shanghai, 1898–1919

Industry affected	Strike cause	Source
Cotton	Wage cut	*ZWRB*, Jan. 10, 1898
Cotton	Wage cut	*SWRB*, June 24, 1898
Cotton	Wage withholding	*SWRB*, June 30, 1898
Cotton	Change from daily to piece rate	*NCH*, Sept. 26, 1898
Silk	Wage cut	*ZWRB*, Nov. 8, 1898
Silk	Injured workers	*ZWRB*, Jan. 25, 1899
Cotton	Wage cut	*ZWRB*, June 4, 1899
Silk	Wage withholding	*Shen bao*, Dec. 15, 1899
Silk	Wage withholding	*NCH*, May 27, 1904
Cotton	Dissatisfaction with foreman*	*NCH*, May 5, 1905
Silk	Wage cut	*NCH*, June 10, 1906
Tobacco	Demand for wage raise*	*NCH*, June 10, 1906
Water	Demand for wage raise*	*NCH*, Sept. 3, 1906
Silk	Wage withholding	*NCH*, May 8, 1909
Silk	Increase in work hours	*NCH*, Aug. 6, 1909
Silk	Wage withholding	*Shen bao*, Jan. 8, 1910
Silk	Fines as punishment	*Shen bao*, Feb. 13, 1910
Silk	Wage withholding	*SB*, Jan. 22, 1911
Silk	Wage cut	*SB*, Feb. 9, 1911
Cotton	Wage withholding	*SB*, Apr. 25, 1911
Silk	Wage withholding	*SB*, May 30, 1911
Silk	Wage withholding	*SB*, June 2, 1911
Silk	Wage cut	*SB*, Aug. 7, 1911
Silk	Wage withholding	*SB*, Aug. 9, 1911
Silk	Wage cut	*SB*, Oct. 8, 1912
Silk	Demand for wage raise*	*SB*, Nov. 2, 1912
Cotton	Injured workers	*SB*, Nov. 2, 1912
Fabric	Wage cut	*SB*, Feb. 25, 1913
Paper	Maltreatment by foreman	*SB*, June 16, 1913
Bathhouse	Dispute between foreman and manager	*SB*, Feb. 1, 1914
Cotton	Wage cut	*SB*, Oct. 9, 1914
Night soil	New public health regulations	*SB*, Oct. 26, 1914
Silk	Wage withholding	*SB*, Oct. 30, 1914

Appendix B, cont.

Industry affected	Strike cause	Source
Night soil	Wage withholding	*SB*, Dec. 8, 1914
Dockers	Demand for wage raise*	*SB*, Dec. 14, 1914
Tobacco	Demand for wage raise*	*SB*, Feb. 2, 1915
Cotton	Wage withholding	*SB*, Apr. 7, 1915
Stevedores	Feud among foremen	*SB*, Dec. 23, 1915
Tobacco	Wage cut	*SB*, Mar. 10, 1916
Cotton	Demand for wage raise*	*SB*, Dec. 2, 1916
Silk	Conflict with foreign manager*	*SB*, Dec. 30, 1916
Tobacco	Wage cut	*SB*, July 21, 1917
Silk	Demand for wage raise*	*SB*, July 30, 1917
Cotton	Demand for wage raise*	*SB*, Sept. 4, 1917
Road Repair	Demand for wage raise*	*SB*, May 22, 1918
Railroad	Fear of end to contract system	*SB*, May 31, 1918
Tobacco	Increase in work hours	*MGRB*, Aug. 4, 1918
Cotton	Demand for wage raise*	*Shen bao*, Aug. 14, 1918
Cotton	Dispute with forewoman*	*MGRB*, Sept. 20, 1918
Cotton	Resignation of foreman	*Shen bao*, Oct. 18, 1918
Cotton	Termination of sick leave	*Shen bao*, Oct. 30, 1918
Cotton	Change from daily to piece rate	*SB*, Feb. 11, 1919
Cotton	Demand for wage raise*	*SB*, Apr. 19, 1919

NOTE: ZWRB = *Zhongwai ribao*; SWRB = *Shiwu ribao*; NCH = *North China Herald*; SB = *Shi bao*; MGRB = *Minguo ribao*.

*"Offensive" demand.

Appendix C

Rickshaws for Hire in Shanghai

Year	International settlement	Frenchtown	Chinese districts
1882	2,500		
1883	2,000		
1884	2,000		
1885	2,100		
1886	2,500		
1887	2,600		
1888	2,682		
1889	2,730		
1890	2,633		
1891	2,723		
1892	3,016		
1893	3,081		
1894	3,218		
1895	3,248		
1896	3,610		
1897	4,074		
1898	4,308		
1899	4,500		
1900	4,647		
1901	5,076		
1902	5,217		
1903	5,323		
1904	6,345		
1905	6,629		
1906	8,129		
1907	8,204		
1908	8,173		
1909	8,471		
1910	7,786		
1911	6,508		
1912	8,445		
1913	8,621		
1914	8,718		
1915	8,920		

Appendix C, cont.

Year	International settlement	Frenchtown	Chinese districts
1916	7,487		
1917	7,954		
1918	8,000		
1919	8,000		
1920	8,000		
1921	8,000		
1922	8,000		
1923	8,000		
1924	11,485		
1925	10,000		
1926	9,953		
1927	9,996	13,188	17,304
1928	9,995	13,717	17,776
1929	9,995	14,076	17,764
1930	10,390	14,193	18,767
1931	9,995	15,597	20,069
1932	9,990		21,220
1933	9,990		22,335
1934	9,990		23,335
1935	9,990		23,335
1936	9,946		23,335
1937	9,609		
1938	9,497		
1939	9,497		
1940	9,498		
1945			20,424
1946			26,890
1947			20,582

SOURCES: Annual Reports of the Shanghai Municipal Council, 1882–1904; Luo Zhiru, ed., *Tongjibiao zhong zhi Shanghai* [Shanghai through statistical tables] (Nanjing, 1932), p. 58; *Zhongyang ribao*, May 7, 1947; archives of the Shanghai Bureau of Public Utilities, #333-1.

NOTE: The table does not include rickshaws for private use. In 1931, for example, privately engaged rickshaws in the International Settlement numbered 11,446, in the French Concession 3,420, and in the Chinese districts 7,523.

Reference Matter

Character List

Ala tongxiangzhe　阿拉同鄉者
Bai shifu　拜師父
Banghui　帮會
Bangkou　帮口
Baozhang renquan　保障人權
Baozhuang bu　包裝部
Buliang fenzi　不良分子
Chewu bu　車務部
Chongchang　冲廠
Chougong　愁工
Choushen　酬神
Dabing　大餅
Dangshi　黨史
Da qingke　大請客
Da yeji　打野鷄
Dingti　頂替
Duizhuang gongren　堆裝工人
Faxing suo　發行所
Fenba　糞霸
Fenjia　分家
Fentou　糞頭
Gailiang　改良
Gaitou　丐頭
Gaizu pai　改組派
Gong　工
Gonghe shijie　共和世界
Gongjiang　工匠
Gongjin dang　共進黨
Gongjin hui　共進會
Gongren fulihui　工人福利會
Gongren jiuchadui　工人糾察隊

Gongsuo　公所
Gongwei　工委
Gongyunshi　工運史
Guizu gongren　貴族工人
Hongyi nülang　紅衣女郎
Hugong dui　護工隊
Huiguan　會館
Hulang chengqun　虎狼成羣
Jiangcha　講茶
Jiefang　解放
Jieji douzheng　階級鬥爭
Jiuji　救濟
Jiwu bu　機務部
Jizhi bu　機織部
Juanyan bu　卷烟部
Juntong　軍統
Kan renao　看热鬧
Laji shenghuo　垃圾生活
Langong　懶工
Laoda　老大
Laodongjia　勞動家
Laogong shensheng　勞工神聖
Laogong xiejinshe　勞工協進會
Laogui　老鬼
Laohu zao　老虎灶
Laozi hezuo　勞資合作
Li laojun　李老君
Lu Ban dian　魯班殿
Maimai hunyin　買賣婚姻
Namowen　拿摩溫
Nannü pingdeng　男女平等

Nongcun baowei chengshi
　農村包圍城市
Penghu qu　棚戶區
Pingtan　平彈
Qiangong　鉗工
Qida gonghui　七大工會
Qingong　勤工
Sanqingtuan　三青團
Shanghai gonghui zhengli
　　weiyuanhui　上海工會整理委員會
Shanghai gonghui zuzhi
　　tongyi weiyuanhui
　上海工會組織統一委員會
Shanghai gongren dixiajun
　上海工人地下軍
Shanghai gongren zonghui
　上海工人總會
Shanghaishi gongren zhongyi jiu-
　guojun　上海市工人忠義救國軍
Shengcun　生存
Shenghuo　生活
Siming gongsuo　四明公所
Tongjiang　銅匠
Tongjiang jian　銅匠間
Tongyi hui　同義會
Tongzhi　同志
Tuanti　團體
Wu qise　無起色
Xiao cao　小草

Xiao chaguan　小茶館
Xiao shimin　小市民
Xibao jian　錫包間
Xiedou　械鬥
Xintu　信徒
Yang shifu　楊師父
Yanye bu　烟葉部
Yaoban　搖班
Yeji　野雞
Yezi jian　葉子間
Yishe　蟻社
Yiyou she　益友社
Yongbang　甬幫
Youyi hui　友誼會
Youyi lianhehui　友誼聯合會
Yueju　粵劇
Zengjin daode　增進道德
Zhengdang　正當
Zhiwei　職委
Zhongguo jishu xiehui　中國技術協會
Zhongguo laodong xiehui
　中國勞動協會
Zhonghua minguo gongdang
　中華民國工黨
Zhonghua minguo guominjun
　中華民國國民軍
Zhongtong　中統
Zhunbei bu　準備部
Zibenjia　資本家

Notes

INTRODUCTION

1. For a sampling of this important literature, see Jeffrey Haydu, *Between Craft and Class: Skilled Workers and Factory Politics in the United States and Britain* (Berkeley, Calif., 1988); Ira Katznelson and Aristide R. Zolberg, eds., *Working-Class Formation: Nineteenth-Century Patterns in Western Europe and the United States* (Princeton, N.J., 1986); Victoria Bonnell, *Roots of Rebellion* (Berkeley, Calif., 1983); Ronald Aminzade, *Class, Politics, and Early Industrial Capitalism* (New York, 1981); Dick Geary, *European Labour Protest, 1848–1939* (London, 1981); Diane Koenker, *Moscow Workers and the 1917 Revolution* (Princeton, N.J., 1981); William P. Sewell, *Work and Revolution in France* (New York, 1980); Michael P. Hanagan, *The Logic of Solidarity* (Urbana, Ill., 1980); I. Prothero, *Artisans and Politics in Early Nineteenth-Century London* (London, 1979); Herbert G. Gutman, *Work, Culture, and Society* (New York, 1977); Bernard H. Moss, *The Origins of the French Labor Movement: The Socialism of Skilled Workers* (Berkeley, Calif., 1976); Joan W. Scott, *The Glassworkers of Carmaux: French Craftsmen and Political Activism in a Nineteenth-Century City* (Cambridge, Mass., 1974).

2. See especially Richard Jules Ostreicher, *Solidarity and Fragmentation* (Chicago, 1986); Charles F. Sabel, *Work and Politics: The Division of Labor in Industry* (New York, 1982); David M. Gordon, Richard Edwards, and Michael Reich, *Segmented Work, Divided Workers* (Cambridge, Mass., 1982); Ira Katznelson, *City Trenches: Urban Politics and the Patterning of Class in the United States* (New York, 1981); Suzanne Berger and Michael J. Piore, *Dualism and Discontinuity in Industrial Societies* (Cambridge, Mass., 1980); and Stanley Aronowitz, *False Promises: The Shaping of American Working-Class Consciousness* (New York, 1973).

3. For background on the 1911 Revolution, see especially Mary C. Wright, ed., *China in Revolution: The First Phase, 1900–1913* (New Haven, 1968); and Joseph W. Esherick, *Reform and Revolution in China: The 1911 Revolution in Hunan and Hubei* (Berkeley, Calif., 1976). For May Fourth, see Chow Tse-tung,

The May Fourth Movement: Intellectual Revolution in Modern China (Cambridge, Mass., 1960); and Vera Schwarcz, *The Chinese Enlightenment: Intellectuals and the Legacy of the May Fourth Movement of 1919* (Berkeley, Calif., 1986). For the Nationalist regime, see Hung-Mao Tien, *Government and Politics in Kuomintang China, 1927–1937* (Stanford, Calif., 1972); Lloyd E. Eastman, *The Abortive Revolution: China Under Nationalist Rule, 1927–1937* (Cambridge, Mass., 1974); and Eastman, *Seeds of Destruction: Nationalist China in War and Revolution, 1937–1945* (Stanford, Calif., 1984). For the Communist revolution, see Lucien Bianco, *Origins of the Chinese Revolution* (Stanford, Calif., 1967); and Ch'en Yung-fa, *Making Revolution: The Communist Movement in Eastern and Central China* (Berkeley, Calif., 1986). And on the post-1949 political system, see A. Doak Barnett, *Cadres, Bureaucracy, and Political Power in China* (New York, 1967); and Franz Schurmann, *Ideology and Organization in Communist China* (Berkeley, Calif., 1970). In none of these important accounts does labor figure centrally.

4. Jeffrey Wasserstrom, *Student Protest in Twentieth-Century China: The View from Shanghai* (Stanford, Calif., 1991), is a fascinating study of the role of Shanghai students during the years 1919 to 1949.

5. Detailed discussion of these events can be found in Jean Chesneaux, *The Chinese Labor Movement, 1919–1927* (Stanford, Calif., 1968).

6. See Suzanne Pepper, *Civil War in China: The Political Struggle, 1945–1949* (Berkeley, Calif., 1978).

7. On Cultural Revolution factionalism, see Hong Yung Lee, *The Politics of the Chinese Cultural Revolution* (Berkeley, Calif., 1978).

8. Personal observation, December 1986–January 1987, Shanghai.

9. Worker support for the protests of 1989 was substantial. See Jeanne L. Wilson, "Labor Policy in China: Reform and Retrogression," *Problems of Communism* September–October 1990: 44–65; and Elizabeth J. Perry, "Casting a Chinese 'Democracy' Movement: The Roles of Students, Workers and Entrepreneurs," in *Popular Protest and Political Culture in Modern China: Learning from 1989,* ed. Jeffrey Wasserstrom and Elizabeth J. Perry (Boulder, Colo., 1991).

10. Important exceptions are Emily Honig, *Sisters and Strangers: Women in the Shanghai Cotton Mills, 1911–1949* (Stanford, Calif., 1986); and Gail Hershatter, *The Workers of Tianjin, 1900–1949* (Stanford, Calif., 1986). Both of these studies offer refreshing "bottom-up" views of Chinese labor, yet in neither is the labor movement a central focus.

11. Fang Fuan, *Chinese Labour* (1931; rpt. New York, 1980), p. 4.

12. Nym Wales, *The Chinese Labor Movement* (New York, 1945), p. 11.

13. Chesneaux, *Chinese Labor Movement*, p. 405. A recent collection of Shanghai factory histories opens with the assertion that "the Chinese labor movement from beginning to end was developed under the direction of the Chinese Communist Party" (*Shanghai gongchang qiye dangshi gongyunshi congshu* [Collection of Party and labor movement histories of Shanghai factories and enterprises], [Shanghai, 1991], Preface, p. 1).

14. James C. Scott, *Weapons of the Weak: Everyday Forms of Peasant Resistance* (New Haven, 1985), is an eloquent presentation of this perspective. See

also Forrest D. Colburn, ed., *Everyday Forms of Peasant Resistance* (Armonk, N.Y., 1989).

15. James E. Cronin, "Theories of Strikes: Why Can't They Explain the British Experience?" *Journal of Social History* 12 (1978): 194.

16. Michelle Perrot, *Les ouvriers en grève*, 2 vols. (Paris, 1974).

17. Gerald Friedman, "The State and the Making of the Working Class," *Theory and Society*, no. 17 (1988): 402. See also Ira Katznelson's introductory essay in Katznelson and Zolberg, eds., *Working-Class Formation*, pp. 3–41.

18. Gordon Marshall, "Some Remarks on the Study of Working-Class Consciousness," *Politics and Society* 12 (1983): 272.

PART I: INTRODUCTION

1. A simplified version of the Marxist thesis can be found in Karl Marx and Friedrich Engels, *Manifesto of the Communist Party* (London, 1848). The modernization argument is put forth in Arthur Ross and Paul A. Hartmann, *Changing Patterns of Industrial Conflict* (New York, 1960); and Clark Kerr, "Industrial Peace and the Collective Bargaining Environment," in *Collective Bargaining*, ed. A. Flanders (London, 1955), pp. 121–37.

2. William T. Rowe, *Hankow: Commerce and Society in a Chinese City, 1796–1889* (Stanford, Calif., 1984), p. 213. Rowe emphasizes the ability of Hankow residents to transcend such divisions (pp. 245–47).

3. Peter Burke, *Popular Culture in Early Modern Europe* (New York, 1978), p. 50.

4. A very partial listing of important studies of working-class culture includes John E. Bodnar, *Immigration and Industrialization: Community and Protest in an Industrial Society, 1900–1940* (Baltimore, 1982); Craig Calhoun, *The Question of Class Struggle* (Chicago, 1981); Milton Canton, ed., *American Workingclass Culture: Explorations in American Labor and Social History* (Westport, Conn., 1979); John Clarke, Charles Critchen, and Richard Johnson, eds., *Working-Class Culture* (New York, 1979); Robert Darnton, *The Great Cat Massacre* (New York, 1984); Natalie Zemon Davis, *Society and Culture in Early Modern France* (Stanford, Calif., 1966); Michael H. Frisch and Daniel J. Walkowitz, eds., *Working-Class America: Essays on Labor, Community, and American Society* (Urbana, Ill., 1983); David Montgomery, *Workers' Control in America* (Cambridge, Mass., 1979); Barrington Moore, Jr., *The Social Bases of Obedience and Revolt* (White Plains, N.Y., 1978); E. P. Thompson, *The Making of the English Working Class* (New York, 1963); Sean Wilentz, *Chants Democratic: New York City and the Rise of the American Working Class* (New York, 1984); and Paul Willis, *Learning to Labour* (Westmead, Eng., 1977).

5. Herbert G. Gutman, *Work, Culture and Society* (New York, 1977), pp. 15, 18.

CHAPTER I

1. Zheng Zuan, "Jindai Shanghai dushi de xingcheng" [The development of the modern city of Shanghai], in *Shanghai shi yanjiu* [Studies in Shanghai history]

(Shanghai, 1984), pp. 172–73. For general overviews of the development of modern Shanghai, see Tang Zhenchang, ed., *Shanghai shi* [The history of Shanghai] (Shanghai, 1989); Liu Huiwu, ed., *Jindai Shanghai shi* [The history of modern Shanghai] (Shanghai, 1985); Rhoads Murphey, *Shanghai: Key to Modern China* (Cambridge, Mass., 1953); F. L. Hawkes Pott, *A Short History of Shanghai* (Shanghai, 1928); and G. Lanning and S. Couling, *The History of Shanghai* (Shanghai, 1921).

2. Zhu Menghua, "Shanghai nanshi jiuhua" [Old tales of Shanghai's Nanshi], *Shanghai difangshi ziliao*, 1982, no. 1, pp. 43–47.

3. Hu Xianghan, *Shanghai xiaozhi* [Little gazetteer of Shanghai] (Shanghai, 1930), chap. 10.

4. Quan Hansheng, "Shanghai zai jindai Zhongguo gongyehua zhong de diwei" [Shanghai's position in the industrialization of modern China], *Zhongyang yanjiuyuan lishi yuyan yanjiusuo jikan* 29 (1958): 461–62.

5. Zou Yiren, *Jiu Shanghai renkou bianqian de yanjiu* [Studies in the population change of old Shanghai] (Shanghai, 1980), pp. 90–91.

6. John K. Fairbank, *Trade and Diplomacy on the China Coast* (Cambridge, Mass., 1953), pp. 394–96.

7. Leung Yuen Sang, "Regional Rivalry in Mid-Nineteenth-Century Shanghai," *Ch'ing-shih wen-t'i* 4, no. 8 (1982): 30; Wu Zude, "Jiulou fanguan yibie" [A look at restaurants], *Gemingshi ziliao* 2, no. 5 (1987): 146–51.

8. A useful listing of the major Shanghai guilds appears in *Shanghai beike ziliao xuanji* [Selected materials from Shanghai stele inscriptions] (Shanghai, 1980), pp. 507–13. On the guild tradition in Guangdong, see Edward J. Rhoads, *China's Republican Revolution: The Case of Kwangtung, 1895–1913* (Cambridge, Mass., 1975), pp. 24–25.

9. *Shanghaixian xuzhi* [Shanghai county gazetteer], ed. Wu Xin (Shanghai, 1918), chap. 3, pp. 2–8; *Jindai Shanghai diqu fangzhi jingji shiliao xuanji* [Selections of gazetteer materials on the economic history of the modern Shanghai region] (Shanghai, 1984), p. 58.

10. James R. Green, *The World of the Worker* (New York, 1980), p. 28.

11. The following discussion of the Small Sword Rebellion is drawn mainly from the massive compilation of primary sources edited by the Shanghai Academy of Social Sciences: *Shanghai xiaodaohui qiyi shiliao huibian* [Compendium of historical materials on the Shanghai Small Swords Uprising] (Shanghai, 1980). Specific citations and further discussion of the rebellion may be found in Elizabeth J. Perry, "Tax Revolt in Late Qing China: The Small Swords of Shanghai and Liu Depei of Shandong," *Late Imperial China* 6, no. 1 (1985): 83–112. An interesting interpretation of the Small Swords as a labor movement can be found in Wang Ermin, "Wukou tongshang chuqi Shanghai diqu baoluan shijian suo fanying mimi huishe zhi shengji" [Violence in the Shanghai area during the early five-treaty-port period as a reflection of the vitality of secret societies], *Zhongguo wenhua yanjiusuo xuebao* 12 (1981): 65–90.

12. Frederic Wakeman, Jr., *Strangers at the Gate* (Berkeley, Calif., 1966), chaps. 1–3; Ming K. Chan, "Popular Mobilization and Labor Resistance in the Canton Delta, 1831–1927," paper presented at the annual meeting of the Association of Asian Studies, 1989.

13. The fall of Nanjing to the rebels resulted in a substantial flight of skilled workers from Nanjing to the safety of Shanghai. For examples of a cabinetmaker, members of a weavers' guild, and other educated refugees, see *North China Herald,* Aug. 30, Nov. 15, 1856, May 16, 1857.

14. Jen Yuwen, *The Taiping Revolutionary Movement* (New Haven, 1973), chap. 19.

15. Susan Mann Jones, "The Ningbo Pang and Financial Power at Shanghai," in *The Chinese City Between Two Worlds,* ed. Mark Elvin and G. William Skinner (Stanford, Calif., 1974), pp. 73–96.

16. Leung Yuen Sang, "Regional Rivalry in Mid-Nineteenth-Century Shanghai," p. 40; *Shen bao* [Taipei reprint], 7: 4161, 4170, 4217, 4242, 4265. The British press was also inclined to paint the Cantonese in an unfavorable light, blaming their "cruelty" for an increase in crime in the mid-1860's. See *North China Herald,* Mar. 25, 1865.

17. Yu Qian, "Chunfengdeyi lou ji qita" [The Chunfengdeyi tower and more], in *Shanghai zhanggu* (Shanghai, 1982), pp. 65–68; Qian Huafo, *Sanshi nianlai zhi Shanghai* [Shanghai of the past thirty years] (Shanghai, 1947), pp. 23–24.

18. On the tradition of guilds and native-place associations in Zhejiang, see R. Keith Schoppa, *Chinese Elites and Political Change: Zhejiang Province in the Early Twentieth Century* (Cambridge, Mass., 1982), pp. 27–31.

19. Shiba Yoshinobu, "Ningbo and Its Hinterland," in *The City in Late Imperial China,* ed. G. William Skinner (Stanford, Calif., 1977), p. 437.

20. *Shanghai yanjiu ziliao* [Shanghai research materials] (Shanghai, 1937), 2: 295–96.

21. Jones, "Ningbo Pang," pp. 86–88; Fang Teng, "Yu Xiaqing lun" [On Yu Xiaqing], *Zazhi yuekan* 12, nos. 2–4 (1943): 59–63; *Yongguang chuji* [Preliminary compilation of the glory of Ningbo] (Shanghai, 1941).

22. James L. Watson and Evelyn S. Rawski, eds., *Death Ritual in Late Imperial and Modern China* (Berkeley, Calif., 1988).

23. Pott, *Short History of Shanghai,* p. 98.

24. Wu Zude, "Jiulou fanguan yibie," pp. 146–51. On the influx of wealthy refugees from Suzhou following its fall to the rebels, see *North China Herald,* Jan. 28, 1865.

25. By the 1920's, some 200,000 to 300,000 of Shanghai's inhabitants were living in 50,000 such huts. A survey of shantytown residents conducted in 1926 by the International Settlement revealed a 77 percent employment rate—mainly as factory workers, rickshaw pullers, and dockers (*Shanghai penghuqu de bianqian* [The transformation of Shanghai's shantytowns] [Shanghai, 1962], p. 34).

26. Zhu Maocheng, *Diaocha Shanghai gongren zhuwu ji shehui qingxing jilüe* [Outlines of a report on housing and social conditions among industrial workers in Shanghai] (Shanghai, 1926), pp. 4–12; Tang Hai, *Zhongguo laodong wenti* [Chinese labor conditions] (Shanghai, 1926), pp. 9–10; Yang Meizhen, "Yangshupu nügong zhuangkuang" [Conditions of women workers in Yangshupu] (Pujiang University graduation thesis, 1930).

27. Inoue Kobai, *Shanhai no himinsō* [The face of Shanghai's poor] (Tokyo, 1934), pp. 31–32.

28. Wu Zude, "Jiulou fanguan yibie," p. 149.

29. Zheng Zuan, "Jindai Shanghai dushi de xingcheng," pp. 172–73.

30. Xue Gengshen, "Jindai Shanghai de liumang" [The gangsters of modern Shanghai], *Wenshi ziliao xuanji*, no. 3 (1980): 160–62.

31. D. K. Lieu, *The Growth and Industrialization of Shanghai* (Shanghai, 1936), pp. 175–76. (In the quote romanization has been changed to pinyin.)

32. On rural feuds in North China, see Elizabeth J. Perry, *Rebels and Revolutionaries in North China, 1845–1945* (Stanford, Calif., 1980), pp. 74–80. On the Southeast China tradition, see Harry J. Lamley, "Lineage Feuding in Southern Fujian and Eastern Guangdong Under Qing Rule," in *Violence in China: Essays in Culture and Counterculture*, ed. Jonathan N. Lipman and Stevan Harrell (Albany, N.Y., 1990), pp. 27–64.

33. Chen Gang, *Shanghaigang matou de bianqian* [Changes on the docks of the port of Shanghai] (Shanghai, 1966), pp. 46–47; *Shanghaigang shihua* [Historical tales of the port of Shanghai] (Shanghai, 1979), p. 297.

34. Emily Honig, "The Politics of Prejudice: Subei People in Republican-Era Shanghai," *Modern China* 15, no. 3 (1989): 259–62.

35. Jean Chesneaux, *The Chinese Labor Movement, 1919–1927* (Stanford, Calif., 1968), pp. 393–400.

36. Emily Honig, *Sisters and Strangers: Women in the Shanghai Cotton Mills, 1911–1949* (Stanford, Calif., 1986), p. 245; Gail Hershatter, *The Workers of Tianjin, 1900–1949* (Stanford, Calif., 1986), p. 7.

37. For other recent studies that emphasize variation within the Chinese working class, see Lynda Shaffer, *Mao and the Workers: The Hunan Labor Movement, 1920–1923* (Armonk, N.Y., 1982); and Ming Kou Chan, "Labor and Empire: The Chinese Labor Movement in the Canton Delta, 1895–1927" (Ph.D. dissertation, Stanford University, 1975).

38. John Cumbler, "Migration, Class Formation and Class Consciousness: The American Experience," in *Confrontation, Class Consciousness, and the Labor Process*, ed. Michael Hanagan and Charles Stephenson (Urbana, Ill., 1986), p. 53.

39. Lieu, *Growth and Industrialization of Shanghai*, p. 166.

40. See Michael Hanagan and Charles Stephenson, eds., *Proletarians and Protest* (New York, 1986), p. 4, for an argument—contra E. P. Thompson—that social solidarity, more than ideology, stands as the critical mediating link between past experience and proletarian protest.

41. A similar pattern has been observed among skilled workers in other settings. See especially David Montgomery, *Workers' Control in America: Studies in the History of Work, Technology, and Labor Struggles* (Cambridge, England., 1979).

CHAPTER 2

1. William T. Rowe, *Hankow: Commerce and Society in a Chinese City, 1796–1895* (Stanford, Calif., 1984), p. 252.

2. Whether guild power hindered or furthered economic development in China has been the subject of controversy in the secondary literature. For contrasting

views, see Imahori Seiji, *Chūgoku no shakai kōzō* [Chinese social structure] (Tokyo, 1953); Peng Zeyi, "Shijiu shiji houqi Zhongguo chengshi shougongye shangye hanghui de chongjian he zuoyong" [The reconstruction and functioning of urban handicraft and commercial guilds in late nineteenth-century China], *Lishi yanjiu*, no. 91 (1965): 71–102; and Ho Ping-ti, *Zhongguo huiguanshi lun* [A historical survey of landsmannschaften in China] (Taipei, 1966).

3. For the European case, see esp. Bernard Moss, *The Origins of the French Labor Movement, 1830–1914: The Socialism of Skilled Workers* (Berkeley, Calif., 1976).

4. The contrast between European and Chinese guilds is made in Peter J. Golas, "Early Ch'ing Guilds," in *The City in Late Imperial China*, ed. G. William Skinner (Stanford, Calif., 1977), p. 563.

5. Chinese Academy of Social Sciences, ed., *Shanghai minzu jiqi gongye* [Shanghai's national machine industry] (Beijing, 1979), pp. 59–60; *Shanghai chuanchang gongyunshi* [The history of the labor movement at Shanghai's shipyards] (Shanghai, 1984), p. 16.

6. *Shanghai minzu jiqi gongye*, p. 60; *Shanghai chuanchang gongyunshi*, p. 16. According to stele inscriptions, a construction guild (also known as *Lu Ban dian*) had been founded in the city as early as 1823 for merchants and workers from Shanghai, Ningbo, and Shaoxing. See *Shanghai beike ziliao xuanji* [Selected materials from Shanghai stele inscriptions] (Shanghai, 1980), p. 509.

7. *North China Herald*, Jan. 10, 1879; *Zhongguo jindai gongyeshi ziliao* [Materials on the history of China's modern industry] (Beijing, 1957–61), 4 volumes, 1:1224–46.

8. *North China Herald*, Nov. 4, 1880; *Zhongguo jindai gongyeshi ziliao*, 1:1247–48.

9. *All About Shanghai and Environs* (Shanghai, 1935), p. 60. [Transliteration changed to pinyin.]

10. Mao Qihua, "Da geming chuqi Shanghai Zhonghua shuju zongchang de dang, tuan zuzhi yu gongren yundong" [Party and league organization and the labor movement at the Shanghai Zhonghua Book Company in the early period of the great revolution], *Shanghai gongyunshi yanjiu ziliao*, 1984, no. 4, pp. 2–3.

11. Chinese Academy of Social Sciences, ed., *Shanghai minzu jiqi gongye*, p. 19.

12. Li Cishan, "Shanghai laodong zhuangkuang" [Shanghai labor conditions], *Xin qingnian* 7, no. 6 (1920): 44.

13. Shen Xiaokun, Shao Xingbei, and Xie Zuoming, "Jiefangqian Shanghai wujin shangye gaikuang" [Conditions in the Shanghai metalworking trade before Liberation], in *Shanghai wujin shangye zhigong yundong shiliao* [Materials on the labor movement in the Shanghai metalworking trade] (Shanghai, 1985): pp. 20–23.

14. *Minguo ribao*, June 21, 1920. Subservience to the master did not end with the initiation ceremony. At mealtime in the factory cafeteria, apprentices respectfully entered the dining hall first so they would be on hand to serve rice to their masters.

15. Economics Institute of the Shanghai Academy of Social Sciences, ed., *Jiangnan zaochuanchang changshi* [Factory history of the Jiangnan Arsenal] (Nanjing, 1983), pp. 86–91.

16. Gary G. Hamilton, "Why No Capitalism in China?" *Journal of Developing Societies* 1 (1985): 204.

17. Charles Tilly, "Collective Violence in European Perspective," in *The History of Violence in America*, ed. Hugh Davis Graham and Ted Robert Gurr (New York, 1969), pp. 4–45.

18. Chinese Academy of Social Sciences, ed., *Shanghai minzu jiqi gongye*, p. 786.

19. *Shen bao*, Nov. 11, 1879.

20. *North China Herald*, May 11, 1883.

21. Economics Institute of the Shanghai Academy of Social Sciences, ed., *Jiangnan zaochuanchang changshi*, p. 92.

22. *North China Herald*, Sept. 5, 1890; *Zhongguo jindai gongyeshi ziliao*, 1:1250.

23. *North China Herald*, May 21, 28, 1902; *Zhongguo jindai gongyeshi ziliao*, 2:1260.

24. Ming K. Chan, "Popular Mobilization and Labor Resistance in the Canton Delta, 1831–1927," paper presented at the annual meeting of the Association of Asian Studies, 1989. In 1858, within a month more than 20,000 of the total of 70,000 Cantonese workers in Hong Kong returned to their native towns in Guangdong as part of a retaliatory strike against the British.

25. *North China Herald*, Sept. 23, 30, 1911.

26. Negishi Tadashi, *Shanhai no girudo* [The guilds of Shanghai] (Tokyo, 1951), pp. 325–27. As Negishi points out, construction guilds that brought together carpenters and masons (and sometimes painters) were also formed in Beijing and Wuxi at around the same time for the same purpose of resisting foreign competition.

27. *Shanghai beike ziliao xuanji*, pp. 321–22.

28. On the relationship between an artisanal language of association and the French Revolution, see William H. Sewell, Jr., *Work and Revolution in France: The Language of Labor from the Old Regime to 1848* (New York, 1980).

29. *Shi bao*, Nov. 8, 1911.

30. Yang Shaoying, *Zhongguo gongren de bagong douzheng* [Strike struggles of Chinese workers] (Nanjing, 1957), preface.

31. Shanghai Academy of Social Sciences History Institute, ed., *Xinhai geming zai Shanghai shiliao xuanji* [Compilation of historical materials on the 1911 Revolution in Shanghai] (Shanghai, 1981), pp. 892–93; Chen Minglu, "Minguo chunian laogong yundong de zaipinggu" [A reevaluation of the labor movement in the early years of the republic], paper presented at the Conference on the Early History of the Republic of China, Taipei, 1983, p. 4; Zhu Dalu, "Shanghai hongmen xinhai yuxue ji" [Record of the 1911 bloodbath of the Shanghai Red Gang], in *Shanghai yishi* [Shanghai anecdotes] (Shanghai, 1987), pp. 169–75. Fan Songfu, "Shanghai banghui neimu" [Inside the Shanghai gangs], *Wenshi ziliao xuanji*, no. 3 (1980), p. 155, notes that in Shanghai the Mutual Advancement Society was

composed largely of "wharf officers" (*matou guan*) whose positions had been eliminated by the overthrow of the Qing dynasty. These wharf officers were also gang leaders.

32. Further discussion of the exclusivist character of the Labor Party can be found in S. Kojima, "Shingai kakumeiki ni okeru Kōtō to Nōtō" [The Labor Party and the Peasant Party at the time of the 1911 Revolution], *Rekishi hyōron*, no. 256 (1971).

33. *Xinhai geming zai Shanghai shiliao xuanji*, pp. 903–6; *Minli bao*, Jan. 2, 8, 25, Feb. 10, 21, June 23, 1912; *Minquan bao*, Dec. 21, 1911, Apr. 25, 27, May 23, June 13, Dec. 15, 1912; *Taipingyang bao*, July 6, 1912; Li Shiyue, "Xinhai geming qianhou de Zhongguo gongren yundong he Zhonghuaminguo Gongdang" [The Chinese labor movement and the Chinese Labor Party around the time of the 1911 Revolution], *Shixue jikan*, 1957, no. 1, pp. 63–86; Ma Chaojun et al., *Zhongguo laogong yundongshi* [A history of the Chinese labor movement] (Taipei, 1959), 5 volumes, 1:73–78.

34. *Minquan bao*, June 12, July 15, 16, 17, 1912; *Taipingyang bao*, July 15, 1912; *Shi bao*, Dec. 2, 1912. Nine months later, when industry leaders tried to renege on the agreement, the Loyalty Association countered with another successful strike (*Minquan bao*, March 14, 18, 19, 20, 30, 1913).

35. The carpenters' strike is described in *Shi bao*, Nov. 26, 27, 30, Dec. 21, 25, 1912, Jan. 7, 10, 23, 1913; *Minquan bao*, Nov. 24–29, Dec. 2, 11, 1912, Jan. 5, 9, 13, 30, 1913.

36. *North China Herald*, Dec. 11, 1912; *Shi bao*, Dec. 18, 1912.

37. Chinese Academy of Social Sciences, ed., *Shanghai minzu jiqi gongye*, pp. 840–41; Luo Chuanhua, *Jinri Zhongguo laogong wenti* [Labor problems in today's China] (Shanghai, 1933), p. 153. Yuan was reportedly particularly perturbed by the formation at the Jiangnan Arsenal, probably under Labor Party inspiration, of a vocal union known as the "workers' alliance" (*gongren tongmenghui*). See *Minquan bao*, May 23, 1912.

38. *Minquan bao*, May 30, 31, June 1, 2, 3, 5, 6, 10, 15, 1913.

39. *Zhongguo jindai gongyeshi ziliao*, 2:1299–1301; Liu Mingkui, ed., "1911–1921 nian Zhongguo gongren bagong douzheng he zuzhi qingkuang ziliao huibian" [Compilation of materials on the strikes and organizations of Chinese workers, 1911–1921], *Zhongguo gongyun shiliao*, 1960, no. 3, pp. 91–159, no. 4, pp. 29–85; Ma Honglin, Ji Guozhong, and Chen Shulin, "Diyici shijie dazhan qijian Shanghai gongren jieji de zhuangda he gongren yundong de fazhan" [The strength of the Shanghai working class and the development of the labor movement during the period of World War I], *Shixue yuekan*, 1964, no. 7, p. 11.

40. Ma Honglin, Ji Guozhong, and Chen Shulin, "Diyici shijie dazhan," p. 12.

41. *Shi bao*, Oct. 29, 31, Nov. 8, 10, 11, 13, 1914.

42. Ibid., Nov. 19, 20, 21, 1914.

43. Ibid., Nov. 22, 23, 1914, Sept. 3, 1916.

44. Ibid., Nov. 21–26, 1914.

45. Ronald Aminzade, "The Transformation of Social Solidarities in Nineteenth-Century Toulouse," in *Consciousness and Class Experience in Nineteenth-Century Europe*, ed. John M. Merriman (New York, 1979), pp. 85–105;

William H. Sewell, Jr., "Artisans, Factory Workers, and the Formation of the French Working Class, 1789–1848," in *Working-Class Formation: Nineteenth-Century Patterns in Western Europe and the United States,* ed. Ira Katznelson and Aristide R. Zolberg (Princeton, N.J., 1986), pp. 45–70.

46. *Taipingyang bao,* July 2, 1912, reprinted in *Zhongguo jindai gongyeshi ziliao,* 2:1278.

47. *Shangwu yinshuguan gonghui shi* [A history of the Commercial Press union] (Shanghai, 1924), pp. 1–2.

48. Ronald Aminzade, *Class, Politics, and Early Industrial Capitalism: A Study of Mid-Nineteenth Century Toulouse, France* (New York, 1981), p. 78.

49. Sewell, *Work and Revolution in France,* pp. 1, 179.

CHAPTER 3

1. A. M. Kotenev, *Shanghai: Its Municipality and the Chinese* (Shanghai, 1927), pp. 13–14; Nym Wales, *The Chinese Labor Movement* (New York, 1945), p. 9.

2. *Zhongguo jindai gongyeshi ziliao* [Materials on the history of China's modern industry] (Beijing, 1957–61), 2:1299–1301.

3. Cui Xilin, "Wo suo zhidao de Qinghongbang" [The Red and Green gangs I knew], *Jiangsu wenshi ziliao xuanji,* 1987, no. 20.

4. Wu Yuanshu and Jiang Sitai, "Shanghai qibaige qigai de shehui diaocha" [A social survey of 700 Shanghai beggars], Pujiang University graduation thesis, 1933. In 1926, Green Gang chieftain Du Yuesheng founded the Shanghai beggars shelter as a benevolent gesture (Mei Zhen and Shao Pu, *Haishang wenren Du Yuesheng* [Seaside celebrity Du Yuesheng] [Henan, 1987], p. 38).

5. Gail Hershatter's work in progress promises greatly to improve our understanding of this important topic.

6. Cang Haisheng, *Xianhua changmen* [Gossip about prostitution] (Shanghai, 1935), p. 7; Bao Zubao, *Changji wenti* [The prostitute problem] (Shanghai, 1935).

7. Yang Jieceng and Jia Yuannan, *Shanghai changji gaizao shihua* [Historical tales of the reformation of Shanghai prostitutes] (Shanghai, 1988), pp. 17–19.

8. *Shanghai wuchaoan neimu* [The inside story of Shanghai's dancers' incident] (Shanghai, n.d.).

9. Li Cishan, "Shanghai laodong zhuangkuang" [The condition of Shanghai labor], *Xin qingnian* 7, no. 6 (1920): 76–77; Xue Gengshen, "Jindai Shanghai de liumang" [The gangsters of modern Shanghai], *Wenshi ziliao xuanji,* 1980, no. 3, pp. 171–72; Shanghai Municipal Bureau of Health, ed., *Shanghaishi qingchu fenbian gongzuo gaikuang ji gaijin jihua* [Conditions and plans for reform of Shanghai sanitation work] (Shanghai, n.d.); *Shen bao,* June 22, 23, 24, 25, 27, 28, 29, 30, 1912; Zhu Menghua, "Jiu Shanghai de sige feipin dawang" [Four great garbage kings of old Shanghai], *Shanghai difangshi ziliao,* 1984, no. 3, pp. 162–63.

10. Further cases of protest by night-soil carriers against government health regulations occurred in 1913, 1914, and 1919 (*Shi bao,* Dec. 14, 1913, Aug. 18, Oct. 26, 29, Nov. 5, 23, 1914; *Minguo ribao,* June 9, Dec. 15, 16, 1919, Jan. 4, 1920). Night-soil workers were not the only group to react against newly imposed

sanitation regulations. In 1910, fruit sellers struck to protest a regulation requiring the use of glass cases, butchers struck in opposition to a ban on private pig slaughtering, and shop owners closed their doors to avoid a health inspection aimed at reducing the incidence of plague in the city (*Shi bao*, Apr. 2, July 8, Oct. 12, 1910).

11. Interviews with labor movement authorities at the Port of Shanghai, May 26, 1987, and Sept. 26, 1988.

12. See Number Two History Archives, Nanjing, no. 722: 4-503, for examples of serious feuds between dockers of Shandong and Hubei origin.

13. *Shanghaigang shihua* [Historical tales of the Port of Shanghai] (Shanghai, 1979), pp. 298–300; *Shi bao*, Dec. 14, 15, 16, 1914, Jan. 1, 17, 18, 20, 21, 22, 24, 1915.

14. David Montgomery, *Workers' Control in America: Studies in the History of Work, Technology, and Labor Struggles* (Cambridge, England, 1979), p. 42.

15. See, for example, Fu Daohui, *Wusa yundong* [The May Thirtieth Movement] (Shanghai, 1985); Ren Jianshu and Zhang Quan, *Wusa yundong jianshi* [A brief history of the May Thirtieth Movement] (Shanghai, 1985).

16. *Minguo ribao*, May 1, 1922.

17. Fang Lanying, Apr. 16, 1958, transcript of interview, Labor Movement Archives of the Shanghai Academy of Social Sciences Institute of History.

18. Emily Honig, *Sisters and Strangers: Women in the Shanghai Cotton Mills, 1911–1949* (Stanford, Calif., 1986).

19. Liu Ajiu, Apr. 16, 1958, transcript of interview, Labor Movement Archives of the SASS Institute of History.

20. Li Cishan, "Shanghai laodong zhuangkuang," pp. 10–11; *Minguo ribao*, May 1, 1922.

21. Mary Ninde Gamewell, *The Gateway to China* (New York, 1916), p. 226.

22. Zhu Bangxing, Hu Linge, and Xu Sheng, eds., *Shanghai chanye yu Shanghai zhigong* [Shanghai industry and Shanghai workers] (Shanghai, 1984), p. 47.

23. Fang Fuan, "Shanghai Labor," *Chinese Economic Journal* 7, nos. 2 and 3 (1930): 882, 998, 1008–9.

24. Zhu Maocheng, *Diaocha Shanghai gongren zhuwu ji shehui qingxing jilüe* [Outlines of a report on housing and social conditions among workers in Shanghai] (Shanghai, 1926), pp. 4–12.

25. Zhu Bangxing et al., *Shanghai chanye*, pp. 93–95; Fang Fuan, "Shanghai Labor," p. 877; Yang Meizhen, *Yangshupu nügong zhuangkuang* [The condition of women workers in Yangshupu] (Shanghai, 1930).

26. Zhu Bangxing et al., *Shanghai chanye*, p. 87.

27. Honig, *Sisters and Strangers*, p. 5.

28. Li Cishan, "Shanghai laodong zhuangkuang," pp. 9–11.

29. Xu Weiyong and Huang Hanmin, *Rongjia qiye fazhanshi* [A developmental history of the Rong family enterprises] (Beijing, 1985), p. 265.

30. Honig, *Sisters and Strangers*, p. 212.

31. Yang Meizhen, 1930.

32. Zhu Bangxing et al., *Shanghai chanye*, p. 107.

33. Liu Mingkui, ed., "1911–1921 nian Zhongguo gongren bagong douzheng

he zuzhi qingkuang ziliao huibian" [A compilation of materials on the strikes and organizations of Chinese workers, 1911–1921], *Zhongguo gongyun shiliao*, 1960, nos. 3 and 4, pp. 91–159, 29–85.

34. *Shanghai Strike Statistics, 1918–1940* (see footnote, p. 7).

35. *Zhongguo jindai gongyeshi ziliao*, 2:1236, 1257–60, 1268, and 1286–92 provide good examples of late nineteenth- and early twentieth-century strikes among women factory workers in Shanghai.

36. See *Shi bao*, June 16, 1913, for the case of an all-women's strike at the Longzhang paper mill to protest abuse by male workers.

37. In 1898, strikes at several British cotton mills in Yangshupu were aimed at preventing a switch to piecework wages. The British enterprises advocated the new system so that workers might "get the most out of their machines," thereby improving competitiveness with the Indian cotton market (*North China Herald*, Sept. 26, 1898).

38. For strikes to protest imposition of the "baby ban" and piece rates in the Japanese-owned Rihua cotton factory, see *Minguo ribao*, Aug. 13, 14, 15, 16, 1918, Feb. 10, 1919; *Shen bao*, Aug. 5, Sept. 22, 1918; and *Shi bao*, Feb. 2, 11, 13, 16, 1919.

39. See *Zhongguo jindai gongyeshi ziliao*, 2:1291, for a case in 1898 of a cotton mill forewoman leading a strike to protest a wage reduction.

40. *Shen bao*, Aug. 16, 1918; *Minguo ribao*, Sept. 21, 1918.

41. C. L'estrange Malone, *New China Report of an Investigation* (London, 1926), pt. 2, pp. 11–13.

42. Foreigners were not the only capitalists who engaged in discriminatory practices. For a discussion of prejudice against Subei workers by Jiangnan mill owners, see Honig, *Sisters and Strangers*, p. 76.

43. In analyzing the development of the contract labor system in Shanghai cotton mills, Honig (ibid., p. 130) points out that "the significance in this context of the workers' movement, beginning May 30, 1925, is that mill owners opted for an alliance with the Green Gang in order to control the workers."

PART II: INTRODUCTION

1. For the period between 1919 and 1927, we have Jean Chesneaux's path-breaking study, *The Chinese Labor Movement, 1919–1927* (Stanford, Calif., 1968). For the years 1928–48 there is S. Bernard Thomas, *Labor and the Chinese Revolution* (Ann Arbor, Mich., 1983). The entire period is covered in the multi-volume work by Ma Chaojun et al., *Zhongguo laogong yundongshi* [A history of the Chinese labor movement] (Taipei, 1959).

2. Orley Ashenfelter and George E. Johnson, "Bargaining Theory, Trade Unions and Industrial Strike Activity," *American Economic Review* 59 (1969): 35–49; John I. Griffin, *Strikes: A Study in Quantitative Economics* (New York, 1939); Alvin Hansen, "Cycles of Strikes," *American Economic Review* 11 (1921): 616–21; K.G.J.C. Knowles, *Strikes* (Oxford, 1952); Jack W. Skeels, "Measures of U.S. Strike Activity," *Industrial and Labor Relations Review* 24 (1971): 515–25; John Vanderkamp, "Economic Activity and Strikes in Canada," *Industrial Relations* 9

(1970): 215–30; Andrew Weintraub, "Prosperity Versus Strikes: An Empirical Review," *Industrial and Labor Relations Review* 19 (1966): 231–38; Dale Yoder, "Economic Change and Industrial Unrest in the United States," *Journal of Political Economy* 48 (1940): 222–37.

3. Edward Shorter and Charles Tilly, *Strikes in France, 1830–1968* (Cambridge, Mass., 1974), p. 104.

4. Robert W. Barnett, *Economic Shanghai: Hostage to Politics, 1937–1941* (New York, 1941), p. 59.

5. *Jiefangqian de Shanghai wujia* [Commodity prices in preliberation Shanghai] (Shanghai, 1961).

6. On the theory behind the GMD-sponsored labor movement, see especially Pan Gongzhan, *Zhongguo Guomindang laogong zhengce de yanjiu* [A study of the labor policies of the Chinese Guomindang] (Shanghai, 1930); and Lu Jingshi, *Zhongguo laogong zhengce zhi lilun yu shiji* [The theory and practice of Chinese labor policy] (Taipei, 1954).

7. On ink workers, see Liu Shih-chi, "Yijiuersinian Shanghai Huibang mojiang bagong fengchao—jindai Zhongguo chengshi shouyi gongren jiti xingdong zhi fenxi" [The 1924 strike wave among Shanghai's Hui-gang ink workers—an analysis of collective action by urban handicraft workers in modern China], paper presented at the conference on Regional History in Modern China, Academia Sinica, Taipei, 1986.

CHAPTER 4

1. The classic study of this event remains Chow Tse-tung, *The May Fourth Movement* (Cambridge, Mass., 1960).

2. Joseph Chen, *The May Fourth Movement in Shanghai* (Leiden, 1971).

3. *Wusi aiguo yundong ziliao* [Materials on the May Fourth patriotic movement] (Beijing, 1979), pp. 461, 463–64, 466, 475–76, 487, 514; *Wusi yundong zai Shanghai shiliao xuanji* [Collection of historical materials on the May Fourth Movement in Shanghai] (Beijing, 1980, pp. 328, 356–57; *Xinwen bao*, June 7, 1919.

4. *Shen bao*, June 9, 1919; *Xinwen bao*, June 11, 1919.

5. *Wusi aiguo yundong ziliao*, p. 494.

6. Ibid., pp. 496, 514–15, 531.

7. *Wusi yundong zai Shanghai*, p. 372.

8. *Shishi xinbao*, June 11, 1919.

9. Ibid., June 13, 1919.

10. Li Lisan, "Zhongguo zhigong yundong gailun" [A general discussion of the Chinese labor movement], 1919, quoted in Wang Jianchu and Sun Maosheng, *Zhongguo gongren yundongshi* [A history of the Chinese labor movement] (Shenyang, 1987), p. 53.

11. James E. Cronin, "Labor Insurgency and Class Formation," *Social Science History* 4 (1980): 126.

12. See *Minguo ribao*, Oct. 12, 1919, for a discussion attributing the underlying cause of labor strife in both Europe and China to wartime inflation.

13. *Shi bao*, Oct. 20, 21, 1919.

14. *Xinwen bao,* Jan. 3–4, 6, 10, 19, 1920.

15. See Arif Dirlik, *The Origins of Chinese Communism* (New York, 1989), for a discussion of the pivotal role of the May Fourth Movement in generating a momentous alliance between the intelligentsia and workers.

16. The findings of the survey appeared in *Xin qingnian* [New youth] 7 (May 1920): 1143–1245. On the Marxism Study Society, see *Shanghai gongchanzhuyi xiaozu* [The Shanghai Communism small group] (Shanghai, 1988), pp. 6–12.

17. *Shanghai gongchanzhuyi xiaozu,* p. 101; Dirlik, *Origins of Chinese Communism,* p. 161. On the association's involvement in May Fourth, see *Wusi aiguo yundong ziliao,* pp. 459–60.

18. Shao Weizheng, "Jiandang qianhou de Shanghai gongren yundong" [The Shanghai labor movement around the time of the founding of the party], *Dangshi ziliao,* 1983, no. 3, pp. 76–80. Yu Xiusong, a member of the Marxism Study Society and originally from Zhejiang, revealed in a letter of April 1920 that he had recently left Beijing for Shanghai to work in a machine factory (Yu Xiusong, April 4, 1920, correspondence held in the archives of the First Party Congress Museum, Shanghai).

19. *Laodong jie* [Labor world], nos. 9 and 19; "Shanghai jiqi gonghui kai faqihui jilüe" [Annals of the inaugural meeting of the Shanghai Mechanics Union], reprinted in *Zhongguo gongren yundongshi cankao ziliao* [Reference materials on the history of the Chinese labor movement] (Beijing, 1980), 1:43–47. The manifesto also eschewed control by capitalists, politicians, or native-place associations, thereby disavowing the traditional guild style of organization.

20. Chen Duxiu, "Shanghai shehui" [Shanghai society], *Xin qingnian* 8, nos. 1–4 (1920), reprinted in *Shanghai gongzhanzhuyi xiaozu* [The Shanghai Communist small group] (Shanghai, 1988), pp. 67–71. Emphasis added.

21. *Zhonggong zhongyang guanyu gongren yundong wenjian xuanbian* [Selected documents from Party Central concerning the labor movement] (Beijing, 1985), 1:1.

22. *Bao Huiseng huiyilu* [The memoirs of Bao Huiseng] (Beijing, 1983), p. 67.

23. Ibid.; Bao Huiseng, "Erqi huiyilu" [Memoirs of February Seventh] in *Erqi dabagong ziliao xuanbian* (Beijing, 1983): 605–23; Chang Kuo-t'ao, *The Rise of the Chinese Communist Party* (Lawrence, Kan., 1971), 1: 170–74; Cai Shaoqing, "Secret Societies and Labor Organizations in the Early History of the Chinese Communist Party," in *Working Papers in Asian/Pacific Studies* (Durham, N.C., 1986), p. 11.

24. Jiang Peinan and Chen Weimin, "Shanghai zhaopai gonghui de xingwang" [The rise and fall of Shanghai's signboard unions], *Jindaishi yanjiu,* 1986, no. 6, pp. 46–47, provides a description of several of the more important of these unions.

25. *Minguo ribao,* June 16, 30, July 7, 14, Aug. 4, 11, 18, Sept. 8, 29, 1919.

26. Ibid., Sept. 15, 1919; *Shen bao,* Oct. 16, 1919.

27. *Minguo ribao,* Aug. 5, 8, 21, Sept. 16, 1919; Ma Chaojun, *Zhongguo laogong yundongshi* [A history of the Chinese labor movement] (Taipei, 1959), 1:139.

28. *Xinwen bao,* Mar. 6, Apr. 3, 1920; Ma Chaojun, *Zhongguo laogong yundongshi,* 1:139.

29. *Xinwen bao,* Apr. 5, 1920.

30. Shi Bing, *Zhongguo gongren yundong shihua* [Historical tales of the Chinese labor movement] (Beijing, 1985), 1: 68.

31. Chen Weimin, "1922 nian Shanghai bagong yundong de xingqi" [The rise of the Shanghai labor movement in 1922], *Shilin*, 1986, nos. 1–2, pp. 126–35; Jean Chesneaux, *The Chinese Labor Movement, 1919–1927* (Stanford, Calif., 1968), chap. 8.

32. *Minguo ribao*, Oct. 7–Nov. 5, 1922.

33. Deng Zhongxia, *Zhongguo zhigong yundong jianshi* [A brief history of the Chinese labor movement] (Beijing, 1949), p. 136.

34. Su Qiming, "Beifa qijian gongyun zhi yanjiu" [A study of the labor movement during the Northern Expeditionary period] (M.A. thesis, Zhengzhi University, Taipei, 1984), pp. 94–100; Chesneaux, *Chinese Labor Movement*, p. 225.

35. "Shanghaishi dangyuan diaochabiao" [Survey tables of party members in Shanghai municipality], Party History Archives, Taipei, nos. 435/218, 435/232.

36. Wang Jiagui and Cai Xiyao, eds., *Shanghai daxue* [Shanghai University] (Shanghai, 1986), p. 16.

37. Ibid., pp. 1–20.

38. Ibid., pp. 20–22.

39. Xu Haojiong, "Liu Hua," in *Shanghai yinglie zhuan* [Biographies of Shanghai martyrs], ed. Zhang Yiyu (Shanghai, 1987), pp. 45–70; Zhang Deqing, "Tao Jingxuan lieshi" [Martyr Tao Jingxuan], *Shanghai dangshi ziliao tongxun*, 1985, no. 5, pp. 39–41.

40. *Minguo ribao*, Feb. 6, 12, 1925; Ren Jianshu and Zhang Quan, *Wusa yundong jianshi* [A brief history of the May Thirtieth Movement] (Shanghai, 1985), pp. 37–40.

41. Liu Guanzhi, "Guanyu 1924–1925 nian Shanghai gongren yundong de huiyi" [Memoirs concerning the Shanghai labor movement, 1924–1925], *Zhongguo gongyun shiliao*, 1960, no. 1, pp. 34–82.

42. Emily Honig, *Sisters and Strangers: Women in the Shanghai Cotton Mills, 1911–1949* (Stanford, Calif., 1986), p. 8.

43. Chen Weimin, "Zhongguo gongchandang jianli chuqi de Shanghai gongren yundong pinggu" [An evaluation of the Shanghai labor movement in the early period of the Chinese Communist Party], *Shilin* 4, no. 11 (1988): 78.

44. Su Qiming, *Beifa qijian gongyun zhi yanjiu*, p. 94; Chesneaux, *Chinese Labor Movement*, pp. 223–27, 252.

45. *Zhonggong zhongyang guanyu gongren yundong wenjian xuanbian* [Selected Party Central documents on the labor movement] (Beijing, 1985), 1: 48–49, 54.

46. *Zhongguo lici quanguo laodong dahui wenxian* [Documents from successive national labor congresses] (Beijing, 1957), pp. 8–35.

47. Wang Jiagui and Cai Xiyao, eds., *Shanghai daxue*, pp. 31–36, 54.

48. *Minguo ribao*, May 26, 1925.

49. Shen Mengxian, "Guanyu wusa fandi xuanchuan shiwei de huiyi" [Memoir concerning the May Thirtieth demonstration against imperialism], reprinted in *Wusa yundong shiliao* (Shanghai, 1981), 1: 663.

50. Zhu Bangxing, Hu Linge, and Xu Sheng, eds., Shanghai chanye yu Shanghai Zhigong [Shanghai industry and Shanghai workers] (Shanghai, 1984), p. 543;

Shanghai gongren yundong lishi dashi ji [Annals of the history of the Shanghai labor movement] (Shanghai, 1979), 1: 78–79.

51. *Minguo ribao,* Aug. 6, 7, 1925.

52. Jiang Weixin, "Cong eryue bagong dao wusa yundong" [From the February strike to the May Thirtieth Movement], *Wenshi ziliao xuanji,* 1980, no. 3, pp. 48–49; Zhang Weizhen, "Zhang Weizhen tongzhi tan Shanghai wusa yundong" [Comrade Zhang Weizhen talks about Shanghai's May Thirtieth Movement], *Dangshi yanjiu ziliao* (Sichuan), 1982, no. 1, pp. 304–12. Li Lisan's involvement with gangsters dated back to the Anyuan coal miners' strike of 1922, when he had developed close relations with the Red Gang. See Cai Shaoqing, "Secret Societies," pp. 11–13.

53. *Police Daily Report,* Aug. 3, 1925, Shanghai Municipal Archives, no. 1-1-1147.

54. On Li Lisan's reliance on Green Gang support during the May Thirtieth Movement, see Zhu Xuefan, "Shanghai gongren yundong yu banghui ersan shi" [Two or three things about the Shanghai labor movement and the gangs], *Jiu Shanghai de banghui* [The gangs of old Shanghai] (Shanghai, 1986), p. 1.

55. *Wusa yundong shiliao* [Historical materials on the May Thirtieth Movement] (Shanghai, 1986), 2:70.

56. *Police Daily Report,* July–August 1925.

57. Zhang Weizhen, "1928 nian yiqian Shanghai gongyun de yixie qingkuang" [Some conditions of the Shanghai labor movement before 1928], *Gemingshi ziliao,* 1980, no. 1, p. 47; Zhang Weizhen, "Zhang Weizhen," pp. 304–12; *Police Daily Report,* July 9, 1925.

58. *Police Daily Report,* July 16, 28, 1925; *Minguo ribao,* Sept. 1, 1925.

59. *Police Daily Report,* Aug. 23, 25, 1925; Liu Guanzhi, "Guanyu 1924–1925," p. 71.

60. *Police Daily Report,* July 29, Aug. 12, 13, 1925; Yang Ruiliu, "Shanghai bagong de zhenxiang ji qi yingxiang" [The actual conditions and impact of the Shanghai strike], *Xiandai pinglun* 2, no. 35 (1925): 7.

61. Transcript of interview, Zhu Lianke, May 6, 1958; Labor Movement Archives of the SASS Institute of History.

62. Chesneaux, *Chinese Labor Movement,* p. 282.

63. Wang Jianchu and Sun Maosheng, *Zhongguo gongren yundongshi,* p. 124.

64. Chesneaux, *Chinese Labor Movement,* p. 284.

65. *Shanghai gongren sanci wuzhuang qiyi yanjiu* [A study of the Shanghai workers' Three Armed Uprisings] (Shanghai, 1987), pp. 61–72; Feng Shoucai and Shi Quanping, "Shanghai gongren disanci wuzhuang qiyi de zuzhi lingdao jigou gaikuang" [The leadership system of the third Shanghai workers' armed uprising], *Wenshi ziliao,* 1985, no. 3, pp. 73–76; Huang Yifeng, "Shanghai gongren disanci wuzhuang qiyi de qianqianhouhou" [Before and after the third Shanghai workers' armed uprising], *Wenshi ziliao xuanji,* 1978, no. 1, pp. 1–5; Wang Jianchu and Sun Maosheng, *Zhongguo gongren yundongshi,* pp. 136–37.

66. Xu Hongsheng, Apr. 25, 1957, and Jiang Zhonglin, May 2, 1957, transcripts of interviews, Labor Movement Archives of the SASS Institute of History.

67. Ma Chaojun et al., *Zhongguo laogong yundongshi,* 2:622.

68. Ren Qixiang et al., "Zhuiji Shangwu jiuchadui de douzheng" [Remembering struggles of pickets at the Commercial Press], *Shanghai gongyun shiliao*, 1987, no. 2, p. 10; Mao Chaojun et al., *Zhongguo laogong yundongshi*, 2:643–45.

69. Xie Qingzhai, Feb. 25, 1957, transcript of interview, Labor Movement Archives of the SASS Institute of History.

70. *Shanghai youzheng zhigong yundong shiliao* [Historical materials on the Shanghai postal workers' movement] (Shanghai, 1986), 1: 56.

71. "Yang Peisheng lieshi xiaozhuan" [Brief biography of martyr Yang Peisheng], *Shanghai gongyun shiliao*, 1984, no. 2, pp. 34–47; Huang Hezhi, "Yang Peisheng," *Shanghai yinglie zhuan* [Biographies of Shanghai martyrs] (Shanghai, 1987), pp. 21–34.

72. *Shanghai gongren sanci wuzhuang qiyi yanjiu* [A study of the Shanghai workers' Three Armed Uprisings] (Shanghai, 1987), pp. 156–57, 209.

73. Shanghai Municipal Archives, ed., *Shanghai gongren sanci wuzhuang qiyi* [The Shanghai workers' Three Armed Uprisings] (Shanghai, 1983), pp. 220, 262, 273. Not all gangsters were as cooperative as Huang and Du. During the three uprisings some gang members reportedly served as mercenaries for foreign capitalists and others posed as GLU pickets to undermine their reputation by depredations. See *Yijiuerqi nian de Shanghai shangye lianhehui* [The Shanghai Chamber of Commerce in 1927] (Shanghai, 1983), pp. 229, 225.

74. Chesneaux, *Chinese Labor Movement*, chap. 14.

CHAPTER 5

1. Harold R. Isaacs, *The Tragedy of the Chinese Revolution*, rev. ed. (Stanford, Calif., 1951), remains the standard English-language account of this event.

2. Fan Songfu, "Shanghai banghui de neimu" [Inside the gangs of Shanghai], *Wenshi ziliao xuanji*, 1980, no. 3, p. 156.

3. "Siyier shibian de qianqian houhou" [Before and after the April 12 incident], *Shanghai gongren yundong lishi ziliao* 4 (1953): 1.

4. Xue Gengshen, "Jindai Shanghai de liumang" [The gangsters of modern Shanghai], *Wenshi ziliao xuanji*, 1980, no. 3, pp. 162–63; Cheng Xiwen, "Wodang Huang Jinrong guanjia de jianwen" [What I saw and heard as Huang Jinrong's butler], in *Jiu Shanghai de banghui* [The gangs of old Shanghai] (Shanghai, 1986), pp. 144–48.

5. *Shanghai Municipal Police Files*, D-9319; Shanghai Academy of Social Sciences, ed., *Da liumang Du Yuesheng* [Big gangster Du Yuesheng] (Shanghai, 1965), pp. 1–7; Huang Guodong, "Dumen huajiu" [Old tales of the Du residence], in *Jiu Shanghai de banghui*, p. 248.

6. Zhu Jianliang and Xu Weizhi, "Zhang Xiaolin de yisheng" [The life of Zhang Xiaolin], in *Jiu Shanghai de banghui*, pp. 343–44.

7. Xiang Bo, "Huang Jinrong shilüe" [An account of Huang Jinrong], in *Jiu Shanghai de banghui*, p. 134; "Siyier shibian de qianqian houhou," pp. 1–5.

8. *Police Daily Report*, Apr. 3, 1927, quoted in *Shanghai gongren sanci wuzhuang qiyi yanjiu* [A study of the Shanghai workers' Three Armed Uprisings] (Shanghai, 1987), p. 294.

9. Su Zhiliang, "Shanghai liumang shili yu 'siyier' zhengbian" [Shanghai gangster power and the April 12th coup], *Jindaishi yanjiu*, 1988, no. 2, pp. 217–20. Rumors that the Mutual Advancement Society was subsidized by the Shanghai bourgeoisie or by Chiang Kai-shek himself are probably incorrect. More likely, as Du Yuesheng claimed, the gangsters provided most of the financial wherewithal for the venture. See ibid., p. 221; and Zhang Jungu, *Du Yuesheng zhuan* [Biography of Du Yuesheng] (Taipei, 1968), 2: 32.

10. Xiang Bo, "Huang Jinrong shilüe," p. 134.

11. "Siyier shibian de qianqian houhou," pp. 12–35; Wang Jianchu and Sun Maosheng, *Zhongguo gongren yundongshi* [A history of the Chinese labor movement] (Shenyang, 1987), p. 138.

12. A useful study of Shanghai labor under the GMD is Edward Hammond, "Organized Labor in Shanghai, 1927–1937" (Ph.D. dissertation, University of California, Berkeley, 1978).

13. On corporatism, see Suzanne Berger, ed., *Organizing Interests in Western Europe: Pluralism, Corporatism and the Transformation of Politics* (Cambridge, 1981); Philippe C. Schmitter, *Corporatism and Public Policy in Authoritarian Portugal* (London, 1975); Schmitter, *Trends Toward Corporatist Intermediation* (London, 1979); Schmitter and Gerhard Lembruch, *Patterns of Corporatist Policy-Making* (London, 1982), and Alfred Stepan, *The State and Society: Peru in Comparative Perspective* (Princeton, N.J., 1978).

14. Ma Chaojun et al., *Zhongguo laogong yundongshi* [A history of the Chinese labor movement] (Taipei, 1959), 2: 658–60; Wang Jianchu and Sun Maosheng, *Zhongguo gongren yundongshi*, p. 146.

15. "Shanghai zonggonghui baogao" [Report of the Shanghai General Labor Union], in *Zhongguo lici quanguo laodong dahui wenxian* (Beijing, 1927), p. 188.

16. Ma Chaojun et al., *Zhongguo laogong yundongshi*, 2: 734–36.

17. Ibid., 3: 807–10.

18. Ibid., pp. 810–11; *Shanghai Municipal Gazette*, June 22, 1928.

19. Number Two History Archives, #722:4-506, reports by Zhou Feng, July 31, Aug. 4, 27, 1928.

20. *Shanghai Municipal Gazette*, Nov. 23, 1928.

21. The laws included labor dispute regulations (June 1928), a labor union law (October 1928), a factory law and guidelines for its enforcement (December 1929), regulations for labor associations (October 1930), a factory inspection law (February 1931), and guidelines for enforcing the labor union law (1932). See Wang Jianchu and Sun Maosheng, *Zhongguo gongren yundongshi*, p. 147; and Zhang Peide, "Guomindang tongzhi qianshinian (1927–1937)" [Shanghai's labor problems during the first ten years of Guomindang rule, 1927–1937], unpublished manuscript (Shanghai, 1989).

22. *Shanghai Municipal Gazette*, Dec. 12, 1928, Mar. 22, 1929.

23. Pan Gongzhan, "Shanghai tebieshi shehuiju zhi zuzhi ji gongzuo" (The organization and work of the Shanghai Bureau of Social Affairs), *Qingnian jinbu*, 1930, no. 133, pp. 34–41.

24. See Bradley Kent Geisert, "From Conflict to Quiescence: The Kuomintang, Party Factionalism and Local Elites in Jiangsu, 1927–31," *China Quarterly*, 1986,

no. 108, pp. 681–92, on the activities of the left-wing GMD in the Jiangsu countryside during this period. A general overview is Yamada Tetsuo, *Chūgoku Kokumintō saha no kenkyū* [Studies of the left wing of the Chinese Guomindang] (Tokyo, 1980).

25. Jiang Hao, "Guomindang gaizupai zai Shanghai de huodong" [The activities of the Guomindang Reorganization Faction in Shanghai], *Shanghai difangshi ziliao* [Materials on Shanghai local history], 1982, no. 1, pp. 197–205; Jiang Hao, "Qingbang de yuanliu ji qi yanbian" [The origins and transformation of the Green Gang], in *Jiu Shanghai de banghui*, p. 65.

26. Chen Gang, *Shanghaigang matou de bianqian* [Changes on the docks of the Port of Shanghai] (Shanghai, 1966), p. 46.

27. Huang Yongyan, "Du Yuesheng dajin Dada lunchuan gongsi jingguo" [The process by which Du Yuesheng broke into the Dada Steamship Company], in *Jiu Shanghai de banghui*, pp. 284–92.

28. Number Two Archives, #720-33.

29. Chen Yun remained active in the publishing union of Commercial Press, for example. Likewise, BAT, the Post Office, and the newspaper unions all had remnant Communist activists. See Shen Yixing, "Dierci guonei geming zhanzheng shiqi de Shanghai gongren yundong" [The Shanghai labor movement during the period of the second internal revolutionary war], *Shanghai gongyunshi yanjiu ziliao*, 1981, no. 2, p. 10.

30. Wang Jianchu and Sun Maosheng, *Zhongguo gongren yundongshi*, pp. 157–58; *Shanghai gongren yundong* [The Shanghai labor movement] (Nanjing, 1935), p. 313; Bo Gesen, *Zhongguo laodong yundong de xianzhuang* [The current condition of the Chinese labor movement] (Beijing, 1930), pp. 101–5.

31. Zhang Jungu, *Du Yuesheng zhuan*, 2; 151–55; Zhu Xuefan, "Shanghai gongren yundong yu banghui ersan shi" [Two or three things about the Shanghai labor movement and the gangs], in *Jiu Shanghai de banghui*, p. 5.

32. Wang Zhenya, "Di yige Zhonggong Shanghai youju zhibu" [The first CCP branch at the Shanghai Post Office], in *Shanghai youzheng zhigong yundong shiliao* [Historical materials on the labor movement at the Shanghai Post Office] (Shanghai, 1986), pp. 13–14.

33. Wang Ruogu, "Yi 'wusa' douzheng" [Remembering the "May Thirtieth" Struggle], in *Shanghai youzheng zhigong yundong shiliao*, p. 33.

34. "Shanghai youwu gonghui de jianli" [The establishment of the Shanghai postal union], *Shanghai gongyun shiliao*, 1984, no. 1, pp. 2–15; "Kangri zhanzheng yiqian Shanghai youzheng zhigong de douzheng qingkuang" [Struggle conditions among the Shanghai postal workers prior to the war of resistance against Japan], *Shanghai gongren yundong lishi ziliao*, 1954, no. 4, pp. 4–19.

35. Zhu Xuefan, "Shanghai gongren yundong yu banghui ersan shi," pp. 6–9.

36. Ilona Ralf Sues, *Shark's Fins and Millet* (Boston, 1944), p. 78.

37. George F. Nellist, ed., *Men of Shanghai and North China* (Shanghai, 1933), p. 110.

38. Sues, *Shark's Fins and Millet*, p. 68.

39. Walter E. Gourlay, " 'Yellow Unionism' in Shanghai: A Study of Kuomintang Technique in Labor Control, 1927–1937," *Papers on China* 7 (1953): 104.

40. For an analysis of the complexities inherent in the operation of corporatist politics, see especially Howard J. Wiarda, *Corporatism and Development: The Portuguese Experience* (Amherst, Mass., 1977).

41. Shen Tiansheng, "Huiyi yijiuerqi dao saner nian de Shanghai youwu gong-hui" [Remembering the Shanghai post office union from 1927 to 1932], in *Shanghai youzheng zhigong yundong shiliao*, pp. 77–82.

42. Rao Jingying, "Guanyu 'Shanghai youwu gonghui'—Zhongguo huangse gonghui de yige pouxi," [Concerning the "Shanghai postal union"—analysis of a Chinese yellow union], *Shilin*, 1988, no. 2, p. 117.

43. *Shanghai Municipal Police Files*, D-4611, D-9319.

44. Zhu Xuefan, "Shanghai gongren yundong yu banghui ersan shi," pp. 6–7.

45. Zhang Jungu, *Du Yuesheng zhuan*, 2:155.

46. Sues, *Shark's Fins and Millet*, p. 75.

47. Zhu Xuefan, "Shanghai gongren yundong yu banghui ersan shi," p. 7.

48. Number Two History Archives, Nanjing, #1: 2-746.

49. Zhu Bangxing, Hu Linge, and Xu Sheng, ed., *Shanghai chanye yu Shanghai zhigong* [Shanghai industry and Shanghai workers] (Shanghai, 1984), p. 359; Xue Gengshen, "Wo yu jiu Shanghai fazujie" [The old French Concession of Shanghai and I], *Wenshi ziliao xuanji*, 1976, no. 6, pp. 157–58; Brian G. Martin, "Tu Yueh-sheng and Labour Control in Shanghai: The Case of the French Tramways Union, 1928–32," *Papers on Far Eastern History* 32 (1985): 133–35.

50. "Kangri zhanzheng yiqian Shanghai youzheng zhigong de douzheng qing-kuang," pp. 1–30; Shen Tiansheng, "Huiyi 1927–1932 nian Shanghai youwu gonghui qingkuang" [Remembering the situation in Shanghai's postal workers' union, 1927–1932], *Shanghai gongyunshi yanjiu ziliao*, no. 6 (1981), p. 29.

51. Joel S. Migdal, *Strong Societies and Weak States* (Princeton, N.J., 1988), p. 141.

52. *Da liumang Du Yuesheng*, pp. 50–51; Zhu Xuefan, "Shanghai gongren yundong yu banghui ersan shi," p. 8.

53. Zhu Xuefan, "Shanghai gongren yundong yu banghui ersan shi," p. 5.

54. Fan Shaozeng, "Guanyu Du Yuesheng" [Concerning Du Yuesheng], in *Jiu Shanghai de banghui*, pp. 221–29.

55. Harold R. Isaacs, *Five Years of Kuomintang Reaction* (Shanghai, 1932), p. 97.

56. Guo Lanxin, "Du Yuesheng yu Hengshe" [Du Yuesheng and the Constant Club], in *Jiu Shanghai de banghui*, pp. 300–320; Fan Shaozeng, "Guanyu Du Yuesheng," p. 206; Zhu Xuefan, "Shanghai gongren yundong yu banghui ersan shi," p. 6; "Hengshe sheyuanlu" [Record of the Constant Club membership], in *Jiu Shanghai de banghui*, pp. 369–82; *Hengshe qiuji lianhuan dahui tekan* [Special issue on the autumn get-together of the Constant Club] (Shanghai, 1934).

57. Huang Guodong, "Dumen huajiu," p. 253.

58. *Shanghai Municipal Police Files*, D-9319.

59. Guo Lanxin, "Du Yuesheng yu Hengshe," pp. 306–7.

60. For case studies of the impact of this process on different Shanghai industries see especially Zhu Bangxing et al., *Shanghai chanye*.

61. Luo Gengmo, "Muxia laogong shenghuo huitan," *Zhongguo jingji lun-wenji* [Collection of essays on the Chinese economy] (Shanghai, 1936), 2: 309.

62. An attempt to implement scientific management at the Commercial Press generated a strong reaction from printers in 1931. See "Shangwu yinshuguan jiufenan jiejue" [Resolution of the dispute at the Commercial Press], *Gongshang banyue kan* 3, no. 4 (1931): 27–28; and Zhang Xinyi et al., "Shangwu yinshuguan chongjian dang zuzhi yihou" [After the reestablishment of a Party branch at the Commercial Press], *Shanghai gongyunshi yanjiu ziliao*, 1983, no. 1, pp. 5–6.

63. Underground Party cadres hoped that large-scale strikes in the Shanghai textile industry would spark an urban uprising that would also gain widespread peasant support. See *Jiangsu nongmin yundong dang'an shiliao xuanbian* [A compilation of archival materials on the Jiangsu peasant movement] (Beijing, 1983), pp. 31–51.

64. *Shanghai Municipal Police Files*, #D-4820.

65. James Pinckney Harrison, *The Long March to Power: A History of the Chinese Communist Party, 1921–72* (New York, 1972), pp. 161–62; *Hu Chao* [Shanghai Tide], May 8, 1930, no. 14.

66. *Shanghai Municipal Police Files*, #D-4820.

67. Wang Jianchu and Sun Maosheng, *Zhongguo gongren yundongshi*, pp. 161–76; S. Bernard Thomas, *Labor and the Chinese Revolution* (Ann Arbor, Mich., 1983), chap. 2. During this period veteran labor leader Liu Shaoqi continued to call for a more moderate program of cooperation with yellow unions. Several essays written by Liu in late 1931 and early 1932 strongly criticized the reckless policies of the day. See *Liu Shaoqi lun gongren yundong* [Liu Shaoqi on the labor movement] (Beijing, 1988), pp. 50, 61, 68–69, 88–93.

68. *Shanghai Municipal Police Files*, #D-4820.

69. Wang Jianchu and Sun Maosheng, *Zhongguo gongren yundongshi*, p. 176.

70. Shen Yixing, *Gongyunshi mingbianlu* [Controversies in labor movement history] (Shanghai, 1987), pp. 143, 162.

71. Zhang Weizhen, "Yijiuerba nian yiqian Shanghai gongyun de yixie qing-kuang" [Conditions in the Shanghai labor movement before 1928], *Gemingshi ziliao*, 1980, no. 1, pp. 60–61.

72. Their confessions appear in *Zhuanbian* [Conversion], 1933, in the archives of the Bureau of Investigation, Taiwan, #245.3/841.

73. Office of Strategic Services, "Political Implications of Chinese Secret Societies" (1945), in Department of State Decimal File on China, #097.3, Z1092, 2254/45.

74. For discussion of a comparable process elsewhere, see James M. Malloy, "Authoritarianism, Corporatism and Mobilization in Peru," in *The New Corporatism: Social-Political Structures in the Iberian World*, ed. Frederick B. Pike and Thomas Stritch (Notre Dame, Ind., 1974), pp. 52–84.

75. Philippe C. Schmitter, "Still the Century of Corporatism?" ibid., pp. 93–94.

76. The interpretation of the GMD as representative of the Chinese bourgeoisie or landlord classes can be found in Robert W. Barnett, *Economic Shanghai: Hostage to Politics* (New York, 1941), p. 12; Isaacs, *Tragedy of the Chinese Revolution*, p. 182; Barrington Moore, Jr., *The Social Origins of Dictatorship and Democracy* (Boston, 1966), p. 196; and Mao Zedong, *Selected Works* (Beijing, 1967), 1:55. For a refutation of this position, see especially Parks Coble, *The Shanghai Capitalists and the Nationalist Government* (Cambridge, Mass., 1980).

77. The autonomy thesis can be found in Lloyd Eastman, "New Insights into the Nature of the Nationalist Regime," *Republican China* 9, no. 2 (1984): 11. See also his *The Abortive Revolution* (Cambridge, Mass., 1974).

78. Charles Bright and Susan Harding, eds., *Statemaking and Social Movements* (Ann Arbor, Mich., 1984), p. 4.

79. Karl Marx, *The Eighteenth Brumaire of Louis Bonaparte*, in *Selected Works* (New York, 1977), p. 178.

80. James C. Scott, *Comparative Political Corruption* (Englewood Cliffs, N.J., 1972), p. 114.

CHAPTER 6

1. For an analysis of the decline of Nationalist power in this period, see especially Lloyd E. Eastman, *Seeds of Destruction* (Stanford, Calif., 1984). On the rebuilding of the Communist labor movement, see Qi Wu, *Kangri zhanzheng shiqi Zhongguo gongren yundong shigao* [A draft history of the Chinese labor movement during the anti-Japanese war] (Beijing, 1986).

2. The reaction of labor was part of a much broader nationalistic coalition in which students, businessmen, and other social groups played key roles. For students, see Jeffrey Wasserstrom, *Student Protest in Twentieth-Century China: The View from Shanghai* (Stanford, Calif., 1991); for businessmen, see Parks Coble, *The Shanghai Capitalists and the Nationalist Government, 1927–1937* (Cambridge, Mass., 1980).

3. *Yier jiu yihou Shanghai jiuguohui shiliao xuanji* [Selected historical materials on the Shanghai National Salvation Association after December Ninth] (Shanghai, 1987), pp. 108–15, 268–311, 424–29.

4. "Kangri zhanzheng shiqi Shanghai gongren yundong" [The Shanghai labor movement during the period of the War of Resistance], *Shanghai gongyun shiliao*, 1988, no. 1, p. 3.

5. Zhang Weizhen, Han Nianlong, and Zhou Lin, "1936 nian Shanghai fanri dabagong huiyi" [Memoir of Shanghai's great anti-Japanese strike of 1936], in *Kangri fengyun lu* [Annals of the war of resistance] (Shanghai, 1985), p. 57. For an analysis of the strike that stresses the limited role of the Communists, see Matthew H. Sommer, "Strikes in Shanghai Cotton Mills During the Nanjing Decade: A Case Study of the November 1936 Anti-Japanese Strike Wave," unpublished University of Washington seminar paper (1988).

6. Liu Shaoqi, "Guanyu baiqu zhigong yundong gongzuo de tigang" [Outline for labor movement work in the white areas], 1936, reprinted in *Shanghai gongyunshi yanjiu ziliao*, 1980, no. 1, pp. 1–8.

7. Zhang Chengzong, "Liu Changsheng tongzhi he Shanghai ju" [Comrade Liu Changsheng and the Shanghai bureau], *Shanghai gongyun shiliao*, 1987, no. 1, pp. 8–9.

8. Ma Chungu, *Shanghai gongyun de xianzhuang baogao* [Report on the current condition of the Shanghai labor movement] (Yenan, 1941), p. 62.

9. Jiang Kelin and Wu De, "Shanghai gongren jiuguohui jianjie" [A brief introduction to the Shanghai Workers' National Salvation Association], *Shanghai gongyun shiliao*, 1986, no. 2, pp. 17–23.

10. See Xu Deliang, "Yishe lishi de huigu" [Recollections of the history of the Ant Society], *Shanghai gongyunshi yanjiu ziliao*, 1981, no. 4, pp. 1–39.

11. "Kangri zhanzheng shiqi Shanghai gongren yundong" [The Shanghai labor movement during the anti-Japanese war], *Shanghai gongyun shiliao*, 1988, no. 1, pp. 32–33; Lu Renzhi, "Ji yiyoushe" [Remembering the Helpful Friend Society], *Shanghai dangshi ziliao tongxun*, 1988, no. 10, pp. 1–9.

12. Wu Chengfang, "Zai geming gongzuo zhong yunyong banghui guanxi de pianduan ziliao" [Fragmentary materials on the use of gang connections in revolutionary work], in *Jiu Shanghai de banghui* [The gangs of old Shanghai] (Shanghai, 1986), p. 25.

13. "Kangri zhanzheng shiqi Shanghai gongren yundong," pp. 6–14; Wang Jianchu and Sun Maosheng, *Zhongguo gongren yundongshi* [A history of the Chinese labor movement] (Shenyang, 1987), p. 209; Ma Chungu, *Shanghai gongyun de xianzhuang baogao* [Report on the current condition of the Shanghai labor movement] (Yenan, 1941), p. 62; Shanghai Academy of Social Sciences, ed., *'Bayisan' kangzhan shiliao xuanbian* [Selections of historical materials on the "August 13" war of resistance] (Shanghai, 1986), p. 309.

14. Eleanor Hinder, *Social and Industrial Problems of Shanghai* (New York, 1942), pp. 49–51; Robert W. Barnett, *Economic Shanghai: Hostage to Politics, 1937–1941* (New York, 1941), pp. 57, 51, 46.

15. Zhang Xinyi et al., "Shangwu yinshuguan chongjian dang zuzhi yihou" [After the reestablishment of Party organization at the Commercial Press], *Shanghai gongyunshi yanjiu ziliao*, 1983, no. 1, pp. 1–26.

16. In December 1941, 214 factories in the International Settlement closed, putting 22,000 laborers out of work. The decline continued through 1942 and 1943. See Qi Wu, *Kangri zhanzheng*, pp. 184–86.

17. Wang Jianchu and Sun Maosheng, *Zhongguo gongren yundongshi*, pp. 236–37. A notable example of ostensibly "spontaneous" strikes under CCP influence was the so-called "headless struggles" that erupted at the Shanghai Power Company in 1942 and 1944. See "Shangdian gongren de 'wutou douzheng'" [The 'headless struggles' of SPC workers], *Shanghai gongyunshi yanjiu ziliao*, 1982, no. 1, pp. 42–46.

18. These cooperative gang chieftains hailed from Hubei, Hunan, and Anhui. Several boasted revolutionary connections going back to Sun Yat-sen. See Wu Chengfang, "Zai geming gongzuo zhong yunyong banghui guanxi de pianduan ziliao," pp. 24–26.

19. Lin Zhenfeng and Du Boru, "Huainian Hu Yongqi tongzhi" [Cherishing the memory of comrade Hu Yongqi], in *Shanghaishi baoxianye zhigong yundong shiliao* [Historical materials on the labor movement in the Shanghai insurance business] (Shanghai, 1987), pp. 146–50.

20. Shanghaishi baoxianye dangshi ziliao zhengjizu, "Shanghai shi baoxianye yeyu lianyihui jianshi" [A brief history of the Shanghai Insurance Business Federation], ibid., pp. 5–22; Shi Zheming and Wang Yizhou, " 'Baolian' geyongzu he kouqinzu huodong pianduan" [Fragments regarding the activities of the song group and the harmonica group of the "Insurance Federation"], ibid., p. 125.

21. Shanghaishi baoxianye dangshi ziliao zhengjizu, "Zhonggong Shanghai baoxianye dixiadang zuzhi de jianli he fazhan" [The CCP's establishment and

development of an underground party organization in the Shanghai insurance business], ibid., pp. 31–53.

22. Yang Qing, " 'Xiao Cao' chengzhang shi" [History of the development of "Little Grasses"], *Shanghai gongyunshi yanjiu ziliao*, 1981, supplemental issue, pp. 1–5.

23. Lu Renzhi, "Youguan Shanghai baihuoye zhigong yundong shiliao de jige wenti" [Several questions concerning historical materials on the Shanghai department store workers' movement], *Shanghai gongyunshi yanjiu ziliao*, 1982, no. 3, pp. 1–17.

24. *Shanghai chuanbo gongye gongyun ziliao huibian* [Compilation of materials on the Shanghai shipbuilding industry] (Shanghai, 1986), pp. 73–185.

25. Weng Sanxin, "Kangri zhanzheng shiqi Shanghai dang zuzhi gaikuang," [Overview of Shanghai party organization during the anti-Japanese war], *Shanghai dangshi ziliao tongxun*, 1988, no. 10, pp. 30–34.

26. Of the 69 members of the workers' army on whom data are available, only 2 were from Subei, 6 were from Shandong, and the remaining 61 were from Jiangnan locations ("Shanghai gongrendui duiyuan mingdan" [Name list of members of the Shanghai workers' brigade], *Shanghai gongyun shiliao*, 1988, nos. 2–3, pp. 52–54).

27. "Zongshu Shanghai gongren dixiajun" [Overview of the Shanghai workers' underground army], ibid., pp. 1–7; Zhang Chengzong, "Zuzhi dixiajun, zhunbei wuzhuang qiyi" [Organizing the underground army, preparing for armed rebellion], ibid., pp. 8–12; Zhang Qi, "Huiyi Shanghai gongren dixiajun" [Remembering the Shanghai workers' underground army], ibid., pp. 13–18. *Jiefang ribao*, Aug. 23, 1945, and *Xinhua ribao*, Aug. 28, 1945, reported the news under the headline "50,000 Shanghai Workers Rebel."

28. A listing of these returnees is in Shanghai Municipal Archives, #12-1-52.

29. Including captives from the Eighth Route Army, most of these individuals had been working in Hokkaido for several years before being sent home (ibid., #11-1, 11-9).

30. *Zhongguo jishu xiehui banian* [Eight years of the China Technical Association] (Shanghai, 1987).

31. *Jiefangqian de Shanghai wujia* [Commodity prices in preliberation Shanghai] (Shanghai, 1961), p. 330.

32. *Shanghai baihuoye zhigong yundong shiliao* [Historical materials on the workers' movement in Shanghai department stores] (Shanghai, 1986), pp. 86–87. In some of the more traditional artisan trades, such as the soy sauce industry, Communists made substantial inroads among white-collar shop clerks. See "Shanghai jiangyuanye zhigong douzheng qingkuang" [The conditions of struggle among workers in the Shanghai soy sauce trade], *Shanghai gongren yundong lishi ziliao*, 1954, no. 4, pp. 31–59.

33. Mao Qihua, "Lüetan jiefang zhanzheng shiqi Shanghai gongren yundong de yixie qingkuang" [A summary discussion of conditions in the Shanghai labor movement during the war of liberation], *Shanghai gongyunshi yanjiu ziliao*, 1982, no. 2, p. 1.

34. Qi Wu, *Kangri zhanzheng shiqi zhongguo gongren yundong shigao*, p. 188.

35. Shanghai gongren yundong shiliao weiyuanhui, "Guanyü Shanghai liuda

gongyong shiye gonghui lianyihui de yixie qingkuang" [Conditions in the federation of labor unions at Shanghai's six major public utilities], *Zhongguo gongyun shiliao* 2 (1980): 164–71.

36. Shanghai Municipal Archives, #1-7-48.

37. *Shanghai Municipal Police Files*, #D-5310-1.

38. Shanghai gongren yundong shiliao weiyuanhui, "Shanghai dianli gongsi gongyun lishi jishi" [A historical record of the labor movement at the Shanghai Power Company], *Zhongguo gongyun shiliao* (Beijing, 1984), 2:173–208.

39. Zhang Xianhao, "Jiefang zhanzheng shiqi Zhonggong Shanghai shiwei zuzhi gaikuang" [Overview of the municipal committee organization of the Shanghai CCP during the war of liberation], *Shanghai dangshi ziliao tongxun*, 1988, no. 12, pp. 30–34.

40. On the wartime activities of the *juntong*, see Yeh Wen-hsin, "Dai Li and the Liu Geqing Affair: Heroism in the Chinese Secret Service During the War of Resistance," *Journal of Asian Studies* 48 (1989): 545–62.

41. Mao Qihua, Lüetan jiefang zhanzheng shiqi Shanghai gongren yundong de yixie qingkuang," pp. 3–5.

42. Shui Xiangyun, "Shanghaishi liangnianlai de gongyun" [The Shanghai labor movement in the past two years], *Shizheng pinglun* 11, nos. 1–2 (1949): 8; Shao Xinshi and Deng Ziba, eds., *Shanghai laogong nianjian* [Shanghai labor yearbook] (Shanghai, 1948), p. 38.

43. Fan Shaozeng, "Guanyu Du Yuesheng" [About Du Yuesheng], in *Jiu Shanghai de banghui*, p. 241.

44. Guo Lanxing, "Du Yuesheng yu Hengshe" [Du Yuesheng and the Constant Club], ibid., p. 316.

45. Jiang Menglin and Mao Zipei, "Kangzhan shenglihou Shanghai Guomindang neibu de paixi douzheng" [Factional struggles within the Shanghai Guomindang after the victory of the War of Resistance], *Wenshi ziliao xuanji*, 1979, no. 3, pp. 182–84. The loss of the GMD post was particularly galling to Wu, for it was announced by his erstwhile backer, Chen Lifu.

46. "Guanyu Shanghai liuda gongyong shiye gonghui lianyihui de yixie qingkuang" [Conditions in the friendly society of Shanghai's six major public utilities], *Zhongguo gongyun shiliao*, pp. 167–68.

47. "Zhide jiqu de yige jiaoxun" [A lesson worth remembering], *Shanghai gongyun shiliao*, 1986, no. 2, pp. 29–32; Liang Cheng, "Shangdian gongren zai 'Futong shijian' zhong" [Shanghai Power workers during the 'Futong incident'], *Shanghai gongyun shiliao*, 1987, no. 5, pp. 9–14.

48. Zhang Qi, "Huiyi Shenjiu erer douzheng" [Recalling the struggle of February 2 at Shenxin Number Nine], *Shanghai gongyun shiliao*, 1986, no. 1, p. 20.

49. Jin Di, "Shanghai wuchaoan" [The case of the Shanghai dancers' upsurge], *Wenshi ziliao xuanji*, 1981, no. 1, pp. 152–60; Fan Xipin, "Shanghai wuchaoan qinliji" [A personal record of the Shanghai dancers' upsurge], *Wenshi ziliao xuanji*, 1979, no. 3, pp. 190–99; *Shanghai wuchaoan neimu* [The inside story of the Shanghai dancers' upsurge] (Shanghai, n.d.), pp. 4–21.

50. Quoted in Zhang Qi, "Huiyi Shenjiu erer douzheng," p. 28.

51. Fan Shaozeng, "Guanyu Du Yuesheng," pp. 239–42. Du may have begun to lean toward the Communists. According to his accountant, Du had developed

contacts among future leaders of both the Shanghai municipal and the central People's Republic government. See Huang Guodong, "Dumen huajiu," in *Jiu Shanghai de banghui*, pp. 265–67.

52. Jiang Menglin and Mao Zipei, "Kangzhan shenglihou Shanghai Goumindang neibu de paixi douzheng," p. 184.

53. Gu Shuping, "Wo liyong Gu Zhuxuan de yanhu jinxing geming huodong" [I used the cover of Gu Zhuxuan to carry out revolutionary activities], in *Jiu Shanghai de banghui*, pp. 363–66. Another helpful gangster convert at this time was Xiang Haiqian, a major Red Gang leader in the Shanghai area who had participated in the 1911 Revolution. See *Gemingshi ziliao* [Materials on revolutionary history], 1981, no. 5.

54. Lu Xiangxian, *Zhongguo laodong xiehui jianshi* [Brief history of the China Labor Association] (Shanghai, 1987), pp. 20–22, 39.

55. Ibid., pp. 35–36, 102.

56. Lu Xiangxian, *Zhongguo laodong xiehui jianshi*, pp. 103–21; Zhu Xuefan, "Liang'an gonghui hezuo, gongtong zhenxing Zhonghua" [Cooperation between unions on both shores, working together to strengthen China], *Renmin ribao*, Aug. 25, 1988.

57. E. Perry Link, Jr., *Mandarin Ducks and Butterflies: Popular Fiction in Early Twentieth-Century Chinese Cities* (Berkeley, Calif., 1981), p. 5; Yeh Wen-hsin, "Shanghai's Petty Urbanites: Cultural Mobilization in Republican China," paper presented at the International Symposium on Modern Shanghai, 1988, p. 2; E. P. Thompson, *The Making of the English Working Class* (London, 1966).

58. For the rural Communist movement, see especially Ch'en Yung-fa, *Making Revolution: The Communist Revolution in Eastern and Central China, 1937–1945* (Berkeley, Calif., 1986).

59. For a preliminary discussion of this issue, see Elizabeth J. Perry, "Labor Divided: Sources of State Formation in Modern China," in a forthcoming volume edited by Joel Migdal, Atul Kohli, and Vivienne Shue. The argument will be developed in a second volume of this study.

PART III: INTRODUCTION

1. Michael Burawoy, *Manufacturing Consent* (Chicago, 1979); Richard Edwards, *Contested Terrain* (London, 1979); Charles F. Sabel, *Work and Politics: The Division of Labor in Industry* (New York, 1982); Michael Hanagan and Charles Stephenson, eds., *Confrontation, Class Consciousness, and the Labor Process: Studies in Proletarian Class Formation* (New York, 1986); P. K. Edwards, *Conflict at Work* (Oxford, 1986).

2. See Michael Hanagan, "Solidary Logics: Introduction," *Theory and Society*, no. 17 (1988): 309–12, for a review of this issue.

CHAPTER 7

1. *Zhongguo jindai gongyeshi ziliao* [Materials on the history of China's modern industry] (Beijing, 1957–61), vol. 4, no. 1, p. 455.

2. Ibid., p. 446; "Hatabako" [Leaf tobacco], *Shanhai Mantetsu chōsa shiryō*, 1939, no. 29, pp. 63–113; Sherman Cochran, *Big Business in China* (Cambridge, Mass., 1980), chaps. 2–3.

3. Cochran, *Big Business in China*, pp. 176–85, 188–95; *Zhongguo jindai gongyeshi ziliao*, vol. 4, no. 1, p. 447.

4. See Part II, Introduction, n. 2.

5. *Shanghai Strike Statistics, 1918–1940.*

6. *Shanghai juanyan gongye gaikuang* [Conditions in the Shanghai rolled tobacco industry] (Shanghai, 1950), pp. 35–42; *Yan yu yanye* [Tobacco and the cigarette industry] (Shanghai, 1934), p. 49; Hao Lixiang, June 10, 1958, transcript of interview, Labor Movement Archives of the SASS Institute of History.

7. BAT Pudong archives, #75/33, #60/8, SASS Institute of Economics.

8. Ibid., #214c.

9. Ibid., #75/33, #60/8; *Yingmei yangongsi zaihua qiye ziliao huibian* [Collected materials on BAT business activities in China] (Beijing, 1983), pp. 223–24.

10. Lin Xinbao, Aug. 11, 1958, transcript of interview, Labor Movement Archives of the SASS Institute of History.

11. Lu Daxiu, Aug. 24, 1958, transcript of interview, ibid.

12. *Shanghai gongren yundong lishi ziliao* [Historical materials on the Shanghai labor movement], no. 9 (1956), pp. 6–8. This practice was discontinued after a protest in which workers urinated on the tobacco leaves and defecated into the spittoons.

13. BAT Thorburn Road archives, July 6, 1938, SASS Institute of Economics.

14. Lu Daxiu, Aug. 8, 1958, transcript of interview, Fan Zijun, Sept. 2, 1958, transcript of interview, Zhang Yongsheng, Aug. 17, 1958, transcript of interview, ibid. On a comparable process in the cotton industry, see Emily Honig, *Sisters and Strangers: Women in the Shanghai Cotton Mills, 1911–1949* (Stanford, Calif., 1986), pp. 65–66, 79–87.

15. Hao Lixiang, interview, June 10, 1958.

16. *Zhandou de wushi nian* [Fifty years of struggle] (Shanghai, 1960), p. 8.

17. April 1932 Riddick report, BAT archives.

18. *Shangyan erchang minzhu tuanjie yundong cailiao* [Materials on the movement for democratic unity at Shanghai's Number Two Tobacco Factory] (Shanghai, 1957), p. 1957.

19. Zhu Bangxing, Hu Linge, and Xu Sheng, eds., *Shanghai chanye yu Shanghai zhigong* [Shanghai industry and Shanghai workers] (Shanghai, 1984), p. 582.

20. *Yingmei zaihua*, pp. 1051–52.

21. Lu Daxiu, transcript of interview, Aug. 8, 1958.

22. *Minguo ribao*, June 28, 1921.

23. BAT Pudong archives, #155/24.

24. *Yingmei zaihua*, p. 1028; Zhao Qizhang, Oct. 28, 1958, transcript of interview, Huang Zhihao, July 23, 1963, transcript of interview, Zhang Yongsheng, Aug. 7, 1958, transcript of interview, all in the Labor Movement Archives of the SASS Institute of History.

25. *Yingmei zaihua*, p. 1027.

26. Ye Shilin, Aug. 13, 1963, transcript of interview, SASS Institute of Economics; *Yingmei zaihua,* p. 225.

27. Shan Genbao, Sept. 2, 1958, transcript of interview, Labor Movement Archives of the SASS Institute of History.

28. *Shanghai gongren yundong lishi ziliao,* no. 9 (1956), pp. 6–8; Zhu Bangxing et al., *Shanghai chanye,* pp. 587–88; Luo Chuanhua, *Jinri Zhongguo laogong wenti* [Labor issues in contemporary China] (Shanghai, 1933), p. 105; Cochran, *Big Business in China,* pp. 137ff.

29. Bureau of Investigation archives, Taipei, #556.282/810.

30. *Yingmei zaihua,* pp. 1036–37, 1042. This estimate was made in 1924.

31. Zhu Bangxing et al., *Shanghai chanye,* pp. 582, 587; BAT Pudong archives, #55/24, #2/19; BAT Thorburn Road archives, #758.

32. Zhu Bangxing et al., *Shanghai chanye,* pp. 575, 577.

33. Zhu Bangxing et al., *Shanghai chanye,* p. 589.

34. Chen Qingbiao, Apr. 29, 1958, transcript of interview, Labor Movement Archives of the SASS Institute of History.

35. *Shi bao,* June 13, 1906, Feb. 2, 1915, Mar. 3, 1916.

36. *Minguo ribao,* July 21, 24, 25, Aug. 2, 10, 1917, May 2, 1918.

37. *Zhandou de wushi nian,* pp. 16–17; *Minguo ribao,* Aug. 4, 1918; *Shi bao,* Aug. 5, 6, 9, 1918; Zhang Yongsheng, Aug. 7, 1958, transcript of interview, Labor Movement Archives of the SASS Institute of History.

38. *Shi bao,* Oct. 8, 1919.

39. *Minguo ribao,* Nov. 10, 14, 1919.

40. Ibid., June 23, 1920, Mar. 7, 18, June 25, 28, 29, 1921.

41. Rose Glickman, *Russian Factory Women: Workplace and Society, 1880–1914* (Berkeley, Calif., 1984), pp. 162, 165.

42. Louise A. Tilly, "Paths of Proletarianization: Organization of Production, Sexual Division of Labor, and Women's Collective Action," in *Women's Work,* ed. Eleanor Leacock and Helen I. Safa (South Hadley, Mass., 1986), p. 37. See also Michelle Perrot, *Les ouvrières en grève,* 2 vols. (Paris, 1974); Patricia A. Cooper, *Once a Cigar Maker: Men, Women, and Work Culture in American Cigar Factories, 1900–1919* (Urbana, Ill., 1987).

43. *Shen bao,* July 21, 24, 1921; *Minguo ribao,* July 21, 1921; *Zhandou de wushi nian,* pp. 19–20.

44. *Zhandou de wushi nian,* pp. 20–22; *Zhongguo gongyun ziliao* [Materials on the Chinese labor movement], no. 1 (1958), pp. 58–59, 70–72; *Minguo ribao,* Aug. 2, 6, 1921.

45. Li Qihan, "Huanying Wang Fengshanjun de fanhui" [Welcoming Mr. Wang Fengshan's change of heart], *Laodong zhoukan,* 1921, no. 12.

46. Si Bingwen, "Li Qihan," in *Zhongguo gongren yundong de xianqu* [Pioneers of the Chinese labor movement] (Beijing, 1983), 2:156–68.

47. Chang Kuo-t'ao, *The Rise of the Chinese Communist Party* (Lawrence, Kan., 1971), 1: 174–75.

48. *Zhandou de wushi nian,* p. 31.

49. *North China Herald,* Sept. 2, 1922.

50. *Zhandou de wushi nian,* pp. 32–37; *Minguo ribao,* Nov. 3, 5, 24, 1922;

"Shangyan yichang gongchangshi" [Shanghai Number One Tobacco Factory's history], n.d., unpublished ms. in the archives of SASS Institute of Economics.

51. *Minguo ribao,* Nov. 8, 21, 25, 1922; Cochran, *Big Business in China,* p. 139; *Zhandou de wushi nian,* p. 38.

52. Zhang Yongsheng, Aug. 9, 1958, transcript of interview, Labor Movement Archives of the SASS Institute of History.

53. *Zhandou de wushi nian,* pp. 43–45; Fan Zijun, Sept. 2, 1958, transcript of interview, Labor Movement Archives of the SASS Institute of History. As Sherman Cochran has pointed out, BAT's workers constituted nearly 10 percent of the total number of Shanghai strikers (160,000) during the May Thirtieth Movement (*Big Business in China*), p. 177.

54. Wang Jiagui and Cai Xiyao, *Shanghai daxue* [Shanghai University] (Shanghai, 1986), p. 96.

55. Ma Chungu and Zhang Yun, *Huiyi Yang Zhihua* [Remembering Yang Zhihua] (Hefei, 1983), p. 28.

56. Ibid., pp. 1–28; *Shanghai minzu jiqi gongye* [Shanghai's national machine industry] (Beijing, 1979), p. 58.

57. Yang Longying, Apr. 11, 1958, transcript of interview, Labor Movement Archives of the SASS Institute of History.

58. Zhu Quanfa, June 10, 1958, transcript of interview, ibid.

59. Li Xinbao, Aug. 11, 1958, transcript of interview, ibid.

60. Yang Longying, interview, Apr. 11, 1958.

61. Zhu Quanfa, interview, June 10, 1958.

62. Cochran, *Big Business in China,* p. 184.

63. *Yingmei zaihua,* p. 1176; *Shanghai Strike Statistics, 1918–1940.*

64. Hao Lixiang, interview, June 10, 1958.

65. *Zhandou de wushi nian,* pp. 69–84.

66. Lu Daxiu, interview, Aug. 24, 1958.

67. Ibid.

68. Zhu Quanfa, interview, June 10, 1958.

69. *Shangyan yichang gongchangshi;* Zhang Ruilin, Sept. 4, 1958, transcript of interview, Labor Movement Archives of the SASS Institute of History.

70. Harold R. Isaacs, *The Tragedy of the Chinese Revolution* (New York, 1966), chaps. 10–11.

71. Luo Chuanhua, *Jinri Zhongguo laogong wenti,* pp. 97–102.

72. Cochran, *Big Business in China,* pp. 188–95; Parks M. Coble, *The Shanghai Capitalists and the Nationalist Government, 1927–1937* (Cambridge, Mass., 1980).

73. *Shen bao,* July 27, Aug. 16, 1927.

74. Ellis Goldberg, *Tinker, Tailor and Textile Worker: Class and Politics in Egypt, 1930–1952* (Berkeley, Calif., 1986), p. 177.

75. Zhang Tinghao, n.d., transcript of interview, Archives of the SASS Institute of Economics.

76. *Shangyan yichang gongchangshi.*

77. BAT Pudong archives, #35: 42–13.

78. *Minguo ribao,* Oct. 8, 1927.

79. Number Two History Archives, #1: 2-746.

80. *Shen bao*, Oct. 25, 1927.

81. *North China Daily News*, Oct. 14, 1927; *North China Herald*, Aug. 6, 1927; *Xinwen bao*, Dec. 15, 1927, Jan. 11, 1928. BAT's management observed, "According to recent editorials in Chinese newspapers, it seems this is not a dispute between us and our workers, but is instead a struggle between China and the imperialist nations, of which we have been chosen as chief representative" (*Yingmei zaihua*, p. 1205).

82. Lu Daxiu, interview, Aug. 24, 1958.

83. *North China Daily News*, Jan. 18, 1928; *Shangyan yichang gongchangshi*.

84. Zhang Tinghao, interview, n.d.

85. Zhang Ruilin, Sept. 4, 1958, transcript of interview, Labor Movement Archives of SASS Institute of History.

86. Zhang Yongsheng, interview, Aug. 7, 1958; Lu Daxiu, interview, Aug. 24, 1958.

87. Xue Gengxin, "Wo jiechuguo de Shanghai banghui renwu" [Shanghai gangsters I have known], in *Jiu Shanghai de banghui* [The gangs of old Shanghai] (Shanghai, 1986), p. 92.

88. August 1933 report of I. G. Riddick, BAT Pudong archives.

89. Li Xinbao, interview, Aug. 11, 1958.

90. BAT Pudong archives, #24: 8–9.

91. *North China Herald*, Dec. 22, 1931.

92. *Laogong yuekan*, May 1, 1933, vol. 2, no. 5, p. 95.

93. *Xinwen bao*, May 20, 1933; Number Two History Archives, #9: 8093. Among those arrested was Qiang Lei, a copper fitter at BAT who was also secretary of the East Shanghai branch of the Communist Party (*Zhongguo xiandai zhengzhishi ziliao huibian* [Compendium of materials on contemporary China's political history], vol. 2, no. 44, document 5414).

94. Number Two History Archives, #722: 4-225.

95. *Shangyan yichang gongchangshi*.

96. *Shanghai Municipal Police Files*, D-5844.

97. *Zhandou de wushi nian*, pp. 114–26; Yao Haigen, Oct. 28, 1958, transcript of interview, Labor Movement Archives of the SASS Institute of History.

98. Hong Benkuan, Oct. 24, 1958, transcript of interview, Labor Movement Archives of the SASS Institute of History.

99. *Zhandou de wushi nian*, pp. 136–44.

100. Ibid., p. 165; Shan Genbao, interview, Sept. 2, 1958.

101. Archives of the Bureau of Investigation, Taipei, #556.282/810.

102. *Zhandou de wushi nian*, pp. 169–84.

103. Huang Zhihao, Sept. 2, 1958, transcript of interview, Labor Movement Archives of the SASS Institute of History.

104. Ibid.; *Zhandou de wushi nian*, pp. 195–98.

105. *Shanghai gongren yundong lishi ziliao*, 1956/9, pp. 62–65.

106. *Zhandou de wushi nian*, p. 202.

107. *Yingmei zaihua*, p. 1278.

108. *Zhandou de wushi nian*, pp. 207–8.

109. *Yingmei zaihua*, pp. 1119–21; Huang Zhihao, interview, Sept. 12, 1958.
110. Cochran, *Big Business in China*, pp. 207–8, 232.

CHAPTER 8

1. Robert Y. Eng, *Economic Imperialism in China: Silk Production and Exports, 1861–1932* (Berkeley, Calif., 1986), pp. 38, 56; "Shanghai zhi siye" [The silk industry of Shanghai], *Shehui banyuekan* 1, no. 19 (1935): 45–46; Lillian Li, *China's Silk Trade: Traditional Industry in the Modern World* (Cambridge, Mass., 1981), pp. 33, 164–71, 204; Liu Dajun, *Shanghai gongyehua yanjiu* [A study of the industrialization of Shanghai] (Shanghai, 1940), pp. 23–24. On the Shanghai cotton industry, see Emily Honig, *Sisters and Strangers: Women in the Shanghai Cotton Mills, 1911–1949* (Stanford, Calif., 1986), chap. 1.

2. Zhu Bangxing, Hu Linge, and Xu Sheng, eds., *Shanghai chanye yu Shanghai zhigong* [Shanghai industry and Shanghai workers] (Shanghai, 1984), pp. 186–89; Li Cishan, "Shanghai laodong zhuangkuang" [Labor conditions in Shanghai], *Xin qingnian* 7, no. 6 (1920): 30–31.

3. D. K. Lieu, *The Silk Reeling Industry in Shanghai* (Shanghai, 1933), p. 69.

4. Eleanor Hinder, *Social and Industrial Problems of Shanghai* (New York, 1942), p. 18. Nearly twenty years earlier, the Shanghai Municipal Council had decried the maltreatment of child workers in the silk industry. See *Municipal Gazette*, July 19, 1924. Further discussion of the inhumane conditions in Shanghai filatures can be found in Mary Ninde Gamewell, *The Gateway to China: Pictures of Shanghai* (London, 1916), pp. 230–33.

5. *Zhongguo jindai gongyeshi ziliao* [Materials on the history of China's modern industry] (Beijing, 1957–61), 2: 1299–1301.

6. *Shanghai Strike Statistics, 1918–1940*.

7. *Shi bao*, Sept. 22, 1912; *Minli bao*, Jan. 4, 1913; *Xinwen bao*, Jan. 12, 1913; Ma Chaojun, et al., *Zhongguo laogong yundongshi* [A history of the Chinese labor movement] (Taipei, 1959), 1: 80–81.

8. *Shi bao*, Apr. 24, 1921. A silk filature strike for higher wages in the summer of 1920 was attributed to gangster leadership (*Minguo ribao*, July 17, 1920).

9. Jian Meng, "Cong sichang nügong bagongzhong delai de jiaoxun" [Lessons gained during the women silk workers' strike], *Funü zazhi* [Women's journal] 8, no. 10 (1922): 17; Mi Bi, "Shanghai sichang nügong de tongmeng bagong" [The general strike of Shanghai women silk workers], ibid., pp. 63–65; Ci Chang, "Nüzi gongye jindehui yu funü laodong zuhe wenti" [The women's industrial advancement society and the issue of associations of women laborers], ibid., no. 11, p. 46.

10. *Xinwen bao*, Aug. 12, 1922.

11. *Minguo ribao*, May 1, 1923.

12. Ibid., Jan. 16, Feb. 28, 29, Mar. 4, 5, 1924.

13. Ibid., July 1, 2, 3, 8, 1924.

14. Ibid., Aug. 7, 12, 25, 1924.

15. Zhu Yingru, Mar. 14, 1957, transcript of interview, Labor Movement Archives of the SASS Institute of History.

16. Cocoon Guild Archives, file #516. Mu Zhiying and the Cocoon Guild later charged that the strike had been instigated by one Sun Zongfang, a Communist who had come to Shanghai for the purpose of establishing a rival union. The Chinese police were unable to verify Sun's role in the strike, however. See Cocoon Guild Archives, files #516, 517.

17. *Minguo ribao,* Aug. 7, 12, 1925.

18. Yang Zhihua, "1926 nian Shanghai sichang nügong bagong yundongzhong zhi ganxiang" [Thoughts during the strike movement of Shanghai women silk workers in 1926], in *Huiyi Yang Zhihua* [Remembering Yang Zhihua] (Hefei, 1983), p. 247; reprint of an article published by Yang in 1927 in *Chinü zazhi* [Red women's journal].

19. *Minguo ribao,* June 10, 11, 12, 16, 19, 28, 29, 30, 1926; Cocoon Guild Archives, file #520.

20. *Minguo ribao,* July 1, 1926.

21. Cocoon Guild Archives, file #523; *Minguo ribao,* July 16, Sept. 22, 1926; *Xinwen bao,* Aug. 13, 1926.

22. Yang Zhihua, "1926 nian Shanghai sichang nügong bagong yundongzhong zhi ganxiang," p. 248.

23. Zhu Yingru, interview, Mar. 14, 1957; Shen Yihong, "Muqin Zhu Yingru zhandou de yisheng" [Mother Zhu Yingru's lifetime of struggle], *Fuyunshi ziliao,* 1981, no. 1, pp. 56–57; "Zhandou zai sanci wuzhuang qiyizhong de Shanghai nügong" [Shanghai women workers fighting in the Three Armed Uprisings], ibid., p. 47.

24. "Zhonggong Shanghai quwei youguan Shanghai gongren sanci wuzhuang qiyi de wenxian qipian" [Seven documents of the Shanghai district Party committee concerning the Shanghai workers' Three Armed Uprisings], *Dang'an yu lishi,* 1987, no. 1, p. 11.

25. Cocoon Guild Archives, file #528.

26. *Minguo ribao,* Nov. 6, 1927; Shen Yihong, "Muqin Zhu Yingru zhandou de yisheng," pp. 57–58.

27. *Shanghai Strike Statistics, 1918–1940; Shen bao,* Mar. 10, June 10, 15, 23, July 5, 14, Oct. 7, 1928; *Minguo ribao,* June 25, 28, July 1, 4, Aug. 3, 21, 1928.

28. *Shen bao,* June 22, 1928.

29. Criticisms of the Hongkou union were especially numerous. See Cocoon Guild Archives, file #48.

30. Ibid., file #72-1.

31. Chen Xiuliang, "Lisan luxian yu xingdong weiyuanhui" [The Li Lisan line and the action committee], *Wenshi ziliao xuanji,* 1981, no. 1, pp. 14–16.

32. *Shangye yuebao* [Business monthly], 1937, no. 7.

33. Robert W. Barnett, *Economic Shanghai: Hostage to Politics, 1937–1941* (New York, 1941), pp. 96–97.

34. *Zhongguo jindai gongyeshi ziliao,* 2: 1299–1301.

35. Yang Shaoying, *Zhongguo gongren de bagong douzheng* [The strike struggles of Chinese workers] (Nanjing, 1957), preface. Suzhou artisans undertook large-scale guild-based strikes in 1693, 1701, 1715, 1720, 1730, and 1756.

36. Zhu Bangxing et al., *Shanghai chanye,* pp. 132–34; *Shanghai sichou*

gongye jieduanshi [A periodized history of the Shanghai silk-weaving industry] (Shanghai, n.d.), pp. 1–3.

37. *Shanghai Strike Statistics, 1918–1940.*

38. *Shanghai zhi jizhi gongye* [Mechanized industry in Shanghai] (Shanghai, 1933), p. 175; Zhu Bangxing et al., *Shanghai chanye*, p. 133; Luo Gengmo, "Meiya gongchao shimo" [The Meiya workers' tide from beginning to end], *Zhongguo jingji lunwen ji* (Shanghai, 1936), p. 227; D. K. Lieu, *The Silk Industry of China* (Shanghai, 1940), p. 191; Zhang Shouyu, *Jindai Jiangnan sizhi gongyeshi* [A history of the modern Jiangnan silk-weaving industry] (Beijing, 1988); *Meiya qikan* [Meiya journal], Nov. 16, 1933 (in Shanghai Municipal Archives, #199-48-258 and #199-48-259).

39. *Meiya qikan*, Aug. 16, 1934, p. 2.

40. *Shanghai sichou gongyunshi* [The labor movement among Shanghai silk weavers] (Shanghai, 1985), pp. 13–17.

41. *Shanghai Strike Statistics, 1918–1940;* Number Two Archives #722: 4-226.

42. "Sizhiye" [The silk-weaving industry], 1982, manuscript in the archives of the Shanghai Number Four Silk-Weaving Factory.

43. Zhu Bangxing et al., *Shanghai chanye*, p. 142.

44. Shanghai Municipal Archives #199-48: 1–6.

45. Zhu Bangxing et al., *Shanghai chanye*, p. 146.

46. Zhu Bangxing et al., *Shanghai chanye*, p. 143.

47. Xu Xijuan, June 2, 1987, interview conducted at the Shanghai Number Nine Silk-Weaving Factory; *Sizhiye;* A Ying, "Chouchang de nügong" [Women workers in the silk-weaving factories], *Shenghuo zhishi,* 1946, no. 39, p. 4.

48. Zhu Bangxing et al., *Shanghai chanye*, p. 142.

49. Xie Qingzhai, Feb. 25, 1957, transcript of interview, Labor Movement Archives of the SASS History Institute.

50. Zhu Bangxing et al., *Shanghai chanye*, p. 142.

51. Li Shufa, Dec. 24, 1969, transcript of interview, and Shen Rongqing, n.d., dossier in the archives of the Shanghai Number Four Silk-Weaving Factory.

52. Zhou Zhixin, June 5, 1982, transcript of interview, ibid.

53. Zhu Bangxing et al., *Shanghai chanye*, pp. 141–43.

54. Wan Wenhua, July 21, 1982, transcript of interview, archives of the Shanghai Number Four Silk-Weaving Factory.

55. Zhang Shouyu, *Jindai Jiangnan sizhi gongyeshi;* Yi Wei, "Meiya chouchang bagong de yanzhongxing" [The seriousness of the Meiya silk factory strike], *Nüsheng* 2, no. 12 (1934): 2.

56. *Meiya qikan*, Aug. 16, 1934.

57. Zhu Bangxing et al., *Shanghai chanye*, p. 151.

58. Ibid., p. 162.

59. Zhou Zhixin, Dec. 21, 1981, transcript of interview, archives of the Shanghai Number Four Silk-Weaving Factory.

60. Zhang Qi, June 16, 1987, interview at the Shanghai Federation of Labor Unions.

61. Zhu Bangxing et al., *Shanghai chanye*, p. 152.

62. Ibid.; *Shanghai Municipal Police Files*, D-5802.

63. Yu Lin, May 8, 1982, transcript of interview, archives of the Shanghai Number Four Silk-Weaving Factory.

64. Zhang Qi, interview, June 16, 1987.

65. Ge Sulan, July 17, 1982, transcript of interview, archives of the Shanghai Number Four Silk-Weaving Factory.

66. Luo Gengmo, "Meiya gongchao shimo," pp. 229–31.

67. Number Two Archives, #722: 4-224.

68. Luo Gengmo, "Meiya gongchao shimo," pp. 228–29.

69. Ibid., pp. 230–31.

70. Zhu Bangxing et al., *Shanghai chanye*, pp. 153–54; *Shanghai Municipal Police Files*, D-5802.

71. *Shanghai Municipal Police Files*, D-5802.

72. Number Two Archives, #722: 4-224.

73. *Shanghai Municipal Police Files*, D-5802; Zhu Bangxing et al., *Shanghai chanye*, p. 165.

74. *Shanghai Municipal Police Files*, D-5802; *Hongse Zhonghua* [Red China], Jiangxi, nos. 162, 169, 171, 178, 180, March–April 1934; *Douzheng* [Struggle], Shanghai, Apr. 19, 1934.

75. *Tuan de jianshe* [League construction], Shanghai, no. 13, Mar. 12, 1934, no. 15, Apr. 13, 1934, no. 16, Apr. 27, 1934; *Qunzhong de tuan* [League of the masses], Shanghai, no. 3, Apr. 6, 1934.

76. *Shanghai Municipal Police Files*, D-5802.

77. Ibid.; *Meiya qikan*, Aug. 16, 1934, pp. 3–7.

78. Luo Gengmo, "Meiya gongchao shimo," p. 234; *Shanghai Municipal Police Files*, D-5802; Zhu Bangxing et al., *Shanghai chanye*, p. 155.

79. *Shanghai Municipal Police Files*, D-5802; Zhu Bangxing et al., *Shanghai chanye*, pp. 155–56; Luo Gengmo, "Meiya gongchao shimo," p. 234.

80. *Shanghai Municipal Police Files*, D-5802; Zhu Bangxing et al., *Shanghai chanye*, p. 153.

81. Bai Shi, "Zai Meiya bagong zhong duiyu nügong de renshi" [Understanding women workers in the Meiya strike], *Nüsheng* 4, no. 10 (1934): 2.

82. Number Two History Archives, #722: 4-224.

83. *Shanghai Municipal Police Files*, D-5802.

84. Lieu, *Silk Industry of China*, p. 222; Zhu Bangxing et al., *Shanghai chanye*, p. 140; Ma Chaojun, *Zhongguo laogong yundongshi* [History of the Chinese labor movement] (Taipei, 1954), p. 1190.

85. *Shanghai Municipal Police Files*, D-5802.

86. Zhu Bangxing et al., *Shanghai chanye*, pp. 156–57. The parallel with Nanyang Brothers' assistance to BAT strikers in 1927 (see Chapter 7) is notable.

87. *Shanghai Municipal Police Files*, D-5802.

88. Zhu Bangxing et al., *Shanghai chanye*, pp. 157–58; *Meiya disi zhichouchang* [The Meiya Number Four Silk-Weaving Factory] (Shanghai, 1982), p. 33.

89. Luo Gengmo, "Meiya gongchao shimo," p. 235; *Meiya disi zhichouchang*, pp. 33–34.

90. Ma Chaojun, *Zhongguo laogong yundongshi*, p. 1191; "Shanghai dijiu

sizhichang gongren yundong douzhengshi" [A history of labor movement struggles at the Shanghai Number Nine Silk-Weaving Factory] (Shanghai, 1983), p. 23, in the archives of the Shanghai Number Nine Silk-Weaving Factory; *Meiya disi zhichouchang*, p. 34.

91. *Shanghai Municipal Police Files*, D-1791.

92. Ibid., D-5802; Zhu Bangxing et al., *Shanghai chanye*, p. 159.

93. Shanghai Municipal Archives, #199-48-207.

94. *Meiya disi zhichouchang*, p. 28; Jiang Hongjiao, "Ziwo pipan" [Self-criticism], n.d., in the archives of the Shanghai Number Four Silk-Weaving Factory.

95. *Shanghai Municipal Police Files*, D-5802.

96. Ibid.

97. Zhu Bangxing et al., *Shanghai chanye*, pp. 160–61.

98. Number Two History Archives, #722: 4-224.

99. *Shanghai Municipal Police Files*, D-5802; Zhou Zhixin, Dec. 21, 1981, transcript of interview, archives of the Shanghai Number Four Silk-Weaving Factory.

100. G. Crossick, *An Artisan Elite in Late Victorian Society* (London, 1980); Robert Gray, *The Aristocracy of Labour in Nineteenth-Century Britain* (London, 1981).

101. Pan Yueying, July 11, 1961, transcript of interview, Labor Movement Archives, SASS Institute of History.

102. *Qunzhong de tuan*, no. 8, Aug. 24, 1934; *Meiya qikan*, Aug. 16, 1934, p. 2.

103. *Meiya disi zhichouchang*, p. 19; *Shanghai dijiu sizhichang*, p. 31; Fu Yuanhua, December 1982, manuscript of interview, archives of the Shanghai Number Four Silk-Weaving Factory; Shanghai Municipal Archives, #199-48-207.

104. *Shanghai zhi jizhi gongye* [Mechanized industry in Shanghai] (Shanghai, 1933), p. 175.

105. Zhu Bangxing et al., *Shanghai chanye*, pp. 163–64.

106. *Shanghai Strike Statistics, 1918–1940*.

107. *Shanghai sichou gongye jieduanshi*, p. 3.

108. *Shanghai Municipal Police Files*, D-7506.

109. *Shanghai Strike Statistics, 1918–1940*; *Shanghai Municipal Police Files*, D-7506.

110. Zhu Bangxing et al., *Shanghai chanye*, pp. 171–72; *Shanghai Municipal Police Files*, D-7744.

111. *Shanghai Municipal Police Files*, D-7744.

112. "Yijiusanqi nian sizhiye dabagong" [The great silk weavers' strike of 1937], 1982, in the archives of the Shanghai Number Four Silk-Weaving Factory, pp. 13–14; Zhang Yuezhen, Sept. 23, 1981, transcript of interview, archives of the Shanghai Number Four Silk-Weaving Factory; Zhou Yunqing, Oct. 4, 1982, transcript of interview, ibid.

113. Zhang Pingshan, Sept. 29, 1981, transcript of interview, archives of the Shanghai Number Four Silk-Weaving Factory; Zhang Yuezhen, interview, Sept. 23, 1981.

114. *Shanghai dijiu sizhichang*, p. 39; He Zhensheng, "Kangri zhanzheng shiqi Shanghai fangzhi gongye yu zhigong de yixie qingkuang" [Conditions of the

Shanghai silk-weaving industry and its workers during the Sino-Japanese War],
Shanghai gongyun shiliao, 1984, no. 4, pp. 14–15.

115. Zhang Yuezhen, interview, Sept. 23, 1981.

116. Zhu Boqing, Aug. 22, 1961, transcript of interview, Labor Movement
Archives, SASS Institute of History.

117. Zhu Bangxing et al., *Shanghai chanye*, p. 173.

118. *China Press*, Mar. 31, 1937; *Shanghai Evening Post and Mercury*, Mar. 31,
1937; Zhu Bangxing et al., *Shanghai chanye*, pp. 174–75; *Shanghai dijiu sizhichang*, p. 39.

119. *China Press*, Mar. 29, 31, 1937.

120. The totals are found in Zhu Bangxing et al., *Shanghai chanye*, p. 135.

121. "Yijiusanqi nian," pp. 5–6.

122. *Meiya disi zhichouchang*, p. 46.

123. *Shanghai Evening Post and Mercury*, Apr. 5, 1937; *Shanghai sichou
gongye jieduanshi*, pp. 20–21.

124. Zhu Bangxing et al., *Shanghai chanye*, p. 176.

125. *Shanghai Times*, Apr. 14, 1937; Number Two History Archives, #722:
4-519.

126. *Shanghai Municipal Police Files*, D-7744; Zhu Bangxing et al., *Shanghai
chanye*, pp. 177–78.

127. *Shanghai Times*, May 19, Apr. 3, 1937.

128. Zhu Bangxing et al., *Shanghai chanye*, p. 181.

129. *Shanghai Municipal Police Files*, D-7744; *Shanghai sichou gongyunshi*,
p. 50.

130. *China Press*, May 26, 1937; Zhu Bangxing et al., *Shanghai chanye*, p. 179.

131. Shanghai Municipal Archives, #199-48-207.

132. SHCY, pp. 180–81.

133. Bernard H. Moss, "Workers' Ideology and French Social History," *International Labor and Working Class History*, no. 11 (1977), p. 28.

134. Edward Shorter and Charles Tilly, *Strikes in France, 1830–1968* (Cambridge, Mass., 1974), p. 10.

135. *Shanghai dijiu sizhichang*, p. 46.

136. Ma Chungu, *Shanghai gongyun de xianzhuang baogao* [Report on the
current condition of the Shanghai labor movement] (Shanghai, 1941), pp. 17–18.

137. Qian Yukan, "Hunan qingnian jiuwangtuan de chengli ji qi huodong"
[The founding and activities of the south Shanghai youths' salvation association],
Shanghai gongyunshi yanjiu ziliao, 1984, no. 4, pp. 13–14.

138. *Shanghai dijiu sizhichang*, p. 52; *Meiya disi zhichouchang*, p. 55; *Shanghai sizhi gongyunshi*, pp. 69–71.

139. For union involvement in negotations on issues ranging from maternity
leave to cost-of-living subsidies, see Shanghai Municipal Archives, #1-7-50,
#6-9-1625, #6-9-1633.

140. Lu Duanhua, May 9, 1970, transcript of interview, archives of the Shanghai Number Four Silk-Weaving Factory; Wu Yongnian, dossier, ibid.; Shanghai
Municipal Archives, #19-17; *Shanghai dijiu sizhichang*, p. 69; *Sanqu sizhiye
gonghui diaocha baogao* [Investigation report of the District Three silk weavers'
union], Bureau of Investigation, Taipei, #556.18/803. The District Three Union

complained that GMD cadres and Trotskyites often joined forces to keep workers out on strike long after the CCP-led union had negotiated an acceptable settlement.

141. Zhang Shouyu, *Jindai Jiangnan sizhi gongyeshi; Shanghai sichou gongyunshi*, p. 94.

142. *Shanghai sichou gongyunshi*, pp. 101–13; Pan Yueying, Nov. 21, 1982, transcript of interview, Shanghai Number Four Silk-Weaving Factory.

143. Zhang Yongqin, "Cong zhengzhi dao hezuo" [From politics to cooperation], *Shehui yuekan* 2, no. 10 (1947): 40.

144. Shanghai Municipal Archives, #1-7-54; "Yaoqiu jiedong shenghuofei zhishu de douzheng" [The struggle to demand an unfreezing of the cost-of-living index], *Shanghai fangzhi gongyunshi ziliao*, n.d., no. 3, pp. 83–84.

145. Wan Wenhua, June 22, July 21, 1982, transcripts of interviews, archives of the Shanghai Number Four Silk-Weaving Factory; "Yaoqiu jiedong shenghuofei," pp. 81–82.

146. *Shanghai sichou gongyunshi*, p. 127; Lu Duanhua, May 9, 1970, Tao Youlin, Oct. 17, 1982, transcripts of interviews, archives of the Shanghai Number Four Silk-Weaving Factory.

147. Huang Cailin, July 15, 1968, confession, archives of the Shanghai Number Four Silk-Weaving Factory.

148. *Shanghai sichou gongyunshi*, p. 132.

149. See Shanghai Municipal Archives, #6-9-1644 for labor disputes in the silk-weaving industry in the spring and summer of 1948.

150. *Shanghai sichou gongyunshi*, pp. 130–32.

151. Hanagan, *Logic of Solidarity*, pp. 216–17.

152. Crossick, *Artisan Elite*; Gray, *Aristocracy of Labour*.

153. Eric J. Hobsbawm, "The Labour Aristocracy in Nineteenth-Century Britain," in *Labouring Men* (London, 1964).

154. E. P. Thompson, *The Making of the English Working Class* (New York, 1963).

155. Robert J. Bezucha, *The Lyon Uprising of 1834* (Cambridge, Mass., 1974), p. 158.

156. Lu Jialong, Apr. 17, 1958, transcript of interview, Labor Movement Archives of the SASS Institute of History.

157. Jiang Yuanqing and Song Sanmei, Sept. 12, 1957, transcript of interview, ibid.

158. "Shanghai guomian shierchang gongren douzheng changshi ziliao" [Factory history materials of the workers' struggle at Shanghai's Number Twelve Cotton Mill], *Shanghai gongren yundong lishi ziliao*, 1955; no. 1, p. 5.

159. *Shenjiu "erer" douzheng jiyao* [Notes on the February 2 struggle at Shenxin Number 9], 1982, unpublished manuscript in the archives of the Shanghai Number 22 Cotton Mill, pp. 10–22.

CHAPTER 9

1. Zhu Bangxing, Hu Linge, and Xu Sheng, eds., *Shanghai chanye yu Shanghai zhigong* [Shanghai industry and Shanghai workers] (Shanghai, 1984), chaps. 8–10.

2. Several early strikes were instigated by workers in the traffic department to protest the arrests of fellow drivers for traffic infractions. See *Shi bao*, Aug. 18, 1914; *Minguo ribao*, July 2, 1917.

3. Ren Jianshu and Zhang Quan, *Wusa yundong jianshi* [A brief history of the May Thirtieth Movement] (Shanghai, 1985), p. 93.

4. Zhang Xiaofang, Feb. 18, 1957, transcript of interview, Labor Movement Archives of the SASS Institute of History. When two fitters were questioned in connection with Ni Tiansheng's assassination, an all-company strike erupted in January 1927. A handbill issued during the course of the strike pointed out that suspicions between mechanics and traffic department workers were a continuing source of dissension (*Shanghai Municipal Police Files*, D-7587).

5. *Shanghai Municipal Police Files*, D-6449A.

6. Zhu Bangxing et al., *Shanghai chanye*, pp. 382–83.

7. *Minguo ribao*, Mar. 4, 7, 1921.

8. Zhou Guoqiang, *Huiyi Shanghai gongren de sanci wuzhuang qiyi* [Remembering the Shanghai workers' Three Armed Uprisings] (Shanghai, 1957), pp. 1–2.

9. "Shanghai Fashang dianche, diandeng, zilaishui gongsi gongren douzheng jianshi" [A brief history of workers' struggles at the French Tramway, Electric, and Water Company], in *Shanghai gongren yundong lishi ziliao* [Historical materials on the Shanghai labor movement], 1953, no. 2; Jiang Peinan, "Xu Amei," in *Zhongguo gongren yundong de xianqu* [Pioneers of the Chinese labor movement] (Beijing, 1984), 3: 189–90.

10. Miao Yu, "Shanghai gongren yundong de yizuo qiang baolei" [A strong fortress of the Shanghai labor movement] in *Zhongguo gongchandang yu Shanghai gongren*, ed. Liu Changsheng (Shanghai, 1953), p. 13.

11. Zhou Guoqiang, *Huiyi Shanghai gongren*, pp. 12–16; "Shanghai Fashang dianche," pp. 5–6.

12. Zhou Guoqiang, *Huiyi Shanghai gongren*, p. 28.

13. Jiang Peinan, "Xu Amei," p. 199; "Shanghai Fashang dianche," p. 8; Zhou Guoqiang, *Huiyi Shanghai gongren*, p. 31.

14. Zhu Bangxing et al., *Shanghai chanye*, pp. 308–12.

15. See Shanghai Municipal Archives, #6-7-370, #6-7-371, #6-7-372, #6-7-373, #6-7-374, #6-7-375, #6-7-376, #6-8-069, #6-8-483, for handbills calling for opposition to Du Yuesheng and the GMD-sponsored union and advocating a continuation of the strike under CCP leadership. The handbills were concealed inside packets of Chinese herbal medicine and passed along from one comrade to another (Jiang Peinan, "Xu Amei," p. 203).

16. Jiang Peinan, "Xu Amei," pp. 201, 204; Zhu Bangxing et al., *Shanghai chanye*, pp. 312–13.

17. Jiang Peinan, "Xu Amei," pp. 209, 215; Zhu Bangxing et al., *Shanghai chanye*, p. 319.

18. Even the government authorities became sympathetic to the strike. Because the death had been caused by French police, GMD Central instructed the Foreign Ministry to lodge a protest with the French against this "violation of Chinese sovereignty" (Number Two History Archives, #1: 2-747).

19. Jiang Along, "Wushiqitian dabagong" [The 57-day great strike], in *Zai jianku douzheng de suiyue li* (Shanghai, 1958), p. 13.

20. Jiang Peinan, "Xu Amei," pp. 217–18; Zhu Bangxing et al., *Shanghai chanye*, pp. 353–54; Miao Yu, "Shanghai gongren yundong de yizuo qiang baolei," p. 14.

21. Zhu Bangxing et al., *Shanghai chanye*, pp. 354–56.

22. Brian Martin, "Tu Yueh-Sheng and Labour Control in Shanghai," *Papers on Far Eastern History*, no. 32 (1985): 134–35; Xue Gengshen, "Wo yu jiu Shanghai Fazujie" [The old French Concession of Shanghai and I], *Wenshi ziliao xuanji*, no. 6 (1979), pp. 157–58; Xue Gengshen, "Wo jiechuguo de Shanghai ganghui renwu" [Shanghai gangsters I have known] in *Jiu Shanghai de banghui* [The gangsters of old Shanghai] (Shanghai, 1986), pp. 93–94; Zhu Bangxing et al., *Shanghai chanye*, p. 359.

23. Chen Weimin, "Huang Fulin lieshi xiaozhuan," [Brief biography of martyr Huang Fulin], *Shanghai gongyun shiliao*, 1984, no. 4, pp. 41–43.

24. "Shanghai Fashang dianche," pp. 24–25.

25. *Shanghai Fadian gongren yundong lishi ziliao* [Historical materials on the labor movement at Shanghai's French Tramway Company] (Shanghai, 1957), 2:82–95; Quan Linfu et al., "Fadian gongren wei shixian 'sanbuting' er douzheng," [French Tramway workers struggling to implement the three nonstops] *Wenshi ziliao xuanji*, 1979, no. 2, p. 134; Jiang Pengfa, " 'Da qingke' he 'jie Fachang,' " [The "grand invitational" and the "plunder of FTC"], in *Zai jianku douzheng de suiyue li* [In the years and months of difficult struggles] (Shanghai, 1958), pp. 27–34.

26. *Shanghai Fadian*, 2: 96.

27. Miao Yu, "Shanghai gongren yundong de yizuo qiang baolei," pp. 20–21.

28. "Jiefangqian Shanghai Fashang dianche, diandeng gongsi gongchandang zuzhi yange" [Changes in the Communist Party organization at Shanghai's French Tramway and Electric Company before liberation], *Shanghai gongyun shiliao*, 1987, no. 4, pp. 37–38.

29. Miao Yu, "Shanghai gongren yundong de yizuo qiang baolei," p. 22; Quan Linfu et al., "Fadian gongren wei shixian 'sanbuting' er douzheng," p. 137.

30. Quan Linfu et al., "Fadian gongren wei shixian 'sanbuting' er douzheng," p. 138.

31. Li Cishan, "Shanghai laodong zhuangkuang" [The condition of Shanghai labor], *Xin qingnian* 7, no. 6 (1920): 72; Shanghai Bureau of Social Affairs, ed., "Shanghaishi renlichefu shenghuo zhuangkuang diaocha baogaoshu" [Report on a survey of the living conditions of rickshaw pullers in Shanghai], *Shehui banyuekan* 1, no. 1 (1934): 100; Zhu Bangxing et al., *Shanghai chanye*, p. 673; Zhou Jianfeng, "Fashang dianche" [The French Tramway], in *Shanghai de gushi* [Tales of Shanghai] (Shanghai, 1979), 4: 29.

32. Lei Jingdun, "Shanghai Yangshupu renlichefu diaocha" [Survey of rickshaw pullers in Shanghai's Yangshupu] (Graduation thesis, Pujiang University, Shanghai, 1930). The survey revealed that nearly all of the respondents (94 percent) had come to Shanghai as refugees from natural disaster.

33. Shanghai Municipal Archives, #13-1-2131, lists all owners who belonged to the Rickshaw Employers' Association. The great majority were from Yancheng and Funing.

34. Chen Caitu, quoted in Lei Jingdun, "Shanghai Yangshupu renlichefu diaocha."

35. Zhu Bangxing et al., *Shanghai chanye*, p. 676.

36. "Shanghaishi renli chefu shenghuo zhuangkuang diaocha baogaoshu," *Shehui banyuekan* 1, no. 3 (1934): 41–42.

37. Shi Zhilin, quoted in Lei Jingdun, "Shanghai Yangshupu renlichefu diaocha."

38. Chen Yinyu, quoted in ibid.

39. Eleanor Hinder, *Social and Industrial Problems of Shanghai* (New York, 1942), p. 69.

40. Lei Jingdun, "Shanghai Yangshupu renlichefu diaocha."

41. *Shishi xinbao*, Mar. 9, 11, 1919. Fifteen cents of the contracting profits went to the minor contractor and five cents to the major contractor.

42. Ernest O. Hauser, *Shanghai: City for Sale* (New York, 1940), p. 135.

43. Zhu Bangxing et al., *Shanghai chanye*, p. 677.

44. "Shanghai renmin de fandi fanfengjian douzheng" [The Shanghai people's struggles against imperialism and feudalism], *Shanghai difangshi ziliao*, 1983, no. 2, p. 173.

45. *Shi bao*, Dec. 3–9, 1915. To make room for expanded tramway service, the Shanghai Municipal Council mandated a reduction in the number of rickshaws from 10,000 to 6,000.

46. *Minguo ribao*, Apr. 12, 19, 20, 21, 22, 26, 1918; *Shishi xinbao*, Apr. 18, 19, 20, 21, 26, 1918.

47. "Shanghaishi renli chefu shenghuo zhuangkuang diaocha baogaoshu" [Report on an investigation of the living conditions of Shanghai's rickshaw pullers], *Shehui banyuekan* 1, no. 1 (1934), pp. 103, 107.

48. The request was made by Chen Guoliang, a lawyer and GMD member with close connections to some of the rickshaw owners. His petition was denied on grounds that he was not himself a puller (Number Two Archives, #722:4-513).

49. Zhu Bangxing et al., *Shanghai chanye*, pp. 678–79; Luo Gengmo, "Shanghai gonggong zujie renliche jiufen jieshu zhi hou" [After the resolution of the rickshaw dispute in the International Settlement of Shanghai], in *Zhongguo jingji lunwenji* [Collected essays on the Chinese economy] (Beijing, 1936), 1:240–52. See also *Shanghai Municipal Police Files*, D-3482, on collusion between owners and pullers in protesting the recommendations of the Shanghai Municipal Council.

50. *North China Daily News*, Aug. 23, 1935. Since some pullers were fingerprinted as many as nineteen times in the course of the registration drive, their fears were not entirely without basis.

51. *Shanghai Municipal Police Files*, D-5670; *Shen bao*, Aug. 7, 8, 1935.

52. *Dongfang ribao*, Dec. 2, 1939.

53. "Quandang zhengqu huangbaochefu zongbagong de shixian" [The entire Party strives to realize a general strike among the rickshaw pullers], Sept. 20, 1930, archives of the Bureau of Investigation, Taipei, #556.696/817.

54. "Zhongguo xiandai zhengzhishi ziliao huibian" [Compilation of materials on Chinese contemporary political history] (Nanjing) vol. 2, no. 44, document #5551.

55. *Shanghai Municipal Police Files*, D-5864.

56. Ibid., D-5670.

57. Shanghai Municipal Archives, #1-14-237. Even so, the authorities continued to suspect Communist involvement in the small-scale rickshaw strikes that erupted in response to the government ban. See *Xinwen bao*, Nov. 3, 1947.

58. David Strand, *Rickshaw Beijing* (Berkeley, Calif., 1989), pp. 243, 28–64.

59. See *Shanghai Municipal Police Files*, D-5661, for details of a serious fracas in February 1934 between wheelbarrow coolies and rice porters over the unloading of rice on Suzhou Creek.

60. Jiang Yuanqing and Song Sanmei, Sept. 12, 1957, transcript of interview, Labor Movement Archives of the SASS Institute of History.

61. Zhong Shengfa, Jan. 9, 1957, transcript of interview, ibid.

62. Zheng Changshan, Mar. 7, 1957, transcript of interview, ibid. Though somewhat below the daily wages of the bottom rung of factory labor, this strike pay was probably more than a "wild chicken" could otherwise expect in daily income.

63. Interviews at the Port of Shanghai, May 26, 1987, and Sept. 26, 1988.

64. Number Two Archives, #720-33, #722: 4-233, #722: 4-502, #722: 4-504. Green Gang notables Chang Yuqing, Zhu Xuefan, and Lu Jingshi were all involved in deals with contractors to establish unions that would prevent implementation of the government regulation.

65. Interview at the Port of Shanghai, Sept. 26, 1988.

66. Quoted in David M. Mandel, *The Petrograd Workers and the Fall of the Old Regime* (New York, 1983), p. 13.

67. University of Liverpool Department of Social Science, *The Dock Worker* (London, 1956), pp. 5, 74, 78–81, 122–23.

68. *Shanghai Municipal Police Files*, D-8976.

CONCLUSION

1. The trend was initiated by E. P. Thompson, *The Making of the English Working Class* (New York, 1963). A discussion of differences among the American, French, and German labor movements can be found in Ira Katznelson and Aristide R. Zolberg, *Working-Class Formation* (Princeton, N.J., 1986).

2. Kuo-Heng Shih, *China Enters the Machine Age: A Study of Labor in Chinese War Industry* (Cambridge, Mass., 1944), pp. 14–15.

3. Ibid., pp. 16–17.

4. Charles Tilly, "Solidarity Logics: Conclusions," *Theory and Society*, no. 17 (1988), p. 453.

5. Lynda Shaffer, *Mao and the Workers: The Hunan Labor Movement, 1920–1923* (Armonk, N.Y., 1982), p. 210.

6. Gail Hershatter, *The Workers of Tianjin, 1900–1949* (Stanford, Calif., 1986), pp. 49–63.

7. See footnote on p. 40.

8. Ming Kou Chan, "Labor and Empire: The Chinese Labor Movement in the Canton Delta, 1895–1927" (Ph.D. dissertation, Stanford University, 1975), pp. 171, 258–60.

9. See the sources cited in notes 1 and 2 of the Introduction and note 4 of Part I, Introduction.

10. Ronald Aminzade, "French Strike Development and Class Struggle," *Social Science History* 4 (1980): 63–78; James E. Cronin, "Labor Insurgency and Class Formation," ibid., p. 143.

11. William H. Sewell, Jr., *Work and Revolution in France: The Language of Labor from the Old Regime to 1848* (New York, 1980); Ronald Aminzade, *Class, Politics and Early Industrial Capitalism: A Study of Mid-Nineteenth-Century Toulouse, France* (New York, 1981).

12. Dick Geary, *European Labour Protest, 1848–1939* (London, 1981), pp. 40, 72.

13. Eric Hobsbawm, *Labouring Men* (New York, 1963), p. 424; Michael P. Hanagan, *The Logic of Solidarity* (Urbana, Ill., 1980), pp. 10–11.

14. Aminzade, "French Strike Development," p. 76.

15. This point is also made in John French's study of Brazilian labor, which finds that skilled workers were disproportionately active in unions as well as in the Communist Party ("Activism in the Workplace: The Not So Powerless Prevail," unpublished paper, 1991).

16. Jeffrey Haydu, *Between Craft and Class: Skilled Workers and Factory Politics in the United States and Britain, 1890–1922* (Berkeley, Calif., 1988), p. 13.

17. On this point, see Hanagan, *Logic of Solidarity*, p. 210. See also Victoria Bonnell, *Roots of Rebellion: Workers' Politics and Organizations in St. Petersburg and Moscow, 1900–1914* (Berkeley, Calif., 1983), p. 444.

18. Natalie Zemon Davis, "A Trade Union in Sixteenth-Century France," *Economic History Review* 19 (1966), pp. 48–69; Davis, *Society and Culture in Early Modern France* (Stanford, Calif., 1975), pp. 4–10; Robert J. Bezucha, *The Lyon Uprising of 1834* (Cambridge, Mass., 1974); Eric J. Hobsbawm and Joan W. Scott, "Political Shoemakers," in *Workers: Worlds of Labor*, ed. Eric Hobsbawm (New York, 1984), pp. 103–30.

19. Sewell, *Work and Revolution in France*, pp. 155–56. As Sewell notes, the only major exception to this symbiotic relationship between factory and artisanal work was in textiles, where new factories supplanted hand spinning and hand-loom weaving.

20. Hanagan, *Logic of Solidarity*, p. 79; Edward Shorter and Charles Tilly, *Strikes in France, 1830–1968* (New York, 1974), p. 76.

21. Cronin, "Labor Insurgency," p. 138; Hanagan, *Logic of Solidarity*, pp. 12–13; Aminzade, "French Strike Development," pp. 63–78; Sewell, *Work and Revolution in France*, p. 160. A similar argument for the United States is presented in David Montgomery, "Workers' Control of Machine Production in the Nineteenth Century," in *The Labor History Reader*, ed. Daniel J. Leab (Chicago, 1985), pp. 129–30.

22. John Cumbler, "Migration, Class Formation, and Class Consciousness: The American Experience," in *Confrontation, Class Consciousness, and the Labor Process*, ed. Michael Hanagan and Charles Stephenson (New York, 1986), p. 42.

23. Stanley Aronowitz, *False Promises: The Shaping of American Working Class Consciousness* (New York, 1973), chap. 3.

24. The analogy is made in Frederic Wakeman, Jr., "Policing Modern Shanghai," *China Quarterly,* no. 115 (1988): 416.

25. On the role of the Mafia as labor broker, see Howard Abadinsky, *The Mafia in America* (New York, 1981), pp. 4–11; Joseph L. Albini, *The American Mafia* (New York, 1971), p. 72.

26. *New York Times,* Sept. 9, 1923.

27. Jonathan Kwitny, *Vicious Circles: The Mafia in the Marketplace* (New York, 1979), pp. 143–44.

28. Jim Clay, *Hoffa!* (Beaverdam, Va., 1965), p. 163.

29. Fan Shaozeng, "Guanyu Du Yuesheng" [Concerning Du Yuesheng], in *Jiu Shanghai de banghui* [The gangsters of old Shanghai] (Shanghai, 1986), pp. 221–25.

30. Clay, *Hoffa!,* p. 163.

31. Anton Blok, *The Mafia of a Sicilian Village* (New York, 1974), pp. 6–7, 177.

32. See David M. Mandel, *The Petrograd Workers and the Fall of the Old Regime* (New York, 1983), pp. 31–32, for a discussion of the protest patterns of unskilled workers in Russia.

33. Quoted in S. A. Smith, *Red Petrograd: Revolution in the Factories, 1917–1918* (Cambridge, 1983), p. 29.

34. Mandel, *Petrograd Workers,* p. 23.

35. Charles F. Sabel, *Work and Politics: The Division of Labor in Industry* (New York, 1982), p. 134.

36. See Richard Jules Ostreicher, *Solidarity and Fragmentation* (Chicago, 1986), for a fascinating discussion of divisions by age, skill level, and especially ethnic origin among the Detroit working class. For China, Emily Honig's analysis of women cotton workers in Shanghai and Gail Hershatter's study of Tianjin workers both offer rich detail on working-class fragmentation.

37. Diane Koenker, "Moscow in 1917: The View from Below," in *The Workers' Revolution in Russia, 1917* (Cambridge, 1987), p. 90. See also Koenker, *Moscow Workers and the 1917 Revolution* (Princeton, N.J., 1981), p. 359.

38. Smith, *Red Petrograd,* p. 255.

39. See the references in Part II, Introduction, n. 2.

40. James E. Cronin, "Labor Insurgency and Class Formation," *Social Science History* 4 (1980): 144–45.

41. Edward Shorter and Charles Tilly, *Strikes in France* (Cambridge, 1974), p. 104.

42. Victoria Bonnell, *Roots of Rebellion* (Berkeley, Calif., 1983), p. 447.

43. Zhu Lianke, May 6, 1958, transcript of interview, Labor Movement Archives of the SASS Institute of History.

44. Karl Marx and Friedrich Engels, *Manifesto of the Communist Party* (Beijing, 1975), p. 45.

45. Mancur Olson, *The Logic of Collective Action* (Cambridge, Mass., 1977); Russell Hardin, *Collective Action* (Baltimore, 1982).

46. This point is developed in John R. Low-Beer, *Protest and Participation: The New Working Class in Italy* (Cambridge, 1978), p. 175.

47. Haydu, *Between Craft and Class*, p. 212, finds that labor solidarity in the United States and Britain has been accompanied by a concern for economistic, rather than control, issues.

48. David Strand, *Rickshaw Beijing* (Berkeley, Calif., 1989), p. 196.

49. Craig Calhoun, "The Radicalism of Tradition and the Question of Class Struggle," in *Rationality and Revolution*, ed. Michael Taylor (Cambridge, 1988), p. 153.

50. The same dichotomy between the "traditional communities" of the artisan and the "modern associations" of the factory worker appears in Charles Tilly, *From Mobilization to Revolution* (Reading, Mass., 1978), pp. 62–64, and in Edward Shorter, ed., *Work and Community in the West* (New York, 1973), pp. 17–20.

51. Herbert G. Gutman, *Work, Culture and Society* (New York, 1977), p. 41.

52. See "Nuli kaichuang dangshi, gongyunshi ziliao zhengji gongzuo xinjumian" [Strive to open a new chapter in the work of collecting materials on party history and labor history], *Shanghai gongyun shiliao*, 1984, no. 4, pp. 1–7.

53. Jean Chesneaux, *The Chinese Labor Movement, 1919–1927* (Stanford, Calif., 1968).

54. Andrew G. Walder, "The Remaking of the Chinese Working Class, 1949–1981," *Modern China* 10 (1984): 3–48. See also his *Communist Neotraditionalism* (Berkeley, Calif., 1986), p. 85.

55. "Shangwu yinshuguan gonghuishi" [A history of unions at the Commercial Press], Shanghai library, pp. 1–2.

56. David M. Bachman, *Chen Yun and the Chinese Political System* (Berkeley, Calif., 1985), pp. 72–73.

57. The resultant dependence of workers on state enterprises in contemporary China is insightfully analyzed in Andrew G. Walder, *Communist Neo-Traditionalism: Work and Authority in Chinese Industry* (Berkeley, Calif., 1986).

58. Martin King Whyte and William L. Parish, *Urban Life in Contemporary China* (Chicago, 1984), p. 33.

59. Walder, *Communist Neo-Traditionalism*, chap. 4.

60. François Gipouloux, *Les cent fleurs à l'usine* (Paris, 1986), pp. 198–205; see also Lynn White III, "Workers' Politics in Shanghai," *Journal of Asian Studies* 36, no. 1 (1976): 105–7.

61. White, "Workers' Politics in Shanghai," pp. 107–15.

62. Interviews with former Shanghai Red Guards, May 25, July 2, 1987.

63. White, "Workers' Politics in Shanghai," pp. 114–15.

64. Gu Xingsheng, May 13, 1958, transcript of interview, Labor Movement Archives of the SASS Institute of History.

65. On the importance of learned protest repertoires, see Charles Tilly, *The Contentious French* (Cambridge, Mass., 1986). This theme is creatively developed for Shanghai students in Jeffrey Wasserstrom, *Student Protest in Twentieth-Century China: The View from Shanghai* (Stanford, Calif., 1991).

66. Zhang Ben et al., "Shanghai guomian shiqichang gongren douzhengshi"

[The history of labor struggles at Shanghai's Number Seventeen cotton mill], *Shanghai gongren yundong lishi ziliao* (Shanghai, 1953), pp. 61–70.

67. Fan Wenxian, "Shanghaishi zonggonghui beiza jishi" [Annals of the assault on the Shanghai Federation of Labor], *Shanghai gongyun shiliao*, 1986, no. 5, pp. 1–6.

68. "Zhengzheng tiegu chuiqing shi" [In appreciation of martyrdom], ibid., pp. 13–22.

69. Stuart Schram, ed., *Chairman Mao Talks to the People* (New York, 1974), p. 278; Harry Harding, *Organizing China* (Stanford, Calif., 1981), pp. 251–52.

70. Walder, *Communist Neo-Traditionalism*, 1986, chap. 2, offers a helpful overview of the major social divisions (of age, job security, wage grades, and so on) in the contemporary Chinese working class. In his analysis, however, these social groupings do not explain the political networks (of activists, nonactivists, and rival factions).

71. For a discussion of the post-1949 labor movement that links social divisions (of gender, job security, and the like) to political protest, see Gipouloux, *Les cent fleurs.*

Index

In this index an "f" after a number indicates a separate reference on the next page, and an "ff" indicates separate references on the next two pages. A continuous discussion over two or more pages is indicated by a span of page numbers, e.g., "57–59." *Passim* is used for a cluster of references in close but not consecutive sequence.

Library of Congress Cataloging-in-Publication Data

Perry, Elizabeth J.
    Shanghai on strike : the politics of Chinese labor / Elizabeth J.
Perry.
        p.   cm.
Includes bibliographical references and index.
ISBN 0-8047-2063-0 (cl.) : ISBN 0-8047-2491-1 (pbk.)
    1. Strikes and lockouts—China—Shanghai—History—20th century.
2. Working class—China—Shanghai—Political activity—History—20th
century.   I. Title.
HD5430.Z9S535   1992
331.89'2951132—dc20
92-17774
    CIP

⊗ This book is printed on acid-free paper.